The Role of Gender in Practice Knowledge

Garland Reference Library of Social Science
Volume 1086

The Role of Gender in Practice Knowledge

Claiming Half the Human Experience

Edited by
Josefina Figueira-McDonough
F. Ellen Netting
Ann Nichols-Casebolt

Garland Publishing, Inc.
A member of the Taylor & Francis Group
New York and London
1998

Library of Congress Cataloging-in-Publication Data

The role of gender in practice knowledge : claiming half the human experience / edited by Josefina Figueira-McDonough, Ann Nichols-Casebolt, F. Ellen Netting.

p. cm. — (Garland reference library of social science ; v. 1086)

Includes bibliographical references (p.) and index.

ISBN 0-8153-2228-3 (alk. paper)

1. Feminist theory. 2. Social science—Study and teaching. 3. Sex discrimination against women. I. Figueira-McDonough, Josefina. II. Nichols-Casebolt, Ann, 1949– III. Netting, F. Ellen. IV. Series.
HQ1190.R65 1998
305.42—dc21 97-52304
CIP

Printed on acid-free, 250-year-life paper
Manufactured in the United States of America

In memory of women who shaped us—
Ada, Pearl, and Viva

Contents

Preface

All books have a history. This is a book that grew out of a shared uneasiness about the invisibility of women at the core of the curriculum, the "after thought" given to women's issues in our classes, and the divisions between what are supposed to be the central theories we teach and the "special" considerations used to explain how women's issues do not quite fit or are not accounted for by "universal" theories. Subsequent contact with colleagues across the country has reassured us that our uneasiness was not an idiosyncratic concern.

This uneasiness with "what is" and a desire for change motivated us and others to seize an opportunity for a joint women's faculty effort. The opportunity to act on this set of concerns was provided by a reaccreditation evaluation of the school in which we were all faculty members at the time. Following the site visit, the school was asked to present a curricular plan that would pay greater attention to women's issues. The Dean at the time appointed one of us to prepare a plan, and this effort quickly developed into a collaborative task among all the women faculty. Early breakfast meetings brought the group together, setting us in the direction of framing a knowledge-integrated curriculum.

This integration experience was part of a larger, ongoing movement to integrate women's issues into university curricula and was based on several trends specific to social work education. These trends included the push inherent in the 1979 CSWE curriculum statements about minorities and women, the "ecological" approach to theory and practice championed by social work educators, a resurgence of definitions of social justice as paramount within the profession, and a move toward diverse and alternative theories and practice models. We found that despite these positive trends, the social work literature and colleagues with whom we consulted agreed that the integration of women's issues into social work curricula had not been seriously attempted.

Our change effort in this one school resulted in a massive report. We divided up the work and revised all required graduate courses, introducing new language and literature that would facilitate the change. These revisions were produced within a semester. However, the conditions that had triggered this effort changed. In the final reaccreditation negotiations CSWE dropped the requirement of curricular changes for women's issues, and the new administration did not show any commitment to the project. What had begun as a driving force for change, reinforced by our accrediting body, lost momentum. Since this was not something that the site team was inclined to press, in light of numerous other issues that needed to be addressed, the opportunity to examine gender content seriously was no longer a focus of the school's leadership. Disappointed and aware that our concerns were shared by faculty in other schools, we adapted the report into an article that was published by the *Journal of Social Work Education*. In a true spirit of collaboration, this work was co-authored by all the women faculty at the school. Essentially, our initial experience within one school of social work became the first stage in a larger change process.

Once the article appeared in print, readers let us know that sharing our experience and work with others interested in gender curricular integration was helpful. Our hope was that other schools would attempt to push ahead with what we had not been able to implement, or that at least, they would start discussing the possibility of a reconstruction of their curricula.

A few months later, a new opportunity for continuing our project presented itself. David Estrin, Senior Editor at Garland, called to invite us to develop into book form the ideas presented in the article. By now we knew that faculty in various schools around the country were interested in seeing gender content integrated into social work curricula. We invited contributors from across the nation who had special knowledge in different curricular areas and a commitment to gender-integrated knowledge to join us.

We are impressed and excited by the wealth of materials our contributor-colleagues have produced. This book represents the second stage in our joint efforts to target schools of social work for curricular change by providing content that can be integrated into any school of social work curricula. We hope that readers will use these materials to begin to change curricula in their schools.

Josefina Figueira-McDonough
F. Ellen Netting
Ann Nichols-Casebolt

Acknowledgments

The contributors to this volume have put up with more revisions than they bargained for when they accepted our invitation to write chapters for this book. We thank them for tolerating a compulsive threesome who seemed to "never go away," and for the wonderful way in which they have educated us in the process. We are in their debt, for the quality of their work has made this book a resource for all of us.

Special appreciation goes to our colleagues who served as readers for various chapters when we needed additional expertise. Elizabeth "Lib" Hutchison and Elizabeth "Liz" Cramer, both of Virginia Commonwealth University, consulted with us and gave us excellent feedback when we drafted and reviewed materials early in the project. Christina Risley Curtiss at Arizona State University and Mindy Loiselle at Virginia Commonwealth University are due special thanks for serving as informal reviewers of draft chapters. Their insightful comments were invaluable, all the more so because of their timeliness.

To Anne Kisor, we can only say that without her we would still be formatting and working on disk compatibility issues. Anne's patience, compulsiveness, and attention to detail provided us with the expertise to get our final draft completed.

David Estrin, the Senior Editor at Garland, is someone with whom we feel a special bond. David saw the potential in the article we had written with colleagues and had faith in our abilities to organize and coordinate this effort. We thank him for the interest, encouragement, and support that made this project possible.

We want to thank the members of the Council on Social Work Education's Commission on the Role and Status of Women for giving us the opportunity to have a dialogue about gender at annual meetings.

Peter Kettner, previous Acting Dean of the School of Social Work at Arizona State University, took the CSWE requirement for integration of women's issues in the curriculum seriously. He assigned one of us to work on curricular reconstruction, knowing her commitment to the issue. It is thanks to his decision that we launched this enterprise.

In addition, we are grateful to Frank Baskind, Dean of the Virginia Commonwealth University School of Social Work, for his encouragement and support, as well as for the resources needed to express-mail and fax numerous drafts and revisions to our contributors.

Last, and especially, we thank Peter, Karl, and Gordon for their unfailing willingness to watch with puzzlement and curiosity as we approached this effort with zest and commitment. It is they who have offered a supporting presence (and humorous interludes) as we have debated and struggled with the relevance of gender in our professional and personal lives.

The Role of Gender in Practice Knowledge

CHAPTER 1

Toward a Gender-integrated Knowledge in Social Work

Josefina Figueira-McDonough

INTRODUCTION

Meaningful knowledge and education must reflect the diversity of human perspectives and experiences. Therefore, to mainstream content on women (and other excluded groups) into basic academic courses is an epistemological imperative. Women, as the largest group excluded from participation in the construction of knowledge, have pressed academia for a move into gender-integrated knowledge. According to Stimpson (1984), a variety of changes in the contemporary cultural context were favorable to this enterprise, including the large entrance of women into the labor force, democratization of higher education, civil rights ideology, ideologies of value equality and self-realization, emergence of theories questioning the empiricist tradition and recognizing the ideological roots of all knowledge, partial blurring of cultural definitions of masculinity and femininity, and the lessening of prejudice of women in positions of power. Zalk and Gordon-Kelter (1992, pp.1–14) agree that in contemporary times social systems are not inherently unreceptive to feminist revisions. They are, however, basically unable to accommodate such revisions without revolutionary redefinition and reorganization. As Bernard (1987) puts it, this transformation requires methodological and substantive changes of the magnitude of a paradigm shift. To the extent that cultural production is remade into the means of accumulation of a kind of professional academic capital, cultural producers are encouraged to accept commonplace understandings of the world (Calhoun, 1995). Therefore, when fundamental academic tenets are challenged, resentment and opposition will emerge among the defenders of those tenets.

Since achieving gender-integrated knowledge in academic settings is not impossible but difficult, what are the alternatives for feminist scholars? From a 1992 informal survey of women faculty of social work (Carter et al., 1994), we learned that faculty, female and male, who had embraced the feminist paradigm have shaped the content of their courses and adopted a pedagogy consistent with the objective of gender-integrated knowledge. As valiant as such efforts are and as valuable as they may be to the students they reach, it is unlikely that a small group of individuals can achieve acceptance and diffusion of a new paradigm across the academic enterprise.

Women's studies programs and special women's courses within disciplines are another route for inclusion of this scholarship. They also give (self-selected) students the opportunity to be exposed to knowledge and perspectives not otherwise easily available. But they cannot contribute to a general balanced curricula. In fact, they reinforce the idea that women are an atypical subgroup, not integral to the substance of the disciplines. The social sciences and the professional schools using social science knowledge will continue to pursue and teach principles of human behavior, building knowledge and standards based on limited and selective samples, while a majority of humans (women) are treated as special cases or exceptions to the norm. The "ghettoization" of feminist studies both within the disciplines and in the larger institution has functioned to allow the disciplines to maintain the status quo while women's courses are viewed as a symbol of academic tolerance and political necessity rather than a seat of scholarship (Zalk & Gordon-Kelter, 1992, pp. 1–14).

Commenting on the role of black and women's studies, Marable (1995) proposes that their role is to maintain a broad intellectual dialogue and exchange to incorporate divergent perspectives and concerns. Their intellectual anchor rests with a series of themes and questions that cut across disciplines, but they are not disciplines nor can they revolutionize the disciplines. The challenge before us is to create programs designed to have an impact on the disciplines and professional schools linked to that body of knowledge, so that epistemological imperatives of the new paradigm can take place. The task is one of transforming the curricula.

In search of a framework to promote gender integration in the curriculum, this chapter will

1. address some of the shortcomings of dominant knowledge, identify the limitations of its constructions, and question its assumed "universal" nature;
2. argue for the pressing nature of this quest given the embeddedness of gender in all aspects of social life;
3. review recent challenges to traditional knowledge and the alternatives they offer;
4. consider pedagogies that are consistent with the goals of implementing an integrated curriculum; and
5. evaluate the strategic position of social work education to engage in gender-integrated curricular changes.

Each of the subsequent nine chapters addresses a specific curricular area in social work education, critically assessing the content, assumptions, and lag in the knowledge traditionally imparted to social work students. They will suggest and justify needed changes toward the goal of gender integration. The final chapter will discuss strategic issues for the implementation of curricular change.

MISSING HALF OF THE HUMAN EXPERIENCE: LIMITED AND DISTORTED KNOWLEDGE

The assumption of feminist critique is that traditional knowledge, especially in the social sciences, is androcentrist by nature. The social sciences were developed for the most part by a homogeneous group of white, middle-class, Western men who pursued their search for knowledge by building on shared assumptions and observations. Since assumptions shape observations and observations are understood in terms of assumptions, the process constituted a closed circle within which theories were articulated and evidence for confirmation was sought (Zalk & Gordon-Kelter, 1992). Insiders with similar experiences and common history select facts or observations that become meaningful in the contexts of theories or interpretations of these observations, and observations are not independent from interpretation. Therefore, what passes for universal knowledge reflects the experiences and actions of some men. This type of knowledge is necessarily saturated with male perspectives. Netting and Rodwell (Chapter 8) make this abundantly clear in their review of the organizational literature, as do Weil, Williams, Gamble, and Smith (Chapter 7) when analyzing the male dominance in community organization since the middle of the century.

This notion of knowledge construction related to personal history and interpretation dramatizes the exclusion of experiences—women's experiences—that represent more than half of humanity. The history of women's everyday life demonstrates how it has been experienced differently from men's and how it may have produced different types of knowledge and understanding. It is this dissociation between women's experience and traditional knowledge that is conducive to interpretative distortions of women's reality. Since men and women have different experiences and men are predominantly the insiders in knowledge construction, men tend to study women as outsiders. The standard assumptions they use will shape the questions they ask, and this, in turn, will condition the data they collect. A case in point is the construction of mental health diagnostic systems discussed by Ashford and Littrell in Chapter 4.

Gilligan's (1982) critique of Kohlberg's moral development research illustrates this type of distortion. Propositions about the stages of moral development emerged from the male experience and interest in the public arena, and validation for these propositions was obtained from male samples. The program of research was extended to samples of women leading to the "universal" conclusion about the lesser moral development of females.

Simply adding sex as a variable would fail to restructure disciplines that were not designed to study women. Since these approaches were shaped to reflect men's experiences and interpretations, the strategy serves mainly to compare women to the male standard. Inasmuch as theories are supposed to reflect experiences and not the other way around, conceptual approaches that do not include women's experiences cannot claim universality.

The consequences of this selective process of knowledge-building are that it defines males and male experience as standard or normative, and females and female experience as sex-specific deviations from the norm. Men are equated with humans, and women are "other." This gender polarization constructs social reality in such a way that a cultural connection is forged between sex and virtually any aspect of human experience. Women are challenging the "hegemonic universals" of traditional knowledge to give space to other voices and experiences (Lewis, 1992). The experiences of others in turn reflect the historical and structural contexts commonly neglected when only the experiences of insiders are given a voice. This commitment to a plurality of experience is essential to feminist epistemology. The intent is not to exclude the insiders, but to include those excluded, by reason of class, race, and gender, in the construction of knowledge (Stanley, 1992). This is a theme that pervades all the chapters in this book.

Issues of inequality and their causes need to be essential components of any conceptual frame. Some theoretical approaches either omit the issue of inequality or address it separately with little or no link to the central theoretical frame. As Gordon (1990) shows, most of the theories of the welfare state in the Western world do not include gender as a major organizing principle, obscuring the omissions in the policies, the unanticipated consequences of policies, and the very roots of poverty. Dominelli's (1991) study further unveils the international invisibility of women's contributions to welfare regardless of government structure, economic system, and political orientation. This argument is echoed by Nichols-Casebolt in Chapter 9 on social welfare policy.

To the extent that issues of gender and race are addressed as exceptions within the disciplinary theory, they reinforce their exclusion and therefore preserve the status quo. For example, the great books ideal of education, based on the classic canon (Bloom, 1987) imposes Western white middle-class perceptions and experiences on its putative audience. Esthetic tastes and moral values are formed by preferential approach and imposed on all education. Although this hegemony is troublesome in academia, its effects in applied social sciences are still more devastating. Incomplete and distorted conceptual frames create a false consciousness of social reality that results in ineffective interventions reinforcing the status quo. Intervention might lead to entrapment rather than change. For example, Finn, in Chapter 6 on families, argues that the use of the nuclear family standard has resulted in the pathologization of female-headed households and minority kinship arrangements.

THE EMBEDDEDNESS AND PERVASIVENESS OF GENDER

The achievement of gender-integrated knowledge is a difficult enterprise, not only because it requires the inclusion of more than half of human experience, but also because polarization and stratification of gender is present in all aspects of culture and social structure. The exclusion of women's experiences from traditional knowledge construction defines gender polarization that is both the reflection of a societal condition and a reinforcement of it. Gender is a human invention used to organize human social life. The distinctions that it carries are built into the organization and politics of all institutions, and into the interactions of everyday life and self-identity (Lorber, 1994). It is in fact a process of a socially accepted system of stratification, institutionalized in the family, workplace, state, language, and culture. It establishes patterns of expectation for individuals, ordering the social process of everyday life. For example, Janet Finn (Chapter 6) highlights the essential link between the construction of gender and family. Gutierrez, Reed, Ortega, and Lewis (Chapter 5) examine the evidence on differences in gender group participation and relate this gap to socializing reinforcements and institutionalized contexts.

The strength and resilience of this invention comes from pervasiveness in all dimensions of social life and from a belief in its universality and naturalness. The discourses and social institutions in which gender is embedded channel females and males into unequal life situations. During enculturation, the individual internalizes cultural lenses and thereby becomes motivated to construct an identity consistent with them (Bem, 1993). Cross-cultural similarities in divisions of labor and biological differences are joined in an argument that differences are natural and indeed permanent. Men and women become homogenized, the internal differences explained as deviance and intergroup differences as normative. These later become crystallized as opposites such as rational/emotional and/or autonomy/connectedness. More than the construction of difference, gender establishes a hierarchy of power. The genders are not only different, they are unequal. The process establishing gender differentiation establishes at the same time gender inequality. Central to his conception of hierarchy is a knowledge paradigm that defines men as the norm and women as the other.

In spite of evidence that "within" gender differences are as large as "between," the institution of gender continues to create and maintain socially significant differences between men and women as a primary way of signifying relationships of power (Scott, 1988). The gendered division of labor is identified with one institution, patriarchy, and associated with another, capitalism, that place women in vulnerable positions (Lorber, 1994). And it is through apparently gender-neutral policies that the state plays a part in this stratification. For example, the "Contract with America" under the neutral label of welfare reform targets Aid to Families with Dependent Children with the most punitive changes. Nichols-Casebolt expands on this view in Chapter 9.

To the degree that society, as well as knowledge, is organized from a male perspective, men's distinctive needs are taken care of while women's needs are either treated as "special" cases or left unmet (Bem, 1993). This is the case of the frequent exclusion of pregnancy from insurance coverage and the inclusion of prostatectomies and circumcision, the resources devoted to male sports at universities, the mother-teacher meetings set during work hours, GI grants, and so on.

The primacy of inequality over difference in shaping gendered society is defended by Mackinnon (1987). She argues that gender is first a power inequality and that only as a result of this power inequality is gender a question of difference. The difference becomes important only as a consequence of power. "One of the most deceptive anti-feminisms in society, scholarship, politics and law is persistent treatment of gender as if it is truly a question of difference rather than treating the gender difference as a construct of the difference that gender makes" (pp. 8–9). Further, domination is not achieved by force but by winning the hearts and minds of subordinates. This is done especially through the development of institutions and values that make inequality appear the natural order of things, so that open conflicts between dominators and the dominated are rare. It is from this perspective that Carlton-LaNey and Andrews insist on the centrality of empowerment strategies in direct practice (Chapter 3).

At the micro level (family), paternalism is the primary mode of control. From Hegel's view that the family is a unit where husband and wife are united by marital love so that only the husband need have citizenship rights (Pateman, 1988), to the construction of the nuclear family in a market economy, where the division of labor made women's work unpaid and her access to financial resources dependent on the goodwill of the husband-provider, the dominator is depicted as sharing concern for the subordinator in such a way as to preserve the power hierarchy (Chaffetz, 1988). At the macro level, promotion of individualism by the dominators diffuses the subordinate's attempt at collective change of status (Jackman, 1994). This is evident, for example, in the way access to public assistance benefits is structured. Eligibility through means tests by definition instituted individualized evaluations and distribution of benefits (Cates, 1983). This, together with the lack of clarity and mutability of rules, reinforces the power of the front line decision-maker, making the position of clients very precarious and discouraging any form of protest, individual or collective (Cloward & Piven, 1974; Lipsky, 1980).

Lorber (1994) goes further in equating gender with all social relations that separate people into differentiated gender states. She calls attention to the cross-cutting racial and class statuses within each gender status and how these can belie the uniform pattern of men's domination of women by introducing both the domination of men (white) over other men (black) and women (white) over other women or men (black).

Race, class, sexual preference, nationality, and religion will cross-cut the meaning of gender division, but given the pervasiveness of the gender division and the size of the groups, it is important to focus on gender (diLeonardo, 1991; Lerner, 1986). As we examine gender in this book, we might develop methodology to analyze other hierarchies while being aware that dimensions do not necessarily overlap. Gender embeddedness means that all forms of patterned inequality merit analysis. Women perceive and respond to their situation as a result of the intersection of class, culture, and gender that define their multiple stratification. Understanding women's experiences requires awareness of the multiple contexts in which they are located (diLeonardo, 1991). Hutchison and Charlesworth's learning module, at the end of Chapter 2, represents an operational example of this perspective.

It is erroneous to assume that subjugated individuals accept their position passively. Such an assumption dehumanizes victims by denying rational (calculated) resistance. In fact, Jackman (1994), Davis and Fisher (1993, pp. 3–22), and Spencer-Wood (1994) strongly argue and gather evidence that women and others in subjugated positions resist subjugation. This does not mean that they are not victimized but only that they resist and therefore modify domination. Jackman argues that power will adjust to resistance, what Foucault (1980) calls capillary power, while Davis and Fisher give examples of how women negotiate at the margins of power (how women's agency manifests itself even under structured forms of constraint); and Spencer-Wood's research examines the forms of resistance and collective action of Victorian ladies in Boston in the mid-nineteenth century. Work done on the culture of black women (Gilkes, 1992) reveals how that culture itself is a form of resistance built over a long time to cope with the interlocking nature of oppression.

The role of knowledge in justifying and legitimizing gender inequality cannot be overemphasized. Commitment to end gender stratification requires dismantling of the present institutional order and requires a paradigm change in the construction and transmission of knowledge (Lorber, 1994).

IN SEARCH OF INCLUSIVE KNOWLEDGE

The women's movement challenged the hegemonic universals of traditional knowledge and gendered social structure and started a search for knowledge that would not only represent women's subjects and voices but all the other excluded populations. Women scholars have worked hard to achieve knowledge integration. Their struggle against the establishment has been arduous and diverse. It is, however, based on two points:

1. Male orientation to knowledge is systematically distorted and needs to be corrected to include all experience.
2. Knowledge has to be pursued as a means to structural change that will eliminate the subjugation of women.

In their search, women scholars have played a crucial role in the "deconstruction" of traditional theories, methodologies, and practices. They have critically analyzed various assumptions and beliefs on which the paradigms of social sciences are based. They have demonstrated that social knowledge cannot be constructed independently of structural contexts that change with history and culture. Critical analyses have been directed against traditional biological accounts of women's nature (see, e.g., Hubbard, 1988), views of women in psychological and mental health studies (Franks & Rothblum, 1983; Kessler & McKenna, 1978; Parlee, 1992), theories of moral development (Gilligan, 1982), the image of women in gynecological medicine (Fisher, 1987; Scully & Bart, 1973), the invisibility of women in social and historical analyses (Scott, 1988; Smith, 1979), male monopoly of historical representation and creation of patriarchy (Jansen-Jurreit, 1982; Lerner, 1986), systematic discounting of women's work in national and international economy statistics (Waring, 1988, 1992), homogenization of gender stereotypes in anthropology (diLeonardo, 1991), pervasiveness of male metaphors in biological theorizing (Keller, 1985), under representation of women in social science research and marginality of women's issues in sociological analysis (Farrell, 1992; Johnson & Frieze, 1978), misconceptions of family (Zinn, 1992), the exclusion of feminist voice from political theory (Jaquette, 1992; Lewis, 1992; Macaulay, 1985), selective use of deviance and control (Figueira-McDonough & Sarri, 1987), the male-centeredness in sex-role and marital adjustment (Long Laws, 1972), and the pervasive gender and race bias in welfare policy (Abramovitz, 1988; Quadagno, 1994).

New approaches were shaped from a variety of intellectual movements that had already taken hold, themselves the result of various theoretical and methodological contestation, such as Kuhn's (1970) and Manheim's (1954) recognition of the ideological character of knowledge (diLeonardo, 1991; Farrell, 1992); Thompson's (1963) cultural historical frame, a "bottom's up" type of historical interpretation; Mintz and Wolf's (1989) focus on perception and contestative actions and emphasis in phenomenology; Garfinkel's (1967) symbolic interactionism, the literary poststructuralism of the Frankfurt School and Foucault's (1980) view of suppressed knowledge; Mills's (1959) criticisms of the limitations of abstract empiricism, the critical theory mistrust of unexamined assumptions; and finally, Freire's (1973) theory that knowledge and learning should be an active tool for emancipation of oppressed people. The critical theory challenges to enlightenment deserve special attention.

Critical Theory: A Challenge to the Epistemological Foundation of the Enlightenment

The questioning of contradictions of positivism and a commitment to change are at the roots of convergence between critical and feminist theory. The revision of assumptions of universalism, objectivity, and progressivism was the work of the Frankfurt School during the interwar years. The goal of its members was to defend rationality in the midst of contradictions and polarizations of the modern era. In a world of increasing change and diversity, they had to address historical and cultural variation while holding to commonalities of humanity (Arendt, 1958). Challenges to universalism brought inclusion of historical and cultural contexts in theoretical analysis. Questions regarding separation of theory and facts led to the recognition that all social science theories are partially inductive and that they depend on empirical analogies and comparisons rather than lawlike universal statements (Calhoun, 1995). Furthermore, it became clear that while theory guided the empirical search, selecting facts to be observed and how to analyze them, and assumptions on which the theory was built, were taken for granted and not tested. These considerations toned down the fervor of empiricism;

empirical results might be used to generate alternative interpretations rather than exclusively for generalization. The legitimization of multiple theories and the recognition that theories reflect individual perspectives and interests encouraged a dialogue among alternative theories to be guided by criteria of adequacy. Theoretical selection or reframing would be defined by applicability to practical concerns. All chapters in this book embrace this position. Chapters 2 and 8 give special emphasis to legitimacy of multiple theories for practice.

The tension between idiographic and nomothetic reasoning was addressed in part by the concept of intersubjectivity, recognizing historical and cultural constraints. Based on epistemological reformulations, critical theory came to be defined as "self-conscious about its historicity, its place in a culture among cultures [acceptance of multiple theories], its irreducibility to facts and its engagement in the practical world" (Calhoun, 1995, p. 11).

Habermas (1990), the best-known contemporary descendant of the Frankfurt School, was especially interested in the contradiction between the technical progress predicted by the Enlightenment project and the alienation—a strain reflected in the tension between a mass, administered society, and the erosion of public participation and social responsibility. Communication free from domination became the center of Habermas' theory of communication action.

This attention to communication, text, and discourse led to what came to be known as postmodernism. Starting from a critical theory base that theories are supposed to reflect experiences, not the other way around, and that the goal of knowledge is to understand human life experiences, postmodernism saw experiences as mutually constructed conversations (Farrell, 1992; Zalk & Gordon-Kelter, 1992). Committed to the desirability of multitheoretical dialogue, postmodernists argue that all groups have a right to speak for themselves in their own voice, accepted as authentic and legitimate (Harvey, 1992, p. 48). While critical theory shares with postmodernists the notion that knowledge takes multidimensional forms unique to particular times and people, many of the latter reject truth as a goal, since they question logic, rationality, and reason (Rosenau, 1992, p.77). From the postmodernist point of view knowledge can only describe, and all descriptions are equally valid (Newman, 1985). Human knowledge is interpretive and examining discursive processes is the only way of gaining understanding. There are many truths, so no particular belief system has a privileged position that can guide action (Foucault, 1980).

Habermas (1990), on the other hand, remained committed to reason, and his theory was grounded in universal presuppositions about language, denouncing the paralysis of relativism. However, while Habermas was conscious of how the socioeconomic-psychological characteristics of individuals' private and civil life conditioned their degree of autonomy in public life, he has not focused on the basic differences among groups, nor on how groups affect members differently (Calhoun, 1995). The notion that critical consciousness is preserved to a greater degree by deprived groups has its roots in the Marxian stream of the Frankfurt School. Fanon's (1963) work still stands as the most powerful analysis of how the disempowered experience alienation as double consciousness. Weil and colleagues (Chapter 7) often hint at the double vision of the disenfranchised in community development.

Feminist Specifications and Imprint

The results of challenges made to epistemological foundations of the Enlightenment paradigm that became part of critical theory have been endorsed by feminist theory:

1. Critical engagement with the contemporary world.
2. Awareness of historical and cultural contexts in defining the reality to be analyzed.
3. Examination of the assumptions and interests that enter in the formulation of theory.
4. Continuous critical reexamination of categories and conceptual frameworks of different epistemes.
5. Continuous confrontations with multiple theories that are the product of history and context.
6. Awareness that there are alternatives to the present social structure and commitment to action for the resolution of social problems.

Two features of critical theory were very important in the evolution of feminist theory: critical assessment of traditional knowledge and commitment to praxis. From there, feminism followed a line of greater specification, focusing on gender organization as the major obstacle to a just society. The link between knowledge and praxis, a characteristic of social movements, was tighter in this feminist progression. Central to feminism was the goal of doing away with the "woman disadvantage." In searching for a solution, it took several roads that together can be viewed as a near-dialectic process.

While earlier corrections demanded the introduction of gender as a necessary variable in all types of social theorizing and research, later orientations demanded the contextualization of theories and findings through the specification of structural positions, cultural norms, and historical time.

Human Similarities

Confronted with widespread gender inequalities, the second women's movement in the late 1960s and early 1970s pressed for what was most fitting within a liberal system—the Equal Rights Amendment. The goal was to equalize the opportunities of men and women as a means to a just society. The National Organization of Women emerged and took the lead in the fight for equal rights. This was accompanied by an explosion of academic writings arguing and justifying "sameness" between the genders. A just society was a unisex society or a society where gender was as inconsequential as the color of one's eyes. To assert equality, women engaged in dismantling the knowledge that reinforced gender stereotypes. They questioned and demonstrated the distortion of traditional knowledge, absence of parallel studies on both genders, and persistence of separate theories.

Two lines of arguments developed, arguing for the advantages of an androgenous or a pluralistic society. Both proposed erasing the linkages between sexual identity and social roles. Supporters of an androgenous society argued that the ideal human identity was the one that combined the best traits of women and men, that the most highly functioning individuals had such characteristics, and that in fact in most of their samples the male/female mix dominated (Bem, 1976; Heilbrun, 1973; Jaggar, 1983). The pluralist perspective did not depend on a society of ungendered members but, within a liberal principle, proposed that gender should be a matter of individual private choice. Therefore, individuals should not be denied opportunities because of sex nor should society interfere with the choice (Kirp, Yudof & Franks, 1985). Both of these positions seem to treat lightly the embeddedness of gender, the strength of gendered social identity, the multiple ways in which preferences are created and constrained, and the threat of the dominance of the male archetype. Furthermore, while the pluralist argument claims to maximize choice, it remains neutral with regard to outcomes. Examples of this in the social work literature came mostly from writings associated with macro-practice, emphasizing policy fairness, equal rights, and strategies to overcome inequality in predominantly male settings (Baldock & Cass, 1983; Figueira-McDonough & Sarri, 1987; Haynes, 1989; Sainsbury, 1994).

Earlier efforts to include women in traditional knowledge seemed to many women scholars not to be enough to bring forth neglected experiences. The focus changed to interactionist method and phenomenology as a better means to recapture and discover a hidden reality. A group of women scholars argued not only that such methods were necessary but that they were the only valid ones. They called into question the empiricist perspective itself. They argued that the researcher/research neutrality at the basis of positivism is nonexistent, that in fact once an investigator has adopted a given ontology, this system of orientation will define the nature of questions asked, what will count as an event, and the conclusions derived. This criticism emphasizes that facts are indeed products of ideology and that objectivity does not exist (Gergen, 1988). The theorist and the object of knowledge are reconceptualized as historically and culturally variable. The truth can be little more than a discursive effect produced by local heterogenous and cultural discourses (Davis & Fisher, 1993).

This dissatisfaction was best expressed by Harding (1986): "To do research on women will not suffice since existing bodies of knowledge do not simply ignore gender, they distort women's understanding of all social life by ignoring the way women shape social life and by advancing false claims about women and gender" (p. 13). This new vision of how to construct knowledge centered on women's experiences had two consequences: the emphasis on gender differences and feminist postmodernism.

Women's Distinctive Characteristics

In the late 1970s and early 1980s, the emphasis was on difference. Women did not want to become men or ungendered. The new purpose was to make women and their contributions visible and to value their distinctiveness. This led to an explosion of contributions under what Offen (1988) called "relational feminism." Friedan (1981) complained about the entrapment of women in a man's world. Chodorow (1978) and Dinnerstein (1976) analyzed the developmental origins of gender. Rossi (1977) emphasized biological differences; Ehlstain (1982) elaborated on women's capacity for child rearing as the basis for a caretaker vocation and Gilligan (1982) distinguished between men's abstract rules of morality and women's moral responsibility in concrete situations. The focus on women's differences from men carried with it a tendency to homogenize women and therefore impeded the awareness of historical, contextual, and structural differences among women.

Antipositivist reasoning propelled feminist theory to its links with postmodern thought, in which uncertainty prevails concerning the appropriate grounding of scientific propositions. A social epistemology gained ground in which knowledge claims are viewed as quintessential constituents of social interchange (Flax, 1987; Smith, 1979; Stanley & Wise, 1983). While the discovery of a multiplicity of women's voices was the result of this alliance, poststructuralist arguments by their very nature attempt to destabilize received concepts of science, order, society, and self. In its extreme form this approach was anti-science and anti-theory, its logic is disintegration, and therefore, it cannot affirm any truth or claim any political direction (diLeonardo, 1991).

However, women scholars who embraced this approach tended to introduce a direction favoring the privileged perspective of women. This ultimately took the intellectual movement back in the direction of gender polarization by advocating cultural feminism. The merit of this perspective was a research stance, a set of tools for groundbreaking, perspective-altering work. Women are represented as closer to nature and as having developed "double consciousness." Women's experience is tied more closely than man's to the grit of daily relations, to the emotions of nature, more holistic, more in touch with their humanity, and therefore more understanding of others. Most of social work writings that reflect this orientation tend to be more geared to micro practice and are especially concerned with women clients (e.g., Brook & Davis, 1985; Butler & Wintram, 1991; Coles & Coles, 1980; Kamine, 1984; Perry, 1993).

Both feminist essentialists and conservative antifeminists draw from nineteenth-century motherhood symbolism stressing women's innate identity with nurturance and nature; in so doing, they increase the gulf between genders. As Daly (1973) observes, there is a thin line between arguments for "superior" qualities of women and the reinforcement of stereotypes. This orientation increases the dualisms and categorizations that women had promised to decrease. Furthermore, in pursuit of a female-privileged perspective, we return to the argument of "natural" differences, only now the argument is reversed toward women being born superior. This process is not unique, and similar arguments have been developed in relation to the natural superiority of African Americans (Marable, 1995).

The perspective on double consciousness is more challenging and more directly linked to the issue of women's marginality or second-citizenship status. This view posits that women and minorities often hold "outsider within" positions that foster a double vision (Collins, 1991). People at the margin, it is claimed, develop a particular way of seeing reality. They look both from the outside in and from the inside out. They have what Simmel (1921) called the "stranger's greater capability for objectivity." Strangers may be able to see patterns that are invisible to those immersed in them.

As relational feminism criticized the assumptions of the equal rights movement, so it has been criticized for having moved from the consideration of economic-historical factors over the past decades toward almost exclusive attention to "subjectivities." As Bricker-Jenkins, Hooyman, and Gottlieb (1991) suggest, feminist theory is a work-in-progress and appropriately progresses in a dialectic fashion where each new position is in part shaped by arguing against the previous one (p. 5). In the process, goals are reinstated and conceptualizations are refined. Nurius and Franklin offer an insightful discussion on the trends of feminist research in Chapter 10.

New Directions

Feminism in the late 1980s and early 1990s has come out of the previous periods. Recent feminism recognizes the contributions of each previous period and looks beyond sameness and difference. The focus is on the difference of outcomes or, as in Mackinnon's (1987) words, "the difference that difference makes" (p. 10). The goal is to prevent gender differences from becoming social disadvantages. To achieve this, it is clear that mandates of equal treatment do not suffice. Since gender pervades social life, we need more empirically and historically grounded analysis, engaging more participants in the reconstruction of a social structure that promotes not only equality between the sexes but the quality of life for both.

Lorber (1994), diLeonardo (1991), and Bem (1993) offer a dialectic interpretation of feminist theory that moves from doubting the linear and sure knowledge rooted in selective experiences (deconstruction) to the development of an alternative based on the strengths of women's experiences (essentialism) and finally to an integration of a plurality of experiences selected in terms of concrete goals (ongoing dynamic reconstruction). In other words, feminist theory has moved from adjustment to traditional knowledge to creative disorganization to complex specification for action. This later stage, historically contingent and contextually framed, can become a platform toward change.

Contemporary feminism offers "no single view of our appropriate destination but it does suggest certain preferred means of travel. This depends on a careful evaluation of which women benefit, how much, at what costs, compared to which alternatives, and on an analysis of the social conditions that foster or discourage the disadvantage of women" (Rhode, 1989, p. 317).

Some authors writing in social work appear to be moving in this direction. Although mainly focusing on women clients, they attempt to integrate more directly structure and subjectivity. In addition, they use both individual experiences, guarded generalizations, and theoretical approaches in exploring knowledge constructs (e.g., Bricker-Jenkins et al., 1991; Hanmer and Statham, 1988; Langan & Day, 1992).

The dimensions of critical theory consistent with feminist theories were further specified through the changes described earlier, leading to the following intellectual and practice guidelines.

1. Recognition that gender is a complex social, historical, and cultural product.

2. Rejection of the study of unique histories and specific social formations as universal.

3. Recognition of institutionalized perceptions and patterns of behavior that are diverse and changeable without falling into polarizations or homogenized categories.

4. Promotion of methodologies that allow for the study of the relative salience of other divisions within gender.

5. Analysis of gender embeddedness so that other forms of patterned inequality can be assessed.

6. Recognition, exploration, and valuation of women's experience as a precondition to understanding the impact of different and unequal contexts on identities.
7. Initiation of a process of integration in knowledge construction guided by praxis.
8. Awareness that the end of subjugation, not difference, is the target of action.

In this sense, feminism seems to converge again with critical theory's call for greater analytical concreteness, progressing from less-adequate to more-adequate propositions, with criteria of adequacy shaped by practical problems.

Adapting Critical and Liberation Pedagogy

The quest for a new paradigm in knowledge construction carries with it demands of transmitting this new knowledge in a consistent way. The question of how to do this is complex: It requires on the one hand an ability to transmit the complex world that feminism has embraced, keeping its phenomenological strength, avoiding simplified and false dichotomies, maintaining the focus on context, structure, and history, and not imposing the instructor's own view on the students. On the other hand, it has to address how to break with traditional canons of rationality so that new problems can be resolved as they arise in ever-changing circumstances.

Feminist theory, like other contemporary approaches, validates difference, challenges universal claims to truth, and seeks to create social transformation in a world of shifting goals. In search of a pedagogy that would permit the transmission of a complex and changeable vision and at the same time commitment to a more just society, women scholars have found in Freire's (1973) pedagogical theories, with his emphasis on the primacy of experience, both a methodological tool to uncover the world of students' meaning and the ontological ground from which a politics of liberation can be waged. Equally important and in certain ways complementary are the contributions to education of theories of critical reasoning.

Central to Freire's pedagogy is the practice of "conscientialization" of inequality and oppression and the commitment to end it. It calls for the articulation of interest and identity on the part of the teacher and student (Weiler, 1994). Essential to this is learning based on shared experiences. Teacher and student are seen as joint learners. There is not a single master "narrative," but rather multiple narratives as different groups of people define their own identities, social space, and institutional relations, and as they analyze the circumstances of their oppression, and the membership in multiple collectivities, shaped within asymmetrical relations of power (Freire, 1973). The purpose is for students to recognize the historical and cultural specificity of their own lived experiences as an opportunity to acquire a critical praxis, to be transformed into an insurgent instrument for challenging hegemonic ideas, and to create new ideas and social practices. In his earlier work, Freire emphasized the link between material condition and consciousness. In complex societal contexts the conscientialization of institutional and ideological oppression become more central and so does the complexity of the praxis toward justice.

In following this approach, a feminist pedagogy posits that the validity of any strong theory comes from its capacity to explain aspects of reality personally experienced (directly or vicariously). It does accept that learning presupposes guidance in the delivery of information but insists on the conscientialization of self-experience, exposure to experiences of other students, and of texts representing other personal experience (Maher, 1984). The teacher holds authority by virtue of greater knowledge and codified experience and by the attributes given to her/his position by the academic organization. The counterpart to the teacher's claim to authority is the requirement to empower the students.

These principles suggest some general pedagogic guidelines: Participation, for example, is essential for empowerment and self-expression. To maximize learning from participation, class dialogue is a necessary means, and the teacher has a major role as simultaneous translator of the realities shared. To achieve this successfully, the atmosphere of the class has to be cooperative rather than competitive. Strategies of pass/fail, extracurricular assignments to improve grades, and group assignments might prove useful to this end.

Students must feel free to build on their experiences, on that of their peers, and on other related personal experiences transmitted by any medium. Class materials can then be used to interpret the multiplicity of experiences in an exploratory fashion rather than evaluated by standards of correct or incorrect. Experience, recognition, and interpretation will lead to theoretical understanding, the understanding of the facts that affect each student and her/his colleagues' lives and the interpretation of shared experiences. Exposure to multiple experiences demonstrates that subjects are not fixed in a timeless structure and that structures can be re-created through social relationships. Students can then enter a third level of discussion, that of the enquirer, by bringing together theory and experience in examining different interpretations of a controversial issue before taking a stand (Maher, 1984).

Critical reasoning emphasizes more intellectual clarity and is less contingent on experiential knowledge than liberation pedagogy. It involves a skeptical questioning of inadequately substantiated claims and culturally conditioned assumptions. Because ordinary consciousness always starts with a set of meanings conditioned by culture and historical tradition, the first step in critical reasoning is to free ourselves from the prejudices of our worldview, making them thematic and therefore analyzing the suppositions on which they are based (Talaska, 1990). Johnson (1990) proposes that, to do this, one needs further to be aware of one's point of view—a kind of intellectual therapy. Only then can the worldview that is revealed by one's behavior, and the worldview one thinks to hold, be compared. Johnson (1990) also proposes that the use and development of critical reasoning requires training in informal logic along a dialectic process whereby students start by a structural analysis of presenting arguments, then analyze alternatives, dealing with objectives and consequences, and finally decide on the most adequate path to problem solving. Ennis (1990) and McPeck (1990) disagree about the extent to which priority in classrooms should be given to the acquisition of critical reasoning or to the learning of the subject matter. Several proposals exist about how to combine the two. They could be taught separately, that is, with special classes in critical reasoning, or the subject matter should be used for teaching critical reasoning (infusion). Finally, a proposal more in line with the objective of this book is "immersion" in the subject so that learning about the subject will develop both critical reasoning and open new perspectives on how to study the subject content.

While liberation theory moved pedagogy toward capturing multiple experiences and to an awareness of the complexity of inequality on which praxis can be based, critical reasoning is based more on an exhaustive and ongoing intellectual exploration of different theoretical positions and assumptions. The discussion starts with the canon, and then examines conflicting views and moves toward integration in responding to problems that are at the core of specific subject matters. The pedagogical proposals in this book follow either model or a mixture of both. The suggestions of Finn (Chapter 6) and Netting and Rodwell (Chapter 8) lean more toward liberation pedagogy, while Gutierrez, Reed, Ortega, and Lewis (Chapter 5) and Hutchison and Wood (Chapter 2) favor the critical approach.

Pedagogy following either direction involves, therefore, specific ways of presenting the subject matter, of structuring classes and developing assignments (Maher, 1984). The ultimate purpose of these approaches is to establish explicit connections among three conceptual levels: observation and experience, theory, and research.

THE CASE OF SOCIAL WORK EDUCATION: READINESS FOR CHANGE AND NEW CONTRIBUTIONS

The social work profession emerged with a very strong link, even dependence, on the social sciences. This is understandable, since the social sciences themselves emerged from a modernistic worldview intent on solving social problems. Tied to historical, cultural, and structural contexts of the nineteenth century, the new social sciences were embedded in the concerns of everyday problems. It is in fact this problem-solving core of all social sciences that made their disciplines susceptible to the postmodernist reaction. The rising awareness that epistemologies are not neutral and instead reflect interests and experiences of their creators led to questions about their universality.

Reamer (1994) contends that social work has constructed a body of practice knowledge whose common denominator is sensitivity to individually based concerns and the environmental forces that affect them. However, as is true in relation to other professions, applied theories are grounded in knowledge constructs of the disciplines. Can we then assume that the same problem-centeredness that served for a revisionist stance in the social science disciplines is as visible, or more so, in social work? The answer to this question is twofold. There have been developments in practice knowledge that are consistent with the epistemological revolution proposed in this book. On the other hand, some of the disciplines' new directions seem not to have yet filtered into the intellectual context of social work foundations.

Social work curricula should reflect the range of conceptual viewpoints and theoretical perspectives that are germane to the profession, since social workers' effectiveness depends on the growth of knowledge within the profession and allied disciplines. Although

Reamer (1994) promotes this view in the introduction of his book, the other chapters, with the exception of a chapter on diversity dealing with women, do not reflect the move toward integration of women's knowledge in the various topical areas. To reduce women to a topical area jeopardizes the epistemological imperative of integration advocated in this book. Nonetheless, the demographic composition of schools of social work, the problem-solving stance of the profession, its philosophy of social justice, the development of contemporary applied theories, and Council on Social Work Education (CSWE) mandates, favor social work over other professions and disciplines to carry the torch of the paradigmatic revolution for which feminists are calling. Given this, and that women form the numerical majority of social work students, faculty, and clients, it is puzzling that their experiences, needs, and interests have not yet been fully integrated in social work education and services (Hooyman, 1994). If the knowledge transmitted in the education of social workers is limited to or dominated by the experience of a minority of men and their interpretation of women's and subjugated groups' experiences, professional training will be biased and defective. Social workers will not be equipped to empower—personally, interpersonally, institutionally, and politically—the overwhelming majority of their clients.

On the other hand, the increasing awareness on the part of women faculty, women students, and women deans of this contradiction offers good prospects for a move toward knowledge integration. For example, if a critical mass of faculty and students committed to integration is reached, then minimal integration, defined by Abramovitz et al. (1982) as based in instructors' discretion, is likely to be achieved. Also, as deanships become increasingly occupied by progressive educators (women and men), moderate integration (meaning schoolwide policies sanctioning and requiring women's content) is likely to occur.

At the institutional level, the 1979 CSWE curriculum statement made the concern for minorities and women explicit. It called for content on ethnic minorities of color and women, for attention to consequences of discrimination and oppression and understanding of the meaning of reactions to those experiences. More recent statements have reflected the same orientation in specifying curricular requirements (CSWE, 1991, 1994). For example, the 1994 CSWE Curriculum Policy Statement states that students have to be prepared to critically value diversity in terms of gender, race, ethnicity, culture, class, and sexual orientation. It also requires that they be prepared to understand the forms of oppression and discrimination as well as be prepared to use strategies and skills to advance social justice (p. 137). Current evaluation guidelines reflect change in roles and responsibilities of institutions to uphold rights of women in policies, and in procedures concerning patterns of institutional staffing, of student recruitment, and of curricula. The outcomes of these policies are unclear. On the one hand, Vinton (1992) reports that integration within foundation courses has declined since the 1980s. On the other hand, the creation of the National Association of Social Workers' National Commission of Women's Issues and the CSWE Commission on the Role and Status of Women represent the recognition of a vital constituency in the profession. Such developments are important elements for the proposed gender integration of social work knowledge.

Several trends in social work practice knowledge have converged to demand and potentially facilitate integration of women's issues in the curriculum. The development of the "ecological" approach focused the profession's attention on the significance of the individual's socioeconomic and political environment, moving the profession to a more contextualized vision of intervention. The fit between the ecological perspective and the integral concepts of the new paradigm was further increased by an extension of the ecology perspective by Germain and Gitterman (1995), where dimensions of power, history change, and life model were added to the contextual definitions and the dynamic of person/environment interactions.

At the theoretical level, elaboration and definition of social work goals resurrected the primacy of social justice and its connection to self-determination. In this respect, Wakefield's (1988) work is of great importance: It points out (a) that the uniqueness of the social work profession is determined by its goals, not its techniques, and (b) that access to basic goods (distributive justice) is a precondition for self-determination (Rawls, 1971). The social justice view implies that structurally vulnerable populations are the intended focus for social work practice and that intervention should shift from considerations of personal pathologies to promotion of access to resources. Need and structural positioning are seen as interlinked (Wood & Middleman, 1989).

The importance of the development of structural social work with its focus on modifying social situations that limit people's functioning (e.g. Middleman & Goldberg, 1974) is that it opens a new view to macro-practice, although it claims to be generalist in nature, and facilitates the analysis of various forms of oppression as intersecting at numerous points, creating an overarching system of oppression. Structural social work views social problems as arising from a specific societal context and proposes a two-pronged approach for immediate relief and longer-term institutional and structural change. It also posits that the foundation of society consists of a dominant ideology that, through socialization and power, conditions the nature of society's institutions and the relations among its people (Clark & Asquith, 1985; Davis, 1991; Goldberg-Wood & Middleman, 1974; Moreau, 1990; Mullaly, 1993).

There is also a growing push, resulting from broader curricular changes, to compare critically a variety of theoretical and practice models as a challenge to essentialist thinking that treats historical and social constructs as fixed, natural, and absolute. This critical approach—contrary to many postmodernist digressions derived from the humanities (see Nuccio & Sands, 1992)—is rationalist although not linear. Its major contribution lies in its ability to specify circumstances and problems under which different theoretical or practice approaches might be valid. In that sense, it deals with complex diagnoses that are the opposite of conventional taxonomies (Gambrill, 1991). Furthermore, such a perspective facilitates addressing environments of change. Notions of social rights and individual needs change with the emergence of new or newly discovered social problems. It follows that frames of social work intervention need to be sufficiently flexible to absorb change. This means that practice models developed at a specific historical time need to be periodically reevaluated in terms of new knowledge and adequacy of responses to new problems.

It is of interest to note that together these trends in social work education reflect the poststructuralist focus on historico-structural variables that explain diversity. On the other hand, embeddedness of gender in all aspects of life and the role of social workers in addressing the daily oppression of women and people of color has made them resistant to the seductions of postmodernist relativism. This is evident in the last work of Davis and her associates (1994). While dismissing feminist essentialism, they have built on its impetus toward valuation of women's strength and applied it to address social problems, and change the power context of interpersonal and institutional interactions. It is this commitment toward change, this view of knowledge as a social enterprise, that makes the critical reaction to modernism more suitable to the reform of social work curriculum than postmodernism.

The contributors to this book have accordingly focused on five major areas:

1. The imperative of integrating gender in social work education, both as knowledge development and practice.
2. The review of dominant theories in the field and the place of women's issues within them.
3. The critical evaluation of the construction of such theories in terms of assumptions, logical consistency, and empirical validity.
4. The critical reconstruction of alternative theoretical and practice approaches that include the experiences of women in contemporary society.
5. The need for ongoing critical renewal, with a focus on how constructed theories and practice approaches should be open to continuous reevaluation.

Based on principles of critical theory but also contingent on social change, new contexts of gender justice, and new strategies of intervention, the authors offer curricular proposals following the foci just mentioned and share with the readers the sources and arguments that support their suggestions.

There is a great diversity in the ways schools across the nation organize their curricula so what we are presenting here as separate courses might be parts of one course, or the content of one chapter might be relevant to more than one course. For example, many schools have family and group content in direct practice courses, and administration content might be part of both organization and community courses. We believe that the material covered in the chapters can be usefully integrated in various combinations.

In Chapter 2, Elizabeth Hutchinson and Leanne Wood Charlesworth present an extensive and thorough review of the various types of theories that constitute the substance of human behavior and the social environment. Their discussion is interesting as a demonstration of a process of knowledge building. They describe a process of development within each type, whereby reactions to the limitations of earlier formulations lead to refinements and specifications that expand the validity of the type of theory and simultaneously lead to some overlap with other perspectives. Their table on the centrality-marginality of gender across the various theories will be extremely useful for faculty in this field. In a more analytic vein, they offer a framework for locating the various theories based on two vectors: degree of centrality of gender issues and emphasis on praxis versus construction of knowledge.

This field, as demonstrated in the chapter, is rich and complex. The implications for practice in terms of gender are so extensive that it is impossible to specify all of them in the chapter. Furthermore, the authors argue that practitioners should not embrace a single theory, but need to search continuously for a fit between theory or theories and a given situation in a given context. They have given us an updated overview of knowledge available in this area and the place of gender in it.

Chapter 3 addresses direct practice curricula. Iris Carlton-LaNey and Janice Andrews give us a historical overview of the development of social work practice, highlighting the common impact of paternalism on the treatment of women and blacks. Next, they describe the contemporary alternatives that have emerged to undo this legacy. Theories of direct practice dominant in schools of social work are reviewed, and their limitations and strengths in addressing gender are discussed. Their chapter makes a unique contribution by integrating race and gender. In so doing, they have expanded feminist theorizing and practice in an area of acknowledged weakness. In defending the importance of group empowerment in direct practice with women, they go beyond traditional direct practice schema, bringing networks to the center of intervention.

José Ashford and Jill Littrell (Chapter 4) address a part of the social work curriculum that has become controversial in recent times—Psychopathology. The authors stress the need for many social work practitioners to be familiar with the *Diagnostic and Statistical Manual-Fourth Edition* (DSM-IV), and center the discussion around this system of diagnostic classification. First Ashford and Littrell note the contradictions between professional principles of social work and the purpose of the diagnostic scheme, and they go on to use DSM-IV as an example of the construction of mental health definitions. A review of definitions of mental disorders shows the inadequacies of each perspective and hence the vagueness of the bases of diagnostic classifications. This awareness is a necessary background against which to examine gender differences in mental disorders. Interpretation of such differences goes beyond assumed and even verified biological causes to the examination of structural origins. Women's successful fight against some mental disorders typically ascribed to women have been based on proving that they are the result of traumatic experiences (masochist personality disorder) or on the normalcy of biological functions intrinsic to women (PMS). In view of the fact that the construction of mental disorders reflects the power and biases of the creators of diagnostic schemes, students are encouraged to critically question evidence and interpretation supporting the labeling system and examine consequences of its application for women and other powerless groups.

Group work is addressed by Lorraine Gutierrez, Beth Glover Reed, Robert Ortega, and Edith Lewis in Chapter 5. They review the history of group work in social work and underline the preference for this method in feminist practice. It is a type of practice that has the capacity to link personal to group experiences and to insert both in societal contexts. The authors argue that while group work as a separate intervention method has been declining, the relevance of groups to all other forms of intervention has been increasing, making the infusion of group work in all these other courses a necessity. Work with groups is central to the integration of women issues in social work. Research on the marked gender differences in group structure and patterns of participation, and their variation by group composition, is reviewed, as are the theories that attempt to explain these patterns. The authors conclude that the study and practice of groups has a unique potential for raising the awareness of gender interaction and serving as a vehicle for change. Using classes as groups and group assignments can therefore have a major impact in promoting the experiential gender integration of the curriculum.

Janet Finn starts her discussion on the family in Chapter 6 with the premise that both the concept of the family and the concept of gender are constructs aimed at upholding and reproducing stratified, unequal relationships. A case in point is the acceptance of the nuclear family as a standard against which all families are evaluated, in spite of its relatively recent construction and its lack of statistical norm. She proposes that it would be more helpful to view families as "arenas of struggle where power and intimacy, conflict and support play out in shaping gender and generational relations."

Critically reviewing functional, system, exchange, and interactionist family theories, she finds that they are either an outgrowth of political and economic organizations or that they fail to address historical contexts and external constraints. In sum, they are predicated on the U.S. white, middle-class nuclear family model. The impact of this construction on social work practice is the pathologization of female-headed households, of minority kin arrangements, and of gay/lesbian couplings. Finn contends that because kinship and gender are mutually constructed in political and economic systems, the family is a key for exploring the ways in which gendered power relationships are constituted and reproduced. Feminist scholars have identified the key practices in the construction of gender by decoding the politics of every day life and examining the links between family roles and economic and political systems. Students should be imparted strategies to "find" families, participate in experiential learning, and use critical analysis in fieldwork, with the purpose of understanding the construction of difference.

Chapter Seven covers community practice. Marie Weil, Dorothy N. Gamble, and Evelyn Smith Williams argue for the central role of community work for social work in the twenty-first century. Indeed, for practice to be responsive to the impact on the poor—especially poor women, of political, economic, social, and technological changes—social workers need to reengage more forcefully in community practice. The authors present a historical overview of the roots and development of community method in social work. They highlight its origins in the settlement house movement and the influence of women leaders in shaping the values of social reform and democratic participation, intrinsic to this method of intervention. While the presence of women leaders in community practice stayed strong up to the 1930s, their voices began to weaken in the 1940s and 1950s. Finally, during the period of greatest development in schools of social work, the 1960s and 1970s, the field was dominated by male voices. It was the emergence of feminist theories in social work, in the 1980s, and the parallel development of empowerment models of practice, that forms the basis of the models of practice that they propose. Adopting community-practice development models developed by Weil and Gamble (1995), the authors develop feminist applications of such models.

F. Ellen Netting and Mary K. Rodwell begin Chapter 8 on administration with a review of classic and contemporary organization theories highlighting the dominance of male metaphors. They further propose the use of Weick's (1995) "sensemaking" approach as a strategy to evaluate the gender sensitivity of these theories, and they assess the contributions of power/politics and culture conceptualizations to the inclusion of women in organizational theory.

The authors engage in the reconstruction of theories and practice models to meet Weick's framework, and they discuss four assumptions on which such reconstruction will be based: organization/environment interpenetration, the moral and political nature of decision-making, the importance of language in creating and transmitting power, and the awareness of the diversity of organizational cultures. The work of five contemporary authors is selected and discussed to serve as guides for reconstructed practice models. Netting and Rodwell acknowledge that the nature of work in progress of conceptual formulations they are using prevents them from proposing more precise practice guidelines. That is a creative activity to which both faculty and students will contribute.

Ann Nichols-Casebolt starts Chapter 9 on policy by underlying the centrality of social policy for the concerns of women. Teaching of social welfare policy in social work usually follows two vectors: history and analysis. Historical accounts usually describe the impact of liberal ideologies and the emergence of social Darwinism in the nineteenth century, in order to explain the late emergence of the welfare state in the United States. Discussions of the emergence of the two-tier system in Social Security legislation is also central to history courses. Often missing in such accounts, according to Nichols-Casebolt, is the role that women had in shaping welfare policy and the Catch–22 created for women who, according to individualist ideals, are expected to be independent and are put in a position of dependence by the family ethic. In fact, this is the core of the gender inequities in family responsibilities, job-access, and remuneration as well as the contradictions in welfare policy.

Policy analysis courses tend to emphasize rational decision-making whereby information is collected regarding a problem and policies emerge as an informed response to the problem. Although it is admissible that in this process the information might be inadequate and therefore the policy inefficient, decisions are still presented as free of interest, differential power, and established assumptions—therefore gender-neutral. The author gives evidence of the fallacy of such presuppositions and how gender-neutral language hides gender realities such as the huge overrepresentation of women in poverty and the devastating and punitive aspects of recent welfare reforms on women.

In Chapter 10, Paula Nurius and Cynthia Franklin address the role of gender in practice research. They have two goals: (1) to identify the underrepresentation of women and women's issues in social research and suggest strategies to rectify it, and (2) to link the research enterprise in social work with practice effectiveness and social change.

In pursuing the first goal, they analyze limitations of traditional research that account for the exclusion or distortion of women's reality (e.g., gender-limited content, biased designs, illusion of objectivity, improper generalization of findings, exclusion of contexts, dissemination limited to academia). The authors analyze the proposed feminist corrections to these distortions with great clarity. They start by describing the nature of contemporary empiricism, and the many forms of qualitative research, then they demonstrate the danger of both in excluding women as well as their capacity for encompassing women's issues.

Their discussion highlights the advantages of combining multiple designs as a way of compensating for these weaknesses. Strategies for teaching students to evaluate and select the most appropriate method for the problem being studied are suggested, as are guidelines for learning the research process through a dialogic approach to the definition of the research question, selection of appropriate methods, and openness to change and development in research. The links between research and practice, and the location of gender in this intersection, are reinforced. The commitment to social justice moves the inclusion of women's issues to the center of the research-practice concerns in social work.

All the chapters in this book give the authors' critical construction of what needs to be changed in order to move toward curricular gender integration in their specific areas. They also have developed models of courses, teaching and field assignments, teaching and field-orientation strategies, and bibliographies consistent with their arguments. This contribution, we think, can be vital to readers committed to gender-integrated curricula. The link between a conceptual argument and its pedagogical implementation will, we believe, be of great value to faculty and students. The presumption is not that faculty will adopt such course outlines but that they will serve as a useful base for their own creative transformations.

In the final chapter the editors grapple with the issue of implementation of a gender-integrated curricula in social work. How can a second-order change of the type proposed in this book be achieved in a school of social work? Organizational change can be initiated internally, that is, within schools of social work, or externally, from the school's environment, or interactively from both directions.

The environment of schools of social work is constituted by the university hierarchy, the university culture, other departments, and the university environment. School constituencies are very important from this perspective because of the close links of the schools with the network of agencies serving as field placements for social work students, the presence of the CSWE as an accrediting agency, and the professional culture represented by the National Association of Social Workers (NASW). The characteristics of these contexts and the different conditions of influence in schools of social work are discussed. Loci for change internal to the schools can be the administration, the faculty, the students, or the alliances between any of them.

Studies of academic secondary change, as the one proposed here, are rare. However, some of the studies we found are helpful in linking different schools' structures to a sequence of tactics, and they also offer an analysis of the different strengths of a range of strategies. The final chapter gives suggestions of strategic choices within a variety of scenarios. To build more specific knowledge in this area, all of us will depend on the contribution of future experiments in schools of social work engaged in the enterprise proposed in this book.

REFERENCES

Abramovitz, M. (1988). *Regulating the lives of women: Social welfare policy from colonial times to the present.* New York: Columbia University Press.

Abramovitz, M., Hopkins, T.J., Olds, V. & Waring, M. (1982). Integrating content on women into social policy curriculum: A continuum model. *Journal of Education for Social Work, 18* (1), 29–34.

Arendt, H. (1958). *The human condition.* Chicago: University of Chicago Press.

Baldock, C. & Cass, B. (1983). *Women, social work and the state in Australia.* Sidney, Australia: Allen and Unwin.

Bem, S.L. (1976). Probing the promise of androgyny. In A.G. Kaplan and J.P. Bean (Eds.), *Beyond sex-role stereotypes: Readings toward a psychology of androgyny* (pp. 481–502). Boston: Little, Brown.

Bem, S.L. (1993). *The lenses of inequality: Transforming the debate on sexual inequality*. New Haven: Yale University Press.

Bernard, J. (1987). Reviewing the impact of women studies on sociology. In C. Farnham (Ed.), *The impact of feminist research in the academy* (pp. 193–216). Bloomington: Indiana University Press.

Bloom, A. (1987). *The closing of the American mind.* New York: Simon & Schuster.

Bricker-Jenkins, M., Hooyman, N. & Gottlieb, N. (Eds.). (1991). *Feminist social work practice in clinical practice*. Newbury Park, CA: Sage.

Brook, E. & Davis, A. (1985). *Women, the family and social work*. London: Tavistock Publications.

Butler, S. & Wintram, C. (1991). *Feminist group work*. London: Sage.

Calhoun, C. (1995). *Critical social theory: Culture, history and the challenge of difference*. Cambridge, MA: Blackwell.

Carter, C., Coudrouglou, A., Figueira-McDonough, J., Lie, G.Y., Maceachron, A.E., Netting, E.F., Nichols-Casebolt, A., Nichols, A.W. & Rizley-Curtis, C. (1994). Integrating women's issues in the social work curriculum: A proposal. *Journal of Social Work Education, 30*(2), 200–216.

Cates, J. (1983). *Insuring inequality*. Ann Arbor: University of Michigan Press.

Chaffetz, J.S. (1988). The gender division of labor and the reproduction of female disadvantage: Towards an integrated theory. *Journal of Family Issues, 9*(1), 108–131.

Chodorow, N. (1978). *The reproduction of mothering: Psychoanalytic feminism and the sociology of gender*. Berkeley: University of California Press.

Clark, C.L. & Asquith, S. (1985). *Social work and social policy: A guide for practice.* London: Routledge and Kegan Paul.

Cloward, R. & Piven, F. (1974). *The politics of turmoil: Essays on poverty, race and the urban crisis.* New York: Vintage Books.

Coles, R. & Coles, J.H. (1980). *Women of crisis II: Lives of work and dreams*. New York: Delacorte Press.

Collins, P.H. (1991). Learning from the outsider within: The sociological significance of Black feminist thought. In M.M. Fonow & J.A. Cook (Eds.), *Beyond methodology: Feminist scholarship as lived research* (pp. 35–59). Bloomington: Indiana University Press.

Council of Social Work Education. (1979). *Curriculum for the master's degree and baccalaureate degree programs in social work education.* Washington, DC: Author.

Council of Social Work Education. (1991). Curriculum policy statement for the master's degree and the baccalaureate degree programs in social work education. In *Handbook of accreditation standards and procedures.* Washington, DC: Author.

Council of Social Work Education. (1994). Curriculum policy statement for the master's degree and the baccalaureate degree programs in social work education. In *Handbook of accreditation standards and procedures.* Washington, DC: Author.

Daly, M. (1973). *Beyond God the father: Toward a philosophy of women's liberation.* Boston: Beacon.

Davis, A. (1991). A structural approach to social work. In J. Lishman (Ed.), *Handbook of theory for practice teachers in social work* (pp. 70–79). London: Jessica Kingsley Publishers.

Davis, L. (1994). We still need a woman's agenda for social work. In L. Davis (Ed.), *Building on women's strength: A social work agenda for the twenty-first century* (pp. 1–25). Binghamton, NY: Haworth.

Davis, K. & Fisher, S. (1993). Power and the female subject. In. S. Fisher & K. Davis (Eds.), *Negotiating at the margins: The gendered discourses of power and resistance* (pp. 3–22). New Brunswick, NJ: Rutgers University Press.

diLeonardo, M. (1991). Gender, culture, and political economy: Feminist anthropology in historical perspective. In M. diLeonardo (Ed.), *Gender at the crossroads of knowledge: Feminist anthropology in the postmodern era* (pp. 1–48). Berkeley: University of California Press.

Dinnerstein, D. (1976). *The mermaid and the minotaur: Sexual arrangements and the human malaise*. New York: Harper & Row.

Dominelli, L. (1991). Convergence between capitalist and socialist models of welfare. In L. Dominelli, *Women across continents: Feminist comparative social policy* (pp. 1–26). London: Harvester Wheatsheaf.

Ehlstain, J.B. (1982). Feminism, family and community. *Dissent, 19*, 442–447.

Ennis, R. (1990). Conflicting views on teaching critical reasoning. In R. Talaska (Ed.), *Critical reasoning in contemporary culture* (pp. 5–27). Albany: State University of New York Press.

Fanon, F. (1963). *The wretched of the earth.* New York: Grove Press.

Farrell, S.A. (1992). Feminism and sociology. In S. Zalk & J. Gordon-Kelter (Eds.), *Revolutions of knowledge* (pp. 57–78). Boulder, CO: Westview Press.

Figueira-McDonough, J. & Sarri, R. (Eds.) (1987). *The trapped woman: Catch 22 in deviance and control.* Newbury Park, CA: Sage.

Fisher, S. (1987). Good women after all: Cultural definitions and social control. In J. Figueira-McDonough & R. Sarri (Eds.), *The trapped woman: Catch 22 in deviance and control* (pp. 318–347). Newbury Park, CA: Sage.

Flax, J. (1987). Postmodernism and gender relations in feminist theory. *Signs, 12*, 621–633.

Foucault, M. (1980). *Power/knowledge: Selected interviews and other writings.* New York: Pantheon.

Franks, V. & Rothblum, E.D. (1983). *The stereotyping of women: Its effects on mental health.* New York: Springer

Freire, P. (1973). *Education for critical consciousness.* New York: Continuum.

Friedan, B. (1981). *The second stage*. New York: Summit Books.

Gambrill, E. (1991). *Critical thinking in clinical practice.* San Francisco: Jossey-Bass.

Garfinkel, H. (1967). *Studies in ethnomethodology*. Englewood Cliffs, NJ: Prentice-Hall.

Gergen, K. (1988). Feminist critique of science and the challenge of social epistemology. In M. McCanney-Gerden (Ed.), *Feminist thought and the structure of knowledge* (pp. 27–48). New York: New York University Press.

Germain, C.B. & Gitterman, A. (1995). Ecological perspective. In *Social work encyclopedia* (Vol 1., 19th ed., pp .816–824). Silver Spring, MD: NASW Press.

Gilkes, C.T. (1992). A case-study: Race-ethnicity, class, and African-American women: Exploring the community connections. In S.R. Zalk & J. Gordon-Kelter (Eds.), *Revolutions in knowledge: Feminism in the social sciences* (pp. 63–78). San Francisco: Westview Press.

Gilligan, C. (1982). *In a different voice: Psychological theory and women's development.* Cambridge, MA: Harvard University Press.

Goldberg-Wood, G. & Middleman, R. (1974). *The structural approach to direct practice in social work*. New York: Columbia University Press.

Gordon, L. (1990). The new feminist scholarship on the welfare state. In L. Gordon (Ed.), *Women, the state and welfare* (pp. 9–35). Madison: University of Wisconsin Press.

Habermas, J. (1990). *Moral consciousness and communicative action*. Cambridge, MA: MIT Press.

Hanmer, J. & Stanham, D. (1988). *Women and social work: Towards a women centered practice*. London: Macmillan Education.

Harding, S. (1986). *The science question in feminism*. Ithaca, NY: Cornell University Press.

Harvey, S. (1992). *The condition of postmodernity.* Cambridge, MA: Blackwell.

Haynes, K. (1989). *Women managers in human services*. New York: Springer.

Heilbrun, C. (1973). *Toward a recognition of androgyny*. New York: Knopf.

Hooyman, N. (1994). Diversity and populations at risk: Women. In F.G. Reamer (Ed.), *The foundations of social work knowledge* (pp. 309–345). New York: Columbia University Press.

Hubbard, R. (1988). Some thoughts about the masculinity of the natural sciences. In M.M. Gergen (Ed.), *Feminist thought and the structure of knowledge* (1–15). New York: New York University Press.

Jackman, M.R. (1994). *The velvet glove: Paternalism and conflict in gender, class and race relations.* Berkeley: University of California Press.

Jaggar, A. (1983). *Feminist politics and human nature.* Sussex, England: Rowman & Allenhead.

Jansen-Jurreit, M. (1982). *Sexism: The male monopoly on the history of thought*. London: Pluto Press.

Jaquette, J.S. (1992). Political science—whose common good? In C. Kramarae & D. Sender (Eds.), *The knowledge explosion: Generations of feminist scholarship* (pp. 141–153). New York: Teachers College Press.

Johnson, P.B. & Frieze, I.H. (1978) Biases in psychology: What are the facts? In I.H. Frieze (Ed.), *Women and sex roles: A social psychological perspective* (pp. 16–27). New York: Norton.

Johnson, R.H. (1990). Critical reasoning and informal logic. In R. Talaska (Ed.), *Critical reasoning in contemporary culture* (pp. 69–87). Albany: State University of New York Press.

Kamine, W. (1984). *Women volunteering*. Garden City, NY: Doubleday.

Keller, E.F. (1985). *Reflections on gender and science.* New Haven: Yale University Press.

Kessler, S.J. & McKenna, W. (1978) *Gender: An ethnomethodological approach.* New York: Wiley

Kirp, D., Yudof, M.G. & Franks, M.S. (1985). *Gender justice*. Chicago: University of Chicago Press.

Kuhn, T. (1970). *The structure of scientific revolutions*. Chicago: University of Chicago Press.

Langan, M. & Day, L. (Eds.). (1992). *Women, oppression and social work: Issues in anti-discriminatory practice*. London: Routledge.

Lerner, G. (1986). *The creation of patriarchy*. New York: Oxford University Press.

Lewis, J. (1992). Women's history, gender history, and feminist politics. In C. Kramarae & D. Sender (Eds.), *The knowledge explosion: Generations of feminist scholarship* (pp. 154–160). New York: Teachers College Press.

Lipsky, M. (1980). *Street level bureaucracy: Dilemmas of the individual in public services*. New York: Russell Sage Foundation.

Long Laws, J. (1972). A feminist review of marital adjustment literature: The rape of the Locke. *Journal of Marriage and the Family, 33*, 483–517.

Lorber, J. (1994). *Paradoxes of gender*. New Haven: Yale University Press.

Macaulay, J. (1985). Adding gender to aggression research: Incremental or revolutionary change. In V. O'Leary and B.S. Allston (Eds.), *Women, gender and social psychology* (pp. 191–224). Hillsdale, NJ: Erlbaum.

Mackinnon, C. (1987). *Feminism unmodified.* Cambridge, MA: Harvard University Press.

Maher, F. (1984). Appropriate teaching methods for integrating women. In B. Spanier, A. Bloom & D. Boroviak (Eds.), *Toward a balanced curriculum: A sourcebook for initiating gender integration projects* (pp. 101–108). Cambridge, MA: Schenkman.

Manheim, K. (1954). *Ideology and utopia: An introduction to the sociology of knowledge.* New York: Harcourt, Brace.

Marable, M. (1995). Black studies, multiculturalism, and the future of American education. *Items, 49* (2–3), 49–57.

McPeck, J. (1990). Teaching critical reasoning through the disciplines: Content versus process. In R. Talaska (Ed.), *Critical reasoning in contemporary culture* (pp. 31–49). Albany: State University of New York Press.

Middleman, R. & Goldberg, G. (1974). *Social service delivery: A structural approach to social work practice.* New York: Columbia University Press.

Mills, C.W. (1959). *The sociological imagination.* New York: Oxford University Press.

Mintz, S. & Wolf, E. (1989). Reply to Michael Taussig. *Critique of Anthropology, 9* (1), 25–31.

Moreau, M. (1990). Empowerment through advocacy and consciousness-raising: Implications of a structural approach to social work. *Journal of Sociology and Social Welfare, 7*(2), 53–67.

Mullaly, R. (1993). *Structural social work: Ideology, theory and practice.* Toronto, Ontario: McClelland and Stewart.

Newman, L.M. (Ed.). (1985). *Men's ideas/women's realities: Popular sciences, 1870–1915.* New York: Pergamon.

Nuccio, K. & Sands, R. (1992). Using postmodern feminist theory to deconstruct "phalacies" of poverty. *Affilia, 7*(4), 24–48

Offen, K. (1988). Defining feminism: A comparative historical approach. *Signs, 14*, 119–123,

Parlee, M.B. (1992). Feminism and psychology. In S. Zalk & J. Gordon-Kelter (Eds.), *Revolutions of knowledge: Feminism in the social sciences* (pp. 33–55). San Francisco: Westview Press.

Pateman, C. (1988). *The sexual contract*. Oxford, England: Polity Press.

Perry, J. (1993). *Counseling for women*. Philadelphia: Open University Press.

Quadagno, J. (1994). *The color of welfare: How racism undermined the war on poverty*. New York: Oxford University Press.

Rawls, J. (1971). *A theory of justice.* Cambridge, MA: Harvard University Press.

Reamer, F.G. (1994). The evolution of social work knowledge. In F.G. Reamer (Ed.), *The foundations of social work knowledge* (pp. 1–12). New York: Columbia University Press.

Rhode, D.L. (1989). *Justice and gender: Sex discrimination and the law.* Cambridge, MA: Harvard University Press.

Rosenau, P.M. (1992). *Post-modernism and the social sciences*. Princeton, NJ: Princeton University Press.

Rossi, A. (1977). A biosocial perspective on parenting. *Daedalus, 103*, 53–67.

Sainsbury, D. (Ed.). (1994). *Gendering welfare states.* London: Sage.

Scott, J. (1988). *Gender and the politics of history.* New York: Columbia University Press.

Scully, D. & Bart, P.J. (1973). A funny thing happened in the way to the orifice: Women in gynecology textbooks. *American Journal of Sociology, 78,* 1045–1049.

Simmel, G. (1921). The sociological significance of the "stranger." In R.E. Park & E. Burgess (Eds.), *Introduction to the science of sociology* (pp. 322–327). Chicago: University of Chicago Press.

Smith, D. (1979). A sociology for women. In J.A. Sherman & E.T. Beck (Eds.), *The prism of sex: Essays in the sociology of knowledge* (pp. 135–187). Madison: University of Wisconsin Press.

Spencer-Wood, S.M. (1994). Diversity and nineteenth-century domestic reform. In E. Scott (Ed.), *Those of little note: Gender, race and class in historical archeology* (pp. 175–208). Tucson: University of Arizona Press.

Stanley, L. (1992). The impact of feminism on sociology in the last 20 years. In C. Kramarae & D. Sender (Eds.), *The knowledge explosion: Generations of feminist scholarship* (pp. 254–269). New York: Teachers College Press.

Stanley, L. & Wise, S. (1983). *Breaking out: Feminist consciousness and feminist research.* London: Routledge & Kegan Paul.

Stimpson, C. (1984). Where does integration fit: The development of women's studies. In B. Spanler, A. Bloom & D. Boroviak (Eds.), *Towards a balanced curriculum: A sourcebook for initiating gender integrating projects* (pp.11–24). Cambridge, MA: Shenkman Publishing.

Talaska, R.A. (Ed.). (1990). *Critical reasoning in contemporary culture.* Albany: State University of New York Press.

Thompson, E.P. (1963). *The making of the working class*. New York: Random House.

Vinton, L. (1992). Women's content in social work curricula: Separate but equal? *Affilia, 7*(1), 74–89.

Wakefield, J.C. (1988). Psychotherapy, distributive justice and social work: Part I—Distributive justice as a conceptual framework for social work. *Social Service Review, 62*, 187–210.

Waring, M.J. (1989). *If women counted.* San Francisco: Harper & Row.

Waring, M.J. (1992). Economics. In C. Kramarae & D. Sender (Eds.), The knowledge explosion: Generations of feminist scholarship (pp. 303–309). New York: Teachers College Press.

Weick, K.E. (1995). *Sensemaking in organizations*. Thousand Oaks, CA: Sage.

Weil, M. & Gamble, D. (1995). Community practice models. In *Social work encyclopedia* (Vol. 1, 19th ed., pp. 577–594). Silver Spring, MD: NASW Press.

Weiler, K. (1994). Freire and a feminist pedagogy of difference. In P.L. McLaren & C. Lankshear (Eds.), *Politics of Liberation: Paths from Freire* (pp. 12–40). New York: Routledge.

Wood, G.G. & Middleman, R.R. (1989). *The structural approach to direct practice in social work*. New York: Columbia University Press.

Zalk, S.R. & Gordon-Kelter, J. (1992). Feminism, revolution and knowledge. In S.R. Zalk & J. Gordon-Kelter (Eds.), *Revolutions of knowledge: Feminism in the social sciences* (pp.1–14). San Francisco: Westview Press.

Zinn, M.B. (1992). Reframing the revisions: Inclusive thinking for family sociology. In C. Kramarae & D. Sender (Eds.), *The knowledge explosion: Generations of feminist scholarship* (pp. 473–479). New York: Teachers College Press.

CHAPTER 2

Human Behavior in the Social Environment

The Role of Gender in the Expansion of Practice Knowledge

Elizabeth D. Hutchison
Leanne Wood Charlesworth

INTRODUCTION

Meyer (1987, 1993) has noted, with some concern, a trend in contemporary social work curricula to put far greater emphasis on processes of intervention than on content about populations and problems, on "doing" rather than on "thinking about what the matter is" (1993, p. 6). Germain (1994) reminds us, however, that from the earliest days of the social work profession, practitioners were keenly aware of the need for understanding people, situations, and problems. Social work has struggled with the challenge of finding an integrative knowledge base that focuses simultaneously on people and situations to understand problems in living, and a person-in-environment perspective is evolving. Since 1962, the Curriculum Policy Statement (CPS) of the Council on Social Work Education (CSWE) has assigned the task of presenting knowledge about person-in-environment to a curriculum component recently known as Human Behavior in the Social Environment (HBSE). It is, theoretically, in the HBSE sequence that the student develops the knowledge base for focusing on the transactions of people with environments to "think about what the matter is."

Stimulated by recent rapid societal transformations, and by attempts of the social and behavioral sciences to keep abreast of those transformations, the HBSE knowledge base is expanding at an intense pace. The current CSWE CPS requires that the HBSE sequence educate students about the diversity of experience that ensues from the complex confluence of personal and environmental variables. Germain (1994, p. 88) predicted that "a look ahead to the twenty-first century, and social work's second century, the profession's dual, yet one-dimensional, focus appears to be in the process of transformation to a multidimensional focus on 'diverse person(s) in diverse environments.'" There is growing consensus that we cannot "think about what the matter is" without understanding the diversity of experiences that arises when diverse and dynamic persons transact with diverse and dynamic environments.

In social work, as in the social and behavioral sciences, the study of gender has been a major element in the new emphasis on diversity. Relevant to the HBSE curriculum, traditional theories of human behavior have come under attack for their basis in male experience, and for failing to take account of female experience (Bernard, 1975; Gilligan, 1982; Gould, 1984; Miller, 1986). Critics have noted that the theorists have been almost exclusively male, and that they have either ignored gender as an element in human behavior or they have written about gender from their privileged male perspective, with a deficit model of femaleness. These critics have called attention to the social, economic, political, and historical contexts of gender, pointing out that "every society has a gender-based definition of economic and social roles" (Greene, 1994a, p. 7), and noting that both historical and contemporary societies assign the control of social, political, and economic institutions to men. Defined gender roles, and their historical power differential, are a salient element in the person-environment transactions of both men and women. A multidimensional understanding of person-in-environment must recognize the "ways in which gender is created and maintained through interpersonal processes" (Riger, 1992, p. 737). Social work practice is a system of interpersonal processes, and social workers must be alert to the ways in which their processes create and maintain gender.

It is also important to recognize gender as only one dimension of a multidimensional perspective on human behavior. We caution against a one-dimensional focus on between-gender differences that fails to take account of the within-gender differences in experience related to other salient dimensions of person-in-environment, such as social class, race, and national origin. Gender is always salient, but gender is not the only salient dimension, and social workers must remain open to the possibility that gender may not be the most salient dimension of some person-environment configurations.

The purpose of this chapter is to examine social and behavioral science theoretical perspectives currently included in the conceptual base of HBSE curricula for their utility in understanding "diverse persons in diverse environments," with special attention to gender. Applications to social work practice and implications for the HBSE curriculum are also discussed.

There is no generally agreed upon perspective or cluster of perspectives for presenting a multidimensional approach to person-in-environment. Germain's (1994) historical overview of the development of knowledge for social work practice suggests that we moved, over time, from a preference for sociological knowledge to a preference for psychological knowledge, and have come to seek knowledge of both personal and environmental factors. In 1958, Stein and Cloward published an edited reader entitled *Social Perspectives on Behavior: A Reader in Social Science for Social Work and Related Professions*, commenting in the preface that social work had failed, in the midst of its fascination with dynamic psychology, to keep abreast of developments in sociology, cultural anthropology, and social psychology.

A convergence of developments intensified the pressure to "put the social back in social work," and in 1962 a revised CSWE CPS renamed the Human Growth and Behavior (HGB) sequence as Human Behavior in the Social Environment. Since that time, there has been a great deal of tension about the conceptual framework for HBSE. Throughout the 1970s and 1980s, schools of social work tended to resolve this tension by choosing one of two competing theoretical approaches, choosing either a psychodynamic framework or a systems framework. In the 1990s, there is a trend toward a multitheoretical framework (see Greene, 1994b; Greene & Ephross, 1991; Longres, 1995; Schriver, 1995) to facilitate a multidimensional approach. Following this trend, we analyze eight theoretical perspectives that recent social work scholars have identified as necessary elements in a multitheoretical framework. The perspectives are based in both sociology and psychology, as well as social psychology, and several have interdisciplinary roots. The eight theoretical perspectives to be analyzed include: systems perspective, conflict perspective, rational choice

Table 2–1
Central Ideas of Theoretical Perspectives

Systems
- Systems are made up of interrelated members (parts) that constitute an ordered whole.
- Each part of the system has an impact both on all other parts and on the system as a whole.
- All systems are subsystems of other larger systems.
- Systems maintain boundaries that give them their identities.
- Systems tend toward homeostasis, or equilibrium.

Conflict
- Groups and individuals try to advance their own interests over the interests of others.
- Power is unequally divided, and some social groups dominate others.
- Social order is based on the manipulation and control of nondominant groups by dominant groups.
- Lack of open conflict is a sign of exploitation.
- Social change is driven by conflict, with periods of change interrupting long periods of stability.

Rational Choice
- People are rational and goal directed.
- Social exchange is based on self-interest with actors trying to maximize rewards and minimize costs.
- Reciprocity of exchange is essential to social life.
- Power comes from unequal resources in exchange.

Social Constructionist
- Actors are free, active, and creative.
- Social reality is created when actors, in social interaction, develop a common understanding of their world.
- Social interaction is grounded in "linguistic conventions, as well as cultural and historical contexts" (Witkin & Gottschalk, 1988, p. 213).
- People can modify meanings in the process of interaction.
- Society consists of social processes, not social structures.

Psychodynamic
- Emotions have a central place in human behavior.
- Unconscious, as well as conscious, mental activity serves as the motivating force in human behavior.

Table 2–1 *(continued)*

- Early childhood experiences are central in the patterning of an individual's emotions, and therefore, they are central to problems of living throughout life.
- Individuals may become overwhelmed by internal and/or external demands.
- Ego defense mechanisms are frequently used by individuals to avoid becoming overwhelmed by internal and/or external demands.

Developmental

- Human development occurs in clearly defined stages.
- Each stage of life is qualitatively different from all other stages.
- Stages of development are sequential, with each stage building on earlier stages.
- Stages of development are universal.
- All environments provide the support necessary for development.

Social Behavioral

- Human behavior is learned when individuals interact with the environment.
- Similar learning processes taking place in different environments produce differences in human behavior (Thyer, 1994).
- Human behavior is learned by association of environmental stimuli.
- Human behavior is learned by reinforcement.
- Human behavior is learned by imitation.
- Human behavior is influenced by personal expectations and meanings.

Humanistic

- Humans are "spiritual, rational, purposeful, and autonomous" (Monte, 1995, p. 665).
- Human behavior can be understood only from the vantage point of the phenomenal self, from the internal frame of reference of the individual.
- People make psychologically destructive demands on each other, and attempts to meet those demands produce anxiety.
- Human behavior is driven by a desire for growth and competence, and by a need for love and acceptance.

Table 2–2: Summary of Major Theorists According to Attention to Gender and Power Issues

Perspective	Little or No Attention to Either Gender or Power	Emphasizes Gender But Not Gender-Power Issues	Emphasizes Power But Not Gender-Power Issues	Emphasizes Gender-Power Issues
Systems	P. Allen-Meares & B. Lane; U. Bronfenbrenner; C. Germain & A. Gitterman; C. Meyer; A. Pincus & A. Minahan; M. Siporin	T. Parsons	K. Lewin; P. Martin & G. O'Connor	A. Hartman (1987); J. Longres; M. Johnson; D. Luepnitz; C. Germain; M. McGoldrick (1988); M. McGoldrick, C. Anderson & F. Walsh; M. Walters, B. Carter, P. Papp & O. Silverstein; R. Merton
Conflict			L. Coser; R. Dahrendorf; G. Lenski; C.W. Mills; J. Habermas; T. Skocpol; K. Marx; I. Wallerstein; M. Mann	F. Engels; M. Weber; R. Collins; Z. Eisenstein; J. Chafetz; R. Blumberg; L. Vogel
Rational Choice	G. Homans; J. March & H. Simon; J. Coleman; J. Thibaut & H. Kelley; A. Collins & D. Pancoast; E. Tracy & J. Whittaker; C. Streeter & D. Gillespie	K. Gerson; K. Luker	P. Blau; R. Emerson; K. Cook	M. Brinton; R. Blood & D. Wolfe; J. Scanzoni; C. Safilios-Rothschild

Constructionist	P. Berger & T. Luckmann; E. Husserl; J. Dewey; H. Blumer; G. Mead; C. Cooley; R. Imre	E. Goffman; H. Garfinkel	M. Rodwell; D. Saleeby; S. Witkin & S. Gottschalk	J. Laird; P. Collins; D. Smith; A. Weick
Psychodynamic	A. Freud; M. Klein; M. Mahler; H. Hartmann; O. Kernberg; H. Kohut; R. White; D. Winnicott	S. Freud		A. al-Hibri; D. Dinnerstein; N. Chodorow
Developmental	E. Erikson; J. Piaget; H. Sullivan; G. Valliant; R. Gould; L. Kohlberg; R. Havighurst	S. Freud; B. Newman & P. Newman; B. Neugarten; C. Gilligan; J. Jordan; P. Weenolsen	D. Levinson	B. Carter & M. McGoldrick
Behavioral	I. Pavlov; J. Watson: B.F. Skinner; E. Thorndike; C. Hull; J. Dollard & N. Miller;			E. Gambrill & C. Richey; S. Berlin; A. Bandura (1986)
Humanistic	E. Husserl; V. Frankl; R. May; C. Rogers; G. Allport; A. Maslow; J. Taft; V. Robinson; R. Smalley	C. Jung	E. Fromm; R.D. Laing; A. Fontana	S. de Beauvoir; M. Daly; K. Horney

perspective, social constructionist perspective, psychodynamic perspective, developmental perspective, social behavioral perspective, and humanistic perspective.

Seven questions seem particularly pertinent to the analysis of theory from a gender lens and are used to guide this discussion.

1. Have the theory builders paid attention to gender?
2. What are the central ideas of the perspective? Each of the theoretical perspectives to be analyzed include multiple theorists and, consequently, variations and even contradictions in conceptualization. The condensed version of propositions and assumptions, found in Table 2–1, is not intended to capture the diversity and complexity of the perspectives, but to demonstrate the ideas at their core.
3. Does the perspective take account of social, economic, political, and historical contexts of human behavior? Gender, stripped of its contexts, is implicitly attributed to factors internal to the person. We see such attribution as unacceptable reductionism.
4. How well can the perspective accommodate diversity of experience? Primary attention is given to inclusion of women's experiences, but the capacity to accommodate diversity among women is also analyzed.
5. Does the perspective take account of power relationships and the life worlds of members of nondominant groups? We assume that gender cannot be understood without understanding the power relations between men and women. Table 2–2 categorizes major theorists for each perspective, including social work scholars who have adapted the perspective for social work, according to their attention to gender. Theorists are placed in one of four categories, based on the authors' reading of their work: (a) little or no attention to either gender or power issues; (b) emphasizes gender but not gender-power issues; (c) emphasizes power but not gender-power issues; (d) emphasizes gender-power issues.
6. Does the perspective have both logical consistency and empirical support? Although theoretical coherence is valued, it is also recognized that theory often gains coherence by denying

contradictions in person-environment configurations. Empirical support is sought, but we assume that some contradictory data can be expected when studying complex phenomena like human behavior. We are most impressed when empirical support comes from multiple empirical methodologies that enhance the possibilities of being gender-sensitive.

7. Does the perspective suggest principles of action? In particular, what actions might address gender concerns?

Each of the eight perspectives covered in the following analysis is best understood as an unfolding social construction, an emergent way of thinking about person-in-environment. Each of the perspectives has continued to evolve over time, and the current trend is for the perspectives to be reconstructed to accommodate gender and other aspects of diversity. Consistent with Ritzer's (1992) prediction that the 1990s will be an era of theoretical synthesizing, there is also evidence of blurring of the boundaries between perspectives in recent theorizing. We welcome these recent developments, but they increase the complexity of the type of theoretical analysis we undertake. We have attempted to avoid presenting any perspective in stereotypical form while at the same time drawing out any analytically relevant distinctions. That is, at points, a tricky line to walk. To provide a visual starting point, the grid in Table 2–1 organizes the traditional versions of the perspectives along two dimensions, first according to their relative attention to "doing" versus "thinking" and second according to their relative attention to gender issues.

ANALYSIS OF PREVAILING THEORETICAL PERSPECTIVES

Systems Perspective

The systems perspective sees human behavior as the outcome of reciprocal interactions of persons operating within organized and integrated social systems. Its roots are very interdisciplinary, based on contemporaneous developments during the 1940s and 1950s in a variety of disciplines, including mathematics, physics, engineering, biology, psychology, cultural anthropology, and sociology. Social work has drawn most heavily from the work of sociologists Parsons and Merton, psychologists Lewin and Bronfenbrenner, and biologist von Bertalanffy.

Feminist criticisms have attacked the use of a systems perspective in family therapy, on the grounds that it lacks attention to the social, economic, political, and historical contexts of gender (see Hare-Mustin, 1978; Taggert, 1985). Although the perspective inherently recognizes macro-level contexts of family life, it is true that some family therapy models that purport a systems perspective operate on the premise that the family is a closed rather than an open system, and give no attention to context. Recently, there is growing recognition and explication of larger influences on family well-being among family theorists (Hartman & Laird, 1983; Imber-Black, 1988). Early theorizing in the systems perspective did not deal with the time dimension, with the focus always on present time, but recent formulations have attempted to add a time dimension, allowing for historical context (see Bronfenbrenner, 1989; Carter & McGoldrick, 1988; Ford & Lerner, 1992; Wachs, 1992).

The lens of the systems perspective is on the system as a whole, and consequently, diversity of experience is not accommodated in a well-developed manner. However, the systems perspective has excellent potential to accommodate the biological person in the biopsychosocial system, and the use of role concepts (Davis, 1986) suggests different experiences for persons in different role positions, such as those related to gender roles. Those versions of the systems perspective that focus on the multiple memberships individuals hold in different systems alert us to the possibility, even probability, of within-gender differences, and provide an explanation for such differences (see Chestang, 1972; Solomon, 1976). To understand the experience of gender in an individual's life, attention must be directed to the variety of systems in which a specific man or woman interacts, as well as the multiplicity of roles played in those systems.

Power relationships are even less well accommodated than diversity of experience in traditional systems theory based on Parsonian functionalism. Parsons was looking for what holds systems together, and his emphasis on system equilibrium and the objective necessity of traditional roles, including traditional gender roles, has been criticized (Cohen, 1968; Gouldner, 1970). Feminist critics of systemic family therapy have called attention to the lack of recognition of differential power and oppression within family systems. Several feminist revisions of family systems theory have appeared in recent years (Ellman & Taggert, 1993; Luepnitz, 1988; McGoldrick, Anderson & Walsh, 1989; Walters, Carter, Papp & Silverstein, 1988), and recent social work

HBSE texts have recognized both conflict and cooperation as inherent in system interactions (see Longres, 1995; Martin & O'Connor, 1989). The challenge for contemporary systems theorists is to clarify how power affects the model of reciprocal causation proposed by the systems perspective. The fear of feminists is that reciprocal causation can support "blaming the victim" assessments.

Ritzer (1992) notes that one of the more serious conceptual criticisms of the Parsonian model of social systems is that the theory engages in tautology, defining the whole in terms of the parts and the parts in terms of the whole, leaving both, therefore, undefined. This is indeed a challenge for the systems perspective, and it is often criticized as too vague and ambiguous to be applied in practice and research. Early theorists rarely applied their work to the empirical world, so many concepts were not operationalized. However, this aspect of the systems perspective has gained strength in recent years as many contemporary systems theorists have applied systems concepts in research on social support and on the relationship between socioeconomic stressors and social and individual problems (see Garbarino, 1976, 1977; Garbarino & Sherman, 1980; Gelles, 1992; Zuravin, 1986, 1989).

We agree with Germain (1994) that the systems perspective has greater utility for "understanding what the matter is" than for "doing," but we also note that several social work scholars (see Germain & Gitterman, 1980; Meyer, 1983; Pincus & Minahan, 1973; Siporin, 1975) have developed practice approaches based on the systems perspective. The most obvious principle of action that derives from the systems perspective is to widen the scope of assessment and intervention (Allen-Meares & Lane, 1987). This widening of scope allows attention to the social contexts of gender. The perspective also suggests that the most effective outcomes are derived from interventions that are multisystem and multidimensional.

Conflict Perspective

The conflict perspective has emerged over and over again in history to draw attention to conflict, dominance, and oppression in social life (R. Collins, 1994). In sociology, there are two traditions of the conflict perspective, a utopian tradition that foresees a society in which there is no longer a basis for social conflict and a second tradition that foresees conflict as inevitable in social life (Wallace & Wolf, 1995). The roots of contemporary conflict theory are usually traced to the works of Marx and his collaborator Engels, and to the works of Weber. It is interesting to note that Engels and Weber formulated theories of sex stratification; both are said to have been influenced in these endeavors by their feminist wives (R. Collins, 1994).

The conflict perspective looks for sources of conflict, and causes of human behavior, in the economic and political arenas; historical analysis is common. Marx and Engels focused on economic structures, but Weber criticized this singular emphasis and presented a multidimensional perspective on social class. Weber called particular attention to the political arena in his work on sex stratification. Contemporary conflict theory tends to favor Weber's multidimensional approach, calling attention to a confluence of social, economic, and political structures in the creation of inequality (R. Collins, 1994; Ritzer, 1992; Wallace & Wolf, 1995). Eisenstein (1979) and Vogel (1983) represent recent theorizing in the Marxist feminist tradition; Chafetz (Chafetz, 1984; Chafetz & Dworkin, 1986) and Blumberg (1978) are feminists who write in the Weberian tradition.

Power relationships are the focus of the conflict perspective, but the various versions of conflict theory differ in their ability to accommodate diversity of experience. All versions are strong in regard to diversity of experience in relation to position in the power structure, making, therefore, a sound contribution to understanding of between-group differences of status groups, including overall gender differences in life experiences. The conflict perspective is, in general, less useful for understanding within-group differences, but some versions are more useful than others in this regard. Coser (1956) proposes a pluralist theory of social conflict that recognizes more than one social conflict going on at all times, with individuals holding cross-cutting and overlapping memberships in status groups. For example, social conflict exists between economic groups, racial groups, ethnic groups, religious groups, and gender groups, and life experience must be understood by looking at simultaneous memberships. This pluralist theory of social conflict explains why many women of color cannot identify with the agenda of white feminists. Critical theory, such as that proposed by Habermas (1984, 1987), with its emphasis on individual perception and its concern for the linkages between culture, social structure, and personality, opens possibilities for understanding diversity.

Conflict theory has developed, in the main, as theorists have attempted to codify persistent themes in empirical historical research

(R. Collins, 1990). Theorists have been primarily interested in "macro-historical" events, and the preferred research method is historical research that looks at large-scale patterns of history (see Mann, 1986; McCarthy & Zald, 1977; Skocpol, 1979; Wallerstein, 1974–1989). As with other methods of research, critics have attacked some of the interpretations of the historical data, but the historical analyses of Mann, Skocpol, and Wallerstein are some of the most influential works in contemporary sociology. In addition to historical analysis, experimental methods have been used to study reactions to coercive power (see Willer, 1987), and naturalistic inquiry has been used to study social ranking through interaction rituals (R. Collins, 1981). Contemporary researchers in the conflict tradition are also drawing on network analysis, which originated in the rational choice perspective, and finding support for their propositions about power and domination (see Burt, 1983).

Concepts of power and social conflict came into social work curricula in the 1960s, particularly in relation to group and community practice, and helped to advance the person-in-environment perspective (Germain, 1994). In particular, such concepts stimulated various approaches to practice that reacted to the tendency of social workers to define social problems in psychological terms. Citing the need to adjust the environment rather than the individual, approaches such as social action (Youngdahl, 1966), structural social work (Goldberg-Wood & Middleman, 1989; Middleman & Goldberg, 1974), and aggressive advocacy (Galper, 1980) focused their efforts on social change through modification of institutional arrangements and practices. In addition, the conflict perspective also played a role in the development of the political economy approach, with recognition of the permanence of interorganizational conflict, in the social work literature on organizational management (Gummer, 1990; Hasenfeld, 1980).

The conflict perspective, as it currently exists, however, is weak in suggesting principles of action beyond assessment. R. Collins, a conflict theorist himself, suggests that "where conflict theory is weak is in explaining what will happen after the revolution, or after a successful movement has won some power" (1994, p. 178). The conflict perspective is crucial to social work, however, because of its directive to look for domination and oppression in person-environment assessments, because it illuminates processes of personal alienation, and because it suggests the need for social workers to consider the meaning of their power relationships with clients, particularly nonvoluntary clients (Cingolani, 1984). Conflict theory, particularly social movement theories, has some implications for mobilization of oppressed groups, but the conflict perspective, in general, provides little in the way of policy direction.

Rational Choice Perspective

The rational choice perspective views human behavior as based on self-interest and rational choices about effective goal-accomplishment. The perspective is interdisciplinary in nature, with strong roots in utilitarian philosophy, economics, and social behaviorism. Social workers are most familiar with social exchange theory from sociology, rational choice models of organizations, public choice theory from political science, and the emerging social network theory.

In the early development of social exchange theory, Homans (1958) insisted that behavior is understood at the psychological level, specifically denying the relevance of role expectations emanating from sociocultural systems. History, to Homans, was important only because the history of rewards for past behavior informs an actor about what is in her/his best interest. More recent formulations of social exchange theory have moved from this position toward a greater interest in the social patterning of exchanges and the context of exchange decisions (see Levi, Cook, O'Brien & Faye, 1990). Rational choice theories have been developed at all levels of social exchange, and several contemporary theorists have written about gender in the rational choice tradition. For example, several rational choice scholars have explored the power dynamics in marital relationships (Blood & Wolfe, 1960; Brinton, 1990; Gerson, 1985; Luker, 1984; Safilios-Rothschild, 1970; Scanzoni, 1972).

Early theorizing attempted to find basic principles of all human behavior, and negated diversity of experience. Some feminists have criticized exchange theory on the grounds that its emphasis on rational calculation of personal advantage is a male attitude and does not represent the female perspective (R. Collins, 1994). In fact, Homans developed his American version of exchange theory partially in reaction to Levi-Strauss's French collectivist version, which argued that social exchange is driven by collective, cultural, symbolic forces and is not based simply on self-interest (Ekeh, 1974). Recently, Cook, O'Brien, and Kollock (1990) undertook a synthesis of social exchange and symbolic interaction theories, recognizing the possibility of different definitions of positive outcomes in social exchange. Thibaut and Kelley's (Kelley & Thibaut, 1978; Thibaut & Kelley, 1959) contribution of the concepts of "comparison level" and "comparison level alternative" is also useful in accommodating diversity of experience. Comparison level is a standard by which the rewards and costs of a given relationship are evaluated, in terms of what the evaluator feels she/he deserves. Comparison level alternatives is the lowest level of outcomes a person will accept in light of alternative opportunities. The concepts are based on acceptance of difference in individual experience and interpretation.

Beginning with the work of Peter M. Blau, social exchange theorists and researchers have taken a strong interest in how power is negotiated in social exchange. Particularly noteworthy in this regard is Emerson's (1972a, 1972b) power-dependency theory and Cook's (1987) exchange network theory. With its emphasis on the social exchange as the unit of analysis, social exchange theory has great potential in regard to Riger's criterion for helping us understand how gender is "created and maintained through interpersonal processes" (Riger, 1992, p. 737). For example, social exchange theorists suggest that men's and women's sexual behavior converges as social and economic opportunities open for women. They theorize that, in the past, women guarded their sexuality as their major resource for negotiating marriages, given men's greater occupational and wealth resources (Blumstein & Schwartz, 1983).

As the rational choice perspective has developed, two conceptual puzzles have emerged, one at the individual level and one at the collective level. At the individual level, there is the puzzle of the limited capacity of individuals to process information and make rational decisions. At the collective level, there is the puzzle of how collective action is possible if each actor maximizes rewards and minimizes costs. To their credit, recent theorists have embraced these puzzles and are incorporating them into the ongoing conceptual development. Recent developments in the rational choice perspective emphasize the limits to rational choice in social life (see Cook et al., 1990; Levi et al., 1990; March & Simon, 1958). Coleman (1990) is particularly noted for his attempts to move rational choice theory to look at how to stimulate collective action for the purpose of social justice. His emphasis on people's needs for each other, and on rational solidarity, is consistent with the feminist emphasis on human connectedness.

The rational choice perspective has stimulated empirical research at several levels of analysis, with mixed results. Cognitive psychologists (Kahneman & Tversky, 1982, 1984) dealt a blow to the rational choice perspective in the 1980s with research findings that individual choices and decisions are often inconsistent with assumed rationality, and that, indeed, situations are often too complicated for individuals to ascertain what is the most rational choice. On the other hand, more than modest support for the perspective has been found in research on dyads, families, and labor markets (see Adams & Jacobsen, 1964; Becker, 1981; Blood & Wolfe, 1960; Burgess & Nielsen, 1974; Carter & Glick, 1976). R. Collins (1988) notes that a serious problem for the rational choice perspective is the lack of a common metric for calculating the costs and benefits derived from social exchange. Contemporary theorists acknowledge the inherent imprecision of this metric and suggest that the rational choice perspective must find a way to incorporate both what people value and the context of social exchange (see Cook et al., 1990). At the current time, however, the imprecision of metric confounds empirical investigations.

Some versions of rational choice theory serve as little more than defense of the rationality of the marketplace of social exchange, suggesting a noninterventionist approach. Other versions emphasize the ways in which patterns of exchange lead to social inequalities and social injustices. Social exchange theorists who look at "marriage markets" suggest that persons who dominate economic resources will dominate the marriage market and have superior power in the home (Blumstein & Schwartz, 1983). Some theorists, in this latter tradition, have begun to propose solutions for creating social solidarity while recognizing the self-interest that is characteristic of Western, industrialized, capitalist societies. It is these attempts that led R. Collins (1994) to suggest that out of all current social theories, contemporary rational choice theories have the greatest chance for informing effective social policy. One of the most promising approaches is the work of Coleman (1990), who explores possible incentives to encourage actors to behave in ways more beneficial to others. For example, Coleman has explored incentives for persons to provide nurturing care to children and adolescents who are at risk of becoming an economic drain on society, with incentives based on the potential hazard to society. Coleman sees the nurturance of children as a societal issue, not a woman's issue, and he values positive rather than negative sanctions.

Within organizational theory, the rational choice perspective stimulated the development of models of organizational action based on a view of organizations as capable of rational prioritization and decision-making. From this perspective, social service agencies are assumed to be capable of engaging in efficient and purposive action, and the focus of interagency efforts is on the selection and implementation of the most efficient means to desired ends (see Netting, Kettner & McMurtry, 1993).

Social network theory, still in early stages of development, already provides useful tools for person-in-environment assessments and holds greater promise in the future (Specht, 1986). Simply stated, social network theory is interested in "the pattern of ties linking individual and collective members of society" (Ritzer, 1992, p. 489). Social workers make use of social network theory at the micro level to examine, and enhance, the social networks of individual clients and families (see Collins & Pancoast, 1976; Tracy & Whittaker, 1990). Social work administrators and planners use social network theory to examine, and enhance, the exchange of resources in networks of social service providers (see Streeter & Gillespie, 1992).

Social Constructionist Perspective

To understand human behavior, the social constructionist perspective focuses on "actors, the way in which they construct social reality, and the action that results from such construction" (Ritzer, 1992, p. 176). The contemporary social constructionist perspective has roots in symbolic interaction theory as well as in phenomenological philosophy. Because of the extensive involvement of American sociologists such as Cooley, Thomas, Mead, Garfinkel, the ethnomethodologists, and the phenomenologists in the profound transformation of received European theories, R. Collins (1994) suggests that social constructionist theorizing is the type of sociology that American sociologists do best.

To the social constructionist, there is no objective reality, only the shared subjective realities that are created as people interact, and constructionists emphasize the existence of multiple social and cultural realities. Given the guiding premise of the constructed nature of reality, the sociopolitical context and history of any situation play an important role in understanding human behavior. Within social constructionism, there are disagreements about how constraining the contexts of actors are on their behaviors. The dominant position is probably the one presented by Schutz's (1932/1967) phenomenological sociology. While arguing that people shape social reality, Schutz also suggested that individuals and groups are constrained by the preexisting social and cultural processes and structures created by their predecessors. Schutz does not provide theoretical tools for understanding institutionalized social, economic, and political arrangements and their links to individual and group constructions of reality, however.

Both between-gender differences and within-gender differences are well accommodated. Social constructionists favor ethnographic methodology that allows actors to present their own perceptions of their experiences, rather than limit their experiences to the conceptual schemes of a dominant group. For example, Geertz (1983) focuses on gaining entry into the conceptual world of participants in order to understand how meaning is constructed around events in daily life. P. Collins (1990), an African-American feminist, has attempted to capture the intersection of race, social class, and gender, ethnographically, through the stories of African-American women. She attempts to understand the meaning these women make of their cross-cutting and overlapping memberships in different status groups.

In his 1975 presidential address to the American Sociological Association, Coser attacked ethnomethodology, one theory in the social constructionist tradition, for ignoring "institutional factors in general, and the centrality of power in social interaction in particular" (1975, p. 696). In a similar vein, Wallace and Wolf (1995) as well as Ritzer (1992) have suggested that symbolic interactionism, ethnomethodology, and phenomenological sociology all lack the theoretical tools for analysis of power relationships. Middleton (1989) has suggested that many contemporary postmodern versions of social constructionism reduce oppression to difference. These critics propose that the contemporary constructionist emphasis on multiple voices and multiple meanings in the construction of reality obscures the power that some actors have to privilege their own constructions and disadvantage the constructions of other actors.

This criticism cannot be leveled at all versions of social constructionism, however. Smith (1990) has recently married phenomenology to Marxist conflict theory to explain gender-power relationships. She looks at structures of domination to understand oppression of particular groups, but she believes these structures can be known only by studying the everyday worlds of variously situated individuals. Social work scholars have been especially attracted to those versions of the social constructionist perspective that have incorporated pieces of the conflict tradition (Laird, 1994; Saleeby, 1994; Witkin & Gottschalk, 1988), particularly to the early work of Michel Foucault on the relationship between power and knowledge. They propose that in contemporary society, minority or "local" knowledges are denied credibility in majority dominated social arenas. Laird (1994, p. 185) suggests that "women have often been denied their stories" by their exclusion from public domains. Social workers can bring credibility to such knowledges by allowing oppressed individuals and groups to tell their stories/narratives. Certainly, this version of social constructionism takes account of the life worlds of members of nondominant groups in a richer way than any of the perspectives discussed earlier in this chapter. It remains to be seen whether such "restorying" of nondominant groups will significantly alter power arrangements. Exclusive attention to the stories of nondominant groups runs the risk of psychological reductionism, with causal attribution to internal, psychological factors, particularly if nondominant groups are steeped in dominant ideology (Riger, 1992).

Social constructionism, particularly original phenomenological and symbolic interactional concepts, is sometimes criticized as vague and difficult to operationalize. However, many proponents challenge this criticism on paradigmatic grounds and offer alternative criteria for theory evaluation, as well as an alternative research methodology, constructivism (Lincoln & Guba, 1985). Witkin and Gottschalk (1988) recommend that theory should be put to the following tests: Does it recognize humans as active agents? Does it account for the life experiences of the client? The argument made by constructivist researchers is that social constructionism can be supported empirically when ethnographic research methods are used. It is important to note that sociologists in both the conflict and rational choice traditions have begun to incorporate social constructionist ideas and to use a mix of research methodologies to accommodate both objective and subjective reality (see R. Collins, 1990; Cook et al., 1990).

Franklin (1995) suggests that the emphasis on context is the reason that social constructionism is often pointed to as an important theory for social work practice (see Imre, 1984; Laird, 1994; Rodwell, 1987; Saleeby, 1994; Weick, 1994). Social constructionism gives new meaning to the old social work adage "begin where the client is." The social work relationship begins with developing an understanding of how the client views the situation and what the client would like to have happen. In addition to this attention to the client's construction of reality, the social worker should engage the client in thinking about the social, cultural, economic, political, and historical contexts in which this version of reality was constructed. As Laird (1994) and Saleeby (1994) suggest, such conversations with members of oppressed groups may lead to an empowering restorying. Indeed, feminist social work practice, with its acceptance of gender as the most fundamental context, has embraced the social constructionist perspective (Davis, 1993). As van den Bergh (1995) stated in her introduction to *Feminist Practice in the 21st Century*, "feminists have been proposing analyses that are social constructivist in their intonation, such as 'the personal is political,' since the beginning of the second wave of the women's movement in the 1960s" (p. xxi). At the level of groups and organizations, the social constructionist perspective recommends a discourse model in which discordant groups engage in sincere discussion of their disparate constructions of reality and negotiate lines of actions (see Fox & Miller, 1995).

Psychodynamic Perspective

The psychodynamic perspective is concerned with how internal processes such as needs, drives, and emotions motivate human behavior. The perspective has evolved over the years, moving from the classical emphasis on innate drives and unconscious processes toward greater emphasis on adaptive capacities of individuals and on interactions with the environment. Recent formulations of the perspective include ego psychology and object relations theories. Although several women, including A. Freud, Klein, and Mahler, were prominent early theorists in the evolving psychodynamic perspective, Horney, whose ideas bridge the psychodynamic and humanistic perspectives, is noted by contemporary feminists for presenting the earliest feminist challenge to the psychodynamic perspective.

In general, the psychodynamic perspective takes account of the context of behavior only in the sense that context is conceptualized as presenting conflicts with which the individual must struggle. Ego psychology purports to look at person-in-environment (Goldstein, 1984, 1986), but propositions about internal processes predominate. When environmental forces are considered, only passing mention of social forces beyond the family are included. This failure to expand the view of social forces beyond the family has led to accusations that psychodynamic theories are "mother blaming" and "family blaming" (Luepnitz, 1988).

Theorists in the psychodynamic tradition are looking for universal laws of behavior to apply to unique individuals, and understanding of diversity at the group level has been neglected. Indeed, these universal laws have been developed through analysis of males of white, Anglo-Saxon, middle-class culture. Feminists, as well as members of racial and ethnic minority groups, have criticized the bias toward autonomy and differentiation in recent as well as classical theories (Berzoff, 1989; Bricker-Jenkins, Hooyman & Gottlieb, 1991; Gilligan, 1982; Ho, 1992; Sue & Sue, 1990). These critics suggest that when practitioners in the psychodynamic perspective use the standard of autonomy and differentiation as "normal," they are likely to see the high value for connectedness found among many women and members of racial and ethnic minority groups as pathological.

Psychodynamic theories are strong in their recognition of power dynamics in parent-child relationships, and in exploring the life worlds of children. They are weak at looking at power issues in other relationships, however, including gender relationships. S. Freud (1925/1961) set an early example of recognizing gender differences, even gender inequality, but conceptualized these as based on moral deficits within women. Erikson's theory, which emerged within the psychodynamic tradition and has had a significant impact on the developmental perspective, has been widely used in social work curricula, preferred to classical psychodynamic theory because of the increased emphasis on social forces. However, Erikson's work has been criticized for its lack of attention to the life worlds of women, racial minorities, and sexual minorities (Berzoff, 1989; Chestang, 1972; Kravetz, 1982; Kropf & Greene, 1994; Schwartz, 1973; Wesley, 1975). Recently, psychoanalytic feminists have operated within the structure of classical psychodynamic theory to explain patriarchy (see al-Hibri, 1981; Chodorow, 1978; Dinnerstein, 1976). Such explanations conceptualize patriarchy as a by-product of the collective neuroses produced by society's early childhood care-giving arrangements. Specifically, because the mother is the dominant presence throughout childhood, unresolved ambivalence toward the female gender develops, which is then acted out in adult relationships and structural arrangements.

Criticisms in terms of logical consistency and empirical support are primarily directed at the original concepts and propositions of S. Freud, which were not operationalizable and not entirely consistent. Ego psychology and object relations theorists strengthened the logical consistency of the psychodynamic perspective by expanding and clarifying definitions of major concepts, and later psychodynamic theorists translated Freud's ideas into more operationalizable terms. Consequently, much empirical work has been based on the psychodynamic perspective. There are contradictions in the research findings, but this may be related in large part to differential operationalizations. Some concepts, such as mastery, have strong empirical support, but this support has been generated primarily by other schools of thought, such as developmental psychology and social behaviorism.

Most versions of the psychodynamic perspective, such as ego psychology, object relations, and self psychology, have included clinical theory as well as human behavior theory. Differences of opinion about principles of action within the wide spectrum of the perspective reflect the theoretical evolution that has occurred. Principles of action common to all versions of the psychodynamic perspective relate to the centrality of the professional-client relationship, the curative value of expressing emotional conflicts and understanding past events, and the goal of self-awareness and self-control. In general, the psychodynamic perspective does not suggest principles of action at the macro institutional level.

Developmental Perspective

The developmental perspective focuses on how human behavior changes and stays the same across the life cycle. The study of life-cycle development is rooted in S. Freud's theory of psychosexual stages of childhood development, but Erikson has been the most influential developmental theorist to date because his model of development includes adult, as well as child, stages of development. In the past several decades, the developmental perspective has been applied to the study of families, with study of family life stages originating in sociology (Duvall, 1962). Social workers Carter and McGoldrick (1988) continue to make important contributions to the understanding of gender in a family life-cycle perspective. Neugarten (1979) was one of the first developmental theorists to study women as well as men.

A frequent criticism of the developmental perspective is that it fails to take account of the social, economic, political, and historical contexts of human behavior. Many theorists conceptualize stages of development as biopsychosocial phenomena and recognize the contributions of social forces; however, most, including Erikson and Levinson, see the stages as universal, and all traditional developmental theorists ignore macro-economic and -political forces. Failure of developmental theories to deal with historical time prompted researchers of adult behavior to point out the "cohort effects" on human behavior that arise when groups of persons born in the same historical time share cultural influences and historical events at the same period in their lives.

Consistent criticisms of the lack of attention to context in developmental models have helped to stimulate the development of the life-course perspective in sociology. This perspective conceptualizes the life course as a social, rather than psychological, phenomenon that is unique for each individual, with some common life-course markers, or transitions, related to shared social and historical contexts (George, 1993). The evolving life-course model respects the idea of role transition that is so central to the developmental perspective, but it also recognizes the multiplicity of interacting factors that contribute to diversity in the timing and experience of these transitions.

The traditional developmental perspective takes no account of power relationships, with the possible exception of power dynamics in the parent-child relationship. Moreover, it is based on the average white, middle-class, heterosexual, Anglo-Saxon male and ignores the life worlds of members of nondominant groups. In response to these limitations, several women have presented developmental models for women (Gilligan, 1982; Jordan, 1992; Weenolsen, 1988), and family life-cycle theorists have begun to discuss gender in the family life cycle (McGoldrick, 1988). Some of these alternative approaches include more pointed discussion of the impact of oppression than others.

Classical developmental theory's notion of life stages is internally consistent, and many of Erikson's ideas have been employed and verified in empirical research. One example of this is Marcia's (1993) study of identity development. As discussed earlier in this chapter, however, much of developmental research has been based on the experiences of white middle-class males. A very recent and notable exception is Levinson's (1996) biographical study of women's ideas. Another concern is that by defining normal as average, developmental research fails to capture the life worlds of groups who deviate even moderately from the average. For example, in research on stages of moral development, instead of careful examination of the differences between males and females, researchers initially concluded that girls were generally less rational and mature than boys in their ability to make moral judgments. Thus, the consistency and empirical support of the perspective is open to criticism because its strength in these areas is based to some extent on statistical masking of diversity.

Through some lenses, the developmental perspective may be viewed as optimistic. It normalizes life crises and challenges, and many people are reassured to hear that their struggle is "typical." Because individuals are seen as having the possibility to rework their inner experiences, as well as their family relationships, individuals and families may be assisted to reassess strategies for meeting various life crises and getting their lives back "on course." Erikson's model has often been used for assessment purposes in social work practice, and in a positive sense, the model can indirectly aid in the identification of personal and social developmental resources. Traditional developmental theories should be applied, however, only with recognition of the ethnocentrism expressed in them. Although it is harder to extrapolate principles of action from the more complex emerging life-course perspective, it serves as a more promising approach for understanding diverse persons in diverse environments. It suggests that individuals must always be assessed within familial, cultural, and historical contexts. This perspective's increased focus on the link between social issues and individual troubles has particular relevance for women.

Social Behavioral Perspective

Theories in the social behavioral perspective suggest that human behavior is learned as individuals interact with their environments, but there is a great deal of conflict among theorists about the processes by which behavior is learned. Our analysis is based on an inclusive view of behaviorism, comprising both the "hard" behaviorism of classical and operant conditioning, and the "soft" behaviorism of cognitive social learning theory. Although there is general recognition of cognition among contemporary proponents of the social behavioral perspective, a major split has developed over the role of cognition in human behavior. The central question in this split is: Are thoughts antecedents or results of behavior, the independent or dependent variable? The following analysis is based on a synthetic approach that recognizes cognition as both antecedent and consequent of behavior, and includes processes of learning proposed by both hard and soft behaviorism.

Hard behaviorism sees human behavior as totally determined by environment, and soft behaviorism sees human behavior as resulting from reciprocal interaction of person and environment. As typically used, however, the social behavioral perspective is directed to the search for one environmental factor, or contingency, related to one specific behavior. The identified contingency is usually in the micro system (i.e., family), or sometimes messo system (i.e., school classroom), but these systems are seldom placed in larger contexts. One exception is Bandura's (1986) discussion of broad systemic influences on the development of gender roles. Social work scholars have made notable efforts in recent years to incorporate a broader view of behavioral contexts (Berlin, 1983; Gambrill, 1987; Reid, 1985). Differences in behavior, in the social behavioral perspective, occur by the same learning processes used in different environments. There is no room for variations in learning based on biology.

Thyer (1994) suggests that "behavior social work practice is embedded in traditional social work values of respect for individuals, maximizing client autonomy, and working toward the elimination of racism, discrimination, and social injustice" (p. 136). Hard behaviorism provides few theoretical tools for understanding or changing power relationships, however. Operant behavioral theory recommends rewarding reinforcements over punishing reinforcements, but it does not account for the coercion and oppression inherent in power relationships at every system level. It is quite possible, therefore, for the professional behavior modifier to be in service to oppressive forces. In contrast, Bandura (1986), a proponent of cognitive social learning theory, writes specifically about power as related to gender roles. Bandura also presents the concepts of self-efficacy, by which he means a sense of personal competence, and efficacy expectation, by which he means an expectation that one can personally accomplish a goal (1977, 1986). Women are seen as particularly vulnerable to learned helplessness (see Mikulincer, 1994), which occurs when a person's prior experience with environmental forces has led to low self-efficacy and efficacy expectation. Berlin (1983) and Gambrill (1987) are two behaviorist social workers who write about gender-power issues and address their impact on behavioral assumptions. Berlin and Johnson (1989) use a structural analysis of social behavior to discuss issues of autonomy and connectedness in women. Gambrill and Richey (1983) describe how group-leader biases about the social status of women may intrude on the performance of women in social skills training.

Social behavioral concepts are easily operationalized for empirical investigation because theorizing is based, in very large part, on laboratory research. This characteristic is also a drawback of the social behavioral perspective, however, because laboratory experiments by design eliminate much of the complexity of person-environment configurations. Overall, the social behavioral perspective sacrifices multidimensional understanding to gain logical consistency. Monte (1995) suggests that all versions of the social behavioral perspective have had their "share of confirmations and disconfirmations" (p. 769), but it seems fair to say that there is a relatively high degree of empirical support for the propositions of both hard and soft behaviorism (see Thyer, 1991).

A major strength of the social behavioral perspective is the ease with which principles of behavior modification can be extrapolated, and it is probably a rare direct practitioner who has not used social behavioral principles of action at some point. Social behavioral methods have been used by social workers and psychologists, primarily, as a practice method for modifying atypical behavior of individuals, and have not produced the same yield for social reform. Stuart (1989) reminds us, however, that behavior modification was once a "social movement" that appealed to young social reformers who were more interested in changing social conditions that produce atypical behaviors than in changing systems of managing atypical behavior. Skinner's *Walden Two* was impetus for attempts by these young reformers to build nonpunitive communities, which represented modification of social conditions rather than a singular contingency (see Kinkade, 1973; Wheeler, 1973).

Humanistic Perspective

The humanistic perspective is often called the third force of psychology, because it was developed in reaction to the determinism found in early versions of both the psychodynamic and behavioral perspectives (Monte, 1995). We are using the title humanistic perspective to include humanistic and existential psychology, both of which emphasize the freedom of action of the individual. It also includes the existential sociology tradition that counters the structural determinism found in some sociological theories and presents as dominant theme the idea that people are both free and constrained. The humanistic perspective, with its emphasis on search for meaning, is the only perspective under discussion to explicitly recognize the role of spirituality in human behavior.

Like social constructionism, the humanistic perspective is often traced to the German phenomenological philosopher Husserl (Krill, 1986), but it was also influenced by a host of existential philosophers beginning with Kierkegaard, and including Nietzche, Heidegger, Sartre, Camus, de Beauvoir, Buber, and Tillich. Perhaps the most influential contributions to humanistic psychology were made by Rogers, who began his professional career at the Rochester Child Guidance Center, where he worked with social workers who had been trained at the Philadelphia School of Social Work. Rogers has acknowledged the influence of Rank, Taft, and the social workers at the Rochester agency on his thinking about the importance of responding to client feelings (Hart, 1970).

The internal life of the individual is the focus of the humanistic perspective, and as might be expected, most theorists in the tradition give limited attention to the contexts of human behavior. Taking the lead from existential philosophers, Laing sees humans as interrelated with their worlds and frowns on the word "environment" because it implies a fragmented person. In discussions of human behavior, however, Laing (1967, 1969) emphasizes the insane situations in which human behavior is enacted. Fromm was heavily influenced by Marx and is much more inclusive of context than other theorists in the humanistic perspective, emphasizing industrialization, Protestant reformation, capitalism, and technological revolution as alienating contexts against which humans search for meaning (Fromm, 1941). Although existential sociologists emphasize the importance of feelings and emotions, they also focus on the problematic nature of social life under modernization (see Fontana, 1984). A dehumanizing world is implicit in the works of Maslow (1962) and Rogers (1951), but neither theorist explicates contexts of human behavior, nor do they acknowledge that some contexts are more dehumanizing than others.

The humanistic perspective, with its almost singular consideration of internal frame of reference, devotes more attention to individual differences than to between-group differences. The work of Fromm and Horney are striking exceptions to this statement. Horney identified culturally based gender differences at a time when psychology either ignored gender or took a "biology as destiny" approach; she also lost favor by reworking S. Freud's conceptualization of the Oedipus Conflict and of feminine psychology (Horney, 1939, 1967). Her examination of the impact of social and cultural factors on female psychological development led to the belief that self-defeating behaviors and feelings of inferiority were a result of cultural restrictions on women's potential. To Horney, the most appropriate route to elimination of such undesirable personality traits was change in the social and economic opportunities available to women.

Although philosophical existentialists de Beauvoir (1949) and Daly (1973) have written two of the most important feminist analyses of gender oppression, in general far too little attention is given in the humanistic tradition to the processes by which institutional oppression influence the "phenomenol self." Because, from this perspective, the individual is viewed as ultimately free to choose her/his own life course, the role of structural constraints is minimized. For example, clearly demonstrating insensitivity to the impact of institutionalized gender oppression on the "phenomenol" selves of women, May (1969) warned against misguided egalitarianism of the sexes on the basis that it would result in loss of personal identity and uniqueness.

Like the social constructionist perspective, however, the humanistic perspective is sometimes quite strong in giving voice to the life worlds of members of nondominant groups. With the emphasis on the phenomenol self, members of nondominant groups are more likely to have preferential input into the telling of their own stories. Most significantly, Rogers developed his respect for the personal self, and consequently his client-centered approach to therapy, when he realized that his perception of the life worlds of his low-income clients in the Child Guidance Clinic were very different from their own perceptions (Hart, 1970).

Theories in the humanistic perspective are often criticized for being vague and highly abstract, with concepts like "being" and "phenomenol self." Indeed, theorists in the humanistic perspective were not afraid to sacrifice coherence to gain what they saw as a more complete understanding of human behavior. As might be expected, empirically minded scholars have not been attracted to the humanistic perspective, and consequently there is little empirical literature to support the perspective. A notable exception is the clinical side of Rogers's theory. Rogers began a rigorous program of empirical investigation of the therapeutic process, and there is strong empirical support for his conceptualization of the necessary conditions for the therapeutic relationship (Monte, 1995).

If the social constructionist perspective gives new meaning to the old social work adage "begin where the client is," it is social work's historical involvement in the development of the humanistic perspective that gave original meaning. The humanistic perspective suggests to begin by developing understanding of how the client views the situation, and with its emphasis on individual drive for growth and competence, recommends a "strengths" rather than a "pathology" approach. What is missing in the humanistic perspective, added by the social constructionist perspective, is the recommendation to engage clients in thinking about the social, cultural, economic, political, and historical contexts in which their versions of reality were constructed. At the organizational level, the humanistic perspective has been used by organizational theorists, such as McGregor (1960), to prescribe administrative actions that focus on employee well-being as the best route to organizational efficiency and effectiveness. Critical theorists have faulted the organizational humanists, however, for their failure to take account of the ways in which organizations are instruments of domination (Hearn & Parkin, 1993).

IMPLICATIONS FOR ONGOING CHANGE IN THE HBSE CURRICULUM

A few years ago, as a minor piece of Elizabeth D. Hutchison's dissertation research, child welfare workers were asked whether current child protective services are overly intrusive, underprotective, or strike the proper balance between child protection and family privacy. One thoughtful social worker responded, "We tend to provide the same services to both high and low risk cases. Therefore, we are underprotective to the high risk family and overly intrusive to the low risk case" (Hutchison, 1988, p. 119). That type of standardized, often narrowly focused social service delivery, was the impetus for Meyer's lament, cited in the introduction to this chapter, about emphasis on "doing" rather than "thinking about what the matter is" in social work curricula. An overemphasis on doing leads us to "understand" client situations from the perspective of what we know how to do, to the "same solution for all situations."

Unfortunately, however, students often struggle, unsuccessfully, to connect the general knowledge gained in the HBSE curriculum to the specific person-environment configurations that they join in the field. We call attention to two possible reasons for this difficulty. First, behavior settings theory, and research that supports it, suggests that "the place in which we first master information helps recreate the state necessary to retrieve it" (Gallagher, 1993, p. 132). Certainly, the classroom setting differs in many significant ways from the field setting, and that has implications for the structure of social work education. Another possible reason for the difficulty is the unique/general tension that Meyer (1993) identifies as inherent to social work practice. Effective social work practice involves balancing the use of general knowledge about human behavior with an individualized, unique person-environment assessment. Students must learn to move back and forth, dialectically, between unique stories and general knowledge. It is the unique story that suggests what general knowledge is needed to enhance knowing and doing in the specific situation, but general knowledge serves only to provide hypotheses to be explored in the unique situation.

HBSE courses can assist students to become comfortable with this continuous dialectical movement between unique knowledge and general knowledge. Instructors can make this dialectic a major theme of HBSE courses; they can talk about it and demonstrate it in the design of courses. Using narratives, students can be asked to consider what general knowledge is needed to inform practice in specific situations. They may need to be assisted to think comprehensively. While analyzing theory and research, students should be asked, continuously, to check general knowledge hypotheses against the unique situations of narratives. The process of moving back and forth between unique and general knowledge is assisted by including both narrative literature and scientific literature in the required readings. Appendix 2–1 at the end of this chapter is a sample of readings, including both popular and social science selections, that may be used to ensure that HBSE courses are inclusive of the experiences of women. Appendix 2–2 is an example of a course module that integrates unique and general knowledge and demonstrates the dialectical movement between them. Schools may also want to begin to develop ways to have more general knowledge taught in the field, to facilitate marriage of thinking and doing.

To avoid narrowly focused standardized doing, social workers need a multitheoretical framework that will allow them to fit the choice of general knowledge to the unique situation, and to use a multidimensional approach that fosters examination of an idiosyncratic event from several perspectives. This multitheoretical framework must include both personal dimensions and environmental dimensions of the person-environment configuration. It also must facilitate understanding of diversity of experience, specifically representing the experiences of women and other nondominant groups. The eight perspectives discussed in this chapter all provide tools for understanding gender, and for doing social work that respects the experiences of women. You may not choose to include all of them in your HBSE curriculum, but there is an urgency now, just as Stein and Cloward identified in 1958, for social work to keep abreast of developments in sociology, cultural anthropology, and social psychology, to put the social back in social work. Without social dimensions, the understanding of gender is severely limited.

We suggested in the introduction that each of these theoretical perspectives should be thought of as a dynamic social construction. All of them have histories of at least several decades, with intellectual roots that are much older. Although recent developments in each perspective are more inclusive of gender than the traditional theories, we do not recommend exclusive teaching of recent formulations. Students will receive much longer lasting benefits from exposure to the process of unfolding theory. By learning about the confluence of personal, social, cultural, economic, political, and historical factors that influence theoretical development, students will be better prepared to think critically about theory and to anticipate the need to keep current on theoretical revisions.

CONCLUSION

The explosion of theories and empirical data about human behavior presents a formidable challenge for social workers. One solution would be to retreat to one way of thinking about human behavior, with the rationale that it is better to know one way of thinking well than to become overwhelmed by a proliferation of ways of thinking about a situation. If social work takes that path, it will become an irrelevant profession for the twenty-first century. The HBSE curriculum can help to reinvigorate social work by assisting students to embrace the complexity of contemporary life and to understand both the possibilities and limitations of multiple ways of knowing about human behavior, and understanding gender.

APPENDIX 2–1: WOMEN'S STORIES: POPULAR AND SOCIAL SCIENCE LITERATURE ABOUT WOMEN

Popular Literature

Anderson, C. & Stewart, S. (1994). *Flying solo: Single women at midlife.* New York: Norton.

Angelou, M. (1969). *I know why the caged bird sings.* New York: Random House.

Angelou, M. (1993). *Wouldn't take nothing for my journey now.* New York: Random House.

Bernays, A. (1989). *Professor Romeo.* New York: Weidenfeld & Nicolson.

Brooks, G. (1995). *Nine parts of desire: The hidden world of Islamic women.* New York: Anchor Books.

Brown, E. (1992). *A taste of power: A Black woman's story.* New York: Pantheon.

Brown, R. (1977). *Rubyfruit jungle*. New York: Bantam.

Campbell, B. (1989). *Sweet summer: Growing up with & without my dad.* New York: Putnam.

Cary, L. (1991). *Black ice.* New York: Knopf.

Chang, J. (1991). *Wild swans: Three daughters of China.* New York: Simon & Schuster.

Cheever, S. (1994). *A woman's life: The story of an ordinary American and her extraordinary generation.* New York: Morrow.

Conway, J. (1989). *The road from Coorain.* New York: Random House.

Donofrio, B. (1990). *Riding in cars with boys: Confessions of a bad girl who makes good.* New York: Morrow.

Flagg, F. (1987). *Fried green tomatoes at the Whistle-Stop Cafe.* New York: Random House.

French, M. (1977). *The women's room.* New York: Summit Books.

Glancy, D. (1992). *Claiming breath.* Lincoln: University of Nebraska Press.

Golden, S. (1992). *The women outside: Meanings and myths of homelessness.* Berkeley: University of California Press.

Gornick, V. (1987). *Fierce attachments: A memoir*. New York: Farrar Straus Giroux.

Ione, C. (1991). *Pride of family: Four generations of American women of color.* New York: Summit Books.

Kingston, M. (1976). *The woman warrior: Memoirs of a girlhood among ghosts.* New York: Knopf.

Lydon, S. (1993). *Take the long way home: Memoirs of a survivor.* San Francisco: Harper & Row.

Millett, K. (1990). *The loony-bin trip*. New York: Simon & Schuster.

Moody, A. (1968). *Coming of age in Mississippi.* New York: Dial Press.

Ortiz Cofer, J. (1990). *Silent dancing: A partial remembrance of a Puerto Rican childhood.* Houston, TX: Arte Publico Press.

Page, M. (1977). *Daughter of the hills: A woman's part in the coal miners' struggle.* New York: Persea Books.

Saxton, M. & Howe, F. (1987). *With wings: An anthology of literature by and about women with disabilities.* New York: Feminist Press.

Sidransky, R. (1990). *In silence: Growing up hearing in a deaf world.* New York: St. Martin's Press.

Silverzweig, M. (1982). *The other mother.* New York: Harper & Row.

Sone, M. (1953). *Nisei daughter.* Boston: Little, Brown.

Taylor, D. (1995). *My children, my gold: A journey to the world of seven single mothers.* Berkeley: University of California Press.

Walker, A. (1992). *The color purple.* New York: Harcourt Brace Jovanovich.

Williams, T. (1991). *Refuge: An unnatural history of family and place.* New York: Pantheon Books.

Wong, J. (1950). *Fifth Chinese daughter.* New York: Harper & Row.

Social Science Literature

al-Hibri, A. (1981). Reproduction, mothering and the origins of patriarchy. In J. Trebilcot (Ed.), *Mothering: Essays in feminist theory* (pp. 81–93). Totowa, NJ: Rowman and Allanheld.

Beauvoir, S. de. (1949/1961). *The second sex.* (H.M. Parshley, Trans.) New York: Bantam.

Berlin, S. & Johnson, C. (1989). Women and autonomy: Using structural analysis of social behavior to find autonomy within connections. *Psychiatry, 52*(1), 79–95.

Bernard, J. (1975). *Women, wives and mothers: Values and options.* New York: Aldine de Gruyter.

Berzoff, J. (1989). From separation to connection: Shifts in understanding women's development. *Affilia, 4,* 45–58.

Blackshaw, S. & Miller, J. (1994). Boundaries in clinical psychiatry. *American Journal of Psychiatry, 151*(2), 293.

Blood, R. & Wolfe, D. (1960). *Husbands and wives: The dynamics of married living.* New York: Free Press.

Blumberg, R. (1978). *Stratification: Socioeconomic and sexual inequality.* Dubuque, IA: W.C. Brown.

Bricker-Jenkins, M., Hooyman, N.R. & Gottlieb, N. (Eds.). (1991). *Feminist social work practice in clinical settings.* Newbury Park, CA: Sage.

Brinton, M. (1990). Intrafamilial markets for education in Japan. In M. Hechter, K. Opp & R. Wippler (Eds.), *Social institutions: Their emergence, maintenance and effects.* Berlin: Walter de Gruyter.

Chafetz, J. (1984). *Sex and advantage: A comparative, macro-structural theory of sex stratification.* Totowa, NJ: Rowman and Allanheld.

Chafetz, J. (1988). *Feminist sociology: An overview of contemporary theories.* Itasca, IL: Peacock.

Chafetz, J. (1990), *Gender equity: An integrated theory of stability and change.* Newbury Park, CA: Sage.

Chafetz, J. & Dworkin, A. (1986). *Female revolt: Women's movements in world and historical perspectives.* Totowa, NJ: Rowman and Allanheld.

Chodorow, N. (1978). *The reproduction of mothering: Psychoanalysis and the sociology of gender*. Berkeley: University of California Press.

Chodorow, N. (1995). Gender as a personal and cultural construction. *Signs, 20*(3), 516–544.

Collins, P. (1990). *Black feminist thought: Knowledge, consciousness, and the politics of empowerment.* Boston: Unwin Hyman.

Collins, R. (1988). *Sociology of marriage & the family: Gender, love, property.* (2nd ed.). Chicago: Nelson-Hall.

Daly, M. (1973). *Beyond God the Father: Toward a philosophy of women's liberation.* Boston: Beacon.

Davis, L. (1993). Feminism and constructivism: Teaching social work practice with women. In J. Laird (Ed.), *Revisioning social work education: A social constructionist approach* (pp. 147–163). New York: Haworth.

Dinnerstein, D. (1976). *The mermaid and the minotaur.* New York: Harper & Row.

Eisenstein, Z. (1984). *Feminism and sexual equality: Crisis in liberal America.* New York: Monthly Review Press.

Eisenstein, Z. (1994). *The color of gender: Reimaging democracy.* Berkeley: University of California Press.

Eisenstein, Z. (Ed.). (1979). *Capitalist patriarchy and socialist feminism.* New York: Monthly Review Press.

Ellman, B. & Taggart, M. (1993). Changing gender norms. In F. Walsh (Ed.), *Normal family processes* (2nd ed., pp. 377–404). New York: Guilford.

Engels, F. (1884/1970). *The origins of the family, private property, and the state.* New York: International Publishers.

Gambrill, E. & Richey, C. (1983). Gender issues related to group social skills training. *Social Work with Groups, 6*(3–4), 51–66.

Gerson, K. (1985). *Hard choices: How women decide about work, career and motherhood.* Berkeley: University of California Press.

Gilligan, C. (1982). *In a different voice*. Cambridge, MA: Harvard University Press.

Gould, K. (1984). Original works of Freud on women: Social work references. *Social Casework, 65*(2), 94–101.

Hare-Mustin, R.T. (1978). A feminist approach to family therapy. *Family Process, 17*, 181–194.

Hartman, A. (1987). Family violence: Multiple levels of assessment and intervention. *Journal of Social Work Practice, 2*(4), 62–78.

Horney, K. (1967). *Feminine psychology*. New York: Norton.

Johnson, M. (1989). Feminism and the theories of Talcott Parsons. In R. Wallace (Ed.), *Feminism and sociological theory.* Newbury Park, CA: Sage.

Jordan, J. (1992). The relational self: A new perspective for understanding women's development. *Contemporary Psychotherapy Review, 7*, 56–71.

Kravetz, D. (1982). An overview of content on women for the social work curriculum. *Journal of Education for Social Work, 18*(2), 42–49.

Laird, J. (1994). Changing women's narratives: Taking back the discourse. In L. Davis (Ed.), *Building on women's strengths: A social work agenda for the twenty-first century* (pp. 179–210). New York: Haworth.

Luepnitz, D. (1988). *The family interpreted: Feminist theory and clinical practice.* New York: Basic Books.

Luker, K. (1984). *Abortion and the politics of motherhood.* Berkeley: University of California Press.

McGoldrick, M. (1988). Women and the family life cycle. In E. Carter & M. McGoldrick (Eds.), *The changing family life cycle* (pp. 31–68). New York: Gardner.

McGoldrick, M., Anderson, C. & Walsh, F. (1989). *Women in families: A framework for family therapy.* New York: Norton.

Middleton, P. (1989). Socialism, feminism and men. *Radical Philosophy*, *53*, 8–19.

Miller, J.B. (1986). *Toward a new psychology of women* (2nd ed.). Boston: Beacon.

Riger, S. (1992). Epistemological debates, feminist voices: Science, social values, and the study of women. *American Psychologist, 47*(6), 730–740.

Safilios-Rothschild, C. (1970). The study of family power structure: A review, 1960–1969. *Journal of Marriage and the Family, 32*, 539–552.

Scanzoni, J. (1972). *Power politics in the American marriage*. Englewood Cliffs, NJ: Prentice-Hall.

Smith, D. (1990). *The conceptual practices of power: A feminist sociology of knowledge*. Boston: Northeastern University Press.

Taggert, M. (1985). The feminist critique in epistemological perspective: Questions of context in family therapy. *Journal of Marital and Family Therapy, 11*(2), 113–126.

Van den Bergh, N. (1995). Feminist social work practice: Where have we been . . . Where are we going? *Feminist practice in the 21st century.* Washington, DC: NASW Press.

Vogel, L. (1983). *Marxism and the oppression of women: Toward a unitary theory*. New Brunswick, NJ: Rutgers University Press.

Wallace, R. (1989). *Feminism and sociological theory*. Newbury Park, CA: Sage.

Walters, M., Carter, B., Papp, P. & Silverstein, O. (1988). *The invisible web: Gender patterns in family relationships.* New York: Guilford.

Weber, M. (1947/1968). *The theory of social and economic organization.* New York: Free Press.

Weenolsen, P. (1988). *Transcendence of loss over the life span.* New York: Hemisphere.

Weick, A. (1994). Overturning oppression: An analysis of emancipatory change. In L. Davis (Ed.), *Building on women's strengths: A social work agenda for the twenty-first century* (pp. 211–228). New York: Haworth.

Weick, A. & Vandiver, S. (1981). *Women, power, and change: Selected papers from Social Work Practice in Sexist Society.* Washington, DC: NASW Press.

Wesley, C. (1975). The women's movement and psychotherapy. *Social Work, 20*(2), 120–124.

APPENDIX 2–2: HBSE CURRICULUM MODULE: A GENDERED VIEW OF COPING

Purpose: To stimulate critical analysis of the relationship between coping strategies and gender issues, including consideration of the impact of social forces on human behavior.

Estimated Time: Total module time: about 2 hours. Time may vary significantly depending on the range of topics covered and the depth of coverage of each topic.

Required Readings:

Banyard, V. & Graham-Bermann, S. (1993). Can women cope? A gender analysis of theories of coping with stress. *Psychology of Women Quarterly, 17*, 303–318.

Kotlowitz, A. (1991). *There are no children here: The story of two boys growing up in the other America.* New York: Doubleday, Chapters 1–10.

Optional Reading: For an overview of macro-level barriers to effective coping and historical trends related to poverty and gender issues, the following article could also be assigned:

Bowen, G., Desimone, L. & McKay, J. (1995). Poverty and the single mother family: A macroeconomic perspective. *Marriage & Family Review, 20*(1–2), 115–142.

Recommended Use in HBSE Course: This module can be used in HBSE courses in a variety of ways, depending on the design of the HBSE curriculum. Within a life-course design, the module could be used in a unit on Adulthood. Within a theoretical design, the module could be used in a unit on Ego Psychology. Within a systems design, the module could be used in a unit on Role Theory.

Description: This module illustrates a dialectical approach to conveying the relationship of gender to adult development and coping styles. The readings are selected to encourage discussion of the intersect between women's coping responses and external resources and constraints. Previous class discussion and readings on the systems or ecological perspective, as well as on coping, would provide useful background knowledge. Ideally, discussion of the issues raised in the readings should take place in small groups. The following are possible discussion topic areas, each of which could be assigned to a small group. Each group would then be asked to describe their discussion and conclusions to the entire class.

A. Traditional Conceptions of Coping

According to Banyard and Graham-Bermann, coping has traditionally been conceptualized as behaviors that enable the experience of stress to be positive and growth enhancing. In Kotlowitz's *There Are No Children Here*, LaJoe experiences a number of stressors that one could view as potentially growth enhancing.

1. Describe and discuss these stressors and the actions LaJoe takes in response to them. Are the terms "passive" or "avoidance" relevant for describing her behavior, or do you agree with Banyard and Graham-Bermann's assertion that these terms may mask a variety of distinct coping actions?
2. How do you see "such individualizing characteristics as gender, race or class" (p. 304) affecting LaJoe's coping responses?
3. Given the salience of institutional and societal forces in LaJoe's life, what would you describe as the "optimum" coping strategy for LaJoe at this point?

B. Gender, Race & Class

On page 306, Banyard and Graham-Bermann state that "women and men are exposed to different stressors as a result of the different jobs that they perform in society and are thus required to use different coping strategies."

1. Do you think that LaJoe and Paul Rivers are expected to perform different "jobs," or roles, in society? What impact, if any, do such expectations have on their coping strategies?
2. Considering your own social network, do you see a difference in the types of "jobs" that men and women are expected to perform? If so, how do you feel that this has influenced their coping styles?

Banyard and Graham-Bermann go on to assert that a question that remains "unasked is whether there might be fewer differences between the coping strategies of women and men of the same race and social class than between women of different races and classes" (p. 306). Based on your discussion of the above issues, what would your response be to this "unasked" question?

C. Issues of Power

On page 308, Banyard and Graham-Bermann state that currently there is not enough emphasis on the issues of power and how it may act as a mediator in the stress and coping process.

1. In what ways do you think that power influences the coping efforts of LaJoe and other women in the Henry Horner Homes?
2. What implications do the "chronic, overarching stressors" of sexism and racism have for understanding LaJoe's responses to day-to-day hassles? What role, if any, have historical forces played in shaping LaJoe's personal coping strategy?
3. If, as a social worker, you were able to work with the women residing in the Henry Horner Homes, what types of social work interventions would you see as most appropriate?

D. Collective Coping

Banyard and Graham-Bermann describe collective coping as efforts "by multiple persons in conjunction with one another to influence adverse circumstances" (p. 309).

1. How useful is this concept for understanding and explaining the behavior of members of the Rivers family? Does this concept alter your assessment of the family's dynamics and level of functioning? In what sense?

Banyard and Graham-Bermann also describe an individual style of coping in which views of oneself and the actions that result from that view may be highly interdependent, or based on "consideration of one's relationship to others" (p. 310).

2. What evidence, if any, do you see of this style of coping in LaJoe? Given what you know about LaJoe's life, do you think this is an effective strategy? What are the advantages and disadvantages of this style for LaJoe and her family?

E. Social Support

On page 311, Banyard and Graham-Bermann discuss Belle's (1982) work on low-income women and suggest that this work changes the focus of social support from a "completely positive, adjustment enhancing resource to an understanding of its profound costs for women."

1. Who comprises LaJoe's social network? In what ways is this network an "adjustment enhancing resource?" In what ways does it produce "profound costs?"
2. In what ways does the existence of this network directly and indirectly affect LaJoe's coping style? What implications does this network have for your assessment of the adequacy of LaJoe's coping style?

F. Research and Theory

You have received a grant that will allow you to conduct research with single mothers living in poverty. You are interested in using Banyard and Graham-Bermann's ideas to assess which types of coping strategies lead to more favorable psychological outcomes for such women. Your goal is to use the results of your research to inform your agency's practice approaches. You have decided to focus on the women living in the Henry Horner Homes.

1. To carry out this research project, what specific research questions would you identify as most relevant? What research design and instruments would you use?
2. How would you utilize theory in this research project? Would you describe your approach as inductive or deductive? Why?

REFERENCES

Adams, J. & Jacobsen, P. (1964). Effects of wage inequities on work quality. *Journal of Abnormal and Social Psychology, 69,* 19–25.

al-Hibri, A. (1981). Reproduction, mothering and the origins of patriarchy. In J. Trebilcot (Ed.), *Mothering: Essays in feminist theory* (pp. 81–93). Totowa, NJ: Rowman and Allanheld.

Allen-Meares, P. & Lane, B.A. (1987). Grounding social work practice in theory: Ecosystems. *Social Casework: The Journal of Contemporary Social Work, 68,* 517–521.

Allport, G. (1961). *Pattern and growth in personality.* New York: Holt, Rinehart & Winston.

Bandura, A. (1977). Self-efficacy: Toward a unifying theory of behavioral change. *Psychological Review, 84,* 191–215.

Bandura, A. (1986). *Social foundations of thought and action: A social cognitive theory.* Englewood Cliffs, NJ: Prentice-Hall.

Beauvoir, S. de. (1949/1961). *The second sex.* (H.M. Parshley, Trans.). New York: Bantam.

Becker, G. (1981). *A treatise on the family.* Cambridge, MA: Harvard University Press.

Berger, P. & Luckmann, T. (1967). *The social construction of reality.* Garden City, NY: Anchor.

Berlin, S. (1983). Cognitive-behavioral approaches. In A. Rosenblatt & D. Waldfogel (Eds.), *Handbook of clinical social work* (pp. 1095–1119). San Francisco: Jossey-Bass.

Berlin, S. & Johnson, C. (1989). Women and autonomy: Using structural analysis of social behavior to find autonomy within connections. *Psychiatry, 52*(1), 79–95.

Bernard, J. (1975). *Women, wives and mothers: Values and options.* New York: Aldine.

Berzoff, J. (1989). From separation to connection: Shifts in understanding women's development. *Affilia, 4,* 45–58.

Blau, P. (1964). *Exchange and power in social life.* New York: Wiley.

Blood, R. & Wolfe, D. (1960). *Husbands and wives: The dynamics of married living.* New York: Free Press.

Blumberg, R. (1978). *Stratification: Socioeconomic and sexual inequaltiy.* Dubuque, IA: W.C. Brown.

Blumer, H. (1969). *Symbolic interaction: Perspective and method.* Englewood Cliffs, NJ: Prentice-Hall.

Blumstein, P. & Schwartz, P. (1983). *American couples: Money, work, sex.* New York: Morrow.

Bricker-Jenkins, M., Hooyman, N.R. & Gottlieb, N. (Eds.). (1991). *Feminist social work practice in clinical settings.* Newbury Park, CA: Sage.

Brinton, M. (1990). Intrafamilial markets for education in Japan. In M. Hechter, K. Opp & R. Wippler (Eds.), *Social institutions: Their emergence, maintenance and effects.* Berlin: Walter de Gruyter.

Bronfenbrenner, U. (1989). Ecological systems theory. *Annals of Child Development, 6,* 187–249.

Burgess, R. & Nielsen, J. (1974). An experimental analysis of some structural determinants of equitable and inequitable exchange relationships. *American Sociological Review, 39,* 427–443.

Burt, R. (1983). *Corporate profits and cooperation: Networks of market constraints and directorate ties in the American economy.* New York: Academic Press.

Carter, H. & Glick, P. (1976). *Marriage and divorce: A social and economic study.* Cambridge, MA: Harvard University Press.

Carter, B. & McGoldrick, M. (1988). *The changing family life cycle* (2nd ed.). New York: Gardner.

Chafetz, J. (1984). *Sex and advantage: A comparative, macro-structural theory of sex stratification.* Totowa, NJ: Rowman and Allanheld.

Chafetz, J. & Dworkin, A. (1986). *Female revolt: Women's movements in world and historical perspectives.* Totowa, NJ: Rowman and Allanheld.

Chestang, L. (1972). *Character development in a hostile environment* (Occasional Paper No. 3), School of Social Service Administration, University of Chicago.

Chodorow, N. (1978). *The reproduction of mothering: Psychoanalysis and the sociology of gender*. Berkeley: University of California Press.

Cingolani, J. (1984). Social conflict perspective on work with involuntary clients. *Social Work, 29,* 442–446.

Cohen, P. (1968). *Modern social theory.* New York: Basic Books.

Coleman, J. (1990). *Foundations of social theory.* Cambridge, MA: Belknap Press of Harvard University Press.

Collins, A. & Pancoast, D. (1976). *Natural helping networks.* Washington, DC: National Association of Social Workers.

Collins, P. (1990). *Black feminist thought: Knowledge, consciousness, and the politics of empowerment.* Boston: Unwin Hyman.

Collins, R. (1981). On the micro-foundations of macro-sociology. *American Journal of Sociology, 86*, 984–1014.

Collins, R. (1988). *Theoretical sociology*. San Diego: Harcourt Brace Jovanovich.

Collins, R. (1990). Conflict theory and the advance of macro-historical sociology. In G. Ritzer (Ed.), *Frontiers of social theory: The new syntheses* (pp. 68–87). New York: Columbia University Press.

Collins, R. (1994). *Four sociological traditions.* New York: Oxford University Press.

Cook, K. (Ed.). (1987). *Social exchange theory*. Newbury Park, CA: Sage.

Cook, K., O'Brien, J. & Kollock, P. (1990). Exchange theory: A blueprint for structure and process. In G. Ritzer (Ed.), *Frontiers of social theory: The new syntheses* (pp. 158–181). New York: Columbia University Press.

Cooley, C. (1902/1964). *Human nature and the social order.* New York: Scribner.

Coser, L. (1956). *The functions of conflict.* New York: Free Press.

Coser, L. (1975). Presidential address: Two methods in search of a substance. *American Sociological Review, 40*(6), 691–700.

Council on Social Work Education. (1962). *Curriculum policy statement*. New York: Author.

Dahrendorf, R. (1959). *Class and class conflict in industrial society*. Stanford, CA: Stanford University Press.

Daly, M. (1973). *Beyond God the Father: Toward a philosophy of women's liberation*. Boston: Beacon.

Davis, L. (1986). Role theory. In F. Turner (Ed.), *Social work treatment: Interlocking theoretical approaches* (3rd ed.) (pp. 541–563). New York: Free Press.

Davis, L. (1993). Feminism and constructivism: Teaching social work practice with women. In J. Laird (Ed.), *Revisioning social work education: A social constructionist approach* (pp. 147–163). New York: Haworth Press.

Dewey, J. (1922). *Human nature and conduct*. New York: Holt.

Dinnerstein, D. (1976). *The mermaid and the minotaur*. New York: Harper & Row.

Dollard, J. & Miller, N. (1950). *Personality and psychotherapy: An analysis in terms of learning, thinking and culture*. New York: McGraw-Hill.

Duvall, E. (1962). *Family development*. New York: Lippincott.

Eisenstein, Z. (Ed.). (1979). *Capitalist patriarchy and socialist feminism*. New York: Monthly Review Press.Ekeh, P. (1974). *Social exchange theory: The two traditions*. Cambridge, MA: Harvard University Press.

Engels, F. (1884/1970). *The origins of the family, private property and the state*. New York: International Publishers.

Erikson, E. (1950). *Childhood and society*. New York: Norton.

Erikson, E. (1982). *The life cycle completed*. New York: Norton.

Ellman, B. & Taggert, M. (1993). Changing gender norms. In F. Walsh (Ed.), *Normal family processes* (2nd ed.) (pp. 377–404). New York: Guilford.

Emerson, R. (1972a). Exchange theory, part I: A psychological basis for social exchange. In J. Berger, M. Zelditch, Jr. & B. Anderson (Eds.), *Sociological theories in progress, Vol. 2* (pp. 38–57). Boston: Houghton Mifflin.

Emerson, R. (1972b). Exchange theory, part II: Exchange relations and networks. In J. Berger, M. Zelditch, Jr. & B. Anderson (Eds.), *Sociological theories in progress, Vol. 2* (pp. 58–87). Boston: Houghton Mifflin.

Fontana, A. (1984). Introduction: Existential sociology and the self. In J. Kotarba & A. Fontana (Eds.), *The existential self in society* (pp. 3–17). Chicago, IL: University of Chicago Press.

Ford, D.J. & Lerner, R.M. (1992). *Developmental systems theory: An integrative approach*. Newbury Park, CA: Sage Publications.

Foucault, M. (1969). *The archaeology of knowledge and the discourse on language.* New York: Harper Colophon.

Fox, C. & Miller, H. (1995). *Postmodern public administration: Toward discourse.* Thousand Oaks, CA: Sage.

Frankl, V. (1963). *Man's search for meaning*. New York: Simon & Schuster.

Franklin, C. (1995). Expanding the vision of the social contructionist debates: Creating relevance for practitioners. *Families in Society: The Journal of Contemporary Human Services, 76*, 395–407.

Freud, A. (1969). *The writings of Anna Freud*. New York: International Universities Press.

Freud, S. (1925/1961). Some psychical consequences of the anatomical distinction between the sexes. In Vol XIX of *The standard edition*. London: Hogarth.

Fromm, E. (1941). *Escape from freedom*. New York: Avon Books.

Gallagher, W. (1993). *The power of place: How our surroundings shape our thoughts, emotions, and actions.* New York: Poseidon.

Galper, J. (1980). *Social work practice: A radical perspective*. Englewood Cliffs, NJ: Prentice-Hall.

Gambrill, E. (1987). Behavioral approach. In A. Minahan (Ed.), *Encyclopedia of Social Work, Vol. 1* (18th ed., pp. 184–194). Silver Spring, MD: NASW Press.

Gambrill, E. & Richey, C. (1983). Gender issues related to group social skills training. *Social Work with Groups, 6*(3–4), 51–66.

Garbarino, J. (1976). A preliminary study of some ecological correlates of child abuse: The impact of socioeconomic stress on mothers. *Child Development, 47,* 178–185.

Garbarino, J. (1977). The human ecology of child maltreatment: A conceptual model for research. *Journal of Marriage and the Family, 39*, 721–735.

Garbarino, J. & Sherman, D. (1980). High-risk neighborhoods and high-risk families: The human ecology of child maltreatment. *Child Development, 51,* 188–198.

Garfinkel, H. (1967). *Studies in ethnomethodology*. Englewood Cliffs, NJ: Prentice-Hall.

Geertz, C. (1983). *Local knowledge: Further essays in interpretive anthropology*. New York: Basic Books.

Gelles, R.J. (1992). Poverty and violence toward children. *American Behavioral Scientist, 35*, 258–274.

George, L. (1993). Sociological perspectives on life transitions. *Annual Review of Sociology, 19*, 353–373.

Germain, C. (1994). Human behavior and the social environment. In R. Reamer (Ed.), *The foundations of social work knowledge* (pp. 88–121). New York: Columbia University Press.

Germain, C. & Gitterman, A. (1980). *The life model of social work practice.* New York: Columbia University Press.

Gerson, K. (1985). *Hard choices: How women decide about work, career and motherhood.* Berkeley: University of California Press.

Gilligan, C. (1982). *In a different voice*. Cambridge, MA: Harvard University Press.

Goffman, E. (1959). *Presentation of self in everyday life*. Garden City, NY: Anchor.

Goffman, E. (1974). *Frame analysis: An essay on the organization of experience*. New York Harper Colophon.

Goldberg-Wood, G. & Middleman, R. (1989). *The structural approach to direct practice in social work*. New York: Columbia University Press.

Goldstein, E. (1984). *Ego psychology and social work practice.* New York: Free Press.

Goldstein, E. (1986). Ego psychology. In F. Turner (Ed.), *Social work treatment* (3rd ed., pp. 375–406). New York: Free Press.

Gould, K. (1984). Original works of Freud on women: Social work references. *Social Casework, 65*(2), 94–101.

Gould, R. (1978). *Transformations: Growth and change in adult life*. New York: Simon & Schuster.

Gouldner, A. (1970). *The coming crisis of Western sociology.* New York: Basic Books.

Greene, R. (1991). The ecological perspective: An eclectic theoretical framework for social work practice. In R. Greene and P. Ephross (Eds.), *Human behavior theory and social work practice* (pp. 261–295). New York: Aldine de Gruyter.

Greene, R. (1994a). Social work practice within a diversity framework. In R. Greene (Ed.), *Human behavior theory: A diversity framework* (pp. 1–17). New York: Aldine de Gruyter.

Greene, R. (Ed). (1994b). *Human behavior theory: A diversity framework.* New York: Aldine de Gruyter.

Greene, R. & Ephross, P. (Eds.). (1991). *Human behavior theory and social work practice.* New York: Aldine de Gruyter.

Gummer, B. (1990). *The politics of social administration: Managing organizational politics in social agencies.* Englewood Cliffs, NJ: Prentice-Hall.

Habermas, J. (1984). *The theory of communicative action: Vol 1. Reason and the rationalization of society.* Boston: Beacon Press.

Habermas, J. (1987). *The theory of communicative action: Vol. 2. Lifeworld and the system: A critique of functionalist reason.* Boston: Beacon.

Hare-Mustin, R.T. (1978). A feminist approach to family therapy. *Family Process, 17*, 181–194.

Hart, J. (1970). The development of client-centered therapy. In J.T. Hart & T.M. Tomlinson (Eds.), *New directions in client-centered therapy* (pp. 3–22). Boston: Houghton Mifflin.

Hartman, A. & Laird, J. (1983). *Family-centered social work practice.* New York: Free Press.

Hartmann, H. (1964). *Essays on ego psychology: Selected problems in psychoanalytic theory.* New York: International Universities Press.

Hasenfeld, Y. (1980). Implementation of change in human service organizations: A political economy perspective. *Social Service Review, 54*(4), 508–520.

Havighurst, R. (1972). *Developmental tasks and education* (3rd ed.). New York: D. McKay Co.

Hearn, J. & Parkin, W. (1993). Organizations, multiple oppressions and postmodernism. In J. Hassard & M. Parker (Eds.), *Postmodernism and organizations* (pp. 148–162). Newbury Park, CA: Sage.

Ho, M.K. (1992). *Minority children and adolescents in therapy.* Newbury Park, CA: Sage.

Homans, G. (1958). Social behavior as exchange. *American Journal of Sociology, 63* 597–606.

Horney, K. (1939). *New ways in psychoanalysis.* New York: Norton.

Horney, K. (1967). *Feminine psychology*. New York: Norton.

Hull, C. (1952). *A behavior system*. New Haven, CT: Yale University Press.

Husserl, E. (1975). *Ideas: General introduction to pure phenomenology.* New York: Macmillan.

Hutchison, E. (1988). *Factors which influence child protective screening decisions.* Unpublished doctoral dissertation, State University of New York at Albany.

Imber-Black, E. (1988). *Families and larger systems*. New York: Guilford.

Imre, R. (1984) The nature of knowledge in social work. *Social Work, 29,* 41–45.

Johnson, M. (1989). Feminism and the theories of Talcott Parsons. In R. Wallace (Ed.), *Feminism and sociological theory* (pp. 101–118). Newbury Park, CA: Sage.

Jordan, J. (1992). The relational self: A new perspective for understanding women's development. *Contemporary Psychotherapy Review, 7*, 56–71.

Jung, C. (1969). *The collected works of C.G. Jung*. Princeton: Princeton University Press.

Kahneman, E. & Tversky, A. (1982). The psychology of preferences. *Scientific American, 246*, 160–173.

Kahneman, E. & Tversky, A. (1984). Choices, values, and frames. *American Psychologist, 39*, 341–350.

Kelley, H. & Thibaut, J. (1978). *Interpersonal relations: A theory of interdependence*. New York: Wiley.

Kernberg, O. (1976). *Object relations theory and clinical psychoanalysis*. New York: Jason Aronson.

Kinkade, K. (1973). *A Walden Two experiment: The first five years of Twin Oaks Community.* New York: Morrow.

Klein, M. (1975). *The psychoanalysis of children*. London: Hogarth (reissued by Delacorte Press, 1975).

Kohlberg, L. (1979). *The meaning and measurement of moral development.* Worcester, MA: Clark Lectures, Clark University.

Kohut, H. (1971). *The analysis of the self*. New York: International Universities Press.

Kravetz, D. (1982). An overview of content on women for the social work curriculum. *Journal of Education for Social Work, 18*(2), 42–49.

Krill, D. (1986). Existential social work. In F. Turner (Ed.), *Social work treatment: Interlocking theoretical approaches* (pp. 181–217). New York: Free Press.

Kropf, N. & Greene, R. (1994). Erikson's eight stages of development: Different lenses. In R. Greene (Ed.), *Human behavior theory: A diversity framework* (pp. 75–114). New York: Aldine de Gruyter.

Laing, R.D. (1967). *The politics of experience.* New York: Ballantine.

Laing, R.D. (1969). *The politics of the family.* New York: Pantheon.

Laird, J. (1994). Changing women's narratives: Taking back the discourse. In L. Davis (Ed.), *Building on women's strengths: A social work agenda for the twenty-first century* (pp. 179–210). New York: Haworth.

Lenski, G. (1966). *Power and privilege: A theory of social stratification.* New York: McGraw-Hill.

Levi, M., Cook, K., O'Brien, J. & Faye, H. (1990). The limits of rationality. In K. Cook & M. Levi (Eds.), *The limits of rationality* (pp. 1–16). Chicago: University of Chicago Press.

Levinson, D. (1996). *The seasons of a woman's life*. New York: Knopf.

Lewin, K. (1936/1966). *Principles of topological psychology*. New York: McGraw-Hill.

Lincoln, Y. & Guba, E. (1985). *Naturalistic inquiry*. Beverly Hills, CA: Sage.

Longres, J. (1995). *Human behavior in the social environment* (2nd ed.). Itasca, IL: Peacock.

Luepnitz, D. (1988). *The family interpreted: Feminist theory and clinical practice*. New York: Basic Books.

Luker, K. (1984). *Abortion and the politics of motherhood*. Berkeley: University of California Press.

Mahler, M. (1968). *On human symbiosis and the vicissitudes of individuation: Infantile psychosis*. New York: International Universities Press.

Mann, M. (1986). *The sources of social power: Vol. 1*. New York: Cambridge University Press.

March, J. & Simon, H. (1958). *Organizations*. New York: Wiley.

Marcia, J. (1993). The ego identity status approach to ego identity. In J.E. Marcia, A.S. Waterman, D.R. Mattesson, S.L. Arcjer & J.L. Orlofsky (Eds.), *Ego identity: A handbook for psychosocial research*. New York: Springer-Verlag.

Martin, P.Y. & O'Connor, G. (1989). *The social environment: Open systems applications*. New York: Longman.

Marx, K. (1987/1967). *Capital: A critique of political economy. Vol 1*. New York: International.

Maslow, A. (1962). *Toward a psychology of being*. New York: Van Nostrand.

May, R. (1969). *Love and will*. New York: Norton.

McCarthy, J. & Zald, M. (1977). Resource mobilization in social movements: A partial theory. *American Journal of Sociology, 82*, 1212–1239.

McGoldrick, M. (1988). Women and the family life cycle. In E. Carter & M. McGoldrick (Eds.), *The changing family life cycle* (pp. 31–68). New York: Gardner.

McGoldrick, M., Anderson, C. & Walsh, F. (1989). *Women in families: A framework for family therapy*. New York: Norton.

McGregor, D. (1960). *The human side of enterprise*. New York: McGraw- Hill.

Mead, G. (1934/1962). *Mind, self, and society: From the standpoint of a social behaviorist*. Chicago: University of Chicago Press.

Merton, R. (1973). The Matthew effect in science. In N. Storer (Ed.), *The sociology of science: Theoretical and empirical investigations* (pp. 439–459). Chicago: University of Chicago Press.

Meyer, C. (1987). Content and process in social work practice: A new look at old issues. *Social Work, 32*, 401–404.

Meyer, C. (1993). *Assessment in social work practice.* New York: Columbia University Press.

Meyer, C. (Ed.). (1983). *Clinical social work in an eco-systems perspective.* New York: Columbia University Press.

Middleman, R. & Goldberg, G. (1974). *Social service delivery: A structural approach to social work practice.* New York: Columbia University Press.

Middleton, P. (1989). Socialism, feminism and men. *Radical Philosophy, 53,* 8–19.

Mikulincer, M. (1994). *Human learned helplessness: A coping perspective.* New York: Plenum.

Miller, J.B. (1986). *Toward a new psychology of women* (2nd Ed.). Boston: Beacon.

Mills, C.W. (1956). *The power elite.* New York: Oxford University Press.

Monte, C. (1995). *Beneath the mask: An introduction to theories of personality* (5th ed.). Fort Worth, TX: Harcourt Brace College Publishers.

Netting, F.E., Kettner, P. & McMurtry, S. (1993). *Social work Practice.* New York: Longman.

Neugarten, B. (1979). Time, age, and the life cycle. *American Journal of Psychiatry, 136,* 887–894.

Newman, B. & Newman, P. (1987). *Development through life: A psychosocial approach.* (4th ed.). Chicago: Dorsey.

Parsons, T. (1951). *The social system.* Glencoe, IL: Free Press.

Pavlov, I. (1927). *Conditioned reflexes: An investigation into the physiological activity of the cortex.* New York: Dover.

Piaget, J. (1952). *The origins of intelligence in children.* New York: International Universities Press.

Pincus, A. & Minahan, A. (1973). *Social work practice: Model and method.* Itasca, IL: Peacock.

Reid, W. (1985). *Family problem solving.* New York: Columbia University Press.

Riger, S. (1992). Epistemological debates, feminist voices: Science, social values, and the study of women. *American Psychologist, 47*(6), 730–740.

Ritzer, G. (1992). *Contemporary sociological theory* (3rd ed.). New York: McGraw-Hill.

Robinson, V. (Ed.). (1942). *Training for skill in social case work.* Philadelphia: University of Pennsylvania Press.

Rodwell, M. (1987). Naturalistic inquiry: An alternative model for social work assessment. *Social Service Review, 61,* 231–246.

Rogers, C. (1951). *Client-centered therapy.* Boston: Houghton Mifflin.

Safilios-Rothschild, C. (1970). The study of family power structure, a review, 1960–1969. *Journal of Marriage and the Family, 32*, 539–552.

Saleeby, D. (1994). Culture, theory & narrative: The intersection of meanings in practice. *Social Work, 39*(4), 351–359.

Scanzoni, J. (1972). *Power politics in the American marriage*. Englewood Cliffs, NJ: Prentice-Hall.

Schriver, J. (1995). *Human behavior and the social environment: Shifting paradigms in essential knowledge for social work practice.* Boston: Allyn and Bacon.

Schutz, A. (1932/1967). *The phenomenology of the social world.* Evanston, IL: Northwestern University Press.

Schwartz, M. (1973). Sexism in the social work curriculum. *Journal of Social Work Education, 9*(3), 65–70.

Siporin, M. (1975). *Introduction to social work practice*. New York: Macmillan.

Skinner, B. (1953). *Science and human behavior*. New York: Free Press.

Skocpol, T. (1979). *States and social revolutions.* New York: Cambridge University Press.

Smalley, R. (1941). *Meaning and use of relief in case work treatment*. New York: Family Welfare Association of America.

Smith, D. (1990). *The conceptual practices of power: A feminist sociology of knowledge.* Boston: Northeastern University Press.

Solomon, B. (1976). *Black empowerment: Social work in oppressed communities.* New York: Columbia University Press.

Specht, H. (1986). Social support, social networks, social exchange, and social work practice. *Social Service Review, 60*, 218–240.

Stein, H. & Cloward, R. (1958). *Social perspectives on behavior: A reader in social science for social work and related professions.* New York: Free Press.

Streeter, C. & Gillespie, D. (1992). Social network analysis. *Journal of Social Service Research, 16*(1–3), 201–221.

Stuart, R. (1989). Social learning theory: A vanishing or expanding presence? *Psychology: A Journal of Human Behavior, 26*(1), 35–50.

Sue, D. & Sue, D. (1990). *Counseling the culturally different: Theory and practice* (2nd ed.). New York: Wiley.

Sullivan, H. (1953). *The interpersonal theory of psychiatry*. New York: Norton.

Taft, J. (1973). *The dynamics of therapy in a controlled relationship.* Gloucester, MA: P. Smith.

Taggert, M. (1985). The feminist critique in epistemological perspective: Questions of context in family therapy. *Journal of Marital and Family Therapy, 11*(2), 113–126.

Thibaut, J. & Kelley, H. (1959). *The social psychology of groups.* New York: Wiley.

Thorndike, E. (1911). *Animal intelligence*. New York: Macmillan.

Thyer, B. (1991). Behavioral social work: It is not what you think. *Arete, 16*, 1–9.

Thyer, B. (1994). Social learning theory: Empirical applications to culturally diverse practice. In R. Greene (Ed.), *Human behavior theory: A diversity framework* (pp. 133–146). New York: Aldine de Gruyter.

Tracy, E. & Whittaker, J. (1990). The social network map: Assessing social support in clinical practice. *Families in Society, 71* (8), 461–470.

Valliant, G. (1993). *The wisdom of the ego*. Cambridge: Harvard University Press.

Van den Bergh, N. (1995). Feminist social work practice: Where have we been . . . Where are we going? *Feminist practice in the 21st century.* Washington, DC: NASW Press.

Vogel, L. (1983). *Marxism and the oppression of women: Toward a unitary theory*. New Brunswick, NJ: Rutgers University Press.

Wachs, T. (1992). *Individual differences and development series: Vol. 3. The nature of nurture.* Newbury Park, CA: Sage.

Wallace, R. & Wolf, A. (1995). *Contemporary sociological theory: Continuing the classical tradition* (4th ed.). Englewood Cliffs, NJ: Prentice-Hall.

Wallerstein, I. (1974–1989). *The modern world system: Vols. 1 3*. New York: Academic Press.

Walters, M., Carter, B., Papp, P. & Silverstein, O. (1988). *The invisible web: Gender patterns in family relationships.* New York: Guilford.

Watson, J. (1924). *Behaviorism*. New York: Norton.

Weenolsen, P. (1988). *Transcendence of loss over the life span.* New York: Hemisphere.

Weick, A. (1994). Overturning oppression: An analysis of emancipatory change. In L. Davis (Ed.), *Building on women's strengths: A social work agenda for the twenty-first century* (pp. 21–228). New York: Haworth.

Wesley, C. (1975). The women's movement and psychotherapy. *Social Work, 20*(2), 120–124.

Wheeler, H. (Ed.). (1973). *Beyond the punitive society.* San Francisco: Freeman.

White, R. (1975). *Lives in progress.* (3rd ed.). New York: Holt, Rinehart & Winston.

Willer, D. (1987). *Theory and the experimental investigation of social structures.* New York: Gordon and Breach.

Winnicott, D. (1971). *Playing and reality.* London: Pengiun Books.

Witkin, S. & Gottschalk, S. (1988). Alternative criteria for theory evaluation. *Social Service Review, 62*, 211–224.

Youngdahl, B. (1966). *Social action and social work.* New York: Association Press.

Zuravin, S.J. (1986). Residential density and urban child maltreatment: An aggregate analysis. *Journal of Family Violence, 1,* 307–322.

Zuravin, S.J. (1989). The ecology of child abuse and neglect: Review of the literature and presentation of data. *Violence and Victims, 4,* 1010–1020.

CHAPTER 3

Direct Practice

Addressing Gender in Practice from a Multicultural Feminist Perspective

Iris Carlton-LaNey
Janice Andrews

INTRODUCTION

This chapter addresses the importance of gender in practice, explores ways in which "women's issues" have been a part of social work practice, and discusses gender in practice from a multicultural feminist perspective. Despite a general acceptance among social workers of the proposition that gender makes a difference, the legitimacy of a feminist orientation is often not presented in any organized fashion in the curriculum and its content may even be completely absent from many social work programs (Collins, 1986; Hooyman, 1994; Krane, 1991; Lazzair, 1991; Nes & Iadicola, 1989; Van den Bergh & Cooper, 1986). Course content more broadly defined as "women's issues" is likewise sparse. When it does exist, it does not provide a fundamental change in the way that practice content is taught, nor does it reexamine the analytical category of patriarchy (Hooyman, 1994). Most students of social work, then, have had little or no education regarding the importance of gender in direct practice. Particularly absent from their learning is a feminist orientation.

HISTORICAL OVERVIEW OF DIRECT PRACTICE

Social work direct practice has its roots in the social casework method. Greatly influenced by the Social Gospel movement, social Darwinism and the laissez faire philosophy, early models of social work practice took a paternalistic approach. This paternalistic practice, modeled on the parent-child template, was visible throughout the pioneering years of the social work profession. Simon (1994) describes this paternalism as a system of relations in which those in authority act on behalf of other people without their permission to do so, while maintaining a belief that their action is in the best interest of the person in need regardless of that person's belief and wishes. Embracing the paternalistic approach, Charity Organization Society (COS) pioneers like Josephine Shaw Lowell and Mary Richmond targeted individual shortcomings and moral weakness in their casework practice. The avoidance of duplication of services was paramount, and changing individual behavior was entrenched in the COS movement's work. The COS advanced seven fundamental ideas—interagency cooperation, community education, individualization, adequacy of relief, repression of mendicancy, preventive philanthropy, and personal service (Lewis, 1977)—all of which were couched in paternalism. The social settlement house leaders also embraced the notion of paternalism, albeit to a lesser extent. Less prone to direct verbal reproach for "inappropriate" conduct, the settlement house leaders encouraged, cajoled, and massaged newcomers, both immigrants and migrants, to convince them of the merits of assimilation and otherwise acceptable behavior. Simon (1994) noted that some paternalism crept into the various clubs and programs of the settlement houses as the leaders held themselves up as role models and stalwarts of the American dream. While settlement house leaders touted the notion that their residence in the communities of need demonstrated the idea that dependency of the classes on each other was reciprocal, their methods of direct practice reflected paternalism and role modeling for assimilation and protection of the middle and upper classes.

Like the COS and the settlement house movements, the National Urban League (NUL), another major social welfare organization of the Progressive Era, also took a paternal position in its work with African Americans who migrated from the rural South to urban centers in the North. Founded as a result of the merger of three organizations, the Committee for Improving Industrial Conditions for Negroes in New York, the National League for the Protection of Colored Women, and the Committee on Urban Conditions Among Negroes, the NUL worked to intervene directly on behalf of newly urban African Americans. The NUL's method of dealing with societal problems that confronted African Americans was to change private practices rather than public laws. The reality of influencing Congress to enact legislation to protect African Americans was fairly unheard of during the early part of the twentieth century. The NUL's method of service therefore tended to be paternal in its approach, since this practice had a history of some success. As Weiss (1974) describes examples of the NUL's paternalism, "it tried to change individual practices in different businesses or cities by private, individual persuasion. If an employer treated his employee shabbily, the League would dispatch a welfare worker to try to adjust their differences. If a company was reluctant to hire [blacks], the Urban League would try to press for an opening for one particularly capable applicant" (p. 88).

Women

Women, like African Americans, were likewise accorded inferior status and seen as a group in need of protection and a paternal guiding hand. Because gender provided some white women with positions of esteem, they were surprised to find that it also denied them access to resources and opportunities. The Grimké sisters of South Carolina, for example, discovered their devalued status when they became abolitionists. Advocating for the rights of enslaved people forced them to face their own oppressed positions as women.

Women's reproductive freedom was another issue where men exercised their positions of power over women. The activities of Anthony Comstock and his Society for the Suppression of Vice defined writing about birth control as obscene and illegal. In 1873 the organization succeeded in getting federal legislation that banned the importation, mailing, or interstate transportation of any article of medicine for the prevention of conception or for inducing abortion (Farley, 1992).

Women's traditional place as caregivers remained prevalent during the early part of the century. Pioneer social work leaders were often in agreement with this position as it referred to *other* women. However, the Cult of True Womanhood, that assigned to women the role of defenders of the moral order, made it acceptable for them to venture into the world outside the home because their highly evolved spirituality, compassion, nurturance, and morality made them suitable to tackle societal uncleanness and immorality (Day, 1997). Struggling with the themes inherent to womanhood during that time, some leaders like Lillian Wald and Florence Kelley practiced and modeled more integrative roles for women. Others like Elizabeth Ross Haynes, elected "lady coleader" of the 21st Assembly District in Harlem, accepted the roles of wife, mother, community leader, and public office holder. She, furthermore, tried to empower other women by encouraging them to vote and seek office for themselves instead of pushing men forward and standing passively in the background (Carlton-LaNey, 1995).

The brief history of social work discussed earlier illustrates an emerging profession steeped in rapid social change, racism, sexism, and classism. The roots of paternalism became the guiding principle for social change, social treatment, and social policy with some notable exceptions. But as Simon (1994) points out, the winds of empowerment were, nonetheless, prevalent with practitioners and theorists contributing significant elements that influenced the social work tradition. The focus on empowerment, however, is a fairly recent phenomenon (Solomon, 1976). Simon describes social work's emphasis on the process of empowerment as follows:

1. Phasing their interventions, beginning with direct responses to clients' request.
2. Encouraging clients' involvement in peer networks.
3. Acknowledging explicitly clients' knowledge, authority, and centrality in the change process. (p. 177)

Phasing interventions requires that professionals listen to the clients' stories and respect their ability to identify their own needs. Clients will be disinclined to seek professional intervention when they feel that their desires and wishes are overlooked or ignored. Oftentimes, women who feel marginalized and devalued are sensitive to responses that blame them for the problem or seek to reinterpret the real issues for them. Current clinical literature and practice, for example, continue to blame women and mothers for family and child problems (Caplan & Hall-McCorquodale, 1983).

Multiculturalism

Social work has a long history of involvement, albeit not always adequate or effective, with issues of human diversity, particularly in the area of civil rights for people of color. The profession came, much later, on the scene of the women's movement. It was not until the mid–1970s that the National Association of Social Workers' (NASW) journal

Social Work finally addressed this neglect. Recently, the profession has been struggling, along with other disciplines, to define multiculturalism. The literature reflects this struggle as it acknowledges the power and relevance of the interaction of cultural variables and their impact on human behavior (Comas-Diaz & Greene, 1994).

Until recently, race and class have been mentioned in texts as afterthoughts, often as an add-on at the end of a chapter, but seldom integrated into the body of the document. Furthermore, the effects of class position and cultural experiences on all people outside the dominant or majority group are often obscured (Farley, 1992). For example, the literature on race often equates African Americans with being poor and whites with being middle-class. Discussions of African Americans and whites are often discussions of the dominant white group and of all African Americans. Such discussions ignore white ethnics and poor whites and treat African Americans as a homogenous group while ignoring other people of color. The result is a simplistic analysis rendering other groups invisible. This simplistic approach leaves students and practitioners alike with a skewed and inaccurate frame of reference resulting in culturally insensitive and incompetent practice.

Embracing multiculturalism can be an effective strategy to avoid mistakes that can be devastating to the client system. A multicultural interaction insists that it is not enough to know someone's race or ethnic background and assume one knows much about that person or group. Likewise, knowing someone's gender does not necessarily tell one much about a person or group. It is the dynamic relationship of race, ethnicity, and gender to one another with other variables (e.g., age, socioeconomic status, sexual orientation, etc.) that begins to describe and refine a person. What is needed is a systematic analysis of the interaction among those dimensions (Taggart, 1985). Essentially the tenets of competent social work practice require linkages between diversity, historic-structural context, and emerging knowledge (Carter et al., 1994).

Understanding how these variables interlink demands that we think and communicate simultaneously about multiple processes and structures in a way that utilizes a "different mirror" (Takaki, 1993). It demands that we understand the concept of power and the ways in which it affects clients as well as practitioners (Pinderhughes, 1989). It further requires that we engage in practice that is sufficiently flexible to reflect new and changing information and knowledge. Multiculturalism that is truly multicultural rejects single variable analyses and understands the complexities of human interaction.

Feminism

Feminism, too, has been moving to embrace more inclusive models of social work and needs to continue to make a commitment in that direction. The concept of feminism is not easily defined. Most discussions of feminism point to at least three different perspectives: liberal, socialist, and radical feminism (Nes & Iadicola, 1989; Van den Bergh & Cooper, 1986; Walters, Carter, Papp & Silverstein, 1988). Within each of these perspectives, there can be a great deal of diversity. All definitions of feminism have common principles that include an action orientation, the recognition of oppression against women, the belief that the personal is political, and the assumption of a patriarchal society. "Womanism," or black feminism, reflects this general definition of feminism and also describes a consciousness that incorporates racial, cultural, sexual, national, and political considerations of all people. Womanism does not accept the primacy of gender issues over the structured inequalities of race and finds it difficult to emphasize any one over the other. When one is emphasized, it is invariably race. Because racism historically has permeated the women's movement, African-American women have been slow to embrace feminism and have questioned the genuineness of the movement in later years as it claims to consider "all people" in its approach. For many African Americans and other women of color, there is the ever-present question that prompts one to wonder if the unspoken caveat is "all people, *except* African Americans or women of color."

Looking at social work practice from a feminist perspective leads one to emphasize those aspects of practice that challenge the status quo and that work to alter the structures in society that oppress women. It also requires acknowledging the fact that traditional knowledge has been formulated by groups of white males who enjoy privilege because of their skin color and gender. Accepting this knowledge as truth has resulted in ignorance, marginalization, and distortion of women's realities (Abbott & Wallace, 1990). By deconstructing the social construction of gender as fixed or absolute, feminists can be open to understanding gender as only one among many elements of one's total self. This understanding leads to a true focus on diversity (Hooyman,

1994). Essentially, deconstruction requires that we critically evaluate the world as described and presented by men. The social worker who engages in practice with women using a feminist perspective addresses the social, political, and cultural origins of the client's presenting issue (the personal is political) and participates in the therapeutic intervention as a co-learner. It is, in essence, a practice of personal and political transformation (Bricker-Jenkins, 1991).

Review of Gender Considerations in Practice

Attention to gender in practice emerged from the second awakening of the women's movement in the late 1960s. Because the roots of theories that explain behavior and describe therapy, for the most part, were conceptualized earlier, much of this early work has been challenged by feminists. There has been an increasing recognition of the limitations of traditional theories of psychological development based on a male model. Family therapist Lois Braverman (1986) asked, "What has taken us so long?" to apply a feminist approach to therapy and concluded that it is too threatening and emotionally loaded to shake "the very precepts upon which our epistemology is based" (p. 6).

Bricker-Jenkins and Lockett (1995) trace the development of feminist social work practice through three phases:

> 1. The "alternative services" phase beginning in the 1960s. In this phase, feminists encouraged an understanding of the special needs of women and offered contributions to practice theory. Many community-based services for women were emphasized such as women's shelters, women's health, and alternatives to traditional counseling;
>
> 2. The "worldview" definitional phase peaked in the mid–1980s. The emphasis of this phase was on advancing a feminist conceptual framework for social work practice. Feminism was distinguished among a continuum from liberal to Marxist. Feminist methods of practice were delineated.
>
> 3. The contemporary "integrative methods development" phase began in the late–1980s. The focus has been on developing a practice model which is "dynamic, multidimensional, situated, and politically shaped." (pp. 2530–2532)

Despite those advances, gender stereotyping remains in social work education and in direct social work practice (Hooyman, 1994). In some cases, there is even a backlash occurring whereby it is becoming difficult to discuss the impact of gender because of a perceived anti-male message in the discussion. Some aspects of the current "men's movement" promote the backlash. A leading social worker and feminist therapist, Marianne Walters (1993), for example, directs criticism at various male movements, but is most critical when discussing Robert Bly (author of *Iron John*) and his movement, which uses myth, poetry, and the pounding of drums to redirect men's connection to the earth and to each other. Walters states:

> I don't believe there would have been a men's movement if not for feminism and the sociopolitical as well as personal changes it has caused. The secure social base on which men rested their authority has been shaken, and many of the customs on which they relied have been brought into question. . . . I believe it has entered that stream of activities we can identify as a backlash to feminism, a phenomenon that not only seeks to restore male privilege but to blame women for every sort of social and emotional malaise. (p. 63)

In the past five years, feminists have been active in more clearly delineating differences between feminist practice and more traditional models of practice (Bricker-Jenkins, Hooyman & Gottlieb, 1991; Hooyman, 1994; Kirst-Ashman, 1992).

MODELS OF PRACTICE AND THEIR THEORETICAL ORIENTATIONS

The psychology of women has not been central to the development of theories underlying our practice models. Therefore, feminists have been skeptical of their use with female clients in particular and with all clients in general. Several psychological attributes such as passivity, dependency, need for social interaction and connection, and emotionality have been viewed as problematic traits of women by many theorists (Schwartz, 1973).

Three broad theoretical approaches—psychotherapeutic, systems, and behavioral/cognitive—are reviewed with issues pertaining to women underscored. It is not the intent of the authors to assume that other approaches are never utilized, nor to encourage the abandonment of all past theoretical work, but, rather, to promote the use of concepts carefully with the full understanding of the important issues being raised by feminists. In order to guide educators and students in asking questions relevant to gender as they examine various theoretical orientations, we pose the following five questions:

1. How does this approach directly respond to the client's request?
2. Does this approach listen to the voices of women?
3. Is this approach helpful in terms of gender?
4. Does this approach reflect an understanding of the context shaping gender and race?
5. Will this approach lead to a gender-sensitive change?

With these questions in mind, we provide a brief overview of models and their theoretical orientations.

Psychotherapeutic Approaches

Feminism focuses on context to a greater extent than can be expected from any of the schools of psychoanalysis. The goal of psychoanalysis is to bring conflict-laden material to consciousness so that it can be resolved. Symbols, metaphors, historical events, and dreams become important resources for the resolution of conflicts (Chin, 1994). This cannot occur absent from an understanding of the multicultural reality of the client. Race, class, gender, socioeconomic status, sexual orientation, among other elements of the context receive primary attention from feminists as they explore with the client—male or female—her/his social situation.

Feminists, and social work in general, have been very critical of Freud's contributions both to psychotherapy and to theories of personality. Major criticism centers around Freud's phallocentrism, his belief that women envy the penis and attempt to compensate by having babies (Luepnitz, 1988). Freud is considered the archetypal patriarch of theory development. Feminists are particularly critical of the impact his work has had on women survivors of child sex abuse. Early in his work, he abandoned the Seduction Theory, which acknowledged that women's neurosis was the result of such abuse. He altered his views when he adopted the Oedipal Theory suggesting that all children desire their parents sexually; when they report sex abuse, they are really imagining such events. This type of criticism has had an impact on social work education in such a way that most students can graduate without ever reading a word of Freud's work.

While the conflicts that feminists have with Freud's work seem insurmountable, Luepnitz (1988) argues that there are, in fact, several similarities between psychoanalysis and feminism:

> 1. Freud attacks Victorian patriarchy pointing out that dualism of normal and abnormal were more apparent than real.
>
> 2. Psychoanalysis redefines issues formerly attributed to women—affect, sexuality, expressiveness, intimacy—as concerns for everyone.
>
> 3. Like feminism, psychoanalysis views the individual as having conflict with the larger society.
>
> 4. Both feminism and psychoanalysis make language a central focus.
>
> 5. Feminism's emphasis on consciousness raising and demystification is similar to Freud's focus on the person's history.
>
> 6. Both perspectives emphasize the importance of the relationship between therapist and client. (pp. 175–177)

The use of psychoanalytic therapy with women of color is explored by Chin (1994), who points to the need to take into consideration the different cultural perspectives and experiences of women. She suggests two approaches: (1) to refine the psychotherapy to include gender differences and (2) to reconceptualize the theory itself to fit the population under consideration (p. 194). In a more homogeneous society, theories are more likely to appear to have universal application. While this is never the case, it is particularly not so with psychoanalysis developed by a white male during a specific historical period who saw clients from a very narrow sociocultural class. All standard rules of practice are culturally rooted. "To be relevant, a psychodynamic approach must use multiple norms to interpret manifestations that arise out of cultural and gender differences" (Chin, 1994, p. 198).

Some feminists have found compatibility with one school of psychoanalysis, the Object Relations School, because of its emphasis on social interaction and relationships. Despite the fact that early members of the school participated in mother-blaming regarding disturbances of children, more recently Nancy Chodorow (1978) has provided a bridge between concepts of the school and feminism. Luepnitz (1988) applauds Chodorow (1978) for showing how enhancing the psychoanalytical/feminist synthesis can be.

> Without feminism, psychoanalytic theories of gender end up with a "deficit" model of femininity, e.g., women as castrated men. Without psychoanalytic theory, social learning theories of gender are behavioristic and superficial, and imply an empty organism, passively conditioned without the capacity to rearrange, refuse, repress, and filter stimuli. Without either feminism or psychoanalytic theory, family therapy is rendered "asexual." It stands without a suitably complex means of talking about the hypostatic reality of gender. (p. 181)

Systems Approaches

Systems theory has had a significant influence on social work practice and has been effective in helping social work to move from a simplistic medical model of causation to a more multicausal way of understanding human behavior. A framework for understanding and examining human behavior, systems theory has been used to explain complex phenomena such as role behavior and gender identity by considering many contributing variables. Systems theory has been useful to social work for two important reasons: (1) an emphasis on interdependence and interaction among systems and (2) a focus on the adaptive or maladaptive nature of systems (Greene & Ephross, 1991).

Social work's reliance on systems theory as the overarching perspective, however, has been problematic for feminists who see in the theory several conceptual problems. The primary concern is systems theory's acceptance of neutrality without understanding the impact of power and control that generally favor males.

Larger system impacts, while acknowledged as crucial in social work systems theories, take on a different meaning when gender and other multicultural variables are emphasized. A feminist view of public service delivery systems, an arena in which many social workers are employed, provides an example. These systems reflect gender-defined roles in the larger society. Generally the direct service workers are women, while the decision makers and power brokers are men. Such hierarchy tends to cause strain within the rank and file. This often results in "a culture that structures conflictual transactions, thus maintaining a diversity process *between* and among *women*" (Walters, 1993, p. 13). In fact, these delivery systems, rather than addressing the social inequities they were created to address, instead often serve to maintain those very same inequities. Women in this system, "either as providers or as recipients, do what people who feel powerless often do: They struggle and experience conflict with one another. Systems that mandate responsibility without authority and expectations without resources tend not only to create victims, but to position them in adversarial relation to one another" (Walters, 1993, p. 13).

Feminist theories in the field of family therapy have been particularly critical of the ways in which family systems theory disadvantages women (Braverman, 1986; Walters, Carter, Papp & Silverstein, 1988). Standard systems concepts like fusion, reciprocity, complementarity, hierarchy, and triangles (Walters et al., 1988) often leave the woman responsible for any dysfunction in the family system. Patterns of women's victimization and exploitation do not emerge. Rather "blame" permeates the helping process and interferes with the relationship while denying a strengths-based perspective of practice.

Taggart (1985) believes that systems theory continues to neglect women's issues and finds that the phenomena of battering, incest, and rape are important locations where systems theory and therapies "most miss the mark." System, the author notes, takes meaning from the contexts that define it. Consequently, problems like family violence cannot be considered as simply *this* family's problem or *this* women's problem. Women's issues in general and family violence in particular are "expressions of the same social frameworks that create and sanction the therapist's total role—theory, practice, language, professional status and livelihoods" (Taggart, 1985, p.122). As a note of caution, Taggart suggests to the reader that the use of dramatic issues like rape and battering should not conceal those "less spectacular but more ubiquitous forms of gender bias in our theoretical clinical and educational practices." Instead we are reminded that clinical practitioners, educators, and researchers alike need to become "sensitive to the violence they perpetrate daily through nothing more sinister than the assumption that their social context is unconnected to what they think, say and do" (p. 122).

The analysis of networking in social support systems is one of the important developments of systems theories that would seem to lead to a consideration of gender. This analysis concerns both planned formal support groups and enabling informal or natural helpers to help friends, neighbors, and family members, as well as communities. This work is both personal and social. The personal component uses the psychological strength and skills of the client to improve her/his competence by enabling self-help and empowerment. Through this process, networking involves social skills training and radical empowerment approaches. Social aspects of helping use nurturing and feedback as a way to stimulate clients' support systems. The personal and the social help that the client gets is an investment in her/him. This investment enables the client to become involved with a network and to offer resources and services to others while being helped her/himself (Payne, 1991).

Behavioral/Cognitive Approaches

Criticized for lacking sensitivity to its sexist knowledge base, cognitive theory focuses on the acquisition and function of human thought including how and what one comes to know and think, and the role this plays in what one does and feels (Greene & Ephross, 1991; Norman & Wheeler, 1996). Thoughts, memories, and reflections of what one feels and does and the ways that one experiences her/his environment form a person's cognition. Greene and Ephross indicate that cognitive theory illuminates areas that are central to understanding human personality and behavior and to designing efforts to create change. They further suggest that understanding an individual's reality and the ways in which this influences feelings provides a point of interface between the person and the situation as well as a focus for a variety of interventive strategies.

Norman and Wheeler (1996) note that the socialization model that developed out of behaviorism lends itself naturally to the consideration of gender, since socialization is known to be an important factor in gender identity. Behaviorists specializing in this approach failed, however, to include gender in their work. But role theory, which contributes to understanding ways that people enter and learn social positions and how they learn to perform in a satisfactory manner in a position, has considered gender-based issues in more recent years (Broverman, Broverman & Clarkson, 1970; Lipman-Bluman, 1984; Scotch, 1971).

Cognitive-behavioral theory has gained acceptance in the past twenty years. Wolpe (1976) asserts that cognition has always been accounted for in the practice of behavior therapy because cognitive processes are acknowledged and used in the behavior change process. This approach has not gone without criticism. Wilson and O'Leary (1980), for example, have provided several distinctions between behavioral therapy and cognitive theory. They argue that the focus on cognition in behavior therapy is concerned with conscious thought processes leaving out unconscious, symbolic meanings.

Dobson and Block (1988, p. 4) identify the following three fundamentals of cognitive-behavioral therapy:

1. Cognitive activity affects behavior.
2. Cognitive activity may be monitored and altered.
3. Desired behavior change may be affected through cognitive change.

Furthermore, the cognitive-behavioral framework views cognition in three ways. First, there are cognitive events that are likely to occur when learning or integrating a new skill, when making choices or judgment, and when anticipating or having a strong emotional experience. Second, cognitive processes are the manner in which we process information, make appraisals, and give meaning to information (Lewis, 1994; Marzillier, 1980; Meichenbaum, 1986). Third, cognitive structures or deep-seated beliefs and assumptions guide our screening, coding, and categorizing of information (Beck, 1976; Meichenbaum, 1986). These beliefs and assumptions are learned early in life and may serve as guides for making sense of the environment.

In recent years scholars such as Wolfe and Fodor (1975) and Fodor (1988) have modified some theoretical foundations of cognitive behavioral theory to address women's issues. They have examined beliefs that women have developed in the process of their role socialization, which are stress inducing and often labeled as irrational. For example:

1. "I must be loved and approved by every significant person in my life" (Wolfe & Fodor, 1975, p. 48).
2. "Other people's needs count more than my own" (Fodor, 1988, p. 98).
3. "It is easier to avoid than to face life's difficulties" (Wolfe & Fodor, 1975, p. 48).

4. "I need a strong person to lean on or provide for me" (Fodor, 1988, p. 99).
5. "I don't have control over my emotions" (Fodor, 1988, p. 99).

> "Disputation for Belief 1: Why would it be terrible if the other person thought I was a 'bitch' or rejected me? How does this make me a worthless, hopeless human being?" (Wolfe & Fodor, 1975, p. 48).
>
> "Disputation for Belief 2: No one else can make me anxious. I make myself feel anxious by the way I view the situation. I can learn to control and change my feelings" (Fodor, 1988, p. 99).

Such an approach is often utilized in assertiveness training with women. Lewis (1994) believes that cognitive behavioral therapy offers strategies for working with women and women of color because the collaborative relationship between therapist and client is guided by respect for the client and acknowledges her ability to be in control of her own life and to make changes where needed. Cognitive behavioral therapy encourages clients to take credit for gains and successes and validates all experiences as useful to the change process and to growth. Lewis (1994) identified possible shortcomings of cognitive behavioral therapy for women of color. Therapists may be unable to understand and appreciate the unique life experiences that have molded women, including the interaction of gender, race, culture, socioeconomics and so on. If this happens, errors in assumptions will lead to damaging therapeutic interventions. Essentially, the therapist must prepare her/himself through self-assessment, education, and openness. The alternative is a gender-insensitive and culturally incompetent clinician who may compound the problem and become part of it.

STRENGTHS AND WEAKNESSES OF THE APPROACHES

While the original forms of psychotherapy were permeated by patriarchal assumptions and attributed women's deficiencies, recent adaptations have emerged with a better potential for addressing women's issues. Psychodynamic modes of intervention focus on psychological context and history. They are able to address gender and multicultural and conflict experiences. Nonetheless, emphasis on structural positioning and change are not part of psychotherapeutic intervention, and the hierarchy between professional and client has been maintained even in the more recent modalities.

The systems approach has contributed to an understanding of gender and multicultural role behavior and identity as adaptations in relational contexts. The framework is useful for comprehending networks and therefore for interventions aimed at strengthening and creating support groups as a self-help strategy. However, the neutrality of the systems approach renders it unable to address inequities in power distribution as sources of conflict. Redressing such inequities lays beyond interventions based on systems theory.

The cognitive-behavioral approach deals with specific changes in person and environment. Because of the emphasis given by cognitive-behavioral modes of intervention to socialization and identity formation, they are well equipped to address gender and multicultural issues. The recent strategies for dealing with women's negative self-beliefs acquired through gendered socialization and lifelong reinforcement are a case in point. While the style of interaction between professional and client is collaborative and clients take credit for change, structural analysis and change is not a component of this approach.

All of the approach described earlier in this chapter, especially their recent developments, have some strengths in addressing questions formulated in the introductory discussion. These approaches, however, seem not to be attentive to women's voice, nor to address the powerlessness of their social position. Since powerlessness pervades the experiences of women and minorities, these approaches need to be infused with the empowerment perspective in order to be effective.

THE EMPOWERMENT PERSPECTIVE

Having focused on three types of models and their theoretical orientations, we now turn to the empowerment perspective that could be used in conjunction with various practice models. The empowerment perspective has been found to include gender determinants. Empowerment is based on a conflict model that assumes that society consists of separate groups possessing different levels of power and control over resources (Fay, 1987). Solomon (1976) defines empowerment as "a process whereby persons who belong to a stigmatized social category throughout their lives can be assisted to develop and increase skills in the exercise of interpersonal influence and the performance of valued social roles" (p. 6). Empowerment, Solomon notes is:

> Culture-specific since it assumes the experience of belonging to a socially stigmatized category; this differential experience of the group leads to differential attitude sets and response sets which may in turn require modification of those goals of intervention or those techniques which have been based on the dominant society's norms. (p. 22)

Solomon's work focused on oppressed communities as the disempowered group. Appropriately, scholars who have built on Solomon's work have applied empowerment to other groups and individuals. In discussing the empowering nature of cognitive-behavior therapy, Lewis (1994) states that clients become empowered when they are able to resolve problems by changing the ways that they think about them. Essentially, cognitive-behavioral therapy fosters a sense of power through "creating new perspectives, facilitating positive self-attribution, and using disappointment as opportunities for growth" (Lewis, 1994, p. 231).

A feminist approach to social work guards against aspects of differential theories, therapies, and techniques whose application may reabuse or revictimize the consumer or reinforce old patterns of exploitation (Morell, 1987). A feminist view demands that we consider the impact of gender on identity, cognition, and behavior. It is imperative to always keep in mind that this must include not only gender, but multiple intersecting factors, such as race, class, age, and other factors that have been historically linked to prejudice, stereotyping, and behavioral discrimination.

Feminists often prefer group intervention because groups can reduce unequal power relationships and can avoid dependence on an individual therapist. Since the beginning of the feminist movement, women understood the importance of the small group as a vehicle for social and personal change. Sharing common experiences promotes an awareness that their problems might not originate in personal deficiencies, but in the constraints that the social context imposes on their gender. Early in the movement, consciousness-raising (CR) groups were common ways in which women began to explore what it means to be a women in the socioeconomic environment. As a result of the "sharing of deeply personal experiences in a warm, supportive, and accepting climate, women are gradually freed from their burdens of guilt and shame, depression, and sense of inadequacy. They 'find their anger' and move toward 'autonomy, activity, self-acceptance" (Loewenstein, 1983, p. 535).

While CR groups and self-help groups, both formal and informal, that address female concerns often have an antiprofessional bias, increasingly they are being incorporated into social work as a viable alternative to traditional counseling. Social work with groups has enjoyed renewed energy and interest in the past ten years in part due to the value of group work with vulnerable populations.

Feminist social work practice is rooted in women's experiences. These experiences include oppression, violence, and denial of access to opportunity. They also include experiences of strength, coping, and support. Women of color have life experiences that are often very different from those of white women. Those differences are important and need to be incorporated into feminist direct practice. The more that we know about others, the more we know about ourselves. For example, traditionally women of color have strong family ties and relationships with other women to whom they turn for concrete and emotional support (Gutierrez & Lewis, 1995). The fictive kin network is very significant to these women. This network includes those individuals who are not related by marriage or bloodline, but are accepted as family and are accorded the privileges, social debts, and responsibilities that other traditional family members enjoy. Such informal ties are nurturing and sustaining. The vignettes below illustrate the experiences of elderly African-American women and the ways that they have provided love, caring, and support to one another. It is based on one of the author's experiences with and observations of a community of women with whom she shared a close and intimate relationship. These vignettes can be used as a model for developing a feminist empowerment group. Furthermore, they illustrate ways to provide strengths to other women who do not have access to similar natural helping systems.

Vignette 1

> About 16 years ago, the women who lived in Crosspoint (pseudonym for a small farming community in southeastern North Carolina) had their last quilting bee. It did not require long planning or preparation. The hostess, my mother, simply made a few telephone calls to her

> sister/friends, asking them to come over to help her "put in a quilt." Mama had made the top of the quilt by sewing together scraps of fabric that she had acquired over time. Making quilt tops was a solitary activity, which Mama had completed before calling on her friends. There was no elaborate design: she simply wanted to be able to give a quilt to each of her daughters. The room was prepared for her guests with the quilt stretched out, attached to a wooden frame pulled tightly and propped up on chairs stationed at each of the four corners. All the chairs from the kitchen and dining room were brought into the family room where the quilt waited. Aunt Eva, Cousin Bertha, Cousin Lucy Mae, and Miss Jewel all arrived about the same time. After greeting them, Mama apologized for the quilt's not being fancy—"just something for the children." As they all took their seats around the quilting frame, Mama offered them coffee and cake. The one can of beer in the refrigerator had been saved for Miss Jewel. "She enjoys a beer," the women remarked to each other.
>
> The quilting went on for hours with little discussion of it save a few comments about Aunt Eva's not being able to see too well and her own complaints that her "lines weren't straight." There were also comments about aching joints, weakness in the hands, and a concern that the thread wouldn't be tight enough. Together, they would periodically roll the frame inward as the quilting progressed closer to the center and would ask Mama for additional thread. Each woman had brought her own quilting needle. The conversation brought the room to life with voices of elderly women laughing and joking but carefully listening as they worked together toward the completion of a common goal. I had no role except to wait on them, to listen, and to observe the beauty of the occasion, which I believe they felt might be their last quilting party together. They talked on for hours about their lives, joys, children and church, with talk of their husbands as the dominant theme. They complained, reminisced, and laughed about their menfolks. Now and then, they'd slip in a little bawdy "sex talk," then, overcome with embarrassment laced with snickers, they'd look over at me and comment that they needed to shut their mouths, "with that young'un sitting over there." The "young'un" was nearly 30 years old. (Carlton-LaNey, 1993, pp. 55–56)

As Vignette 1 illustrates, women of color have drawn strength from their minority status and from each other. Feminist social work practice must be concerned with issues outside the therapy room and recognize the strengths of women of color that are often ignored. While the quilting bee was ostensibly the reason that these women came together, the products of the quilting party were much more than bed covering. Their time together allowed them to talk, to problem-solve, and to strengthen and reinforce healing ties among sisters. One of the quilting bee participants was losing her vision, but to have a quilting bee without her was simply not acceptable, and the idea of doing so was never considered. Her group membership was not based on her ability to contribute to quilt-making, but on an understanding and unconditionally supportive community of women. The quilting bee was just one illustration of the way that these women have worked together to problem-solve and to deal with adversity. They did not perceive of themselves as powerless, but as strong women capable of dealing with many of the blows that they have come to expect from a hostile society. The supportive connection illustrated through the quilting bee is not unusual. Women, according to Sancier (1990), have always found ways of making supportive connections, but the significance of those connections have often been buried in the invisible domestic sphere (p. 5).

In a working class African-American neighborhood in east Baltimore, a similar vignette has been written about the Jonquil Savings Club, an urban, inner-city example of a women's self-help group and social support network.

Vignette 2

> The club consisted of twelve women, all of whom were between the ages of 35 and 45. The objective of the club was to earn and save money that would be equally distributed amongst them at the end of the year. To earn the money, they sponsored dinners, and bus trips to Atlantic City, county fairs and amusement parks. Their meetings were held at a different member's home once a month at which time it was the members' job and duty to serve food and drinks. These meetings were enjoyable, planned with special care, and eagerly anticipated. (Lyles, 1988)

The Jonquil Savings Club lasted for over fifteen years and ended after members became to ill to continue to plan for and participate in group activities. The savings, while useful to women who worked as laborers, soon took a secondary position to the relationships that formed among them. The meetings allowed the women to prepare special meals for each, to "dress-up" for each, and to provide some validation, reinforcement, and legitimation for their feelings and thoughts. Sancier (1990) describes such practices and behaviors among women, whether planned or spontaneous, as "feminism in action." Understanding women's culture as a network of social relationships is fundamental to feminist practice. Feminist practice is a way of viewing the world, not an isolated activity that takes place only on agency time.

Encouraging women to network and form mutual aid groups is an important time-honored strategy for low-power individuals and groups. Mutual aid, natural helping networks, and social support systems, Burwell (1996) notes, are terms used to connote self-help among group members during times of need. Burwell also states that self-help and mutual aid efforts have historically been acts of defiance against oppression and exclusion. Essentially, when the overt and covert dehumanization of the group proved no longer acceptable, individuals and groups have reacted. The foundations of self-help and mutual aid among African-American women, for example, began in colonial America. White (1985) found that social support activities including child care, midwifery, medical care and treatment, and group socialization of children or newcomers were significant elements of the slave communities.

The people described in Vignettes 1 and 2 were part of a strong and resourceful community of women whose legacy of self-help dates back to colonial times. They recognized their sameness and sense of community. The idea of community is central to individual health and well-being as well as to feminist social work practice. McKnight (1987) describes community as "the social place used by family, friends, neighbors, local enterprises, associations as the major social domain" (p. 56). He identifies "associations" as the informal small groups that form the networks of support essential to everyday life. In a community where people are allowed, encouraged, and enabled to contribute their gifts for the survival and success of the group, several elements permeate:

> *Capacity,* the fullness of each member to contribute; *collective effort,* shared work that requires many talents; *informality,* a critical element of the informal economy, authentic, unmanaged relationships, care, not service; *stories,* reaching back into common histories and individual experiences for knowledge about truth and direction for

> the future; *celebration,* associations in community celebrate because they operate by consent and have the luxury of allowing joyfulness to join them in their endeavors; *tragedy,* the explicit common knowledge of tragedy, death, suffering. To be in community is to be part of ritual, lamentation and celebration of our fallibility. (McKnight, 1987, p. 58)

When working with elders of color, like the women in Vignettes 1 and 2, researchers and clinicians should give attention to the shorter life span of this group, their quadruple jeopardy (old age, impoverishment, gender, and color), and the adaptive advantages that they have developed in dealing with age (Padgett, 1988). Ethnicity as well as race contribute differently to the lives of elders. Zuniga (1984) noted that Latino elderly women, for example, share prevalent characteristics that may not be true for others outside that group. According to Zuniga, themes include the (a) sacrifices they make as mother and grandmother; (b) changing cultural arena that presents them with unexpected issues that conflict with their cultural stances as a cohort group; (c) combined sexism and racism they experienced and its effects, which continue to place them in vulnerable situations; and (d) service delivery issues that encumber culturally appropriate interventions (Comas-Diaz & Greene, 1994, p. 345).

Similarly, the African-American women in these vignettes share common characteristics such as a strong work orientation, important links to formal organizations (e.g., secret fraternal orders and church groups), a strong spiritual orientation incorporated into their daily lives, a strong family orientation that included extended family and fictive kin, and a definite system of mutual aid (Carlton-LaNey, 1992). Moreover, these women formed groups out of needs for support and nurturance, personal and communal growth socialization, and self-sufficiency.

In working with women of color, Gutierrez (1990) identifies four associated psychological changes that seem crucial for individual movement from apathy and despair to action: (1) increasing self-efficacy, (2) developing group consciousness, (3) reducing self-blame, and (4) assuming personal responsibility for change. The women described in the vignettes have had a lifetime of experiences including the formation of a natural support group, which illustrate the changes that Gutierrez describes. The group's formation illustrates these women's propensity to involve themselves as participants for change.

Instead of remaining powerless objects, the women in the Jonquil Savings Club, for example, moved to increase their economic base through "savings" and fund-raising. The women in both groups had an awareness of the "shared fate" that allowed them to exert their energies toward problem-solving thus reducing self-blame. The groups' focus on problem-solving and productivity helped to eliminate negative feelings associated with their life situation. Their ability to be productive and to control or regulate their lives was empowering.

Gutierrez (1990) describes specific techniques for empowerment, which include

1. accepting the client's definition of the problem,
2. identifying and building upon existing strengths,
3. engaging in a power analysis of the client's situation,
4. teaching specific skills, and
5. mobilizing resources and advocating for clients.

Practitioners who try to replicate the natural groups described earlier will find Gutierrez's techniques useful as she/he facilitates the group.

Using an empowerment perspective is helpful, but it is also important to focus on how to incorporate empowerment and related approaches into the social work curriculum. We now turn our attention to the task of integrating this content into the curriculum.

Focus on Social Work Education

As in other curricular areas, social work educators have struggled to integrate women's content into the practice curriculum. As noted earlier, however, there is also evidence that many in social work education have not made genuine efforts to include such content partly due to a denial of prevalent societal sexism, lack of adequate information, resistance to "retooling," and professional rigidity and inflexibility. The result is that societal conditions that influence culture and women have not adequately been integrated into the social work curriculum and have thus had little impact on the ways that we prepare students for practice. Some scholars believe that this problem may also stem from our tendency to develop a fragmented curriculum, which segregates content on people of color and women into separate courses (Carter et al., 1994).

In addition to integration of women's content we believe that social work should prepare its students for feminist social work practice that utilizes a multicultural perspective. Such a focus requires faculty to teach from the point of view that an individual's personal problems are interconnected with the larger environment in which she/he lives. Empowerment then becomes a process for helping clients to effect change in their lives and for changing the environment in ways that will improve the lives of our clients. An empowerment approach to teaching practice requires that faculty expand their traditional presentation of micro-practice content to include the broader context in which individuals experience the problems in their lives. This includes the context of racism and sexism within our society.

As faculty we can use the classroom setting to challenge our students to explore their own sense of empowerment and how it is influenced by their race and gender. Students must also be challenged to reflect on how their race and gender—and its meaning to them—affects their interactions and expectations of the clients with whom they work (see exercises contained in Appendix 3–1 for examples of assignments that can be used for this purpose).

A feminist approach to the practice curriculum must incorporate a critical examination of the traditional practice models and their ability to empower our clients. To make this more than an intellectual exercise, the critical examination of practice approaches can be made a required part of the student's field experience. Students can be asked to identify and critique the typical practice interventions used in their field setting and determine the extent to which the agency's approach is empowering to clients and uses a multicultural feminist perspective. This would hopefully not only develop skills and knowledge among our students, but potentially promote change in agency practice as students share their insights with field instructors.

A feminist approach to practice also requires that we have alternative models for practice that value difference and empower our clients. Bricker-Jenkins and Lockett (1995) have formulated "preferred methods and techniques in feminist practice" and "ten propositions and assumptions of feminist practice." These methods are divided into three broad categories: engagement/relationship building, exploration/assessment, and action/ongoing work. The propositions and assumptions are organized according to the elements of a practice model and include (a) basic philosophy, values, and goals; (b) human behavior and the social environment; and (c) practice methods and relationships. While it is acknowledged that these lists are not exhaustive, the work does provide excellent information for developing a feminist practice model that can be personalized and one that is agency/organization sensitive.

Butler (1985) also offers a set of guidelines that distinguishes a feminist therapy approach from other therapeutic approaches. The guidelines emphasize the importance of empowerment, choice, and social action:

1. Recognition of women's oppression based on gender, race, and class.
2. Relevance of the socio-cultural context.
3. Focus on women's empowerment.
4. Diverse therapeutic modalities.
5. Demystification of power.
6. The therapist and other women as role models.
7. The therapist's ongoing self-examination and reflection on her values.
8. Encouragement of growing experiences in addition to therapy.

Because an important component of the practice curriculum is field instruction, it is going to be essential that we not only integrate these models into the classroom for our students, but that we assure it is incorporated in the field as well. This suggests that we need to be developing field instructor training/continuing education that complements changes we make in practice courses (as well as other areas of the curriculum). Unless our field instructors understand, encourage, and teach the kind of practice we want our students to learn, curriculum change is not going to have the desired effect on social work practice.

CONCLUSION

A feminist practice approach requires that the practitioner begin to develop her/his own feminism or womanism, admit that there are social realities of sexism, and move to develop a feminist model of practice that fits her/his circumstances and that embraces the tenets of feminist practice. This involves an acceptance that the practitioner's life experiences may be different from those of the individual whom she/he serves. This means that the practitioners must hear the voices of others and accept their definitions of their problems. Paramount to this is the recognition that individuals come with a history that must be understood and respected.

The history of racism, as well as sexism, in America permeates all that we do and hope to do as feminist practitioners. When people do not understand the complexities of the human experience, simplistic conclusions can be drawn. According to Davis and Proctor (1989), "visual differences that individuals perceive in others are likely to be translated into other underlying differences as well. . . . [For example] perceived differences in skin color. . . largely follow an all or nothing principle: Any perceived difference in color that indicates a racial difference connotes other dissimilarities, such as differences in attitudes, beliefs, and social status" (p. 3).

Findings indicate that perceptions people have of others, race, gender, religion, socioeconomic status, and so on, result in both assumptions as well as expectations about how the other person feels, what that person believes, and whether that person is competent (Davis & Proctor, 1989). This affects the helping relationship as both practitioners and clients struggle to establish a relationship. A multicultural approach avoids dualistic assumptions enabling practitioners to see the layers and complexities of their clients' lives.

We have to look for ways to open up dialogue and interaction between people of color and whites. More knowledge and understanding of our professional history will reveal some legacies and models of interracial cooperation, group work, community organizing, coalition building, and political involvement that may lead to contemporary and creative resolutions to conflicts that are based on gender and racial prejudice/discrimination. Unless or until we acknowledge that as white feminists, we struggle with our racism, and that as feminists of color, we struggle with our distrust of whites, and unless or until we commit to efforts to eradicate those problems of racial hatred, much of our work toward feminist practice will be meaningless or at best inconsequential.

APPENDIX 3–1: EXERCISES TO ENHANCE PRACTICE IN A DIVERSE ENVIRONMENT

Exercise #1: Self-Awareness Journal

> "When you speak, write in your own voice, you become subject rather than object, you transform your own destiny." bell hooks

Keep a journal in which you record new awareness about working with clients and their multicultural elements, being a male or female working with men or women, being a member of your culture (race, gender, ethnic group, sexual orientation, religion), working with clients of your culture as well as clients of other cultures. These may include personal, professional, macro-level, and micro-level issues. The journal should provide you with an opportunity to reflect critically upon and integrate what you are reading for class, what you are learning in class, what you are doing in your practicum, and who you are. Each entry should be dated, and you should include at least two entries per week. Journals will be turned in on a weekly basis so that feedback can be given. The complete journal is to be handed in the last day of class with a final entry that summarizes the journal entries. The journal may be handwritten. It is understood that this is not a finished product that follows proper writing form.

Exercise #2: Self-Awareness of Primary Group Context

If social work practitioners are secure in their own gender and cultural/ethnic identity, they are more likely to act with greater freedom, flexibility, and openness to those of different and diverse backgrounds. Toward this end your assignment is to explore your own family of origin. Include an ecomap and genogram of your family system to enhance clarity. A brief review of literature relevant to your cultural/ethnic background must be included. Be as specific as possible. For example, if you are a Scandinavian American, specifically describe yourself by country of origin, e.g., Sweden, Norway, Denmark, Finland and discuss how long your family has been in this country. Likewise, if you are Caribbean American or Asian American, discuss the country from which your family emigrated and how long they have been here. The following is a list of issues to be addressed:

1. What constitutes a stressful situation or problem in your family? How does gender, culture, and ethnicity influence this situation?
2. How do the individual and group components of your family respond to or cope with problematic situations? How does gender play a role in these responses?
3. Describe any intrafamilial support systems or lack of these systems. Are there networks or supports based on gender?
4. How might your family respond to the prospect of going into family therapy? What are the prevailing attitudes toward seeking help? What therapeutic approaches would be most suitable? How does gender, culture, and ethnicity influence these attitudes?
5. What family values and behaviors are influenced by your ethnic/cultural heritage? How are they influenced?
6. What family values and behaviors are influenced by the composition of your family? How are they influenced?
7. What characteristics of your ethnic/cultural group do you like most? Least? Explain.
8. Who in your family influenced your sense of ethnic/cultural identity? How?
9. Who in your family influenced your sense of gender identity? How?
10. Describe traditions/rituals in your family, e.g., the celebration of holidays. How are gender roles reinforced in these traditions/rituals?
11. Describe the accepted roles of men and women in your family.
12. What signs of ethnic/cultural identity are in your home, e.g., art, books, toys, clothing, language, cooking?
13. What signs of gender identity are in your home?
14. Describe any experiences of prejudice or discrimination you have experienced in regard to gender, culture, or ethnicity?

15. Describe the people who live in your neighborhood and your relationship to them.
16. Describe the role that religion/spirituality plays in your family. How sensitive is your family's faith tradition to gender?
17. What are your family's attitudes toward education, work, upward mobility, physical appearance, politics, expressing emotions, marital intimacy, children's rights to expression?
18. What roles have women in your ethnic group played in the molding of social policy in this country?

Exercise #3: Browsing the Self-Help Industry

Clients often read books that they find in the "self-help" section of the bookstore and draw conclusions about their issues as a result. To be a more effective practitioner with these clients, it is important to understand the messages of these books and to take a critical stance. Read one "self-help" book regarding any issue you choose. You will need to browse through the self-help section to see the wide variety of books before making your selection. How many are written specifically for women? For men? How many address issues of people of color? Poor people? Prepare a brief (3–4 typewritten pages) book review in which you summarize and critically evaluate the book and make recommendations as to the clients for whom this book would be helpful/not helpful.

Exercise #4: Critical Evaluation of Intervention Models

Multiple practice models are used in social work and related fields of study. Select a practice model of your choice and ask the following questions:

1. How does this approach directly respond to the client's request?
2. Does this approach listen to the voices of women?
3. Is this approach helpful in terms of gender?
4. Does this approach reflect an understanding of the context shaping gender and race?
5. Will this approach lead to gender-sensitive change?

Having asked these questions, consider how an empowerment perspective would contribute to how you use this model in practice.

REFERENCES

Abbott, P. & Wallace, C. (1990). *An introduction to sociology: Feminist perceptions.* London: Routledge.

Beck, A. (1976). *Cognitive therapy and the emotional disorders.* Madison, CT: International Universities Press.

Braverman, L. (1986). Reframing the female client's profile. *Affilia, 1,* 30–40.

Bricker-Jenkins, M. (1991). The propositions and assumptions of feminist social work practice. In M. Bricker-Jenkins, N. Hooyman & N. Gottlieb (Eds.), *Feminist social work practice in clinical settings* (pp. 271–303). Newbury Park, CA: Sage.

Bricker-Jenkins, M., Hooyman, N. & Gottlieb, N. (Eds.). (1991). *Feminist social work practice in clinical settings*. Newbury Park, CA: Sage.

Bricker-Jenkins, M. & Lockett, P. (1995). Women: Direct practice. In R. Edwards (Ed.) *Encyclopedia of social work* (19th ed., pp. 2529–2539). Washington, DC: NASW Press.

Broverman, J., Broverman, D. & Clarkson, F. (1970). Sex-role stereotypes and clinical judgments of mental health. *Journal of Consulting and Clinical Psychology, 34,* 1–7.

Burwell, Y. (1996). Lawrence Oxley and locality development: Black self-help in North Carolina, 1925–1928. In I. Carlton-LaNey & N. Burwell (Eds.), *African American Community Practice Models: Historical and Contemporary Responses* (pp. 49–69). New York: Haworth.

Butler, M. (1985). Guidelines for feminist therapy. In L.B. Rosewater & L. Walker (Eds.), *Handbook of feminist therapy* (pp. 32–38). New York: Springer.

Caplan, P. & Hall-McCorquodale, I. (1983). Mother-blaming in major clinical journals. *American Journal of Orthopsychiatry, 55*, 345–353.

Carlton-LaNey, I. (1992). Elderly black farm women: A population at risk. *Social Work, 37*, 517–523.

Carlton-LaNey, I. (1993). The last quilting bee. *Generations, 27*, 55–58.

Carlton-LaNey, I. (March 1995). Elizabeth Ross Haynes: Pioneer reformer and feminist, 1908–1940. Paper presented at the 1995 Annual Program Meeting of the Council on Social Work Education, San Diego, CA.

Carter, C., Coudrouglou, A., Figueira-McDonough, J., Lie, G., MacEachron, A., Netting, F., Nichols-Casebolt, A., Nichols, A. & Risley-Curtis, C.

(1994). Integrating women's issues in the social work curriculum: A proposal. *Journal of Social Work Education, 30,* 200–216.

Chin, J. (1994). Psychodynamic approaches. In L. Comas-Diaz & B. Greene, (Eds.), *Women of color: Integrating ethnic and gender identities in psychotherapy* (pp. 194–222). New York: Guilford.

Chodorow, N. (1978). *The reproduction of mothering.* Berkeley: University of California Press.

Collins, B. (1986). Defining feminist social work. *Social Work, 31*, 214–219.

Comas-Diaz, L. & Greene, B. (Eds.). (1994). *Women of color: Integrating ethnic and gender identities in psychotherapy.* New York: Guilford.

Davis, L. & Proctor, E. (1989). *Race, gender & class: Guidelines for practice with individuals, families, and groups*. Englewood Cliffs, NJ: Prentice-Hall.

Day, P. (1997). *A new history of social welfare.* Englewood Cliffs, NJ: Prentice-Hall.

Dobson, K. & Block, L. (1988). Historical and philosophical basis of the cognitive-behavioral therapies. In K. Dobson (Ed.), *Handbook of cognitive-behavioral therapies* (pp. 3–38). New York: Guilford.

Farley, J. (1992). *American social problems*. Englewood Cliffs, NJ: Prentice-Hall.

Fay, B. (1987). *Critical social science.* Ithaca, NY: Cornell University Press.

Fodor, I. (1988). Cognitive behavior therapy: Evaluation of theory and practice for addressing women's issues. In M.A. Dutton-Douglas & L.E. Walker (Eds.), *Feminist psychotherapies: Integration of therapeutic and feminist systems* (pp. 91–117). Norwood, NJ: Ablex.

Greene, R. & Ephross, P. (1991). *Human behavior and social work practice.* New York: Aldine de Gruyter.

Gutierrez, L. (1990). Working with women of color: An empowerment perspective. *Social Work, 35*, 149–153.

Gutierrez, L. & Lewis, E., (1995). A feminist perspective on organizing with women of color. In F. Rivera & J. Erlich (Eds.), *Community organizing in a diverse society* (pp. 95–112). Boston: Allyn and Bacon.

Hooyman, N. (1994). Diversity and populations at risk: Women. In F.G. Reamer (Ed.), *The foundation of social work knowledge* (pp. 309–345). New York: Columbia University Press.

Kist-Ashman, K. (March 1992). Feminist values and social work: A model for educating non-feminists. Paper presented at the Annual Program Meeting, Council on Social Work Education, New Orleans, LA.

Krane, J. (1991). Feminist thinking as an aid to teaching social work research. *Affilia, 6*, 53–70.

Lazzair, M. (1991). Feminism, empowerment, and field education, *Affilia, 6*, 71- 87.

Lewis, S. (1994). Cognitive-behavioral therapy. In L. Comas-Diaz & B. Greene, (Eds.), *Women of color: Integrating ethnic and gender identities in psychotherapy* (pp. 223–238). New York: Guilford.

Lewis, V. (1997). Charity Organization Society. In J. Turner (Ed.), *Encyclopedia of social work.* (19th ed., pp. 96–100). Washington, DC: NASW Press.

Lipman-Bluman, J. (1984). *Gender roles and power*. Englewood Cliffs, NJ: Prentice-Hall.

Loewenstein, S. (1983). A feminist perspective. In A. Rosenblatt & D. Waldfogel, (Eds.), *Handbook of clinical social work* (pp. 518–548). San Francisco: Jossey-Bass.

Luepnitz, D. (1988). *The family interpreted: Psychoanalysis, feminism, and family therapy.* New York: Basic Books.

Lyles, C. (1988). Interview with Mrs. Willie Edna Carpenter. Presented to the College of Notre Dame.

Marzillier, J. (1980). Cognitive therapy and behavioral practice. *Behaviour Research and Therapy, 18*, 249–258.

McKnight, J. (1987). Regenerating community. *Social Policy, 17*, 54–58.

Meichenbaum, D. (1986). Cognitive-behavioral modification. In F.H. Kanfer & A.P. Goldstein (Eds.), *Helping people change* (pp. 346–380). New York: Pergamon.

Morell, C. (1987). Cause is function: Toward a feminist model of integration for social work. *Social Service Review, 61*, 144–155.

Nes, J. & Iadicola, P. (1989). Toward a definition of feminist social work: A comparison of liberal, radical, and socialist models. *Social Work, 34*, 12–21.

Norman, J. & Wheeler, B. (1996). Gender-sensitive social work practice: A model for education. *Journal of Social Work Education, 32*, 203–213.

Padgett, D. (1988). Aging minority women: Issues in research and health policy. *Women and Health, 14*, 213–225.

Payne, M. (1991). *Modern social work theory: A critical introduction*. Chicago: Lyceum.

Pinderhughes, E. (1989). *Understanding race, ethnicity & power*. New York: Free Press

Sancier, B. (1990). On feminism in action. *Affilia, 5*, 5–7.

Schwartz, M. (1973). Sexism in the social work curriculum. *Journal of Education for Social Work, 9*, 65–70.

Scotch, B. (1971). Sex status in social work: Grist for women's liberation. *Social Work, 6*, 5–11.

Simon, B. (1994). *The empowerment tradition in American social work: A history.* New York: Columbia University Press.

Solomon, B. (1976). *Black empowerment.* New York: Columbia University Press.

Taggart, M. (1985). The feminist critique in epistemological perspective: Questions of context in family therapy. *Journal of Marital and Family Therapy, 11*, 113–126.

Takaki, R. (1993). *A different mirror*. Boston: Little, Brown.

Van den Bergh, N. & Cooper, L. (Eds.). (1986). *Feminist visions for social work*. Silver Spring, MD: NASW Press.

Walters, M. (March/April 1993). The codependent Cinderella and Iron John: A myth for our time. *Networker*, 60–65

Walters, M., Carter, B., Papp, P. & Silverstein, O. (1988). *The invisible web: Gender patterns in family relationship.* New York: Guilford.

Weiss, N. (1974). *The National Urban League, 1910–1040*. New York: Oxford University Press.

White, D. (1985). *Ain't I a woman? Female slaves in the plantation South.* New York: Norton.

Wilson, G. & O'Leary, K. (1980). *Principles of behavior therapy.* Englewood Cliffs, NJ: Prentice-Hall.

Wolfe, I. & Fodor, I.G. (1975). A cognitive/behavioral approach to modifying assertive behavior in women. *Counseling Psychologist, 5*, 45–59.

Wolpe, J. (1976). Behavior therapy and its malcontents: II. Multimodal eclecticism, cognitive exclusivism, and "exposure" empiricism. *Journal of Behavior Therapy and Experimental Psychiatry, 7*, 109–116.

Zuniga, M. (1984). Elderly Latina mujeres: Stressors and strengths. In R. Anson (Ed.), *The Hispanic older woman.* Washington, DC: National Hispanic Council on Aging.

CHAPTER 4

Psychopathology

José B. Ashford
Jill Littrell

INTRODUCTION

The teaching of psychopathology has been altered in many ways since the establishment of university education for social workers. The modifications included not only variations in the content, but also changes in underlying assumptions, philosophy, and even the level of cynicism about what has been taken from the psychiatric literature. Initially, curricula required medical and psychiatric content (Bernard, 1977; Brieland, 1987). Medical information helped students factor in the role of biophysical processes as they evaluated client functioning. For instance, it was recognized that family caseworkers needed to understand the normal processes of physical growth and development to be able to identify life-threatening events (Cabot, 1917). Psychiatric information was also deemed essential because it helped practitioners understand human behavior concerns (Ashford & LeCroy, 1997; Ashford, LeCroy & Lortie, 1997; Jarrett, 1919).

In the early 1900s, medical and disease models played a pivotal role in structuring how behavior problems were viewed in social work education (Hyde & Murphy, 1955). In fact, the medical model was included in the Basic Eight Curriculum of 1933, promulgated by the American Association of Schools of Social Work (AASSW) (Bernard, 1977; Bohem, 1977). This organization was responsible for educational standards prior to the Council on Social Work Education. After the Council on Social Work Education (CSWE) was formed in 1952, it reaffirmed the AASSW's minimum curriculum of 1944, but recommended that schools reorganize their courses on medical and psychiatric information to include a sequence of courses on human behavior. Most programs responded to this requirement by having students take courses on normal psychosocial development with hazards to normal development highlighted in the presentation of this subject matter (Butler, 1959). These courses on normal growth and development were presented to students during their first year of graduate study. In the second year, students were introduced to content on psychopathology. This sequence of courses was initially termed the human growth and behavior sequence (Butler, 1970).

In 1954, CSWE commissioned a special group to identify themes for the organization of curriculum in human growth and behavior. This group, headed by Bohem, recommended that schools include in their curriculum themes on pathology and the health-disease continuum (Butler, 1970). Most of these courses on psychiatric information were taught by psychiatrists prior to the 1960s (Dinerman, 1984). This deference to psychiatric authority stimulated significant controversy. Towle (1960) made a passionate plea to social workers to take responsibility for their own curriculum in Human Behavior in the Social Environment (HBSE). This development, coupled with the antipsychiatry movements (Sedgwick, 1982), had a major impact on the role of psychopathology in social work curriculum. These and other events of the 1960s influenced CSWE's 1969 Curriculum Policy Statement. This statement called for a conversion from a psychiatric model to a more interdisciplinary model (Brooks, 1986, p. 20).

The medical model assumption, upon which psychopathology is based, presumes that it is possible to distinguish "normal" from "abnormal" conditions. The assumption that normal processes can be distinguished from abnormal processes focuses attention on the task of identifying and defining categories of abnormality. What syndromes and dimensions of human behavior are to be lumped under the heading of abnormal? What criteria should be invoked in identifying those behaviors that should be considered abnormal, and who should be empowered to decide? For teachers of psychopathology courses, the question of what dimensions and variations in the human condition to include within the course has already been determined. The American Psychiatric Association (APA) has provided America with the *Diagnostic and Statistical Manual of Mental Disorders* now in its fourth edition (DSM-IV). Because this document has been recognized by insurance companies and Medicare/Medicaid decision-makers as a suitable basis for decisions regarding those treatment activities that can be monetarily compensated, professional schools seeking to instruct students in the rules governing professional practice feel compelled to present and explain the extant system to its initiates.

Most teachers of human behavior courses recognize variations in human behavior and that the etiology and mutability of these variations can be studied. But, the enterprise of differentiating particular behavioral patterns as abnormal or pathological is not the traditional province of social work. Social work teaches respect for human diversity. The notion of person/environment fit reminds us that most human variations can be a strength as well as a weakness depending upon the context of the behavior. Social work eschews the process of negative trait identification, in the belief that helping people identify and maximize their strengths will result in more satisfaction and less distress for all individuals involved (Turner, 1984). The thesis behind the DSM-IV is in fundamental conflict with the strengths' orientation of social work. For this reason, psychopathology has taken on a different meaning in social work from that of psychiatry and other mental health professions.

Psychopathology in social work is not the concept to which medicine and conservative politicians have reduced it. In social work, we are committed to a sense of psychopathology that "harkens back to the original Greek." According to this etymology, the word "psychopathology" refers to the speech or logos of the psyche—that is, all the psyche's ways of hiding, manifesting, expressing, communicating, sharing, and in brief, living out its experience of worldly suffering (pathein) (Levin, 1987, p. 2). This sense of suffering is rooted in the psyche's historical situation. Within these changing historical contexts, social work educators must find places in the curriculum to evaluate the foundation assumptions underlying extant concepts of pathology and other forms of victimization (Ashford, 1994).

So how can a teacher of social work approach the task of integrating gender content into a subject matter that is in conflict with many fundamental social work principles? The task requires a commitment from educators to clarifying how diagnostic and other classification systems are influenced by social processes. Just as history books are written by the victors, the definition of disorder will be a social construction that is significantly influenced by male hegemony. Males and others with power will decide what constitutes a problem. For feminists, of course, there is instant recognition that as a disenfranchised group, women will be infrequently consulted in the process of deciding what is pathological. This responsibility of defining pathology is still left up to "the university educated, economically privileged, predominantly white men who have produced our systems of science and technology" (Hubbard, 1989, p. 119).

In recent years, there has been significant controversy about the inclusion of many proposed diagnoses in the DSM system of classification (Wakefield, 1992a, 1992b). This has included debates about conditions specific to women (DeAngelis, 1993; Zita, 1989). The refinement of mental disorder as a concept is an ongoing process. The philosophic issues are sometimes complex, and the data on relevant gender differences are mounting. But history has had a heavy hand (Ehrenreich & English, 1981), and courses with content on psychopathology rarely share all of the important information on women, or on meaningful gender differences. The information that is presented often perpetuates stereotypes and myths about the biological disadvantages of women (Ussher, 1989). This chapter attempts to remedy this situation in two ways:

1. Key assumptions in extant controversies about defining mental disorders are analyzed to guard against the inclusion of unexamined male biases in determining boundaries between normal and disordered forms of behavior.
2. Summaries are included of extant information about gender differences in various forms of psychopathology.

This chapter also suggests approaches to curriculum organization that challenge inappropriate medicalizations of deviance commonly experienced by women and most persons of color.

THE SOCIAL CONSTRUCTION OF MENTAL DISORDERS

The Medicalization of Deviance

Students of social work cannot wrestle with the issues confronting the validity of various diagnostic categories without examining pros and cons of the "medicalization" of various forms of deviance. In fact, this is an excellent framework for introducing content on psychopathology to social work students. For instance, students can obtain useful insights into issues of medicalization by examining the political implications of medicalization of conditions like premenstrual changes in women. To this end, social work educators can learn much from the approaches being developed by feminists and others in the science technology studies (STS) field (see Biology Gender Study Group, 1989; Hess, 1995). Scholars in this burgeoning area of research are advancing critiques that have uncovered many biases in observations and theory construction of many sacrosanct areas of science (Tuana, 1989), including research on areas of psychopathology (see, e.g., Zita, 1989).

Students in social work and other areas involving science and technology are hungry for content on gender, race, ethnicity, non-Western cultures, and diversity issues as they relate to science (Hess, 1995). To this end, educators must move questions of gender to the forefront by synthesizing some of the research on this topic. "The fundamental starting point for STS today is the idea that theories, observations, methods, machines, social relations, institutions, networks and other aspects of the techno-scientific world are in some sense shaped, negotiated, or otherwise constructed" (Hess, 1995, p. 2). This approach to science does not assume that science and technology are constructed simply on rational principles. Moreover, it challenges the simplistic notion that the making of the science of psychopathology is "in some sense outside society and culture" (Hess, 1995, p. 2). Because it assumes that the making of science involves social processes, its fundamental aim is to identify the politics of facts and artifacts resulting from cultural and social processes (Hess, 1995; McGinn, 1991).

Social work students must understand how gender politics influence evidence used to posit the existence of syndromes that are examined for consideration in the DSM system, like Premenstrual Dysphoric Disorder (also referred to as PMS). Zita (1989) argues that through the gaze of women's approach to science we learn how the observational language of PMS research is replete with biases rooted in a negativity assumption about women's nature. This negativity assumption distorts interpretations about natural premenstrual changes observed in women. Because of such biases, many natural cyclic changes are seen as negative, as are the potentially positive physical processes taking place during the phase of the menstrual cycle that increase women's levels of autonomic arousal. Social work students must learn how to identify similar biases in other disorders in the DSM system. The process of refining concepts of mental illness is ongoing. Feminists in social work should continue to provide input and data to evaluate criteria in defining conditions in the DSMs and in determining whether a category is appropriate for inclusion in the system.

Freud's Concepts Still Linger

The legacy of Western history's treatment of women still influences current clinical labels. Categories of mental illness developed during a time when Freudian concepts held sway have not been purged completely from current categorizations of mental disorder. For instance, we still have terms such as hysteria, whose Latin roots means "of the womb," represented in the Minnesota Multiphasic Personality Inventory (MMPI) even if hysterical personality is no longer a category in the DSM-IV. During the Freudian periods, the notion of penis envy was considered a given and reports of child sexual abuse were attributed to unrequited wishful thinking. These and other assumptions must be challenged by educators of social workers. By exploring the historical development of various categories of mental disorders, educators can confront important issues influencing women and people of color in determining the boundaries between pathology and normal behavior. That is, the historical development of categories of mental illness is an important approach to introducing this content to students. In particular, it affords instructors an opportunity to introduce students to contemporary knowledge of the ways in which a male-dominated culture prioritizes the value placed on male functions to the fundamental disadvantage of women.

Sex Role Stereotypes Influence Judgments and Compromise Diagnostic Reliability

Research suggests that adjectives which are viewed as feminine are more often judged as suggestive of diminished mental health by lay persons (Broverman, Broverman, Clarkson, Rosencrantz & Vogel, 1970; Hamilton & Jensvold, 1992; Kaplan, 1983; Pugliesi, 1992). The priority assigned to "male values" in larger society is clear from this research. Masculine stereotyped adjectives describe traits necessary for achieving in the world (agency). Adjectives involving feminine qualities describe traits needed for forming bonds and getting along in the world (communion) (Katz, Boggiano & Silvern, 1993). In deciding which adjectives represent better mental health, greater value has been ascribed to agency over communion in the Anglo-American practice of mental health.

What do empirical findings say about the health-promoting qualities of feminine versus masculine characteristics? Empirical findings suggest that it is not the presence of femininity that is associated with depression and eating disorders, but rather deficit androgyny (Franks, 1986). Further, for both genders, androgyny is associated with better mental health (Bem, 1977; Kelly, 1983; Maffeo, 1982; Spence, Helmreich & Stapp, 1975).

Franks and Rothblum (1983a, 1983b) have highlighted the difficulties created by the stereotypes associated with gender. Because of the inculcation of these stereotypes in little boys and little girls, children are left without a full set of skills needed to meet life's many challenges. Better mental health is associated with androgyny, that is, possession of both masculine and feminine traits. Gender stereotypes impose constraining expectations on both men and women.

Franks and Rothblum caution that there will be a tendency to view adult persons who fail to conform to sex-role stereotypes as deviant, simply because they fail to conform to gender expectations. The diagnosis of transvestic fetishism (cross-dressing) in the DSM-IV attests to this occurrence. The DSM includes the caveat that distress over cross-dressing must be present to meet criteria for the disorder. This would, on the surface, appear to avoid a charge of gender-role stereotyping. However, if the APA was primarily concerned over distress, distress over cross-dressing could have been accommodated easily under one of the mood disorder categories. There was no real need to create a new category. Thus, the DSM continues to render judgments of deviance when behavior fails to conform to gender stereotypes, albeit in a subtle form.

Feminists are justifiably concerned when organizations such as the APA are empowered to identify deviant or abnormal behavior. This endeavor will entail a value judgment, at least for those categories of mental illness that fail to conform to more universal prototypes rooted in androcentric notions of reality. Fortunately the state of the mental health professions is no longer as biased against women as it once was. The clinicians responsible for the development of the DSM-IV have responded appropriately to some criticism by feminists of earlier versions. For instance, the categories involving premenstrual syndrome, rapistic paraphilia, and self-defeating personality disorder (masochism) were deferred to the Appendix of the DSM-IV, while others were eliminated, because of the lack of sufficient information to warrant inclusion in the system. However, the process of deciding which behavior patterns to include in the DSM is ongoing.

CONUNDRUMS IN DEFINING MENTAL DISORDERS

The concept of mental disorder holds the field of mental health together (Wakefield, 1992a). It is the concept that enables mental health professionals to differentiate disorders from nondisorders. Persons with definable disorders are eligible for valued services by insurance companies and Medicare/Medicaid providers. Deviations of thought, mood, or behavior are not considered a mental disorder if they do not conform to explicit diagnostic criteria of the current DSM system. This criteria involves issues of deviance, distress, and dysfunction, but as Maxmen and Ward (1995, p. 5) point out, not all impairments, deviance, and distress are psychopathological: "Being ugly (not gorgeous), inefficient (not active), and thoughtless (not considerate) are all impairments, but not psychopathology. Being an atheist, punker, crook, or drag queen is deviant, but not psychopathology. Being starved, broke, or lonely is distressing, but not psychopathology" (p. 5). This simple observation encapsulates the fundamental boundary issues confronting any attempts to discriminate between disorders and nondisorders.

Students of social work must be exposed to all the major assumptions underlying the organization of the current DSM system of classification. This system has significant implications for how women are treated by social workers in many areas of social work practice. Critiques of extant labeling practices will lack credibility if they ignore the quasi-revolutionary consequences of the changes in the DSM's definitions of mental disorders. There are many clinical terms that resemble the concept of "mental disorder" as defined in the DSM system, but which are not equivalent (Maxmen & Ward, 1995; Nurcombe & Gallagher, 1986). The concept of "mental disorder" in the DSM system is not analogous to the concepts of disease and illness. Although these terms are often used interchangeably in the literature, the DSM system has a specific definition of what is considered a mental disorder (Ludwig, 1986; Nurcombe & Gallagher, 1986).

> The DSM-IV makes the following points in defining a mental disorder: in the DSM-IV, each of the mental disorders is conceptualized as a clinically significant behavioral or psychological syndrome or pattern that occurs in a person and is associated with present distress (e.g., a painful symptom) or disability (i.e., impairment in one or more important areas of functioning), or a

> significantly increased risk of suffering death, pain, disability, or an important loss of freedom. In addition, this syndrome or pattern must not be merely an expectable culturally sanctioned response to a particular event, for example, the death of a loved one. Whatever its original cause, it must currently be considered a manifestation of a behavioral, psychological, or biological dysfunction in the individual. Neither deviant behavior (e.g., political, religious, or sexual) nor conflicts that are primarily between the individual and society are mental disorders unless the deviance or conflict is a symptom of a dysfunction in the individual, as described above. (APA, 1994, p. xxi)

Establishing Reliability: The Initial Step

One of the major aims of the framers of the DSM-III, DSM-III-R, and the DSM-IV was to develop criteria for defining mental disorders that would increase inter-rater reliability. The fact that little consensus on diagnosis was achieved with the DSM-II constituted a significant threat to the credibility of the psychiatric enterprise in America. Without expert agreement on labels, psychiatric opinion was viewed as meaningless. The framers of the DSM-III and subsequent documents responded to this threat. The descriptive behavioral criteria for diagnosing disorders in the DSM-III was designed to increase inter-rater reliability. Kirk and Kutchins (1992) are social workers who have studied the forces and factors operating within the psychiatric community as the DSM-III and subsequent versions were honed.

The APA has conducted field studies of reliability in assigning diagnostic labels. According to Kirk and Kutchins, the extent to which reliability has actually been achieved is far less than what the APA purports. Kirk and Kutchins list the ways in which the researchers conducting the field studies stacked the deck so that good reliability could be demonstrated. Outcomes were counted as agreement when raters achieved consensus on the overarching category even when specific categories were inconsistent (p. 148). Field study researchers have examined the behavior of raters who were trained in a uniform manner. In the real world, of course, such pristine conditions are never realized. In subsequent studies of actual clinical practice, the reliability achieved was much lower than that reported in field studies (pp. 151–156).

For many of the syndromes that are more often diagnosed in females, the problematic reliability is particularly acute. Inter-rater reliability for the personality disorders is particularly poor, and women are well represented in several categories of personality disorders (Brown, 1992; Kirk & Kutchins, 1992, p. 150). In a specific field study (Spitzer, Williams, Kass & Davis, 1989), on personality disorders, diagnosticians had difficulty distinguishing among the particular categories that have overlapping criteria.

The current DSM has probably, in many cases, succeeded in identifying patterns of behavior that can be reliably identified in individuals. However, creating reliable categories of behavioral patterns, does not address the concern of defining mental illness. How to decide which patterns of behavior (shyness, gregariousness, extroversion, introversion, schizophrenia, manic depression) should be considered variations on normal behavior versus mental illness has been a topic of considerable discussion throughout the literature.

The Role of Deviance in Defining Mental Disorders

Prior to the DSM-III, many critics (Mower, 1960; Szasz, 1960) recommended that mental health professionals do away with the concept of mental illness. Mower (1960) argued that psychologists should move away from the shadow of medicine and view behavior disorders as manifestations of sin rather than disease. He wanted psychologists to focus on the moral dimensions of abnormal or deviant behavior that had been replaced by the ideology of medicine and its putative nonjudgmental therapeutic attitude. In his view, the medical ideology eliminated attributions of fault in its evaluations of behavioral aberrations. Under the medical model, people with personality disorders would not be held accountable because their condition, like other diseases, were outside of their control. In his view, this was potentially dangerous because "to have the excuse of being 'sick' rather than sinful, is to court the danger of also becoming lost" (Mower, 1960, p. 62). He believed that between the concept of sin and mental illness, sin was the lesser of two evils.

The preference for medicine over morals in handling social issues is termed by Boorse (1975) as "the psychiatric turn." By the early 1900s, medicine had achieved great status after its discovery of germ theory and was asked to extend its vast array of technology to deal with other human problems (Zola, 1981). Friedson (1970) and Zola (1972) have referred to this extension of the medical model as "the medicalization of society" (the patient as a passive victim of germs and physical breakdown). Mower (1960) and Szasz (1960) were critical of this psychiatric turn. They did not believe that medicine should replace religion and law as our primary institutions of social control (Zola, 1981).

Szasz (1960) did not agree with treating personality disorders as if they were similar to physical diseases. Indeed he challenged any notion that considered psychiatry as a specialty of medicine. In his view, the subject matter of psychiatry did not deal with issues of physical disease (Sedgwick, 1982). Szasz stated, "As an antidote to the complacent use of the notion of mental illness—whether as a self-evident phenomenon, theory, or cause—let us ask this question: What is meant when it is asserted that someone is mentally ill?" (p. 113). In response to this question, he concluded that mental illness is applied to many problems in living that did not involve any documented disease of the brain. This suggested to Szasz that mental illness had many properties in common with other forms of mythology used to explain undesirable aspects of nature. Was Szasz justified in calling for the elimination of the concept of mental illness simply because there was no documented relationship between forms of mental symptomatology and brain pathology?

Ausubel (1961) is noted for his rebuttal to the Szasz-Mower position on the disease model of personality. In his opinion, the adoption of the Szasz-Mower view of personality disorders would "turn back the psychiatric clock twenty-five hundred years" (p. 55). Ausubel argued that one of the major advances for handling behavioral aberrations has "been in substituting a concept of disease for the demonological and retributional doctrine regarding their nature and etiology that flourished until comparatively recent times" (p. 55). He also saw Szasz's position as being an extreme somatic viewpoint. In his opinion, most theorists recognize that brain pathology is not the most important cause of disturbances in personality or behavior.

Indeed Ausubel's major contribution to the debate about the definition of mental illness was his repudiation of Szasz's argument that a genuine manifestation of a disease must be caused by a physical lesion. "Adoption of such a criterion would be arbitrary and inconsistent both with medical and lay connotation of the term 'disease,' which in current usage is generally regarded as including any marked deviation, physical, mental, or behavioral, from normally desirable standards of structure and functional integrity" (p. 56). The literature is replete with other more recent repudiations of Szasz's lesion requirement for a mental disease or disorder (Kendell, 1975; Maxmen & Ward, 1995).

The notion of brain pathology being a requirement for the definition of a mental disorder is contrasted in the psychopathology literature with another predominant view, value judgment or normativism (Boorse, 1975; Wakefield, 1992a). According to this approach, patterns of behavior that represent gross deviations from behavior patterns deemed desirable by the majority are called mental disorders. "The pure value account of disorder asserts that disorder is nothing (or almost nothing) but a value concept, so that social judgments of disorder are nothing but judgments of desirability according to social norms and ideals" (Wakefield, 1992a, p. 376).

A judgment of undesirability triggers responses to prevent the undesirable consequence of the disordered condition. However, a wide range of responses from control (Conrad & Schneider, 1980; Horwitz, 1982) to abuse or sympathetic care (Horwitz, 1982) can be evoked. Which behaviors should be considered worthy of control or punishment versus sympathetic treatment or care? To date, the APA has not recommended that the criminal justice system be abolished and replaced by mental hospitals. The framers of the DSM indicate that deviant behavior that represents "a conflict between the individual and the society" should not be construed as mental disorder (DSM-IV, p. xxii). Here, a distinguishing criteria for deciding what is the purview of criminology versus mental illness has been volition. The forensic literature is also replete with attempts to grapple with behaviors that distinguish volitional acts from acts that are not under volitional control. These attempts are reflected in legal discussion of insanity and mental illness, conditions whose quintessential feature is a lack of volition therein precluding culpability (Horwitz, 1982, p. 27; Wettstein, 1988). The underlying assumption is that persons cannot choose to have a mental disorder. Of course, volition as a criterion for mental illness is problematic. The issue of whether anybody ever has free will is a long debated philosophical issue (Skinner, 1971).

Statistical deviance is also recognized as a major component of any definition of mental disorder (Boorse, 1975; Horwitz, 1982). But not all forms of statistical deviance constitute psychopathology (Maxmen & Ward, 1995). For instance, physicians are not concerned about treating an inability to run a five- or six-minute mile, but are concerned about a person who is incapable of running. That is, physicians treat persons with conditions that do not meet a minimal expected level of functioning. An additional stipulation is that the significant deviation must be from a minimal level of functioning that would place the organism at some biological disadvantage (Scadding, 1967).

The Dysfunction or Impairment Criterion

Wakefield (1992b) argues that the DSM definition of mental disorders includes another important criterion besides deviance for differentiating disorders from nondisorders: significant dysfunction. He writes: "The dysfunction requirement is necessary to distinguish disorders from any other types of negative condition that are part of normal functioning, such as ignorance, grief, and normal reactions to stressful environments" (1992a, p. 233). In his view, a mental disorder exists when there is an incapacity to perform some natural function that the human body was designed to perform. Lilienfeld and Marino (1995) offer compelling criticism of this criterion. They point out that evolution does not operate in a teleological fashion. It also does not supply a design or function for any particular organism beyond survival and reproduction. The environment, which is always changing, selects for adaptive characteristics to the particular extant environment. Many traits now considered to be essential for a particular species were selected by the environment to achieve a function that can be unrelated to what is currently considered a defining function of that species. Lilienfeld and Marino (1995) provide the example of the feathers of birds, which were probably selected because of their thermoregulation properties, although serendipitously, they allowed for flight. Hence, deciding what functions human beings are designed to perform is virtually impossible and history demonstrates that women often were victims of such evaluative reasoning.

The Role of Distress in Defining Mental Disorders

Another feature that might distinguish criminal behavior (which evokes control) from illness (which evokes sympathy) has been the occurrence of pain and suffering. Pain was once considered one of the key defining features of diseases. But it is assumed in the extant literature on psychopathology that it is not a necessary criterion for defining diseases or disorders (Scadding, 1967). Many people have diseases or disorders that do not present with painful symptoms. Alcoholics and drug addicts may not identify subjective distress (Littrell, 1991a). Persons with antisocial personality disorders, although creating pain and distress for others, may not suffer (subjectively) themselves. An absence of pain is not unique to mental disorders. Conditions viewed as physical diseases, such as essential hypertension (Kendell, 1975), are often not accompanied by distress. In essence, although diseases and disorders frequently involve subjective distress, pain is not considered a necessary or sufficient condition for the definition of disease or disorder.

In reading the prior controversies about establishing boundaries between the normal and the abnormal, the reader should now have a better awareness of the inherent vagueness in the APA's definition of "mental disorder." The DSM-IV's definition contains many terms (dysfunction, impairment, disability, deviant behavior) that have not been defined. Recognizing this vagueness, Blashfield (1991) stated that the concept of mental disorder in the DSM is a Roschian concept (see also Lilienfeld & Marino, 1995). Roschian concepts are "mental constructions typically used to categorize entities in the natural environment (e.g. bird, fruit, mountain), and are characterized by unclear boundaries and an absence of defining (that is, critical) features" (Lilienfield & Marino, p. 416). Roschian concepts can not be defined in terms of rules for inclusion or exclusion. Rather, the process of categorization into a conceptual grouping is made on the basis of whether a given example matches a prototype. The matching process is made difficult by the fact that not all exemplars of a grouping will share all the features of the prototype. Although there will be clear individual examples of a mental disorder, it will be difficult achieving consensus at the margins where some but not all features of the prototype are found (Blashfield, 1991).

Williams (1988) writes that "a common misunderstanding about the disorders in the DSM-III-R is that each category represents a discrete entity with distinct boundaries between it and other disorders and between it and normality" (p. 203). Although sophisticated individuals such as Williams can report that the precise distinction between the different categories of mental illness and between mental illness and normal is blurred, others in the psychiatric community may have operated with assumptions about a far more definitive world. The framers of the DSM have succeeded to some arguable degree in creating a diagnostic system with better reliability than the system that preceded it, and there has been some accretion of factual information regarding etiology, prognosis, and ways to change behavior. The endeavor, however, is orthogonal to the question of whether any category in the DSM is a disease or whether the people satisfying the criteria for a category should be considered sick. Science offers methods for discerning relationships between variables. It provides no mechanism distinguishing the normal from the abnormal, which is an issue of definition.

The authors of the DSM-III took many of these prior issues into account in defining mental disorders. For instance, the definition of mental disorder in this system does not assume that mental disorders are due to biological abnormalities (Spitzer et al., 1989). It also does not assume that "there are sharp distinctions between psychopathology and normality or between different mental disorders" (Maxmen & Ward, 1995; p. 7). In fact, the authors of the DSM-IV make the important point that the concept of mental disorder does not have a precise operational definition that covers all situations. The manual states: "All medical conditions are defined on various levels of abstraction—for example, structural pathology (e.g., ulcerative colitis), symptom presentation (e.g., migraine), deviance from a physiological norm (e.g., hypertension), and etiology (e.g., pneumococcal pneumonia) (APA, 1994; p. XXI). The same is true of mental disorders. Many concepts are needed to define mental disorders: statistical deviance, distress, impairment, dyscontrol, inflexibility, etiology, syndromal pattern, and normative deviations (APA, 1994).

Presently, the APA leaves us with vague criteria for defining a mental disorder: significant dysfunction, disability, deviance, and distress. Of course, determining what constitutes functioning and, its converse, dysfunction involves a value judgment. Should the emphasis be placed on achievement (statistically, more often a male objective) or getting along with other human beings (statistically, more often a female objective)? Who will be empowered to decide? What are the risks that this definition poses for female clients of social workers? Perhaps in instructing student social workers, the teacher is obligated to enhance their awareness of the value judgments that undergird the system. The DSM, like many other documents, is a social construction.

Examination of the philosophical strategies employed by the creators of the DSMs to define disorders and the critiques of these strategies are necessary prerequisites to the examination and analysis of gender variations in psychopathological forms of deviance. Now we will introduce relevant content pertinent to gender differences in the incidence of specific disorders, in the etiology of mental disorders, and in their treatment. This is followed by a presentation of research findings concerning premenstrual and reproductive events, and finally a brief overview of potential strategies for integrating this substantive content into a psychopathology course for social work students.

DIFFERENCES IN RATES BETWEEN THE GENDERS

Although it is beyond the scope of this chapter to detail the historical development of each of the categories in the DSM, it is patently clear, even to students reading undergraduate psychopathology texts, that the categories have changed considerably through the years. New disorders have been added, others dropped, and some patterns of behavior have been dropped only to reappear. What is especially interesting is the recognition of a new behavioral aberration not recognized in previous historical periods. For example, during the nineteenth century there was scant documentation of what might be labeled today as multiple personality disorder or dissociative identity disorder (Spanos, 1994). What accounts for this lack of recognition of an identified mental disorder? How do sociocultural forces determine whether patterns of behavior are recognized as disorders?

When activists have objected to a particular category in the DSM (such as the gay community's successful efforts at having homosexuality expunged from the DSM and when feminists objected to the inclusion of PMS), it is easy to identify the influence of social forces on what is included under the rubric of psychopathology. The influence of social forces on other disorders is perhaps less easily documented. Certainly public attention to alcoholism as a disease emerged only during the 1960s, although it has been present as a problem throughout history and labeled a disease in the 1700s. In order to evaluate these historical developments, students must be made aware of the frequencies of currently labeled conditions. We cannot get into questions of validity or questions of "ought" without exploring questions of "is." In this section, we look at current understandings of gender differences within specific categories of mental disorders in order to alert students to the influence of known frequencies on clinical perceptions. However, it is beyond the scope of this chapter to offer a comprehensive critique of the factors contributing to the social construction of each of these categories.

Clinical social workers are more likely to make diagnoses that comport with gender-frequency-consistent categories. They are less likely to detect problems that have low incidence in a particular gender group. Further, when women are diagnosed with a disorder that has a lower incidence in their gender, the syndrome is viewed as more severe and drugs are more often recommended (Russo & Green, 1993, p. 389; Waisberg & Page, 1988). These biases can hinder the validity of clinical judgment and referral for treatment. Thus, knowledge of statistically reliable gender differences can be both useful (for knowing what to expect) and harmful (when expectations interfere with a clinician's ability to recognize individual differences). These gender biases are as significant as the sociocultural biases influencing the establishment of boundaries between the normal and the pathological.

Depression

The incidence of particular mood disorders (viz., major depression and dysthymia but not manic depressive illness) is twice as high in women as compared to men (Hamilton & Jensvold, 1992). The depressive episodes experienced by women are of longer duration (Sargeant, Bruce, Florio & Weissman, 1990). Studies suggest that this difference in incidence cannot be attributed to willingness to seek treatment or differential willingness to report symptoms (Hamilton & Jensvold, 1992; Nolen-Hoeksema, 1987). Differential rates across genders are found in both community and clinical samples (Kravetz, 1986).

Marital status does influence rates of depression. Married persons of both genders are less likely to be depressed than unmarried (divorced, widowed, never married) persons. However, married females are more likely to experience depression than married males. Within the categories of "widowed" and "never married" men are at greater risk than women. Among those who are divorced, divorced women are at higher risk than divorced men (Kravetz, 1986, p. 109). At highest risk for depression are women who are poorly educated, who have low income levels, and who are single parents (Kravetz, 1986).

Etiological factors that might explain the gender differences in rates of major depression have been examined. Studies suggest that variations of progesterone and estrogen do not reliably affect mood (Nolen-Hoeksema, 1990, pp. 45–72). Hence, hormonal factors cannot explain the higher rates of major depression found in women. There are other competing theories regarding etiology. Women are more often exposed to certain forms of abuse (child sexual abuse, sexual harassment, prejudice in certain occupational arenas) (Kravetz, 1986;

Russo & Green, 1993). The high frequency of trauma and childhood abuse in the history of psychiatric patients suggests that abusive situations might represent a causal factor in the development of mood disorder (Root, 1992, p. 259; Russo & Green, 1993, p. 406). Assuming that women more often exemplify feminine traits, these traits are less likely to be valued in our society (Broverman et al., 1970). The upshot is that they are less likely to develop social identities that might serve as a buffer against stressors. Rothblum (1983) further speculates about the constraining effect of gender role stereotypes in the etiology of depression.

Others have examined particular personality factors (assertion, susceptibility to influence) that occur with differential frequency in females. Because the magnitude of the gender difference in assertion and susceptibility to influence is far smaller than the magnitude observed in the difference for depression, these personality factors fail to provide compelling explanation for the differential rate in depression (Hamilton & Jensvold, 1992).

Nolen-Hoeksema (1990, pp. 178–196) has examined the data pertinent to the age at which differences in depression begin to emerge between boys and girls. She suggests that the time at which differences in depression emerge corresponds to the point at which coping mechanisms for dealing with negative events are learned. Although there are studies to the contrary (Dawes, 1994, p. 213), Nolen-Hoeksema (1990, pp. 169–172; 1993, p. 316) cites studies suggesting that women are more often taught ruminative coping styles for dealing with negative events, that is, little girls are taught to focus on the meaning of negative feelings. In contrast, little boys are taught to engage in vigorous, competitive play and avoid expression of negative emotions when bad things happen to them. Could these coping style differences account for differential rates of depression? Data suggest that rumination can prolong a negative mood (Morrow & Nolen-Hoeksema, 1990; Nolen-Hoeksema, 1991; Teasdale & Fennel, 1982). Nolen-Hoeksema (1990) suggests that ruminative coping style constitutes the causative factor in clinical depression. Indeed, after controlling for difference in ruminative styles, gender differences in depression disappear (Nolen-Hoeksema, 1993, p. 316). Further, men and women differ in their beliefs regarding depression. Men more often endorse the statement, "Depression is just like any other problem that comes up—you just have to find ways to solve it." Women more often believe that depression has biological roots and that it is uncontrollable

(Nolen-Hoeksema, 1993, p. 319). Nolen-Hoeksema's concerns about the role of learned gender-stereotyped coping styles as a contributor to the relatively high rate of depression encountered in women are echoed in similar concerns expressed by Rothblum (1983).

Substance Abuse

It is estimated that males outnumber female alcoholics by a ratio of 4 to 1. Similar differences are found for illegal drugs as well. The differential rates are observed in community samples as well as rates under treatment. Hence, the differential rates cannot be attributed to a tendency for women to less readily seek or be referred into treatment (Russo & Green, 1993).

Although genetic factors for alcoholism have been established for men, the picture is less clear for women (Littrell, 1991b, pp. 80–81). For men, alcoholism is more often a primary diagnosis. However, in a substantial minority of alcoholic men, alcoholism is often viewed as secondary to antisocial personality disorder. That is, the antisocial personality leads to the development of the drinking problem. In women, depression is more often the primary diagnosis with alcoholism being the secondary diagnosis. The hypothesis for women is that for a substantial number of female alcoholics, the drinking was an attempt to cope or control depression (Littrell, 1991a, pp. 140–141).

In addition to differential rates, behavioral aspects of the syndrome of alcoholism tends to be different in women (Littrell, 1991a, pp. 131–136). Whereas men generally indicate a problematic drinking history of several decades when they present for treatment at a mean age of 45, women present for treatment at the same mean age of 45 but with a very much shorter drinking career. Women exhibit drinking problems that, on average, are no less severe than men; they just reach their problematic levels in a much shorter period of time (Littrell, 1991a, pp. 131–136). In terms of severity, on a physical basis, women are more susceptible to the brain damaging and liver disease effects of alcohol than are men (Littrell, 1991b, p. 143). Once in treatment, women are as likely to benefit from treatment as are men (Littrell, 1991a, p. 134).

Alcoholics Anonymous (AA) is a major component in the treatment of alcoholism in this country. AA was developed by men for men. The literature, at least that which was written prior to the 1970s, refers to male alcoholics and their female spouses. The female spouses are depicted as needing to be in the relationship because of their codependent personalities (Collins, 1993). This representation has little empirical support (Littrell, 1991a).

The degree to which the organization of AA can address the special needs of women has been questioned. Research has identified the personality characteristics of individuals who self-select into long-term AA affiliation. Those who have had happy childhoods and who are extroverted have a higher rate of long-term affiliation (Littrell, 1991a, pp. 161–163). Women alcoholics, on average, are unlikely to share these characteristics, since female alcoholics often have been victims of childhood trauma (Carmen & Rieker, 1989; Russo & Green, 1993). For those women who are introverted, AA may present a special challenge because there will be the added barrier of having to bridge a gender difference when joining the AA fellowship. Fortunately, AA has adapted to accommodate the special needs of women. In some localities, female home-groups are available.

The practice of viewing substance abuse as mental illness has met with a great deal of controversy (Fingarette, 1988; Littrell, 1991a; Peele, 1989). None of the empirical findings in the area of addictions necessitates that addictions be viewed from a disease perspective. Although good empirical cases for heredity as an etiological factor and for the efficacy of pharmacological treatments have been advanced, the same findings have been made for shyness (Plomin, DeFries & McClearn, 1990), which is not (yet) seen as a disease. If alcoholism is labeled as a disease, then the social constraints against the occasional intemperate behavior of those who drink infrequently will be weakened. Further, self-labeled alcoholics can give up striving to attain a higher level of conduct having accepted the view that they are fated by their genes. The upshot is that we will continue to debate whether it is functional for society to view addiction from a disease perspective.

Anxiety Disorders

Women do exhibit higher rates of generalized anxiety, panic attacks, posttraumatic stress disorder, and agoraphobia (Fodor, 1992; Hamilton & Jensvold, 1992; Russo & Green, 1993). As with depression, and as with substance abuse, a history of sexual assault is more often found among those diagnosed with phobia, panic disorder, and obsessive compulsive disorder than is found in the general population (Carmen & Rieker, 1989; Russo & Green, 1993). Again, trauma and victimization may constitute risk factors explaining the differential frequency of anxiety disorders in women. Given the occurrence of a traumatic event, some studies have found women are more likely to develop symptoms than are men (Breslau, Davis, Andreski & Peterson, 1991; Cronkite & Moos, 1984), although this is not a consistent finding (Newmann, 1986). Mitral valve prolapse, a congenital heart valve malformation that can trigger panic attacks, and has a higher incidence in females, may also be an etiological factor in agoraphobia (Fodor, 1992).

Fodor (1992) highlights the role that families play in the development and maintenance of panic disorder and agoraphobia. Studies suggest that families who promote dependency, who discourage moving away from the family of origin, and who promote mistrust of the world offer propitious conditions for the development of agoraphobia and panic disorder (Fodor, 1992). Overtraining in passive stereotyped behavior (helplessness, dependency, emotionality, excitability, and the tendency to give up under stress) may all contribute to the development of agoraphobia (Fodor, 1992). Supporting this view are data suggesting that agoraphobic women endorse fewer active traits on personality measures and the fact that under conditions which induce fear, women are less likely than men to approach the feared stimulus (Fodor, 1992, p. 194).

Minor tranquilizers are frequently prescribed for those with anxiety disorders. Women receive more psychotropic medications generally than do men (Russo & Green, 1993) and more tranquilizers (Romach, Busto, Somer, Kaplan & Sellers, 1995). Although anxiolytics will decrease symptoms, they do nothing to train better coping skills. Indeed, they may validate the self-perception of deficit self-efficacy. Relapse rates after discontinuation of benzodiazepines are high (Klinger, 1993). Because of their higher rates of anxiety disorders, women are more at risk for abuse of and addiction to physician-prescribed minor tranquilizers.

Eating Disorders

Higher rates of anorexia and bulimia are observed in women than in men. Approximately 90 percent of persons with eating disorders are women. The rate of disorder is higher in those occupations in which thinness is mandated (modeling, dance, acting, sports). Eating disorder is more likely in those who are young, upper or middle class, and white. The higher rate of eating disorders encountered for women is often attributed to the fact that our society places a higher premium on the thinness ideal for women than for men (Russo & Green, 1993).

Personality Disorders and Dissociative Disorders

Women are more often labeled borderline, as having dependent personality disorder, as having histrionic personality disorder, and as having multiple personalities (Hamilton & Jensvold, 1992; Kass, Spitzer & Williams, 1983). As mentioned previously, research suggests that borderline personality disorder and multiple personalities are often preceded by a history of sexual abuse or other trauma (Brier, Nelson, Miller & Krol 1987; Herman, Perry & van der Kolk, 1989; Ross et al. 1990; Silk, Lee, Hill & Lohr, 1995). Brown (1992, p. 222) has argued that aspects of specific personality disorders and dissociative disorders are in fact normal sequelae to trauma. Root (1992) offers an analysis regarding how these reactions to trauma may constitute adaptive responses to immediate danger. Both writers believe that the victim is blamed a second time when their behavior is branded as a disorder. Further, such pejorative labeling allows the rest of society to skirt responsibility for the victimization (Root, 1992).

Because of the frequently occurring history associated with dissociative and particular personality disorders, van der Kolk (1988) and Brier et al. (1987) have suggested that a diagnosis of posttraumatic stress disorder (PTSD) might be more appropriate than the more stigmatizing personality disorders. The concern here seems to be to destigmatize the syndrome of response to trauma. Whether a diagnosis of PTSD will achieve this goal is unknown. Given the animal literature which suggests that exposure to trauma can create permanent neurotransmitter dysregulation (McIntyre & Edson, 1981; Root, 1992) and the fact that women who were sexually abused as children, on average, display smaller hippocampal volume (Bower, 1996), perhaps a diagnosis of PTSD might have an equally stigmatizing, discouraging impact. Research examining the subjective impact of the various alternatives for conceptualizing a behavioral pattern would be helpful.

Objections to the Masochistic Personality Disorder

The category of self-defeating personality disorder (also known as the masochistic personality disorder) was proffered but ultimately discarded for inclusion in the DSM-IV. This is a case where criticism by feminist authors (Caplan, 1984; Rosewater, 1987; Weasel, 1991) has been heard and acted on. The objection raised was that many of those labeled as having "self-defeating personalities" were, in fact, battered women. By diagnosing the woman, she would be blamed for having been victimized. The society would once again fail to examine structural factors in the abuse of women.

The underlying assumption for personality disorders is that the categories represent structural patterns that will endure despite environmental changes for the better. It is unknown whether this assumption will hold for persons who might be labeled as exhibiting masochistic personalities. The behaviors that constitute criteria for the personality disorder may represent reactions to abusive situations that will disappear given a less oppressive environment (Brown, 1992). Data regarding the frequency with which exposure to victimization can lead to enduring patterns of bad choices for friends and partners (a criterion for the masochistic personality) have not been published.

Beyond the issues of validity of the masochistic personality are concerns regarding the methodology employed to validate the category. In a validation study, a survey was mailed to psychiatrists. These psychiatrists were asked whether (a) in their opinion the category existed and (b) to nominate criteria for the category (Brown, 1992). Rather than studying particular patient samples, the category was operationalized by examining the beliefs of clinicians. Particularly irritating to feminists was that despite the fact that many of the behavioral criteria for this disorder overlap with the battered women's syndrome, field studies did not collect data on the frequency of abuse among those labeled as exhibiting self-defeating personality disorder (Brown, 1992; Rosewater, 1987). Obviously, there were many bases for objecting to the masochistic personality disorder in the DSM.

Concerns Regarding Treatment of MPD and Personality Disorders

As mentioned previously, among those diagnosed with personality disorders and multiple personality disorder (MPD), a history of childhood abuse is often found. Given the statistical correlation, clinicians often assume that such a history may have existed even when the client denies such a history when first asked (Poole, Lindsay, Memon & Bull, 1995). There is an assumption, which has not been tested empirically, that recalling abuse from the past can have an ameliorative effect upon symptoms when accurately recalled (Bowers & Farvolden, 1996). These assumptions have prompted the use of procedures for helping clients recall past abuse. This has raised the possibility of the creation of false memories by overly diligent therapists. This in turn has created controversy within the APA. The resolution of this controversy will undoubtedly have implications for the mental health treatment of women.

Presently, there is a movement spearheaded by an association largely comprised of academic psychologists (American Association of Applied and Preventive Psychology) to introduce legislation to limit mental health professionals to treatments that have been empirically validated. In part, the controversy over repressed memories has been a stimulus to this movement. Controversy over treatment of repressed memory has also led to litigation. The recent Ramona case (involving a father who believed that clinicians employed improper techniques in helping his daughter client to recall memories of childhood incest) may have established the precedent that mental health clinicians can be sued for damage to third parties as well as for damage to the client (Grinfeld, 1994).

Given the much higher rate at which women receive a diagnosis of multiple personality disorder, the controversy surrounding the diagnosis can be seen as a woman's issue (Dell, 1988; McHugh, 1992; Spiegel, 1988). Some have argued that multiple personality does not occur outside the context of psychiatric treatment. Rather, patients are trained to exhibit behavior consistent with the diagnosis by psychiatrists who believe in the existence of the disorder (McHugh, 1992). According to this view, multiple personality disorder is caused by a type of hypnotic phenomenon induced by the treating professional. It will no doubt take a great deal of research to resolve this issue. However, women should be attentive to the controversy, since if critics are correct, they are at greater risk for experiencing iatrogenic problems than men.

PREMENSTRUAL FINDINGS AND OTHER REPRODUCTIVE EVENTS

Feminists have successfully opposed the inclusion of PMS in the DSM-IV. They have opposed the inclusion fearing that attention to the category might be used as a rationale for further discrimination of women (Parlee, 1993). They have pointed out that men as well as women experience circadian and other cyclical changes. They have highlighted the inconsistency in much of the research on PMS (Gallant & Hamilton, 1988). The fact that reports of premenstrual symptoms occur when women are erroneously led to believe they are premenstrual attests to the self-fulfilling nature of the syndrome (Ruble, 1977).

The percentage of women who report minimal mood and somatic changes varies in different studies from 20 percent to 80 percent (Russo & Green, 1993). The percentage of women who meet criteria for premenstrual syndrome is 4.6 percent (Parlee, 1993). That group has a higher incidence of mood disorder generally (Russo & Green, 1993). Given the presence of a mood disorder, symptoms of the disorder may well increase during particular phases of the menstrual cycle. Symptoms of depression and dissociative experience (among women who have been diagnosed as exhibiting these symptoms) are more likely to occur premenstrually than at other times (Hamilton & Jensvold, 1992).

In studies of premenstrual symptoms, results can vary dramatically depending on methodology. Retrospective studies as opposed to daily diary methods increase symptom report. When subjects are aware that the menstrual cycle is the focus of the study, more symptoms are reported. These methodological variations imply that women share the stereotypes about PMS that are found in the culture (Parlee, 1993; Russo & Green, 1993, p. 409). These research inconsistencies suggest that PMS syndrome—that is, the report of distress prior to menstruation—may be a phenomenon caused by a self-fulfilling prophecy. Scientific justification for believing that hormone fluctuation causes symptoms of distress has not been established.

Researchers have recognized another complicating factor in studies attempting to determine what causes distress for women who are premenstrual. There are associations between occurrence of external stressors and the menstrual cycle. The relationship between premenstrual phase of cycle and events holds, whether the events were initiated by the woman or by someone else. Cycles can be disrupted (that is, the internal clock can be reset) given the occurrence of stressful events. It could be that external stressors can both determine when menstruation begins while simultaneously inducing psychological distress. This could make it difficult to disentangle hormonal effects and external stressor effects as causal factors in symptom presentation (Parlee, 1993, p. 334).

Even though scientific findings cannot support the view that hormonal fluctuations induce psychological distress, the belief that hormones influence mood and behavior exists in the culture. Given the belief in PMS, explanations women provide for their feelings will be affected. The impact of cultural stereotypes on how internal events are interpreted can be profound. Since PMS is assumed to evoke anxiety and irritability, and interpersonal events can evoke arousal and irritation, when a women experiences that type of discomfort, the discomfort can either be attributed to an interpersonal situation or PMS. Depending upon the attribution for internal arousal ("my boss is irritating today" versus "my PMS is distressing me"), very different actions can result (Koeske & Koeske, 1975; Rodin, 1976).

Is the lack of the inclusion of PMS as a mental disorder in the DSM a good thing for women? Although feminists are justified in avoiding the stigmatization of a normal function, the other side, in failing to include PMS in the DSM, robs women of the opportunity to receive insurance reimbursement for treatment of distress attributable to premenstrual hormonal changes. The APA recognizes that male-reproductive-system-related functions can cause distress and do emerge as mental health issues. Is it fair that those women who may become distressed premenstrually not be equally entitled to relief from their reproductive system-related problems?

Postpartum Depression

Postpartum depression is a recognized phenomenon. It is reported in 10 percent of childbirth cases, varies in onset between six weeks to three to four months post delivery, and can last from six months to one year (Russo & Green, 1993). The symptoms of postpartum illness include mood changes as well as cognitive changes. Postpartum illness, a more mild syndrome than depression, is reported by 39–85 percent of women, occurs three to four days after delivery, and lasts from one day to several weeks (Russo & Green, 1993). Further, post partum symptoms are more likely to occur among those women in stressful marriages and experiencing stressful life events (Russo & Green, 1993; Terry, Mayocchi & Hynes, 1996), impoverished women, and women without partners (Hobfoll, Ritter, Lavin, Hulsizer & Cameron, 1995).

Menopause

Menopause occurs at about age fifty. Symptoms include "hot flashes," "night sweats," sleep disturbance, fatigue, irritability, and mood changes. Women who have experienced depression prior to menopause are more likely to report symptoms of menopause (Russo & Green, 1993). Those women who have undergone surgical menopause are more likely to report symptoms than those undergoing natural menopause (Russo & Green, 1993).

GENDER DIFFERENCES WITH RESPECT TO ACCESS AND DELIVERY OF TREATMENT SERVICES

Overall, women visit more health providers than men (Travis, 1993). Females are more likely to present for treatment in outpatient mental health facilities and in private mental hospitals (Russo & Green, 1993). However, there are special considerations among the working poor. Because women have lower incomes generally and because they are more likely to be employed part-time or in jobs where health insurance is not provided, unless they are receiving AFDC or are covered under the husband's insurance policy, they will have less access to health care. As such, working poor women may receive less treatment when treatment is needed. When they are treated, they may not be seen as frequently as might be necessary.

Continued Concerns About the Issue of Reliability

Once women enter the mental health treatment system they should inspire special concerns. Despite the fact that the DSM-III and subsequent documents provide precise behavioral criteria for each diagnosis, there is evidence that demographics affect which labels are applied. The sex and race of the client interacting with the race and gender of the diagnostician will influence the label provided (Loring & Powell, 1988). Loring and Powell gave psychiatrists, who were familiar with the DSM-III, a written case study and asked them to render a diagnosis. When there was no information about race or gender, relatively good consensus among subject-psychiatrists on the diagnostic label was achieved. However, consensus attenuated when information about the gender and race of the client was provided. Female diagnosticians assessing female clients tended to provide the less severe diagnosis. Male diagnosticians tended to diagnose histrionic personality disorders more often than female diagnosticians. Weasel's (1991) research also supports the view that race will influence diagnosis. She finds that in public facilities black women are more likely to be diagnosed with bipolar depression or schizophrenia rather than major depression.

In sum, the problems of inadequate reliability will continue to plague diagnosticians. For diagnoses more often provided to women (e.g., personality disorders), inadequate reliability is a particular problem. Assuming that an inappropriate diagnosis can result in harm to the client, there is reason for concern.

Issue of Medication Side Effects Specific to Women

Women are twice as likely as men to receive psychotropic medications. Even after controlling for signs, symptoms, and diagnosis, women are still more likely to receive psychotropic medications than are men (Travis, 1993). The difference in medication status is most pronounced among those over age forty-five. Women are maintained on psychotropic medications for longer intervals than are men (Travis, 1993).

There are special considerations when psychotropic medications for women are prescribed, if pregnancy is a possibility. With SSRI (selective serotonin reuptake inhibitors such as Prozac and Paxil used in the treatment of obsessive compulsive disorder and depression) treatment, there is a danger that infants born to mothers who have taken SSRIs during their pregnancy will be addicted to the SSRIs and will have to be withdrawn (Bromiker & Kaplan, 1994). For those women who are at their child-bearing years, special planning around the prescription of medications must occur. Lithium (the major treatment for bipolar disorder) is a teratogen (Bernstein, 1988). Abrupt withdrawal is associated with rebound manic episodes (Faedda, Tondo, Baldessarini, Suppes & Tohen, 1993). Given the probable interaction of medications with hormonal levels, it is important that more drug trials with female samples be conducted.

FINAL THOUGHTS

Why is a diagnostic system for behavior, creating categories of dysfunction, necessary? Apart from the sometimes overly optimistic hope that correct diagnosis will suggest appropriate treatment, the answer lies in economics (Blashfield, 1991, p. 18). In this country health care is rationed by insurance companies, market forces, and in the case of Oregon, by the state legislature. Since the health care system absorbs 14 percent of the GNP (Grinfeld, 1993), the United States is not willing to spend money on relatively minor matters. Again differentiating between trivial and important requires a value judgment. But, at the limits, reasonable people would probably agree that plastic surgery to repair a cleft palate is a greater necessity than the repair of sagging eyelids in the middle aged. Perhaps the DSM does a reasonable job in presenting a set of behaviors that can be associated with suffering beyond the average state of distress one can anticipate in one's life span.

The assumption is often made that disapproval of a person is more likely to be absent when the person is thought to be burdened by disease, rather than when viewed as morally flawed. When feminists objected to including paraphiliac rapism (raping women) and sadistic personality disorder (a pattern found in wife batterers) in the DSM, they assumed that inclusion in the DSM would decrease disapproval and result in less punishment toward rapists and wife batterers (Williams, 1988). Decreasing blame was the rationale offered for viewing alcoholism as a disease rather than a character flaw. The assumption of less scorn and less punishment when a syndrome is labeled disease has been tested empirically in the case of intemperate drinking. In fact, those viewing alcoholism as a disease do not always respond more kindly or benignly to alcoholics (Littrell, 1991a, pp. 55–61). More research should be conducted as to the connotative fallout attributable to identifying a syndrome as a form of disease or disorder.

In this country, we have relied on labels of disease and disorder to make decisions about whose medical treatment will be compensated. The disease label probably lends an air of credibility and urgency to the process of spending money to eliminate distress. If the public can be convinced that a behavioral syndrome is a disease, there will be more public approval for directing dollars toward research and treatment. Indeed, this thinking was behind the thrust to make violence an issue for medical research at the Alcohol, Drug Abuse, and Mental Health Administration (Wright, 1995). Even with the rubric of disease there are limits to which insurance companies will be willing to direct money for treatment. Insurance companies will not pay for adjustment disorders despite their presence in the DSM.

One problem with the DSM, and mental health diagnostic labels in general, is that labels have impact beyond serving as a mechanism for rationing health care. When individuals are labeled as having a disorder they often assume they have little volitional control over their behavior. In such cases the label can become a self-fulfilling prophesy. When the disorder is also suggested to have a physical basis, there are additional consequences. Research suggests that when people are told their behavior has a physical basis they are less willing to become actively involved in changing their behavior than when they are told they have a behavioral problem (Fisher & Farina, 1979).

In instructing students of psychopathology, the value-laden nature of the enterprise of assigning some variations in the human condition to the category of abnormal should be explained. Although the developers of the DSM caution that they are categorizing disorders and not people (Williams, 1988), emphasizing the arbitrary nature of assigning variations in the human condition to the abnormal category may help students to appreciate that the clients who receive diagnoses should not be viewed or responded to as deviant. Rather, the current system of diagnoses is merely the mechanism the society has constructed for determining whose treatment will be reimbursed. The DSM is just a mechanism for saying "your pain and suffering exceeds that which the average human being should be expected to endure, and therefore you are entitled to financial assistance to relieve your distress."

Along with a recognition that the DSM is a political document, students should be alerted to those DSM categories for which there is special concern for women. The meaning of differential rates for particular categories should be pondered. The need for alterations in the usual manner in which treatment is provided to adapt to the special needs of other groups should also be highlighted. All too often, variations in the presentation of signs and symptoms are ignored by clinicians when they contradict expectations based on group stereotypes. For instance, females with antisocial tendencies are often misdiagnosed, as are males with borderline tendencies. To avoid these common errors in assessment, it is useful to have students evaluate cases that challenge stereotyped views about clinical populations. Moreover, they need to be exposed to assignments that force them to see how gender, race, class, and culture interact with known decision biases in assessment processes. Many inaccurate assessments by novice clinicians are attributable to deficits in their clinical reasoning processes. For this reason, instructors should provide students with assignments that test their logic in assessing cases. Women and persons of color are often the victims of faulty logic with roots in established social processes that perpetuate the privileges of the powerful. The male hegemony often perpetuates views of the nature of women that restrict their opportunities in society. At the same time, other pains and disabilities of women and persons of color that do not serve the interest of clinical authorities are ignored. Thus, extant biases must be challenged in the presentation of content on psychopathology and its processes of identification. This chapter has attempted to highlight some of these biases in the context of a review.

APPENDIX 4–1: PSYCHOPATHOLOGY

Course Description: 3 lecture hours. 3 credits. Employs a social constructionist perspective in examining the influence of social context variables on establishing boundaries between the normal and the pathological. Examines the medicalization of various forms of deviance and the nomenclature, classification systems, and decision rules germane to the study of psychopathology. Stresses gender and cultural variations in clinical symptomatology and factors associated with the etiology, assessment, prognosis, and management of mental disorders from a social work perspective.

Course Objectives: At the end of this course students should be able to:

1. Critically assess the role of social variables (age, gender, race, social class) on the social construction of at least two diagnostic categories in the DSM system of classification.
2. Critically evaluate the pros and cons associated with the medicalization of at least two forms of deviant behavior and its consequences for women and people of color.
3. Describe the politics and other issues involved in establishing boundaries between what is considered normal and what is considered pathological.
4. Identify and contrast key historical contributions to the development of various concepts used in defining mental disorders (deviance, distress, dysfunction, and impairment).
5. Identify and contrast relevant psychiatric, biological, social, psychological, and cultural nomenclature.
6. Identify and contrast legal, cultural, medical, and social definitions of mental disorders.
7. Perform a multiaxial classification.
8. Describe symptoms, prognosis, and treatment for at least three mental disorders.

9. Identify the effects of gender and culture on variations in the presentation of symptomatology in at least two disorders.

Learning Units & Suggested Readings

Unit I: The History and Development of Classification Systems for Mental Disorders: The Politics of Deviance Medicalization

Franks, V. (1986). Sex stereotyping and diagnosis of psychopathology. *Women and Therapy, 5*, 219–232.

Kravetz, D. (1986). Women and mental health. In N. Van Den Begh & L. Cooper (Eds.), *Feminist visions for social work* (pp. 101–127). Silver Spring, MD: NASW Press.

Szasz, T. & Breggin, P. (1991). *Toxic psychiatry.* Part IV. New York: St. Martin's Press.

Tuana, N. (1989). *Feminism & science*. Bloomington: Indiana University Press.

Walsh, M.R. (1987). *The psychology of women: Ongoing debates.* New Haven: Yale University Press.

Weasel, J.W. (1991). Universal mental health classification systems: Reclaiming women's experiences. *Affilia, 6,* 8–31.

Widom, C.S. (1984). *Sex roles and psychopathology.* New York: Plenum.

Unit II: Adult and Childhood Disorders: Symptoms, Signs, and Issues

Broverman, I.K., Broverman, D., Clarkson, F.E., Rosencrantz, P. & Vogel, S. (1970). Sex role stereotypes and clinical judgments of mental health. *Journal of Consulting and Clinical Psychology, 34,* 1–7.

Morrow, J. & Nolen-Hoeksema, S. (1990). Effects of responses to depression on remediation of depressive affect. *Journal of Personality and Social Psychology, 58,* 519–527.

Mower, O.H. (1960). Sin, the lesser of two evils. *American Psychologist, 15,* 301–304.

Newmann, J.P. (1986). Gender, life strains, and depression. *Journal of Health and Social Behavior, 27,* 161–178.

Nolen-Hoeksema, S. (1987). Sex differences in unipolar depression: Evidence and theory. *Psychological Bulletin, 101,* 259–282.

Nolen-Hoeksema, S. (1990). *Sex differences in depression.* Stanford, CA: Stanford University Press.

Nolen-Hoeksema, S. (1991). Responses to depression and their effects on the duration of depressive episodes. *Journal of Abnormal Psychology, 100,* 569–582.

Silk, K.R., Lee, S., Hill, E.M. & Lohr, N.E. (1995). Borderline personality disorder symptoms and severity of sexual abuse. *American Journal of Psychiatry, 152,* 1059–1064.

REFERENCES

American Psychiatric Association. (1994). *Diagnostic and statistical manual of mental disorders* (4th ed.). Washington, DC: Author.

Ashford, J.B. (1994). Child maltreatment interventions: Developments in law, prevention, and treatment. *Criminal Justice Review, 19,* 271–285.

Ashford, J.B. & LeCroy, C.W., (1997). Evolution of HBSE content. In K. Lortie, C.W. LeCroy & J.B. Ashford (Eds.). *Instructors Manual: Human Behavior in the Social Environment*. Pacific Grove, CA: Brooks/Cole.

Ashford, J.B., LeCroy, C.W. & Lortie, K. (1997). *Human behavior in the social environment: A multidimensional perspective*. Pacific Grove, CA: Brooks/Cole.

Ausubel, D.P. (1961). Personality disorder is disease. *American Psychologist, 16,* 69–74.

Bem, S.L. (1977). On the utility of alternative procedures for assessing psychological androgyny. *Journal of Consulting and Clinical Psychology, 45,* 196—205.

Bernard, L.D. (1977). Education for social work. In J.B.Turner et al. (Eds.), *Encyclopedia of social work*. (17th ed., pp. 290–300). Washington, DC: NASW Press.

Bernstein, J.G. (1988). *Handbook of drug therapy in psychiatry* (2nd ed.). Littleton, MA: PSG Publishing.

Biology Gender Study Group. (1989). The importance of feminist critique for contemporary cell biology. In N. Tunana (Ed.), *Feminism and Science* (pp. 172–187). Bloomington: Indiana University Press.

Blashfield, R.K. (1991). Models of psychiatric classification. In M. Hernsen & S.M. Turner (Eds.), *Adult psychopathology and diagnosis* (pp. 3–22). New York: Wiley.

Bohem, W.W. (1977). Education for social work: Studies. In J.B. Turner et al. (Eds.), *Encyclopedia of social work.* (17th ed., pp. 101–127). Washington, DC: NASW Press.

Bohem. W.W. (1959). *Curriculum study*. New York: Council on Social Work Education.

Boorse, C. (1975). On the distinction between disease and illness. *Philosophy and Public Affairs, 5,* 49–68.

Bower, B. (1996). Exploring trauma's cerebral side. *Science News, 149,* (May 18), 315.

Bowers, K.S. & Farvolden, P. (1996). Revisting a century-old Freudian slip—From suggestion disavowed to the truth repressed. *Psychological Bulletin, 119,* 355–380.

Breslau, N., Davis, D.C., Andreski, P. & Peterson, E. (1991). Traumatic events and posttraumatic stress disorder in an urban population of young adults. *Archives of General Psychiatry, 48,* 216–222.

Brieland, D. (1987). History and evolution of social work practice. In A. Minahan (Ed.), *Encyclopedia of social work.* (18th ed., pp. 739–754). Silver Spring, MD: NASW Press.

Brier, J.B., Nelson, B.A., Miller, J.B. & Krol, P.A. (1987). Childhood sexual and physical abuse as factors in adult psychiatric illness. *American Journal of Psychiatry, 144,* 1426–1430.

Bromiker, R. & Kaplan, M. (1994). Apparent intrauterine fetal withdrawal from clomipramine hydrochloride. *Journal of the American Medical Association, 272,* 1722–1723.

Brooks, W.K. (1986). Human behavior/social environment: Past and present, future or folly? *Journal of Social Work Education, 22,* 18–23.

Broverman, I.K., Broverman, D., Clarkson, F.E., Rosencrantz, P. & Vogel, S. (1970). Sex role stereotypes and clinical judgments of mental health. *Journal of Consulting and Clinical Psychology, 34,* 1–7.

Brown, L.A. (1992). A feminist critique of the personality disorders. In L.S. Brown & M. Ballou (Eds.) *Personality and psychopathology: Feminist reappraisals.* (pp. 206–228). New York: Guilford.

Butler, R. (1959). *An orientation to knowledge of human growth and behavior in social work education (Vol. 6).* New York: Council on Social Work Education.

Butler, R.M. (1970). *Social functioning framework: An approach to the human behavior and social environment sequence*. New York: Council on Social Work Education.

Cabot, R. (1917). What of medical diagnosis should the social case worker know and apply? *Proceedings of the National Conference of Social Work.* 101–104.

Caplan, P.J. (1984). The myth of women's masochism. *American Psychologist, 39,* 130–139.

Carmen, E. & Rieker, P.P. (1989). A psychosocial model of the victim-to-patient process: Implications for treatment. *Psychiatric Clinics of North America, 12,* 431–443.

Collins, B.G. (1993). Reconstructing codependency using self-in-relation theory: A feminist perspective. *Social Work, 38,* 470–476.

Conrad, P. & Schneider, J.W. (1980). *Deviance and Medicalization: From badness to sickness*. St. Louis, MO: C.V. Mosby.

Cronkite, R.C. & Moos, R.H. (1984). The role of predisposing and moderating factors in the stress-illness relationship. *Journal of Health and Social Behavior, 25,* 372–393.

Dawes, R.M. (1994). *House of cards: Psychology and psychotherapy built on myth.* New York: Free Press.

DeAngelis, T. (1993). Controversial diagnosis is voted into the latest DSM. *APA Monitor, 24,* 32–33.

Dell, P.F. (1988). Professional skepticism about multiple personality. *Journal of Nervous and Mental Disorder, 176,* 528–531.

Dinerman, M. (1984). The 1959 curriculum study: Contributions of Werner Bohem. In M. Dinerman & L.L. Gesimar (Eds.), *A quarter century of social work education* (pp. 3–24). New York: NASW Press.

Ehrenreich, B. & English, D. (1981). The sexual politics of sickness. In P. Conrad & R. Kern (Eds.), *The sociology of health and illness* (pp. 327–350). New York: St. Martin's Press.

Faedda, G.L., Tondo, L., Baldessarini, R.J., Suppes, T. & Tohen, M. (1993). Outcome after rapid versus gradual discontinuation of lithium treatment in bipolar disorders. *Archives of General Psychiatry, 50,* 448–455.

Fingarette, H. (1988). *Heavy drinking: The myth of alcoholism as a disease.* Berkeley: University of California Press.

Fisher, J.D. & Farina, A. (1979). Consequences of beliefs about the nature of mental disorders. *Journal of Abnormal Psychology, 88,* 320–327.

Fodor, I.G. (1992). The agoraphobic syndrome: From anxiety neurosis to panic disorder. In L.S. Brown & M. Ballou (Eds.), *Personality and psychopathology: Feminist reappraisal* (pp. 177–205.). New York: Guilford.

Franks, V. (1986). Sex stereotyping and diagnosis of psychopathology. *Women and Therapy, 5,* 219–232.

Franks, V. & Rothblum, E.D. (1983a). Introduction: Warning! Sex-role stereotypes may be hazardous to your health. In V. Franks & E.D. Rothblum (Eds.), *The stereotyping of women: Its effects on mental health* (pp. 3–10). New York: Springer.

Franks, V. & Rothblum, E.D. (1983b). Concluding comments, criticism, and caution: Consistent conservatism or constructive change? In V. Franks & E.D. Rothblum (Eds.), *The stereotyping of women: Its effects on mental health,* (pp. 259–270). New York: Springer.

Freidson, E. (1970). *Profession of medicine*. New York: Dodd & Mead.

Gallant, S.J., & Hamilton, J.A. (1988). On a premenstrual psychiatric diagnosis: What's in a name? *Professional Psychology: Research and Practice, 19,* 271–278.

Grinfeld, M.J. (1993). 1993: Health care costs will near $1 trillion. *Psychiatric Times, March,*(10), 44.

Grinfeld, M.J. (1994). Impact of Ramona case uncertain. *Psychiatric Times, October* XI, 3.

Hamilton, J.A. & Jensvold, M. (1992). Personality, psychopathology, and depressions in women. In L.S. Brown & M. Ballou (Eds.), *Personality and psychopathology: Feminist reappraisal* (pp. 116–143). New York: Guilford.

Herman, J., Perry, J. & van der Kolk, B. (1989). Childhood trauma in borderline personality disorder. *American Journal of Psychiatry, 146,* 490–495.

Hess, D.J. (1995). *Science and technology in a multicultural world: The cultural politics of facts and artifacts*. New York: Columbia University Press.

Hobfoll, S.E., Ritter, C., Lavin, J., Hulsizer, M.R. & Cameron, R.P. (1995). Depression prevalence and incidence among inner-city pregnant and postpartum women. *Journal of Consulting and Clinical Psychology, 63,* 445–453.

Horwitz, A.V. (1982). *The social control of mental illness.* New York: Academic Press.

Hubbard, R. (1989). Science, facts, and feminism. In N. Tuana (Ed.), *Feminism & Science*. Bloomington: Indiana University Press.

Hyde, A.B. & Murphy, J. (1955). An experiment in integrative learning. *Social Service Review, 29,* 62–67.

Jarrett, M.C. (1919). The psychiatric thread running through all social casework. *Proceedings of the National Conference of Social Work*, pp. 587–593.

Kaplan, M. (1983). A woman's view of the DSM-III. *American Psychologist, 38,* 786–792.

Kass, F., Spitzer, R.L. & Williams, J.B.W. (1983). The empirical study of the issue of sex bias in the diagnostic criteria of DSM-III Axis II personality disorders. *American Psychologist, 38,* 799–801.

Katz, P.A., Boggiano, A. & Silvern, L. (1993). Theories of female personality. In F.L. Denmaker & M.A. Paludi (Ed.), *Psychology of women: A handbook of issues and theories* (pp. 247–280). London: Greenwood Press.

Kelly, J.A. (1983). Sex-role stereotypes and mental health: Conceptual models in the 1970s and issues for the 1980s. In V. Franks & E.D. Rothblum (Eds.), *The stereotyping of women: Its effects on mental health* (pp. 11–29). New York: Springer.

Kendell, R.E. (1975). *The role of diagnosis in psychiatry* (2nd. ed.). New York: Free Press.

Kirk, S.A. & Kutchins, H. (1992). *The selling of the DSM: The Rhetoric and Science in Psychiatry*. New York: Aldine de Gruyter.

Klinger, E. (1993). Clinical approaches to mood control. In D.M. Wegner & J.W. Pennebaker (Eds.), *Handbook of mental control* (pp. 344–369). Englewood Cliffs, NJ: Prentice-Hall.

Koeske, R.D. & Koeske, G.F. (1975). An attributional approach to moods and menstrual cycle. *Journal of Personality and Social Psychology, 31,* 473–478.

Kravetz, D. (1986). Women and mental health. In N. van den Bergh & L.B. Cooper (Eds.), *Feminist visions for social work* (pp. 101–127). Washington, DC: NASW Press.

Leven, D.M. (1987). Psychopathology in the epoch of nihilism. In D.M. Leven (Ed.), *Psychopathologies of the modern self: Postmodern studies on narcissism, schizophrenia, and depression* (pp. 1–17). New York: New York University Press.

Lilienfeld, S.O. & Marino, L. (1995). Mental disorders as a Roschian concept: A critique of Wakefield's "harmful dysfunction" analysis. *Journal of Abnormal Psychology, 104,* 411–420.

Littrell, J. (1991a). *Understanding and treating alcoholism: An empirically based clinician's handbook for the treatment of alcoholism*. Hillsdale, NJ: Lawrence Erlbaum Associates.

Littrell, J. (1991b). *Understanding and treating alcoholism: Biological, psychological, and social aspects of alcohol consumption and abuse.* Hillsdale, NJ: Lawrence Erlbaum Associates.

Loring, M. & Powell, B. (1988). Gender, race, and DSM-III: A study of the objectivity of psychiatric diagnostic behavior. *Journal of Health and Social Behavior, 29,* 1–22.

Ludwig, A.M. (1986). *Principles of clinical psychiatry* (2nd ed.). New York: Free Press.

Maffeo, P.A. (1982). Gender as a model for mental health. In I. Al-Issa (Ed.), *Gender and Psychopathology*, (pp. 31–50). New York: Academic Press.

Maxmen, J.S. & Ward, N.G. (1995). *Essential psychopathology and its treatment.* New York: Norton.

McGinn, R.E. (1991). *Science, technology, and society.* Englewood Cliffs, NJ: Prentice-Hall.

McHugh, P.R. (1992). Psychiatric misadventures. *American Scholar, 61,* 536.

McIntyre, D.C. & Edson, N. (1981). Facilitation of amygdala kindling after norepinephrine depletion with 6-hydroxydopamine in rats. *Experimental Neurology, 74,* 748–757.

Morrow, J. & Nolen-Hoeksema, S. (1990). Effects of responses to depression on remediation of depressive affect. *Journal of Personality and Social Psychology, 58*, 519–527.

Mower, O.H. (1960). Sin, the lesser of two evils. *American Psychologist, 15,* 301–304.

Newmann, J.P. (1986). Gender, life strains, and depression. *Journal of Health and Social Behavior, 27,* 161–178.

Nolen-Hoeksema, S. (1987). Sex differences in unipolar depression: Evidence and theory. *Psychological Bulletin, 101,* 259–282.

Nolen-Hoeksema, S. (1990). *Sex differences in depression.* Stanford, CA: Stanford University Press.

Nolen-Hoeksema, S. (1991). Responses to depression and their effects on the duration of depressive episodes. *Journal of Abnormal Psychology, 100,* 569- 582.

Nolen-Hoeksema, S. (1993). Sex differences in control of depression. In D. Wegner & J.W. Pennebaker (Eds.), *Handbook of mental control* (pp. 306–324). Englewood Cliffs, NJ: Prentice-Hall.

Nurcombe, B. & Gallagher, R.M. (1986). *The clinical process in psychiatry: Diagnosis and management.* New York: Cambridge University Press.

Parlee, M.B. (1993). Psychology of menstruation and premenstrual syndrome. In F.L. Denmark & M.A. Paludi (Eds.), *Psychology of women: A handbook of issues and theories* (pp. 325–378). London: Greenwood Press.

Peele, S. (1989). *The diseasing of America: Addiction treatment out of control.* Lexington, MA: Lexington Press.

Plomin, R., DeFries, J.C. & McClearn, G.E. (1990). *Behavioral genetics: A primer.* New York: Freeman.

Poole, D.A., Lindsay, D.S., Memon, A. & Bull, R. (1995). Psychotherapy and the recovery of memories of childhood sexual abuse: U.S. and British practitioners' opinions, practices, and experiences. *Journal of Consulting and Clinical Psychology, 63*, 426–437.

Pugliesi, K. (1992). Women and mental health: Two traditions of feminist research. *Women & Health, 19*, 43–68.

Rodin, J. (1976). Menstruation, reattribution, and competence. *Journal of Personality and Social Psychology, 33*, 345–353.

Romach, M., Busto, U., Somer, G., Kaplan, H.L. & Sellers, E. (1995). Clinical aspects of the chronic use of alprazolam and lorazepam. *American Journal of Psychiatry, 152*, 1161–1167.

Root, M.P.P. (1992). Reconstructing the impact of trauma on personality. In L.S. Brown & M. Ballou (Eds.), *Personality and psychopathology: Feminist reappraisal* (pp. 229–265). New York: Guilford.

Rosewater, L.B. (1987). A critical analysis of the proposed self-defeating personality disorder. *Journal of Personality Disorders, 1,* 190–195.

Ross, C.A., Miller, S.D., Reagor, P., Bjornson, L., Fraser, G.A. & Anderson, G. (1990). Structured interview data on 102 cases of multiple personality disorder from four centers. *American Journal of Psychiatry, 147*, 596–601.

Rothblum, E.D. (1983). Sex-role stereotypes and depression in women. In V. Franks & E.D. Rothblum (Eds.), *The stereotyping of women: Its effects on mental health* (pp. 83–111). New York: Springer.

Ruble, D. (1977). Premenstrual symptoms: A reinterpretation. *Science, 197,* 291–292.

Russo, N.F. & Green, B.L. (1993). Women and mental health. *Psychology of women: A handbook of issues and theories* (pp. 379–436). London: Greenwood Press.

Sargeant, J.K., Bruce, M.L., Florio, L.P. & Weissman, M.M. (1990). Factors associated with 1-year outcome of major depression in the community. *Archives of General Psychiatry, 47,* 519–526.

Scadding, J.G. (1967). Diagnosis: The clinician and the computer. *Lancet, 2,* 877–882.

Sedgwick, P. (1982). Antipsychiatry from the sixties to the eighties. In W.R. Grove (Ed.), *Deviance and mental illness* (pp. 199–233). Beverly Hills, CA: Sage.

Silk, K.R., Lee, S., Hill, E.M. & Lohr, N.E. (1995). Borderline personality disorder symptoms and severity of sexual abuse. *American Journal of Psychiatry, 152*, 1059–1064.

Skinner, B.F. (1971). *Beyond freedom and dignity*. New York: Knopf.

Spanos, N.P. (1994). Multiple identity enactments and multiple personality disorder: A sociocognitive perspective. *Psychological Bulletin, 116*, 143–165.

Spence, J.T., Helmreich, R. & Stapp, J. (1975). Ratings of self and peers on sex role attributes and their relation to self-esteem and conceptions of masculinity and femininity. *Journal of Personality and Social Psychology, 32,* 29–39.

Spiegel, D. (1988). The treatment accorded those who treat patients with multiple personality disorder. *Journal of Nervous and Mental Disorders, 176,* 535–536.

Spitzer, R.L., Williams, J.B., Kass, F. & Davis, M. (1989). National field trial of the DSM-III-R diagnostic criteria for self-defeating personality disorder. *American Journal of Psychiatry, 146,* 1561–1567.

Szasz, T. (1960). The myth of mental illness. *American Psychologist, 15,* 113–118.

Teasdale, J.D. & Fennell, M.J.V. (1982). Immediate effects of depression on cognitive therapy interventions. *Cognitive Therapy and Research, 6,* 613–617.

Terry, D.J., Mayocchi, L. & Hynes, G.J. (1996). Depressive symptomatology in new mothers: A stress and coping perspective. *Journal of Abnormal Psychology, 105,* 220–231.

Towle, C. (1960). A social work approach to courses in growth and behavior. *Social Service Review, 34,* 402–414.

Travis, C.B. (1993). Women and health. In F.L. Denmark & M.A. Paludi (Eds.), *Psychology of women: A handbook of issues and theories* (pp. 283–323). London: Greenwood Press.

Tuana, N. (1989). *Feminism & Science*. Bloomington: Indiana University Press.

Turner, F.J. (1984). Mental disorders in social work practice. In F.J. Turner (Ed.), *Adult psychopathology: A social work perspective* (pp. 1–5). New York: Free Press.

Ussher, J.M. (1989). *The psychology of the human body*. New York: Routledge.

Van der Kolk, B.A. (1988). The trauma spectrum: The interaction of biological and social events in the genesis of the trauma response. *Journal of Traumatic Stress, 1,* 273–290.

Waisberg, J. & Page, S. (1988). Gender role nonconformity and perception of mental illness. *Women & Health, 14,* 3–16.

Wakefield, J.C. (1992a). Disorder as harmful dysfunction: A conceptual critique of DSM-III-Rs definition of mental disorder. *Psychological Review, 99,* 232–247.

Wakefield, J.C. (1992b). The concept of mental disorder: On the boundary between biological facts and social values. *American Psychologist, 47,* 373–388.

Weasel, J.W. (1991). Universal mental health classification systems: Reclaiming women's experiences. *Affilia, 6,* 8–31.

Wettstein, R.M. (1988). Psychiatry and the law. In J.A. Talbott, R.E. Hales & S.C. Yudofsky (Eds.), *Textbook of psychiatry* (pp. 1059–1084). Washington, DC: American Psychiatric Press.

Williams, J.B.W. (1988). Psychiatric classification. In J.A. Talbott, R.E. Hales & S.C. Yudofsky (Eds.), *Textbook of psychiatry* (pp. 201–224). Washington, DC: American Psychiatric Press.

Wright, R. (1995). The biology of violence. *New Yorker,* March, 68–77.

Zita, J.N. (1989). The premenstrual syndrome: "dis-easing" the female cycle. In N. Tuana (Ed.), *Feminism & science* (pp. 188–210). Bloomington: Indiana University Press.

Zola, I. (1972). Medicine as an institution of social control . *Sociological Review, 20,* 487–504.

Zola, I.K. (1981). Medicine as an institution of social control. In P. Conrad & R. Kern (Eds), *The sociology of health and illness*. New York: St. Martin's Press.

CHAPTER 5

Teaching About Groups in a Gendered World

Toward Curricular Transformation in Group Work Education[1]

Lorraine Gutiérrez
Beth Glover Reed
Robert Ortega
Edith Lewis

INTRODUCTION

Knowledge about groups and methods for working with groups is critical when the goal is to transform practice paradigms to address issues of gender and other forms of social diversity (Garvin & Reed, 1994). Practice in a group context has been a central element of feminist practice whether the form is support groups, consciousness raising, or social action. If social work students are to learn to work effectively from a "gendered" framework, information about groups and group work must be included in their practice knowledge.

Knowledge about groups is also becoming increasingly important for social workers in all areas of practice. The impetus for this shift toward groups is multifaceted. It is located in the movement of mental health services to cost containment, in consumer-facilitated self-help and support groups, in total quality management (TQM) methods, and

---

1. Special thanks to the following individuals who assisted in the development of this chapter: Charles Garvin, Richard Tolman, Diane Naranjo, and Kylo-Patrick Robert Hart.

in the focus on participatory methods in community organization. Group work skills are needed by those who work with individuals or families but who find themselves conducting group treatment or organizing self-help or support groups. These skills are needed by community organizers, who work with groups in community meetings, committees, or task forces. Trends in social administration focus on organizational development, total quality management, and multicultural issues point to an increasing need for group skills. The ability to work with groups can be considered a critical skill for all forms of social work practice (Garvin & Reed, 1994, 1995).

Despite the centrality of group work practice, group work education has been on the decline within the past 40 years (Birnbaum & Aurbach, 1994). With the decline of settlement work and the move toward generic methods, group work specializations and specialized courses have become less common (Parry, 1995). Currently, only 7 percent of all MSW degree programs offer a group work concentration, and 19 percent of MSW programs require courses on groups (Birnbaum & Aurbach, 1994). These trends are mirrored in field education: Only 34 percent of MSW programs require experience in conducting groups (Birnbaum & Aurbach, 1994). Although we believe that social work education would be strengthened by more courses specific to group practice, these curriculum patterns suggest that if students are to learn to practice effectively with groups, group work education must be infused throughout all practice teaching areas on both the micro and macro levels.

Developing education for group-oriented practice must be focused on both content and process. We must simultaneously consider content of courses on groups and how they reflect the knowledge and skills required of practitioners, and the process of teaching and how this process can encourage critical awareness and skills development. Both of these areas are equally important and involve gender-relevant content (well-conceptualized content will not enhance practice if our method of education does not enhance translation of theory into practice methods and development of skills). Learning to recognize and influence the gendered dynamics of the social work classroom or field setting can also help students to translate these concepts into specific intervention skills. Therefore, this chapter will look equally at these two dimensions by sharing strategies used by social work educators teaching group theory, practice, and research from a gendered perspective.

The first section of this chapter looks at the history of group work in social work and how knowledge of gender issues can reformulate our thinking about groups. Our reformulation is based in a multicultural feminist perspective—one that integrates critical thinking, content on gender and gendered relationships, the interaction of gender with other status characteristics, and collaborative skill-building for students and instructors (Garvin & Reed, 1995; Gutiérrez & Lewis, in press; Lewis, 1995). We describe some knowledge and theory about gender and groups that is important for a social work curriculum, and then delineate relevant skills for practice.

The second section of the chapter is concerned with the practice of teaching. It is built upon the assumption that in order to teach about groups effectively, educators must be able to model the behaviors expected of future group workers. In other words, social work group educators must be able to understand and model methods of balancing multiple identities of group members and group leaders. Even when social work educators are teaching about group theory, or group research, or about other knowledge and skills for social work practice, it is still necessary to model the types of behavior expected by future group workers. In this section we build upon work by Lee (1994) and others to describe a critical education and empowerment group-processes framework that focus attention on the classroom as part of a learning environment.

Unfortunately, limited space does not allow for full discussion of all knowledge and skills relevant for a social work curriculum for educating social workers to attend competently to gender and multicultural issues in groups. Therefore, this chapter should be seen as presenting illustrative concepts, tasks, and teaching options in several required curricular areas, with examples of gender-related questions, knowledge, skills, and issues important for each. We urge the reader to use our examples and develop others for the multiple topics we have not been able to address.

OUR FOUNDATIONS: SOCIAL GROUP WORK

Many of the first people to develop and discuss group work practice were women involved in settlement work (Garvin & Reed, 1995). The focus of many early settlements was on the acculturation of immigrants and rural arrivals to urban life. Additional concerns focused on social isolation as a function of industrialization, character building, leisure time interests and skills, recreation, social action, and social reform (Halpern, 1995; Middleman & Goldberg, 1987). The goal of settlements was the improvement of society by enhancing development of individuals, families, groups, and committees.

Through their work in the social settlements, women were active in the formulation of traditional group work practice. In many ways their experiences as women in a patriarchal society influenced and informed their work (Garvin & Reed, 1995). Jane Addams, for example, insisted on referring to participants as members rather than clients, recognizing the extent to which labels both reflect and shape power imbalances and assumptions. Grace Coyle is also recognized as a major contributor to the conceptualization of social work with groups. In her early work, she stressed such principles as the need for the worker to consider simultaneously the activities of the group, social relationships among members, and wholeness of each person incorporating her/his body, mind, and emotions. Coyle stressed the idea that growth of individuals must be toward identifying with the good of the social whole, to use their capacities for social ends beyond themselves (Garvin & Reed, 1995). Although many early group workers actually agreed with contemporary discriminatory beliefs related to race and ethnicity, processes of collaborative practice, holism, and integration of personal and political issues that are now considered central elements of feminist practice were also the concern of settlement group workers (Bricker-Jenkins & Hooyman, 1986; Garvin & Reed, 1994, 1995; Iglehart & Becerra, 1995).

Group work did not formally become linked with social work until the National Conference of Social Work took place in 1935, and this identification increased significantly during the 1940s and 1950s (Toseland, 1995). During this period of development in group work the social goals, remedial, and reciprocal models evolved separately. Each model differed in goals, theoretical base, and methods. The focus of the social goals model was on assisting individuals to engage in activities for the common good, the remedial model on altering and reinforcing individual level changes, and the reciprocal model on negotiating interactions between individuals and the social environment (Middleman & Goldberg, 1987). Each model came to be associated with different schools of social work and arenas for practice.

However, with the decline of the settlements and the movement of social work into mental health roles, group work has changed and lost some of its initial predominance in the field. Contemporary group work practice builds upon the traditional models while incorporating other aspects of practice such as an understanding of cognitive behavioral or social systems processes. Most group practice involves a goal-directed, planned process (Garvin, 1996). The goals can be educative, affiliative, supportive, treatment-oriented or task-focused. In addition, a growing body of knowledge exists about small groups and the ways in which the group context influences change. Concepts such as group structure, process, development, and culture have emerged to alert the social worker to important dynamics of the group that are key to understanding the change process (Garvin, 1996).

During the past two decades, attempts to revitalize group work within social work have continued. For example, the Association for the Advancement of Social Work with Groups has expanded into an international association and includes a liaison to the Council on Social Work Education (CSWE). There are also standards for practice for group-work education. A recent review of the group work literature found that the growth in volume of group work literature over the past decade occurred as the number of journals promoting group work emerged. The increase in group work research articles also occurred over the study period with a closer review indicating the need for more theory-building articles (Feldman, 1986). This literature suggests that small groups can be powerful change agents that promote social contact and that they are a means through which an individual's attitudes, relationship skills, and coping abilities can be influenced (Garvin, 1996).

A FEMINIST PERSPECTIVE ON GROUP WORK PRACTICE

Only recently have issues of race, ethnicity, and gender been given specific attention in studies of group work practice (Davis & Proctor, 1989; Garvin, 1996; Garvin & Reed, 1994; Lee, 1994). Traditional theorists and practitioners have assumed that one who is adequately trained in group work will be able to work effectively with all people, regardless of race or gender. Current thinking on group work has identified ways in which one's social identity can have an impact on group structures and processes. This literature has focused on the many elements of identity—gender, race, ethnicity, age, and other ways in which our social location will affect interaction (Davis & Proctor, 1989; Lee, 1994; Lewis and Kissman, 1989).

Our perspective on gender in group work emerges from a feminist understanding of the impact of social location on individual and community experience (Collins, 1990; Lewis & Kissman, 1989). We consider gender—the sociocultural meaning given to sex differences—to be one of many significant social identities to be considered in practice. Our perspective draws upon the work by Lee (1994), who emphasizes the importance of having a "fifocal vision" that considers five perspectives simultaneously on any given practice situation: history, social ecology, ethclass, feminism, and critical theory. Attending to these different dimensions of human experience provides depth and richness to the practice encounter.

This feminist multicultural perspective on group work involves linking group methods to an individual's social, historical, and political environments to affect change, for both facilitators and members (Garvin & Reed, 1995; Lee, 1994). Practice should focus on change on all levels—personal, interpersonal, and political. Group work interventions must address issues of power, consciousness-raising, self-identification, bicultural (or multicultural) socialization, and oppression (Garvin & Reed, 1995; Gutiérrez, 1990; Lee, 1994; Lewis, 1992). The impacts and influences that larger societal patterns and inequities have had on group members are important. Feminist group work strategies include the ability to identify "invisible group members"—that is, those extended family, significant other, and friend networks that influence the group member's behavior and actions in the group. A significant consideration is the inherent power discrepancy between professional leader and lay group member.

In order to engage in this form of practice, students must learn to understand the impact of these dynamics on practice and ways to work effectively with these issues. A feminist perspective on groups transforms our understanding of critical areas of teaching for group practice, the purpose of the group, appropriate roles for leaders, and desirable group structures. Our knowledge of gender dynamics in groups provides important information for effective social work practice.

KNOWLEDGE FOR CURRICULAR TRANSFORMATION

This section has two major parts. The first focuses on scholarship, including theory and important knowledge, and the second on skills. Our definition of inclusion of gender into group work curricula includes special issues both for women and for men, as well as ways that gendered assumptions and gendering dynamics may be manifested in groups of all types. Thus, we use gender as both a noun and a verb to indicate (1) that gender is a social construction of biological sex and (2) that processes that create and re-create a range of characteristics and inequities associated with gender are active, recurring, and continuous.

Scholarship on Gender and Groups

Theoretical Perspectives

All of the social sciences, including history, have contributed to the knowledge base that is important for understanding smaller and larger groups. As in most bodies of knowledge, attention to gender and to women in unstereotyped ways is relatively recent and inconsistent. Most texts on group theory and knowledge still address gender primarily with regard to group composition, and even that is usually brief. Attention to race, ethnicity, sexual orientation, and other social identities are more absent. Recent works in cultural studies, women's studies, and from multicultural and feminist critiques of work in various disciplines and professions, including social work, are beginning to remedy earlier omissions. Some of this work focuses specifically on research on groups (see, e.g., Ridgeway, 1992), but other work that is relevant can be found in many theoretical traditions that have informed development of group work theories (e.g., systems theory, behavioral theories, and psychodynamic theories).

Principles of psychoanalytic theory can be used to understand how earlier social experiences and unconscious processes affect group formation and interaction. The nature of emotional ties between members and the leader and processes such as scapegoating, cohesion, contagion, and conflict among members are interpreted using psychoanalytic principles. For example, interpreting member behavior as a reenactment of family life, where members form transference reactions to the leader and particular members, can be used to explore unresolved conflicts by linking past behaviors with current ones. Through a deliberate process of gaining insight, members modify behaviors both within and outside the group. In addition to Freud (1922), the work of Bion (1959), Slavson (1946), Whitaker and Lieberman (1964), and Yalom (1985) have been most influential in applying psychoanalytic principles to groups.

The emphasis on psychoanalytic traditions on primitive drives ignores the importance of group dynamics such as roles, norms, power, consensus, and valence (Lewin, 1951). In addition, by viewing the group as a recapitulation of the family experience, the group leader is assumed to be associated with an all-powerful parent figure, usually the father, so that transference reactions to the group leader (and other members) and members' struggle for the leader's attention (e.g., sibling rivalry) center around a male ego ideal. From this perspective, stereotypes of a dominant male are more likely to be conjured up, and members will behave accordingly. Scheidlinger (1974), on the other hand, discusses the concept of the "mother group" within the psychoanalytic tradition, whereby members enter the group, experience anxiety upon group formation, and regress into interactions in search of a nonconflict, need-gratifying union with "mother." From this perspective, the group leader is seen as the benevolent mother, re-created for the needs of the individuals in the group (Duncan, 1995). Again, gender-role stereotypes of the nurturing female are thought to emerge. Feminist critiques of psychoanalytic approaches have identified these gaps and biases and have begun to develop transformed approaches to psychodynamic group work (de Chant, 1996).

Important contributions from learning paradigms have also influenced social group work practice. Learning theory (Bandura, 1977) explains group member behavior in terms of simple stimulus and conditioned responses or else through observation or vicarious reinforcement and punishment. Many contemporary models of group work within social work have incorporated behavioral practices such as setting measurable goals and using reinforcers to shape members' behaviors, including group norms and expectations and use of constructive feedback. Rarely do these approaches incorporate a gender analysis and critique into all aspects of the behavior-shaping process. A gender analysis would include examination of biases, shaping of goals and expectations, and what gender-related factors may provide, enhance, or inhibit positive and negative reinforcers (Gambrill & Richey, 1983).

Criticisms of learning theory call attention to the focus on individual behavior rather than behavior of the group so that a discussion of group dynamics is relatively absent (Toseland & Rivas, 1995). Another limitation is the total emphasis of learning theories on behaviors based on environmental contingencies that seem linear and mechanical, as opposed to behaviors based on one's free will.

Cognitive-behavioral approaches have emerged in an attempt to respond to such criticisms of learning theory by taking into account the individual's motivations, expectations, and other cognitive aspects of behavior, although little attempt is made to move this discussion into group-level functioning. Despite shifts in learning paradigms, these approaches typically do not fully incorporate our understanding of the ways in which gender-role socialization influences our beliefs, attitudes, and motivations. The section on gender and groups explores this notion in greater detail.

From the early influence of Coyle, groups have been considered to create a reciprocal process between the individual members, the group, and the social system in which the group is embedded. This conceptualization set the stage for social work's emphasis on a systems perspective that takes into account both group participants and complex processes operating both within the group and between the group and the social environment. Parsons (1951) is perhaps most influential in applying systems principles to groups, although Bales (1950) and Homans (1950) developed interpretations of systems approaches. Conceptually, the various systems approaches emphasize the group as a dynamic whole emerging from member interactions. Such dynamism constantly affects group equilibrium and existence. A systems approach acknowledges the transaction between the group and external environment in which it is embedded, as well as internal influences, and the powerful effects of group forces on member behaviors. A systems approach also highlights the developmental nature of the group. This approach can be supportive of a feminist understanding because it is built upon a holistic foundation. However, it is limited by the degree to which it does not incorporate a gendered understanding of ways in which power differentials in gender, race, class, or other factors will influence group process. In the following section we note how all aspects of these interacting subsystems are shaped by gendering processes.

Students must ask critical questions about the absence of gender-related knowledge so that they can identify the potential biases in theories. Perhaps then they will be able to contribute to the development of gender-informed knowledge. What is now known about the impact of gendering processes can serve as examples, especially if the instructor can reflect with students about the origins of this knowledge.

Knowledge About Gender and Groups

Knowledge and theory on small groups include methods used to generate knowledge about groups, theoretical approaches to the understanding of groups, types of groups, goals of groups, phases of group development, group structures (e.g., communication, sociometric, power, role), group processes (e.g., managing member relationships, decision-making), and such key concepts as group norms, cohesiveness, deviance, and culture. In addition to within-group issues, knowledge should include attention to the group's transactions with its environment and its relationships with other groups. Gender, race, and other inferred status characteristics are relevant to these transactions.

Gendering Before Members Enter a Group

The social work curriculum on groups should include gender-related aspects that members and leaders bring to groups from their past experiences. Relevant illustrative topics include the impact of gendered socialization, different societal role expectations (Eagly, 1987), and experience with gender-segregated peer groups (Maccoby, 1990). This literature suggests that both genders tend to have differential strengths and limitations. For example, women and girls tend to be stronger in intimacy skills and define themselves more "in-relationship-with others," while men and boys have more experience with working in competitive teams and define themselves more through "competition-with-others" or in relation to an abstract ideal (Jordan, Kaplan, Miller, Stive & Surrey, 1991; Maccoby, 1990). Research is beginning to document women's different "ways of knowing" (Belenky, Clinchy, Goldberger & Taruli, 1986) and gendered patterns of language and communication (Tannen, 1990). Women and girls are also more likely than men or boys to have experienced past or current family or sexual violence (child sexual abuse, rape, domestic violence), a situation that can create special safety issues in many kinds of groups.

Gendering Outside the Group

Members and the group itself will also be influenced by how gender is defined and experienced outside the group. For instance, some tasks and contexts are associated with one gender more than the other, which influences one's perception of who has more authority and skills on these tasks (Bartol & Martin, 1986; Butler & Geis, 1990; Carli, 1990;

Kent & Moss, 1994; Martin, 1992). Other illustrative topics include the literature on diffuse status characteristics (Berger & Zelditch, 1985; Fisek, Berger & Norman, 1991; Lockheed, 1985; Meeker & Weitzel-O'Neill, 1985), which includes considerable evidence that much of what is characterized as feminine behavior also characterizes the behavior of anyone who occupies positions with lower status in a society or social structure. Gender is a diffuse status characteristic because expectations associated with it are often broad and general. Every culture also has cognitive schema and expectations associated with each gender that differ from each other. In most cultures, female is less valued than male. These forces operate within groups, are brought into the group from the outside, and are reinforced outside the group even if they are challenged and changed within the group (Ridgeway, 1992). Gendered violence and social policies also will influence group members, even if the tasks of the group are unrelated to these forces or policies. This dimension most directly reflects the feminist axiom, "the personal is political."

The Effects of Gender Composition

Multiple types of research have informed the literature on group gender composition. Four types of groups have been researched: (1) groups in which one gender is a token presence within a group, (2) groups with skewed compositions (usually over 60% and under 85% of one gender), (3) balanced groups (containing from 40% to 60% of each gender), and (4) single-gender groups (all men or boys; all women or girls) (Kanter, 1977a, 1977b). The gender composition strongly influences the behaviors, perceptions, and effectiveness of the group.

In groups dominated by one gender, the token member(s) is especially stereotyped; the majority membership downplays its internal differences while focusing on its collective difference from the token. These dynamics interfere with the learning of all members and with group problem-solving. If the token is a valued male, then stereotyped dynamics may confer more power and influence on him. When women are tokens they are often greatly limited in their roles in the group and relegated to less powerful caretaking or sex-object roles (Kanter, 1977a, 1977c). In skewed groups, vestiges of token dynamics remain.

Single-gender groups differ substantially (Aries, 1977; Bartol & Martin, 1986; Carlock & Martin, 1977). Groups comprised of men tend to develop influence structures relatively quickly that remain stable over the life of the group. The members are often highly competitive, and have difficulty expressing feelings related to intimacy or vulnerability. Such groups can be very effective in task performance, although sometimes task performance is disrupted by inflexible power structures or competition (Stein, 1983).

By contrast, members of all-women groups tend to share personal information readily, and to participate in the group relatively equally over time. Conflict may present a special threat to group cohesiveness, since group members rather quickly develop personal relationships that they perceive will be jeopardized by conflict. Task performance may be less effective than for mixed groups and some all-men groups because relationships within the group may be as important to group members as task completion (Hagen, 1983).

Mixed groups also develop relatively stable influence structures, with some members speaking more and differently in the beginning and over the life of the group. Women are limited more to socioemotional roles in mixed groups compared to all-women groups, and are less likely to share personal information in mixed groups. This is especially the case with information about relationships and violence in past and present lives. On the other hand, men in mixed groups seem to be more relaxed with women present, compete less with each other, and share more personal information than they do in all-men groups. These differences are difficult to change, even when all group members are working to change them (Tower, 1979; Wood, 1987). Given the challenge of compositional dynamics, it has been suggested that mixed-gender groups should alternate with single-gender subgroups so that members can become aware of and examine their behavior in groups with different power compositions (e.g., Bernardez & Stein, 1979).

Gendering Processes Within the Group

Interactions within the group often illustrate and re-create gendering forces outside the group, even if group members are determined to operate differently. These include many of the dynamics and roles noted earlier, plus differences in ways that women and men express themselves and interact (see, e.g., Tannen, 1990), in the ways that sociometric structures develop and are structured, and in leadership patterns and relationships with the group's external environment. Studies suggest that differential patterns of participation between women and men in mixed groups, for instance, move toward more equitable proportions after a group is given feedback, but the participation rates of the two genders still differ markedly (see, e.g., Tower, 1979). Research in small groups on emerging influence and leadership is demonstrating that very complex patterns of relationships exist between the nature of the task, how competence is defined in the group, the group's composition, and its environment (Bartol & Martin, 1986; Eagly & Karau, 1991; Ridgeway, 1992).

Gender and Leadership

Gender and leadership has been studied along many fronts including: how leadership is defined; who emerges with influence within groups; behaviors of assigned or emerging leaders; and perceptions of the group members related to the gender (and race) of the group's leaders (Davis, Cheng & Strube, 1996; Eagly & Johnson, 1990; Eagly & Karau, 1991; Fagenson, 1991; Helgesen, 1990). If the group's task is perceived as a female task, one or more women members are more likely to be perceived as the most influential. Leadership is shared more equitably in all-women groups than in any of the other group compositions. Interestingly, women leaders need to be more interactive for group members of subordinates to feel as comfortable with them as they do with men leaders who are less interactive (Garvin & Reed, 1994). All of these findings have great implications for the education of social work students being trained to provide leadership within groups of various types.

A small body of research explores the impact of leader gender on member satisfaction and perceptions of the group and its leader and on group effectiveness. The research results vary depending on the style of leader behavior, the nature of the task, and how the research was conducted (Kent & Moss, 1994). Race and gender of the leader also interact in complex ways that are not yet well understood (Brower, Garvin, Hobson, Reed & Reed, 1987). What is clear, however, is that leader gender strongly influences many things in a group, and the impact may be greatest in the early stages of the group. In groups with women leaders, group members report feeling more anxiety early on, especially when the leader is not very interactive or nurturing (Garvin & Reed, 1994). Most of the research on gender and leadership suggests that unless one or more women have particular qualifications for leadership, men are perceived as more competent leaders (Butler & Geis, 1990; Carli, 1990; Eagly & Johnson, 1990; Eagley & Karau,

1991; Kent & Moss, 1994). Note in the following examples that these conflicts will have differential impact depending on a group's purpose.

Some investigators have posited a social role explanation for some findings: Expectations for a woman are not consistent with expectations for a leader. For instance, members in groups with women leaders may have greater expectations of being nurtured, and may experience anger or anxiety if this does not occur. People become uncomfortable when they cannot make consistent sense of a situation. If the goal of the group is learning about the self, such conflicts can make the potential for learning greater, while they could interfere with task performance if a group is working on a time-limited task (Garvin & Reed, 1994; Shimanoff & Jenkins, 1991).

Others have posed a status conflict explanation—the status of women is low and that of leaders is high—and that people are uncomfortable with this inconsistency (Ridgeway, 1992). Since gender is a stronger and more pervasive marker of status than group leader (which is relevant only within the group), gender-related assumptions about status and power may undermine people's willingness to cede leadership. In a group that values participation by all members, perceiving the leader as a lesser authority might help to facilitate member responsibility for the group. At minimum, women learning to be group leaders must understand that the authority dynamics are likely to be different for them than for their male peers, and from most of what is depicted in the literature (Reed & Garvin, 1984; Shimanoff & Jenkins, 1991).

Gender and Group Development

While there is limited research on this topic, available literature suggests that the usual "forming, storming, norming, performing" sequence is complicated by gender composition, and perhaps by the gender and other characteristics of designated leaders (Hagen, 1983). All-women groups and groups with women leaders may develop an emphasis on intimacy earlier, which will have implications when differences and conflicts emerge.

Alternative Explanations for Gender Differences

There is no consensus about why these systematic patterns of gendering in small groups occur. One approach argues that children learn pervasively about themselves, social relationships, and the larger society in gender-segregated peer groups, and thus learn different interaction rules and patterns. For example, boys use speech to assert positions of dominance and compete for attention, while girls use speech to maintain relations of closeness and equality, and nonchallenging criticism (Maccoby, 1990). Thus, each gender develops a subculture and theory about how culture can be used to explain resulting patterns (Maltz & Borker, 1982).

The social role approach focuses on the situation roles that men and women play. Different expectations and cognitive schemes that exist relative to these roles influence expectations in groups and shape behaviors in complex ways (Eagly, 1987; Eagly & Karau, 1991). Ridgeway (1992) observes in work, status, and power dynamics that what are considered appropriate feminine behaviors are also behaviors exhibited by those in lower status positions. Numerous studies have been conducted in which group leaders and members were given information that increased the perceived expertise of a designated woman leader. Both her behavior and group members' behaviors changed with relatively minimal interventions. Such work provides substantial evidence for power and status explanations, since we would expect cultural and role determinants to be less easily changed. The most relevant reviews yield evidence for all three of these theories, individually and jointly. Social work instructors should stay up-to-date on the developing research, and consider the implications for social work as new knowledge and theories emerge.

Practice-related Approaches and Skills

Social work has generated several distinct and overlapping approaches to group-work practice, including reciprocal groups, social goals groups, remedial groups, and self-help groups (Garvin, 1996; Magen, 1992). How gender is relevant will vary somewhat depending on the approach and on what theories a worker espouses. In remedial groups, for instance, a worker can exercise considerably greater control over most elements of a group. How authority in the group is defined, roles that members are likely to take, and the tasks and sequence of the group's work can vary substantially according to the approach taken. In this way skills required for students can vary, although certain skills are important regardless of the type of group. In this section we describe those skills we believe to be particularly important.

Self-Knowledge

The group worker is visible to all members, and is likely to receive both verbal and nonverbal feedback about how members are reacting to the group and its worker(s). In all forms of practice, knowledge of oneself is important—of one's skills and limitations, and how one's background and conflicts can influence judgments. Self-knowledge is especially important for group work, since the group worker operates with many individuals at once. Her/his characteristics are much more likely to be factors affecting both the members and the group as a whole.

If we are to work from a feminist and multicultural perspective, self-knowledge must include our own gender socialization, the various cultures in our background, and resulting social values and expectations that one has about human behavior. We must learn to recognize areas of privilege and disadvantage in our lives and how they have shaped us (McIntosh, 1992). We need to know how we are typically perceived by others who are similar to and different from us, and behaviors we are likely to elicit from others. We also need to understand deeply how societal forces shape all of us, although this shaping differs depending on our identity characteristics.

Developing, sustaining, and deepening these areas of knowledge requires ongoing cycles of action and reflection, often with others who are similar and different from us so we can learn from their experiences and feedback. We call this particular type of self-awareness, "critical consciousness" (Reed, Newman, Suarez, & Lewis, 1996). It involves a regular critique of our own and other's behaviors within their societal context. It also requires skills to become aware of forces that usually operate outside of our awareness, especially if we have experienced privilege on key dimensions. Group supervision, classroom activities, readings, and assignments should all assist group work students to develop and deepen critical consciousness.

Group Observation Skills

An absolute requirement for group facilitation is to learn to recognize key group dynamics and to collect information through observation and monitoring of one's own reactions. This information then must be synthesized to make hypotheses about what is going on in a group and develop an appropriate intervention to help the group with its tasks. Because they are often embedded in complex ways with other factors, learning to recognize gender-related dynamics can be difficult. As we are better at noticing those things that disadvantage us, men may need to work very hard to recognize dynamics that privilege them. Gendering processes occur so frequently that we take them for granted, and we either never learn to see them or mislabel them as arising from other sources. In fact, behaviors and processes with gendered components are also likely to be determined from multiple sources and have other elements active within them as well. Instructors concerned about gender in their teaching about group work will need to develop multiple ways for students to practice observing and giving each other feedback about what they observe. This can occur within the classroom or via assignments in their field settings.

Group Facilitation and Leadership Skills

Some kinds of group facilitation involve learning particular language that can catalyze a group to examine behaviors and understand them differently, or to move to another phase or level of work. Facilitation skills can focus on the overt task or purposes of the group, or on the multitude of processes necessary to help a group to form and work effectively. What is needed from a facilitator will vary depending on the purpose of the group and the phase of development, and whether the group is open-ended with some membership turnover or maintains a stable membership throughout. Resources are beginning to be available to provide some guidance for what Van Nostrand (1993) calls "gender responsible leadership." There is also a growing feminist group work literature (Butler & Wintram, 1991; Reed & Garvin, 1996), that addresses gender-related issues within therapeutic groups (de Chant, 1996) and gender-related dynamics within groups formed for social action.

Skills for Different Stages and Tasks of Groups

Skilled group workers can modify how they approach groups to fit the goals, composition, and issues of a group. Part of the knowledge and skills needed will be an ongoing awareness of how one's gender, age, ethnicity, disability status, and other characteristics are likely to be important in a group. Sometimes the most effective intervention is to make the element of concern salient for all group members so that they can be aware of potential positive and negative effects, and so that destructive dynamics can be confronted together.

Since gender membership is so important, this should be considered in composing a group. In general, it is best to avoid token dynamics, since they are very difficult to manage or change and almost never have positive consequences. What is needed from leaders for other compositions differs. All-men groups often need strong leadership that confronts tendencies to intellectualize and compete and role models of cooperative behavior and openness. All-women groups may need special attention to norms and skills to address differences and conflict. Mixed groups need special vigilance so that women are not relegated to secondary roles; in fact, this so often happens that some recommend that mixed groups be done only if single-gender subgroupings occur periodically to surface the gendered dynamics within the mixed group.

In orientation to the group, it is important to develop ground rules that support examination of gender-related dynamics informed by the different needs of both female and male members. These ground rules will need to be revisited and updated as a group progresses. The development of group norms and expectations can take place collaboratively with group members creating rules that relate to current group concerns and conditions. In order for them to be effective, it is important that ground rules be updated and analyzed during the life of the group.

Many other skills are necessary for group leadership, including facilitating member participation and common gender schema, dealing with the scapegoating of tokens and others who are deviant or threatening to a group, developing member skills and empowerment, addressing issues of authority and power, developing group cohesiveness without destructive conformity, managing member intimacy within the context of a group's goals, and helping a group to develop roles and procedures that facilitate task performance. Finally, a group worker has to learn to monitor and evaluate a group's performance, factoring in measures that can track gender-related dynamics.

This brief discussion of the content for group courses suggests that students become familiar with knowledge regarding the impact of gender on group interaction and be prepared to intervene effectively with the dynamics that develop. Female students should be prepared to understand that gender, and gender role expectations, could lead to different reactions by male and female members. All students should be familiar with ways that group composition affects interaction. If they understand that men in predominantly male groups are unlikely to recognize the contributions of females, they can build in group tasks and norms that encourage balanced interaction and intervene if women's contributions are overlooked. This knowledge is equally applicable for group practice on all levels.

TEACHING ABOUT GENDER AND GROUP WORK

Locating Gender and Groups in the Social Work Curriculum

Where and how can we best introduce material on group work in the social work curriculum? We believe there is much merit in specialized courses on group work in which students and faculty can focus on approaches to practice and techniques for groups of various types. Knowledge can be developed in more depth and in ways that stress the importance of gender and other identity dimensions that can be explored across many topics. In specialized courses, readings and classroom activities can be linked with experiences in the professional practicum in multiple ways. Class demonstrations can illustrate key readings, and class members can be asked to observe (and code) gender-related dynamics in groups willing to be observed. Activities to develop critical consciousness and skills in recognized gender-based dynamics are especially important.

However, specialized courses on group work are unlikely to reach everyone and may not help students to see the relevance of group work in many settings, fields, and modes of practice. In addition, as we have noted, only a proportion of social work schools offer separate group-work courses. Thus, it is important to consider how to infuse gender and group-work education throughout a curriculum. Exactly how to organize group-work knowledge and skills within a curriculum will depend on how a particular curriculum is organized and what it emphasizes. We present here some examples and principles of relevant group knowledge and where it might be located, as well as some gender issues that are important for each.

Since groups of many kinds mediate between the person and her/his environment, content about groups must be introduced initially and throughout the curriculum. Foundation human behavior and social environment courses should include basic group concepts such as membership, boundaries, cohesion, norms, roles, influence, and leadership. Courses should also incorporate knowledge about how groups affect their members, how members affect each other, how members contribute to groups, and how gender operates in each area. Methods for studying groups should be introduced, perhaps by reviewing some classic experiments and approaches that have generated some of our most basic knowledge about groups. Noting the absence of attention to gender when relevant, and asking about patterns related to gender (and other social and status categories), will help students to notice and track these patterns early.

Methods courses should incorporate the use of groups in interventions of different types, including prevention that builds on social support, individual change and growth, community mobilization and change, organizational planning and coordination, policy development and enactment. Basic skills in group observation and participation should be emphasized in these courses so that gendered patterns within groups can be identified and observed, and so that interventions can be developed to either build on them or work to change them. Methods courses can also assist students to develop skills for groups with different tasks, for different stages in group development, and for groups with different durations and structures. These activities can take place in both micro and macro methods courses. For example, students in administration courses can be involved in observing processes in task groups at their field placements and learn skills for working with these dynamics. Courses should introduce the fact that groups are important elements in all forms of social work methods.

Courses on community and community organizing can include theory, research, and content on neighborhood groups (anomie and affiliation) and on intergroup relations (conflict and cooperation). Gendered dynamics within groups can be discussed and studied, as can community-related issues that have a greater impact on one gender in a community. Courses on human service organizations can include information on roles and groups within organizations, including teams, task forces, and boards. Much of the work on gender composition in formal organizations, and gendered dynamics in management and supervision, will be relevant in such a course (see, e.g., Fagenson, 1991; Martin, 1992).

Courses on the family should include the perspective that families are groups and can be described and analyzed using most concepts, dimensions, and methods employed in the study of groups. Gendered patterns throughout the life cycle usually include peer relations at different ages, with peer and referent groups as important elements in social influence and social support. Members of both genders spend much time in single-gender peer groups, especially during childhood and adolescence, but also later in the life cycle. Peer group size, common tasks, norms, and structures differ substantially depending on the group's gender, and these differences have many implications for the skills that members are learning and practicing. Girls and women form smaller groups and focus more on intimacy and relationships, while boys and men, in larger groups, learn much about participating in teams, negotiating conflicts, and developing hierarchies and rules to manage complex tasks and conflicts.

Using Group Methods in Teaching Group Work Practice

Teaching methods for group work often involves "parallel processes." This refers to using the classroom as a group laboratory with students involved in facilitating and participating in groups in the classroom. This teaching method has been historically used with the understanding that only through action and reflection can students fully appreciate the complexity of understanding groups and develop the ability to intervene with groups.

The methods that we discuss here build upon that tradition while incorporating the feminist understandings which have just been discussed. They are based in notions of feminist pedagogy which suggest that principles of feminist practice can inform methods of education (Dore, 1994). A feminist pedagogical approach encourages students and faculty alike to experience groups within the classroom while taking time to analyze critically and act upon the gender dynamics they observe. The incorporation of a feminist perspective in group work education forces people to recognize the way in which "the personal is political" and how attention must be paid to the perspectives the worker/teacher brings to the practice setting. This method for education is one that can bring theories of gender and groups to life.

A feminist perspective suggests that we must ask participants to risk fully participating in the group, that attention to "direct and indirect power blocks" on the basis of social group membership be addressed, and that the group begin with a mutually chosen theme (Dore, 1994; Garvin & Reed, 1995; Lee, 1994). These principles can be used by group work co-learners in preparation for and in early stages of group work courses.

Tuning into Student Concerns

To be attuned to the needs, desires, concerns, and joys of participants' lives means immersing ourselves in the realities of our students. When most of us began the higher education enterprise we were not forced to work full-time jobs. Yet the soaring costs of education means that many of our students do find full-time work necessary. With the erosion of social welfare service delivery, recent social work graduates with little experience face a shrinking market and are often anxious about their job prospects. The presence of students of color, first-generation college students from working-class backgrounds, and openly gay/lesbian/transgender and bisexual students also bring different concerns about worldview and available options to the social work classroom. Grounding our methods of teaching and learning in the lived reality of ourselves and our students requires using material brought by students into our pedagogy.

Tuning into students can take place if we begin a class by scheduling time for sharing and discussion of emerging concerns related to the purpose of the course. Building this time into a class invites diverse inputs and discussion. This time can involve both small group discussions or discussions involving the entire class. These formats can be integrated as well. For example, in a course on generalist practice, students were divided into small groups to discuss issues that had emerged in their field placements. During this discussion one student expressed frustration that her field supervisor had forbidden her to discuss issues of sexual orientation with an adolescent female client. Group members encouraged the student to bring this issue to the class. With the support of her group, the student brought the issue to the entire class for discussion, support, and problem-solving. The instructor used the class as a group to analyze the issue and generate alternative actions. An environment of open discussion was encouraged so that all students could speak on the topic and present diverse viewpoints. Issues concerning sexual orientation, gender, power relationships in the field, and professional ethics were raised. The student and instructor developed a plan to bring this issue to the attention of the field instructor and the field office if necessary.

Understanding Social Location

Identifying common ground and interest so that all group members can risk full participation, applies to all class participants, including the instructor. Using didactic discussions and writing exercises can help to develop some of this common ground, but the class as an entity can use the fifocal approach to position itself within the social work program, the educational institution, the state, the country, and the global community. Similarities and strengths must be identified within the class in this beginning phase, which may allow for more comfortable discussion of differences at later points, and this identification can be accomplished through using the global rather than the individual lens. Class exercises focusing on social location are useful for supporting this kind of discussion and modeling how these discussions can take place.

Many exercises exist that can assist students to identify and explore their social identities and how they relate to social location (McIntosh, 1989; Schoem, Frankel, Zuñiga & Lewis, 1995). For example, the Twenty Statements Test can be used as a preliminary exercise. In this simple exercise for exploring social identity, students are asked to provide twenty replies to the question "Who am I?" Individuals typically respond to this question with social roles, social identities, and characteristics. Responses to this question can then be shared, categorized, and discussed. Differences and similarities between groups of students may be discussed; for example, women are more likely to identify gender and gender-related roles than men. The implications of these responses for interactions in groups may then be identified and discussed.

The extent to which professors can use themselves as a mirror for students by modeling behavior can also influence this growth in the beginning class sessions. If we model our own ability to take risks and make mistakes, we are more likely to cultivate that behavior with other co-learners. Modeling this kind of behavior can be invaluable for students if they are learning to work in multicultural settings (Schoem et al., 1995).

Using Groups in the Classroom

Most instructors of social work routinely have students divide into groups for various class activities. Students also often work in groups on class assignments. These are invaluable opportunities for students to learn about group work and gendered dynamics, but such learning requires that the instructor prepare for the development of group-observation and feedback skills among class members and the time and materials to observe and review regularly what is occurring in these classroom and task groups.

Classroom and group observers can be selected for every activity, to watch and record what occurs within groups or the class. Everyone will need training on how to observe, and what to observe, and how to give feedback in the ways most easily heard. Learning to distinguish between group level and individual level observation and feedback can take time, and interpersonal tensions must be managed. Group-observation forms can be developed for specific exercises that observers use to document observations.

Groups can also observe each other's work on the same tasks, to view similarities and differences. The competition that often develops between them can facilitate the quality of their work if it does not become too extreme. Group members can also be given questionnaires about their work and their perceptions of their group, which can be summarized and fed back to them to help them look at member satisfaction and participation.

Group activities can be incorporated into courses focused on any level of intervention: individual, family, group, community, or organization. They take a gendered focus when students are asked to attend actively to ways in which group composition affects patterns of participation. Using group assignments in this way reinforces theoretical material while encouraging students to explore the linkages between theory and practice.

Group observation and analysis can be built into class assignments. For example, in a course on advanced generalist practice, undergraduates worked together in small groups on a project that involved writing a paper and developing a class presentation. In preparation for working together, the class was assigned readings on group process and on task groups, and a class session was devoted to this topic. Throughout the term, students kept a journal of their group interactions that was handed into the instructor for comments and dialogue. Task groups were also required to videotape one of their planning meetings. Each student reviewed the tape to analyze their group interactions. Observations focused on dimensions such as stage of group development, leadership patterns, methods for dealing with conflict, and participation/communication patterns associated with race, ethnicity, and gender. At the end of the semester students wrote a brief paper reporting on their analysis.

Using Field Experiences

A high percentage of students receive an MSW without education and training for groups within their field placement. If we are to educate students for competent work with groups, then field activities must include a group component. Appropriate group experiences can include participation in task groups, observing community and organizational meetings, facilitating self-help or support groups, or facilitating treatment groups. Field experiences can all be useful for identifying ways in which gender roles and composition have an influence on group process and outcomes. Even if students observe groups only within an organization or community, they will have an opportunity to learn.

Using Gender Dynamics in the Classroom

Teaching about groups from a gendered perspective requires using a gendered perspective while teaching. Therefore, faculty should use their knowledge of issues such as group purpose, group leadership, and group composition when organizing the course. Attention should be paid to factors such as the gender, ethnicity or race, sexual orientation, and age of the instructor, and how these factors will influence the perceptions, expectations, and interactions of students. For example, students will have different reactions to female and male faculty when issues of gender equity are discussed. Male faculty may be viewed as "sensitive," while female faculty may be viewed as "strident" or "whining" about social conditions. Similarly, class members may expect female faculty to be more understanding and less challenging in their teaching style. Calling attention to how these factors affect classroom dynamics is a means for modeling the behaviors expected of group facilitators.

SUMMARY

This chapter begins with a question regarding content and strategies for integrating gender content into courses on groups. We have presented a number of ideas and strategies, as well as current knowledge regarding the significance of gender to group work. We would particularly like to underline the importance of teaching about groups for those of us concerned about issues of gender and gender equity. Group work with individuals, families, organizations, and communities has been an integral element of feminist practice. Given the small and decreasing number of schools offering specific courses on groups and group practice, it is incumbent upon those of us concerned with gender issues to ensure that group content is integrated into all areas of the curriculum—particularly micro *and* macro practice courses. If we are to use groups as a means for achieving greater gender equity, we need to place a priority on group work education for all students.

APPENDIX 5–1: INTEGRATING GENDER INTO AN EXISTING SOCIAL WORK COURSE WITH GROUP CONTENT

The course depicted here is built on HBSE foundation and practice content, and uses concepts derived from group dynamics and small group theory. The entire course outline includes sessions on the following sections and topics:

Section I: Knowledge Base of Groups and Group Work

1. Definition of a Group
2. Social Work with Groups: From Theory to Practice
3. Values, Ethics, and Professional Guidelines
4. Group Work and Underrepresented Populations

Section II: Achieving Change Through Small Groups

5. Group Structure and Formation
6. Group Process and Development
7. Group Leadership: Roles, Functions, and Guidelines
8. Task Groups: Foundation and Specialized Methods
9. Self-Help/Mutual Aid Groups

Section III: Phases of Group Work Practice

10. Pregroup and Beginning Phases
11. Group Transitions
12. Ending Groups

13. Assessment and Evaluation in Groups

We have chosen in this appendix to highlight how one standard objective might be operationalized in a general course. This objective assesses the impact of social group memberships such as gender, race, ethnicity, and social class on various aspects of group functioning. Three specific sessions are outlined below, with illustrations of readings and assignments related to the integration of content about gender in the course.

Week 5: Group Structure and Formation

Readings

Toseland, R. (1995) Chapter 5, The planning stage. In R. Toseland (Ed.), *An introduction to group work* (2nd ed., pp. 141–171).

Forsyth, D. (1990). *Group dynamics* (2nd ed.). Pacific Grove, CA: Brooks/Cole. Chapter 3(pp. 51–73); Chapter 5, Group structure (pp. 109–133).

Brower, A. (1989). Group development as a constructed social reality: A social-cognitive understanding of group formation. *Social Work with Groups, 12* (2): 23–41.

Carlock, C.J. & Martin, P.Y. (1977). Sex composition and the intensive group experience. *Social Work, 22*, 27–32.

Chau, K. (1992). Needs assessment for group work with people of color: A conceptual formulation. *Social Work with Groups, 15* (2/3), 53–66.

Corey, M. & Corey, G. (1992). *Groups: Process and practice* (4th ed). Pacific Grove, CA: Brooks/Cole. Chapter 3, Forming a group, (pp. 41–103).

Wood, W. (1987). Meta-analytic review of sex differences in group performance. *Psychological Bulletin, 102*, 53–71.

Session Outline

- The Relationship Between Group Structure and Outcomes
- The Role of Pregroup Assessment: Understanding Social Location
- Gender and Group Development
- Self-Assessment: Roles of Social Workers in Groups

In-Class Exercise: "Who Am I?"

The Twenty Statements test is an exercise used to help individuals identify their various social identities. Students list 20 answers to the question "Who Am I?" Answers can be as diverse as students' experiences allow, but each answer should reflect some attribute of importance to the individual. The purpose is to analyze the individual's social and gender identities.

After each student completes their list, responses are shared, and then categorized and discussed as a group. Common categorics include: family roles (daughter, sister, brother), social roles (worker, student, renter), or those related to social categories (woman, Latina, lesbian). Responses to this question will reflect those most salient to the individual student and roles related to the social context. A "fishbowl" is then used to help students explore the implications of the categories of their responses for group formation and group structure. A fishbowl exercise allows a group to observe and analyze group process. In a fishbowl exercise, two groups are formed. These two groups then sit in concentric circles. The outside group will silently observe and take notes. In some versions of a fishbowl exercise, the facilitator of the exercise will invite members of either group to stop the process to make comments and suggestions, or perhaps to move from one group to the other. At the end of the fishbowl exercise, the debriefing will focus on both the observations of the topic and on the experience of sitting within or outside of the "bowl." At the same time, students not actively participating in the fishbowl are instructed to create seating charts for the fishbowl and identify the frequency and patterns of communication among its members, as well as patterns related to gender, power, and status. Outer circle students then switch places with those in the original fishbowl and report their findings. The entire class will then engage in a debriefing discussion that will focus on the following: the gendered patterns of group communication; comparisons of the two "fishbowl" groups, and the participants' comfort/discomfort with the process of listening and speaking.

Week 6: Group Process and Development

Readings

Forsyth, D. (1990). *Group dynamics* (2nd ed.). Pacific Grove, CA: Brooks/Cole. Chapter 4, Development and Socialization, (pp. 75–99); Chapter 10, Decision-making, (pp. 283–315); Chapter 12, Conflict, (pp. 351–387).

Aries, E. (1977). Male-female interpersonal styles in all male, all female and mixed groups. In A. Sargent (Ed.), *Beyond sex roles* (pp. 292–298). St. Paul, MN: West Publishing.

Brower, A.M., Garvin, C.D., Hobson, J., Reed, B.G. & Reed, H. (1987). Exploring the effects of leader gender and race on group behavior. In Lassner, J., Powell, K., and Finnigan, E. (Eds.). *Social group work: Competence and values in practice* (pp. 129–148). New York: Haworth.

Budman, S., Soldz, S., Demby, A. & Merry, J. (1993). What is cohesiveness? An empirical examination. *Small Group Research, 24*(2), 199–216.

Corey, M. & Corey, G. (1992). *Groups: Process and practice* (4th ed.). Pacific Grove, CA: Brooks/Cole. Chapter 8, Group process and practice in perspective, (pp. 247–280).

Fisek, M.H., Berger, J. & Norman, R.Z. (1991). Participation in heterogenous and homogenous groups: A theoretical integration. *American Journal of Sociology, 97*, 114–142.

Gummer, B. (1987). Groups as substance and symbol: Group process and organizational politics. *Social Work with Groups, 10*(2), 25–39.

Kroon, M., VanKreveld, D. & Rabbie, J.M. (1992). Group versus individual decision making: Effects of accountability and gender on groupthink. *Small Group Research: 23*(4), 427–458.

Woolsey, L. & McGain, L. (1987). Issues of power and powerlessness in all woman groups. *Women's Studies International Forum, 10*(6), 579–588.

Session Outline

- Participation in homogenous and heterogenous groups
- Power in groups
- Methods of building cohesion
- Leadership of groups: The impact of social group membership

Assignment

The purpose of this assignment is to gain skills in observing group process and interaction in a variety of settings. In order to conduct this assignment, each student will select and participate in an open membership group that will be the focus of the observation. This group could include an ongoing staff meeting or task group at the field placement, a self-help group, or a treatment group conducted by the student. Group observation reports will be completed and turned in three times over the term. These reports will include the following:

1. A breakdown of the gender, ethnic/racial, and age composition of the group.

2. A sociometric diagram of the communication patterns and participation.
3. Description of the quality of communication in the group—e.g., emotional tone, level of involvement by members.
4. Discussion of how norms have been established, renegotiated, and enforced.
5. Analysis of leadership styles and ethical dilemmas that arise.
6. Discussion of the stage of group development.
7. Examples of how conflict arises and its management.
8. Ways in which individuals leave the group—how is termination managed?

The report should include two or more concluding pages that integrate and summarize this material around important questions. How well is this group functioning? How does this group conform to or conflict with the theories discussed in class? In what ways do gender, ethnic/racial, or other dimensions of difference affect group interaction?

Week 11: Group Transitions

Readings

Corey, M. & Corey, G. (1992). *Groups: Process and practice* (4th ed.). Pacific Grove, CA: Brooks/Cole. Chapter 5, Transition stages of a group, (pp. 145–188).

Berman-Rossi, T. & Cohen, M. (1988). Group development and shared decision-making working with homeless mentally ill women. In J. Lee (Ed.), *Group work with the poor and the oppressed* (pp. 63–78). Binghamton, NY: Haworth.

Galinsky, M. & Schopler, J. (1989). Developmental patterns in open-ended groups. *Social Work with Groups, 12*(2): 99–114.

Hagan, B. (1983). Managing conflict in all women's groups. In B. Reed & C. Garvin (Eds.), *Groupwork with men/groupwork with women* (pp. 95- 104). Binghamton, NY: Haworth.

Martin, P. & Shanahan, K. (1983). Transcending the effects of sex composition in small groups. *Social Work with Groups, 6*(3/4), 19–32.

Milgram, D. & Robin, J. (1992). Resisting resistance: Involuntary substance abuse group therapy. *Social Work with Groups, 15*(1), 95–110.

Session Outline

- Types of group transitions
- Preparing for transitions in groups
- Recognizing a readiness within the group for transitioning
- Leader and member roles in group transitions

Assignment

A. The class will be divided into four working groups. Each group represents a phase in the group work method: pregroup preparation, beginnings, transitions, and endings and termination.

B. Each of these phases will be the focus for discussion in one class. The working group assigned to a particular phase will be responsible for planning, presenting, and leading the class discussion on the topic for that week. Each group should prepare to do the following:

1. Present material on a particular phase and how it takes place in the agencies in which the students are placed. Describe how the phase relates to work with individuals, families, groups, communities, and organizations. Give examples of how human diversity (e.g., gender, race, ethnicity, and sexual orientation) plays a role in this work. Students can use a variety of methods to present this information, including panels, role plays, group exercises, handouts, transparencies, etc.

2. Facilitate a class discussion on this phase. Some options for the discussion include identifying critical questions for the class to explore, soliciting input on how the phase takes places in other agencies, or involving students in a skills-based exercise or role play.

C. Carrying out this assignment will require being able to work in a small group and to facilitate a large group discussion in class. Both skills are central to social work practice. Therefore, each small group will need to pay attention to their group process and ways they work together and use group knowledge to design the class presentation. All groups are required to videotape one of their planning sessions in the Media Center. Individual class members will then review their planning tape to analyze their own group process.

D. In your paper you should briefly summarize what you learned about the phase of the general model and group process through preparing and presenting the material. Analysis of your group process should use the group observation guide included in the assignment for the session on process and development.

REFERENCES

Aries, E. (1977). Male-female interpersonal styles in all male, all female and mixed groups. In A.G. Sargent (Ed.), *Beyond sex roles* (pp. 292–299). St. Paul, MN: West Publishing.

Bales, R. F. (1950). *Interaction process analysis: A method for the study of small groups*. Redding, MA: Addison-Wesley.

Bandura, A. (1977). *Social learning theory*. Englewood Cliffs, NJ: Prentice-Hall.

Bartol, K.M. & Martin, D.C. (1986). Women and men in task groups. In R.D. Ashmore & F.K. Del Boca (Eds.), *The social psychology of female-male relations* (pp. 259–310). Orlando, FL: Academic Press.

Belenky, M.F., Clinchy, B., Goldberger, N.R. & Taruli, J.M. (1986). *Women's ways of knowing: The development of self, voice, & mind.* New York: Basic Books.

Berger, J. & Zelditch, M. (Eds.). (1985). *Status, rewards, and influence.* San Francisco: Jossey-Bass.

Bernardez, T. & Stein, T.S. (1979). Separating the sexes in group psychotherapy: An experiment with men's and women's groups. *International Journal of Group Psychotherapy, 29*(4), 493–502.

Bion, W. (1959). *Experiences in groups and other papers.* New York: Basic Books.

Birnbaum, M.L. & Aurbach, C. (1994). Group work in graduate social work education: The price of neglect. *Journal of Social Work Education, 30*(3), 325–335.

Bricker-Jenkins, M. & Hooyman, N.R. (1986). *Not for women only: Social work pracitce for a feminist future*. Silver Spring, MD: NASW Press.

Brower, A.M., Garvin, C.D., Hobson, J., Reed, B.G. & Reed, H. (1987). Exploring the effects of leader, gender, and race on group behavior. In J. Lassner, K. Powell & E. Finnigan (Eds.), *Social group work: Competence and values in practice* (pp. 129–148). New York: Haworth.

Butler, D. & Geis, F. L. (1990). Nonverbal affect responses to male and female leaders: Implications for leadership evaluations. *Journal of Personality and Social Psychology*, *58*(1), 48–59.

Butler, S. & Wintram, C. (1991). *Feminist groupwork.* London: Sage.

Carli, L.L. (1990). Gender, language and influence. *Journal of Personality and Social Psychology, 59*(5), 941–951.

Carlock, C.J. & Martin, P.Y. (1977). Sex composition and the intensive group experience. *Social Work, 22*(1), 27–32.

Collins, P.H. (1990). *Black feminist thought: Knowledge, consciousness and the politics of empowerment.* Boston: Unwin Hyman.

Davis, L., Cheng, L. & Strube, M. (1996). Differential effects of racial composition on male and female groups: Implications for group work practice. *Social Work Research, 20*(3), 157–167.

Davis, L.E. & Proctor, E.K. (1989). *Race, gender and class: Guidelines for practice with individuals, families, and groups.* Englewood Cliffs, NJ: Prentice-Hall.

de Chant, B. (Ed.). (1996). *Women and group psychotherapy: Theory and practice.* New York: Guilford.

Dore, M. (1994). Feminist pedagogy and the teaching of social work practice. *Journal of Social Work Education, 30*(1), 97–106.

Duncan, S.C. (1995). On the group entity. *International Journal of Group Psychotherapy, 45*(1), 37–54.

Eagly, A.H. (1987). *Sex differences in social behavior: A social-role interpretation*. Hillsdale, NJ: Erlbaum Associates.

Eagly, A.H. & Johnson, B.T. (1990). Gender and leadership style: A meta-analysis. *Psychological Bulletin, 108*(2), 233–256.

Eagly, A.H. & Karau, S.J. (1991). Gender and the emergence of leaders: A meta-analysis. *Journal of Personality and Social Psychology, 60*(5), 685–710.

Fagenson, E. (Ed.). (1991). *Women in management: Trends, perspectives and challenges.* Newbury Park, CA: Sage.

Feldman, R. (1986). Group work knowledge and research: A two-decade comparison. *Social Work with Groups, 9*(3), 7–14.

Fisek, M.H., Berger, J. & Norman, R.Z. (1991). Participation in heterogeneous and homogeneous groups: A theoretical integration. *American Journal of Sociology, 97*(1), 114–142.

Freud, S. (1922). *Group psychology and the analysis of the ego.* London: International Psychoanalytic Press.

Gambrill, E. & Richey, C. (1983). Gender issues related to group social skills. *Social Work with Groups, 6*(3–4) 51–66.

Garvin, C.D. (1996). *Contemporary group work* (3rd ed.). Boston: Allyn & Bacon.

Garvin, C. & Reed, B. (1994). Small group theory and social work practice: Promoting diversity and social justice or recreating inequities? In R. R. Greene (Ed.), *Human behavior theory: A diversity framework* (pp. 173–201). New York: Aldine de Gruyter.

Garvin, C. & Reed, B. (1995). Sources and visions for feminist group work: Reflective processes, social justice, diversity and connection. In N. van Den Bergh (Ed.), *Feminist practice in the 21st Century* (pp. 41–69). Washington, DC: NASW Press.

Gutiérrez, L. (1990). Working with women of color: An empowerment perspective. *Social Work, 35*, 149–153.

Gutiérrez, L. & Lewis, E. (in press). *Empowering women of color*. New York: Columbia University Press.

Hagen, B.H. (1983). Managing conflict in all-women groups. In B.G. Reed & C. Garvin (Eds.), *Groupwork with women/Groupwork with men* (pp. 95–104). New York: Haworth.

Halpern, R. (1995). *Rebuilding the inner city: A history of neighborhood initiatives to address poverty in the United States*. New York: Columbia University Press.

Helgesen, S. (1990). *The female advantage: Women's ways of leadership*. New York: Doubleday.

Homans, G. (1950). *The human group*. New York: Harcourt Brace Jovanovich.

Iglehart, A.P. & Becerra, R.M. (1995). *Social services and the ethnic community*. Boston: Allyn & Bacon.

Jordan, J.V., Kaplan, A.G., Miller, J.B., Stive, I.P. & Surrey, J.L. (1991). *Women's growth in connection*. New York: Guilford.

Kanter, R.M. (1977a). Some effects of proportions in group life: Skewed sex ratios and responses to token women. *American Journal of Sociology, 82*, 965–990.

Kanter, R.M. (1977b). Women in organizations: Sex roles, group dynamics, and change strategies. In A. Sargent (Ed.), *Beyond sex roles* (pp. 371–386). St. Paul, MN: West Publishing.

Kanter, R.M. (1977c). *Men and women of the corporation*. New York: Basic Books.

Kent, R.L. & Moss, S.E. (1994). Effects of sex and gender role on leader emergence. *Academy of Management Journal, 37*, 1335–1346.

Lee, J. (1994). *The empowerment approach to social work practice*. New York: Columbia University Press.

Lewin, K. (1951). *Field theory in social science: Selected theoretical papers* (1st ed.). New York: Harper.

Lewis, E. (1992). Regaining promise: Feminist perspectives for social group work practice. *Social Work with Groups, 15*(2/3), 271–284.

Lewis, E. (1995). Toward a tapestry of impassioned voices: Incorporating praxis into teaching about families. *Family Relations,44 (2)*, 149–152.

Lewis, E. & Kissman, K. (1989). Factors in ethnic-sensitive feminist social work practice. *Arete, 14(2).* 23–31.

Lockheed, M.E. (1985). Sex and social influence: A meta-analysis guided by theory. In J. Berger & M. Zelditch (Eds.), *Status, rewards, and influence* (pp. 406–429). San Francisco: Jossey-Bass.

Maccoby, E.E. (1990). Gender and relationships: A developmental account. *American Psychologist, 45* (4), 513–520.

Magen, R.H. (1992). Practice with groups. In C.H. Meyer & M.A. Mattaini (Eds.), *The foundations of social work practice: A graduate text* (pp. 156–175). Washington, DC: NASW Press.

Maltz, D.N. & Borker, R.A. (1982). A cultural approach to male-female miscommunication. (1982). In J.J. Gumperz (Ed.), *Language and social identity* (pp. 196–266). New York: Cambridge University Press.

Martin, P. (1992). Gender, interaction, and inequality in organizations. In C. Ridgeway (Ed.), *Gender, interaction, and inequality* (pp. 208–226). New York: Springer-Verlag.

McIntosh, P. (1989). White privilege: Unpacking the invisible knapsack. *Peace and Freedom*. London: Women's International League for Peace and Freedom.

McIntosh, P. (1992). White privilege and male privilege: A personal account of coming to see correspondences through work in women's studies. In M.L. Anderson, & P.H. Collins (Eds.), *Race, class, and gender: An anthology* (pp. 70–81). Belmont, CA: Wadsworth.

Meeker, B.F. & Weitzel-O'Neill, P.A. (1985). Sex roles and interpersonal behavior in task-oriented groups. In J. Berger & M. Zelditch (Eds.), *Status, rewards, and influence* (pp. 379–405). San Francisco: Jossey-Bass.

Middleman, R. & Goldberg, G. Social work practice with groups. (1987). In A. Minahan (Ed.), *Encyclopedia of social work* (18th ed., vol. 2, pp. 714–729). Silver Spring, MD: NASW Press.

Parry, J. (1989). Social group work, sink or swim: Where is the group in a generalist curriculum? In M. Feit, J. Ramey, J. Wodarski & A. Mann (Eds.), *Capturing the power of diversity* (pp. 37–46). New York: Haworth.

Parsons, T. (1951). *The social system*. New York: Free Press.

Reed, B.G. & Garvin, C.D. (1984). *Groupwork with women/Groupwork with men*. New York: Haworth.

Reed, B.G. & Garvin, C.D. (1986). Feminist thought and group psychotherapy: Feminist principles as praxis. (1996). In B. de Chant (Ed.), *Women and group psychotherapy: theory and practice* (pp. 15–49). New York: Guilford.

Reed, B.G., Newman, P.A., Suarez, Z. & Lewis, E. A. (1996). Interpersonal practice beyond diversity and towards social justice: The importance of critical consciousness. In C. Garvin & B. Seabury (Ed.), *Interpersonal practice* (2nd ed., pp. 44–76). Englewood Cliffs, NJ: Prentice-Hall.

Ridgeway, C. (Ed.). (1992). *Gender, interaction, and inequality*. New York: Springer-Verlag.

Scheidlinger, S. (1974). On the concept of the "mother group." *International Journal of Group Psychotherapy*, *24*(4), 417–428.

Schoem, D., Frankel, L., Zuñiga, X. & Lewis, E. (1995). *Multicultural teaching in the university.* Westport, CT: Praeger.

Shimanoff, S.B. & Jenkins, M.M. (1991). Leadership and gender: Challenging assumptions and recognizing resources. In R.S. Cathcart & L.A. Samovar (Eds.), *Small group communication: A reader* (6th ed., pp. 504–522). Dubuque, IA: William C. Brown.

Slavson, S. (1946). *Creative group education.* New York: Association Press.

Stein, T. (1983). An overview of men's groups. In B.G. Reed & C. Garvin (Eds.), *Groupwork with women/groupwork with men* (pp. 149–162). New York: Haworth Press.

Tannen, D. (1990). *You just don't understand: Women and men in conversation.* New York: Ballentine Books.

Toseland, R. (1995). *An introduction to group work* (2nd ed.). Boston: Allyn & Bacon.

Toseland, R.W. & Rivas, R.F. (1995). *An introduction to group work practice* (2nd ed.). Boston: Allyn & Bacon.

Tower, B. (1979). *Communication patterns of women and men in same-sex and mixed-sex groups*. Harrisburg, PA: Women's Training Support Program.

Van Nostrand, C.H. (1993). *Gender-responsible leadership: Detecting bias, implementing interventions*. Thousand Oaks, CA: Sage.

Whitaker, D. & Lieberman, M. (1964). *Psychotherapy through the group process*. New York: Atherton Press.

Wood, W. (1987). Meta-analytic review of sex differences in group performance. *Psychological Bulletin, 102*(1), 53–71.

Yalom, I. (1985). *The theory and practice of group psychotherapy.* New York: Basic.

CHAPTER 6

Gender and Families

Janet Finn

INTRODUCTION

This chapter critically develops thinking about gender and family in ways that challenge and expand social work practice knowledge. Issues of family intervention and gender differences are key themes in social work. However, understandings of family and gender are too often assumed rather than critically addressed. I start from the premise that gender and family are social constructions (Collier & Yanagisako, 1987; Ferree, 1990; Ginsberg & Tsing, 1990; Ortner & Whitehead, 1981; Scott, 1988). By recognizing the mutual construction of gender and the family we can develop a more complicated vision of family that better reflects the diverse ways in which people imagine and craft family ties.

First, this chapter defamiliarizes the concept of family as a natural, fixed entity, and reframes it as a socially constructed arena of struggle (Hartmann, 1981; Stacey, 1990; Thorne & Yalom, 1982). I question the certainties that have enabled a very limited, historically specific notion of "nuclear family" to come to stand for and mask a contested terrain of gendered social relations (Nicholson, 1986). Second, I provide an overview of the predominant theoretical perspectives on the family that have informed social work knowledge and practice, situating them in historical context. I address separate spheres—functionalist, exchange, interactionist, developmental/life cycle, and systems theories—of the family. I consider their differences and overlaps and explore ways in which gender and power have been elucidated and obscured in these theoretical perspectives. For the most part, the dominant theoretical models have privileged a white, middle-class ideal family type, and in so doing have failed to recognize not only the inherent (hetero)sexism in their perspectives, but racism and classism as well.

Third, I respond to the shortcomings in these models by drawing on critical understandings of gender and family developed by feminist, practice, and poststructural theorists in a number of disciplines. Several themes resonate through this literature: challenges to the limits of objectivism (Haraway, 1987; Weedon, 1987); attention to relations of power, domination, and resistance (Foucault, 1978; Hare-Muston, 1991; Jennings & Waller, 1990; Komter, 1989) concern with human agency and the structuring of consciousness (Giddens, 1979; Ortner, 1989; Rosaldo, 1989; Sewell, 1992); valuing of experiential knowledge gained through the politics of everyday life (Smith, 1987); and commitment to knowledge for social transformation (Freire, 1990; Hartman, 1992). This rich literature offers new directions to expand social work knowledge and practice. I illustrate the relevance to social work in a number of areas including gender and family welfare; housework, caring, and kinwork; culturally diverse constructions of family; and the meaning and power of family in gay and lesbian relationships. I consider the implications of these insights for family-based social work practice.

Finally, I suggest possibilities for social work education that are informed by and responsive to the mutual construction of gender and family. I consider implications for teaching both in the classroom and in the field placement. Social workers must grapple with critical questions as we challenge our certainties of gender and family. What are the relations of power and forms of hierarchy that are maintained through particular constructions of gender and the family? How have these constructions informed and limited the knowledge base of social work? Perhaps as we engage with these questions we will move beyond expansion to the transformation of practice knowledge.

ARE WE FAMILY?

The concept of family has often been assumed rather than defined in social work literature. The prototype is the nuclear family, an enduring social institution established by ties of marriage and blood that link two heterosexual parents and their offspring. Around that core we elaborate "alternative" forms such as single parent, stepparent, and extended families. More reluctantly, cohabiting couples and gay and lesbian families have been added to the list of "alternatives." Implicit in the notion of alternative is that there is a correct family form, against which others are evaluated. Those who do not fit the prototype have been defined as broken, abnormal, unstable, and generally pathological (Gross, 1992; Schmitz, 1995). The richness of extended kinship systems, sustained among diverse cultural groups in the United States despite disruptive social and political pressures, remains on the margins of social work knowledge (Baca Zinn, 1990; Cross, 1986; Herring, 1989; Stack, 1974).

This fixed image of family has been subject to challenge by those whose visions and practices of lasting connection and support fall outside of its narrow bounds. Confronted with contradictions between the professional discourse and the realities of social practice, a number of social theorists have begun to speak of the "family in transition" (Aponte, 1991; Googins & Burden, 1987; Gross, 1992). Implicit here is a shift from one fixed entity to another equally stable form (Jennings & Waller, 1990; Leslie, 1995). Rather than engaging with multiple family forms and practices, we assume a stable order that has been temporarily disrupted, which will be resored with concerted political and scholarly rigor. Such assumptions lead to a dichotomized view of history that poses current upheaval against past stability. We tend to underestimate the complex dynamics of families in the making over time and overemphasize current struggles as something new. A more helpful view is to conceive of family as an arena of struggle where power and intimacy, conflict and support play out in shaping gendered and generational relations (Baber & Allen, 1992; di Leonardo, 1984, 1987; Ferree, 1990; Stacey, 1990; Thompson, 1992; Thorne & Yalom, 1982).

The contested terrain of family is reflected in debates over definition. Nicholson (1986) described family as a historically and culturally variable concept that connects positions within a kinship system and a household. Di Leonardo (1984, 1987) pointed to the problems of equating family and household. Baber and Allen (1992) describe families as powerful socializing institutions, arenas of affectivity and support, and tension and domination between genders and across generations. Hartmann kept it simple: "Any two or more individuals who define themselves as family" (1981, p. 8). Robson (1994), however, points out that family is a cognitive category enforced by law, noting that the term "family" appears no less than 2,086 times in the U.S. code (p. 980).

The very concept of "family" is not universal (Gittens, 1985). Family does not exist in all languages. Rather family is a culturally and historically located ideology and practice of more or less enduring forms of relationship. Given the ambiguities and contradictions in the ideology and practice of family, it seems that our central question should not be, Whatever happened to the nuclear family?, but rather, How did such a specific and limited view come to stand for and obscure such a complex social reality?

THINKING OF FAMILY: THE DOMINANT THEORIES IN SOCIAL WORK

Social work has drawn historically from sociological and psychological theories of the family in adapting and developing models and interventions. The major theoretical formulations whose premises continue to dominate the bulk of family theory and practice in the United States emerged in the post-World War II era. An ideology of separate spheres, which defined the "public" world of labor and politics as the male domain and the "private" world of home and family as the female domain underpinned theorizing on the family (Bose, 1987; Ferree, 1990; Jennings & Waller, 1990; Thorne & Yalom, 1982). As Baber and Allen (1992) summarize it, "The dual spheres approach attributes the traditional division of labor to industrialization, differential ability, preference, and/or socialization" (p. 178). It depoliticizes and de-economizes family issues (Fraser, 1990). The ideology served to both naturalize and justify the exclusions and divisions made along gender lines. The many poor women and women of color whose paid and unpaid labors transgressed those boundaries were defined as deviant, both their work and their womanhood devalued (Abramovitz, 1988; Dill, 1988; Jones, 1984). The notion of separate spheres was both truism and norm in popular and scholarly discourse of the 1950s that hailed the home as workplace for the woman and refuge for the man. In this context "modern" theories of the family emerged.

Theories of functionalism asserted that social institutions existed to serve a particular purpose (Parsons, 1971). The family was seen as fulfilling social needs of its members through its functions of reproduction, maintenance, social replacement, nurturance and support, and socialization (Bray, 1995; Holman & Burr, 1980). Functionalism focused on the interrelatedness and complementarity of particular functions necessary for meeting particular social needs (Smith, 1995). Emphasis was on the stability and smooth functioning of the system.

Conflict and resistance were seen as deviations from, rather than parts of, the functional process (Schmitz, 1995).

Parsons posited a division of labor in the family between instrumental and expressive functions, and identified them respectively with masculine and feminine family roles (Parsons, 1954; Smith, 1995). This formulation both drew on and reinforced powerful gender ideologies and hierarchies that penetrated the sociopolitical context in which Parsons was developing his theories. The internal division of labor in the family complemented and reinforced the external division between the private and public domains. Functionalists have argued that as society has become more complex, the nuclear family has become the most functional form for meeting those basic social needs (Clayton, 1979; Smith, 1995). Critics of functionalism, however, have pointed out the circular reasoning at work in defining need and function.

Exchange theories, drawing on economic models of rational choice, have also enjoyed popularity in family theory. Social actors are viewed as "profit"-motivated and self-interested (Edwards, 1969). Thus, investments in social relationships are made in terms of what one will gain. Each interaction is a negotiation involving assessment of one's resources, risks, and potential benefits (Cheal, 1991; Ekeh, 1974; Holman & Burr, 1980; Sabatelli & Shehan, 1993; Smith, 1995). Interestingly, this rather stark market analogy brought questions of power asymmetry into the family discourse. Conflict and competition, neglected by functionalism, could be addressed.

Exchange theory's prominence in the 1970s was not without criticism. The theory was important in understanding precarious human relationships such as courtships or marriages in crisis, but it proved harder to get at the complex, subtle, long-term exchange processes of relationships and the "(n)onrational factors such as love, jealousy, (and) self-esteem" (Holman & Burr, 1980, p. 732). Perhaps these insights speak more to the certainties of the dominant economic order in which exchange theory was embedded than to the dynamics of family.

By the 1970s, symbolic interactionism, which emphasized the human capacity for creating and negotiating meaning in interpersonal interactions, enjoyed popularity among family theorists (Holman & Burr, 1980; Stone, 1977). This interest was in part a response to the structural-functionalists who had privileged reified concepts and ignored the actors who constituted family. From the symbolic interactionist perspective, meaning is constituted through social interaction as social actors interpret the signs and symbols they encounter (Smith, 1995; White & Tyson-Rawson, 1995). This approach challenged fixed concepts of the "family unit" and looked instead to the multitude of ways that meaning and power may be negotiated between and among family members in their day-to-day interactions (Luckenbill, 1979). Their contributions have informed more recent discursive forms of family practice that look at people's lives as structured through language (White & Tyson-Rawson, 1995). However, symbolic interactionism neglected the larger systemic forces that shaped the meaning and power of gender and the family writ large (Hutter, 1981).

In 1980, systems theory was pronounced the "wave of the future" in family theory (Holman & Burr, 1980). Building from models of physics, general systems theory focused on systems as interacting sets of elements, exchange of energy and information within the system, hierarchical relationships between systems and subsystems, and the relationships among systems (Kuhn, 1974). Systems theory provided a compelling analogy for depicting family structure and function, envisioning the family as a "complete system." The family system was a dynamic whole greater than the sum of its constituent parts. It was also part of larger systems that could impact internal balance.

The simple and scientific nature of the systems analog lent it both appeal and authority. The discourse of systems has penetrated social work thinking and practice on the family. A family systems approach fit well with the more encompassing ecosystems perspective gaining prominence in social work in the 1970s (Lewis, 1991). This approach developed connections between human ecology and general systems theory to articulate a coherent view of person-environment interaction. The family systems perspective provides very salient discourse for representing intrafamily interactions and the relationship of the family and its members to a larger social environment.

Systems theories have been both praised and criticized for their encompassing generality (Broderick & Smith, 1979). They have also been faulted for lacking a temporal context. Models of family life-cycle development have sought to address this by theorizing families as "systems moving through time" (Carter & McGoldrick, 1989, p. 4). Family life-cycle models focus on the family as a unit and argue that families go through predictable changes over time (Aldous, 1990; Carter & McGoldrick, 1989; Glick, 1955). Drawing from Eriksonian models of individual psychosocial development, theorists have defined series of life stages that families "normally" pass through, from marriage to childbearing, child rearing, regrouping as a couple, retirement, and old age (Elder, 1985). Particular developmental tasks are associated with particular stages. Family crises may ensue if these "normal" transitions are not successfully negotiated.

The family life-cycle model, like the individual model on which it is premised, assumes a "normal" and linear progression for families. Those who are not constituted as a nuclear "unit" or who deviate from the trajectory have failed in their appropriate developmental tasks. Some theorists have sought to broaden the approach by considering life-course development (Aldous, 1990). This perspective incorporates three perspectives of time: individual, familial, and historical. It attempts to make meaningful connections between family development, the social and economic conditions that constrain and enable that development, and the personal crises and stresses that confront individual family members.

These diverse and at times overlapping theoretical perspectives generated debate and knowledge development among family theorists and practitioners that at times implicated gender more directly. For example, sex-role theorists of the 1970s drew from and critiqued functionalist models that had naturalized separate spheres and role complementarity. They began to articulate the gender stratification of society and division of labor by sex as historical rather than natural (Scanzoni & Litton-Fox, 1980; Ferree, 1990). Theorists began more systematic investigations of "gender norms" that raised questions about ideologies that shaped gendered behavior (Holter, 1970). These efforts tended to center around questions of preference, subjective assessment of interests, and socialization of gender roles (Scanzoni & Litton-Fox, 1980). Critiques of power and relations of domination were not part of the discourse.

The separate-spheres ideology has been soundly critiqued for obscuring links between home and the workplace, negating the internal politics of family life, and reinforcing notions of a single, unitary "family interest" (Ferree, 1990). However, as the notion of separate spheres began to be conceived as a normative ideology rather than a reflection of essential reality, it became a way of framing analyses that explored the meaning and power of this dividing line. For example, conflict theorists used a separate-spheres model to articulate the "role strain" experienced by women as they negotiated their labors in both the public and private domains. Family theorists drawing on Marxist critiques of capitalism addressed the connections between the gendered division of labor that accompanied industrial capitalist development and women's subordination in home and workplace (Hartmann, 1981; Sacks, 1975).

Likewise, social exchange theorists were expanding theory to address more complicated questions of choice and the negotiation and balancing of resources over time (Chafetz, 1988; Ekeh, 1974; Holman & Burr, 1980; Sabatelli & Shehan, 1993). These more nuanced analyses of social and economic exchange in the family laid the groundwork for making connections between gender stratification in the home and in the larger society and the mutually reinforcing relationship between them (Chafetz, 1988). They brought questions about the definition and deployment of power in families to the fore (Komter, 1989; Mizan, 1994).

Systems theory allowed theoretical space for the interplay among internal and external forces on family members. However its gender-neutral language omitted power and depoliticized relationships (Barrett, Trepper & Fish, 1990; Goodrich, 1991). Its application was often guided by certainties about boundaries, roles, and balance that implicitly encoded rather than explicitly challenged assumptions that reflected the gender stratification of the larger society (Walters, Carter, Papp & Silverstein, 1988).

Family life-cycle theorists have also worked to incorporate gender as well as issues of race, ethnicity, and class into their thinking and practice (Carter & McGoldrick, 1989). In *The Invisible Web* (1988), Walters et al. brought a feminist perspective to the family life-cycle model, challenged the patriarchal assumptions embedded in family systems theory, and showed how those assumptions disadvantaged women. They addressed gender-based difference in socialization, and the resulting inequalities. Drawing on Gilligan's (1982) gender-based analysis of moral development, Walters et al. questioned the gender-neutral assumptions of the family life-cycle model. For example, by privileging the "masculine" values of autonomy and independence, the "feminine" experiences of intimacy and relationship have been systematically undervalued.

In sum, the dominant theories of the family that have informed social work practice have been predicated on a white, middle-class U.S. nuclear family model. This very particular model has been universalized as the norm against which "deviant" family forms are evaluated (Rapp, 1982; Schmitz, 1995). Institutionalized systems of racism, (hetero)sexism, and classism that shaped the context of theory and practice and the privileged (white male) subject positioning of the majority of the theorists remain outside the bounds of the theoretical discourse (Baca Zinn, 1990; Hare-Muston, 1991). With few exceptions, the dominant theoretical models have not only been insensitive to gender issues. They have uncritically incorporated ideologies of gender and racial inequality that reflect and reinforce the structures and practices of gender and race stratification embedded in the social and historical context from which they emerge (Baca Zinn, 1990; Demos, 1990; Jennings & Waller, 1990; Jones, 1984).

THE FAMILY/GENDER SYSTEM

Since the second wave of feminism emerging in the 1970s, we have seen a broad range of knowledge development that promotes nuanced understanding of gender and the family. This important body of work has explored the social, political, and economic contexts in which gender and family are constituted; challenged the ideology of separate spheres; examined ways in which sex/gender systems are produced, internalized, and maintained; exposed the politics of motherhood; and critically addressed the reproduction of and resistance to gendered identities (Dill, 1988; Ginsberg & Tsing, 1990; Hartmann, 1981; Ortner & Whitehead, 1981; Reiter, 1975; Rosaldo & Lamphere, 1974).

Poststructuralists have focused on questions of language, subjectivity, discourse, and power in the construction of social reality (Weedon, 1987). They have argued that language constitutes, rather than reflects, social reality. The social world is produced through the ongoing negotiation of meaning and power. Similarly, subjectivity, the making of social selves, is a social and political process. The social world is discursively constructed, where "discourse" refers to the structuring of knowledge, modes of thought, social institutions, and fields of practice in ways that reinforce particular relations of power and forms of subjectivity (Foucault, 1978; Weedon, 1987). A number of feminist theorists have turned to poststructuralist insights in order to critique and "deconstruct" masculinist discourses and expose the power relations encoded in supposedly neutral representations of social reality (Weedon, 1987).

Practice theorists have grappled with the mutual constitution of structure and agency, the internalization of external systemic forces, and the remarkable capacity for creative human agency to change the conditions that shape consciousness and action (Bourdieu, 1977; Giddens, 1979; Ortner, 1989; Sewell, 1992). The notion of agency refers to the capacity of human actors to engage in critical, strategic action, even as powerful social forces shape the contours of their subjectivity and social reality. This concept of agency recognizes both the power and indeterminacy of structural forces in the making of social subjects. Taken together, these theoretical contributions provide creative possibilities for transforming social work thinking about gender and family. They provide the tools for deconstructing the dominant professional discourse on gender and family and critiquing the power behind the words.

A number of theorists have engaged in the critical deconstruction of gender as a contested social category and have called for rethinking the family as a political arena (Scott, 1988; Thorne & Yalom, 1982). Some have framed family as the place for social and historical analysis of power negotiated along gender and generational lines. As Flax (1982) argued, families produce *persons* who produce relations of gender, race, and class-based domination and subordination. Others have addressed the sexism and racism inherent in functionalist privileging of the nuclear family (Stack, 1974). For example, Stack documented the networks of exchange and support through which poor African-American women maintained extended bonds of kinship that crossed biological, generational, and household boundaries. She brought a "strengths perspective" to understanding the intersections of race, gender, and economy in the construction of family long before the term was a buzzword of social work.

One of the most cogent statements of the need to systematically address the relationship of gender and family was put forth by anthropologists Collier and Yanagisako (1987). They argued that kinship and gender are mutually constructed, realized together in cultural, political, and economic systems. They called for examination of how families both reproduce and resist forms of gender and class inequality at the same time that they nurture children. Gender and kinship need to be an integrated field of study in order to grasp their fundamental interdependent relationship.

In short, critical theorists have expanded the terrain of thought and action as they recognized gender as a relational process of negotiation rather than an essential quality. They traced the fundamental connections between the construction of gender and the family, and asserted that gender in families included "structural constraints, and opportunities, beliefs, ideologies, actual arrangements and activities, meanings and experiences, diversity and change, interaction and relation" (Thompson & Walker, 1989, p. 846). They have identified family as a key site for exploring the ways in which gendered power relations are constituted, reproduced, and contested over time.

ENGENDERING THE FAMILY IN SOCIAL WORK

Unfortunately, much of this critical knowledge remains tangential to mainstream social work practice with families. When gender is addressed in the family systems literature, it is more often additive than integrated. A chapter on "working with women" may be included, but questions of gender, power, discourse, and commitment to changing existing social relations are seldom addressed. Family-based practice continues to be informed more by models of psychotherapy than by theories of cultural politics.

Reporting on the state of the art in the 1990s, Leslie (1995) wrote that family therapy has ignore, or worse, pathologized three groups: women in families, racial/ethnic minorities, and gay and lesbian families. She contends that a monolithic family form still dominates and that family troubles generally remain relegated to the presumed private realm, devoid of their broader social and economic context. She pointed to the persistent tendency to conceptualize "problem families," such as "alcoholic" or "abusive" families, in language that suggests all members share equal responsibility. At an even more insidious level, the discourse and practice of family therapy sanctions homophobia and secrecy. Assumptions of heterosexism still go without saying (Leslie, 1995, p. 360).

Leslie's assessment of family practice at the close of the century is sobering. It calls for critical attention to the history of our practices in the hopes that we might develop other ways of knowing gender and family for the future. I turn now to key social work issues where uncritical assumptions have left a legacy of damage. I point to the alternative constructions of both problem and intervention that have been articulated by feminist theorists and practitioners.

Gender and Family Welfare

The field of child welfare is fraught with certainties about gender and the family (Sarri & Finn, 1992). "Traditional" ideologies of family and motherhood and practices of mother blaming persist in the mental health and child welfare fields (Carter, 1993). In the case of incest, for example, "good" mothers are expected to have something of an in-bred anticipatory response system. The good mother would surely know if her child were being victimized, and would intervene. Helping systems often perpetuate existing notions of mothering, leaving women disempowered at a time when they are in greatest need of social and emotional support (Carter, 1993).

The U.S. foster care system is also embedded in certainties about gender and family. The system is predicated on the moral overloading of motherhood and the economic undervaluing of women's work as caregivers (Meyer, 1985). As powerful cultural scripts about gender and family play out, birth mothers, foster mothers, and social workers often find themselves at odds in a contest of caring in which neither women nor children are winners (Finn, 1994). Deeply ingrained beliefs have constrained rather than enabled strengths-oriented solutions to child welfare problems. A discourse of "caring" is often used to mask practices of control aimed at women and children (Armstrong, 1996).

These critiques challenge us to rethink the language and practice that shape our definition of child welfare problems and guide the course of interventions. How might we be further endangering women as we attempt to "rescue" their children or preserve the family? How might we construct interventions that allow space for competing discourses of motherhood rather than imposing a single socially acceptable response and blaming those who resist the definition? And as we examine the construction of motherhood, we can also question the assumptions behind fatherhood.

A number of scholars have taken a historical approach to the deconstruction of gender and family ideologies in social welfare (Abramovitz, 1988; Gordon, 1990). Abramovitz's classic work, *Regulating the Lives of Women,* brought a gender lens to the history of social welfare policy in the United States. She traced the ideology of the "family ethic" and the "family wage," illustrating how they justified and reinforced particular constructions of manhood, womanhood, and worthiness. She exposed the racist and classist underpinnings of these ideologies that further marginalized poor women and completely excluded women of color from the rights of womanhood.

Fraser and Gordon's (1994) discursive analysis of gender, family and dependency laid bare the power relations encoded in the language of social welfare. They traced the "genealogy" of dependency, a key word in understanding the mutual construction of gender and family.

Keywords are those that become focal points in struggles, sites where the meaning and power of social experience are contested (Williams, 1976). They examined ways in which dependency has been mapped on to racialized discourses in which women have been villainized as either too dependent or too independent vis-à-vis the family. Fraser and Gordon's discursive turn prompts new questions about gender, family, and welfare. What images are encoded in the dominant discourse? What is at stake? How might "resistance" be reframed, not as pathology but as struggle to change the terms of debate that shape the "common sense" about gender and family?

Social workers can participate as active agents of change by challenging the politics of language and the language of politics that shape the meaning and practice of family. For example, our political leaders make frequent reference to "family values," "personal responsibility," and "legitimacy" as they try to outdo one another in demonizing social welfare. Social workers have a responsibility to unmask the contradictions and expose the assumptions behind the simplistic slogans. We need to offer an alternative common sense, one that respects family as a complex arena of struggle and support, and rejects the oppressive nostalgia of a mythic past.

GENDER, FAMILY, AND LABOR: POLITICS OF THE EVERYDAY

In addition to a critical sense of history and social context, social workers need an appreciation of the myriad daily activities that encode and enforce gendered identities and power relations that families maintain (and that maintain families). It is through the activities, habits, and dispositions of daily life that arbitrary certainties are internalized, naturalized, and contested (Bourdieu, 1977; Ortner, 1984; Sewell, 1992). The politics of everyday life encode and reflect the gendered subtext in the structure and practice of family (Smith, 1987). This section explores the construction of gender and family through three key practices: housework, caring, and kinwork.

Housework

"Housework," women's classic realm of unpaid labor, has been the subject of extensive feminist analyses (Googins & Burden, 1987; Hartmann, 1981; Oakley, 1974; Strasser, 1982). The popular media tells us that the times, they are a changin', and the postmodern men of the 1990s are, really, carrying their share. However, before celebrating this gender transformation, we need to look at what has remained the same. Demo and Acock (1993) found that, across family arrangements, and regardless of women's paid employment status, women performed two to three times more housework than their husbands or cohabitating partners. They concluded that "increasing family diversity has not changed the division of domestic labor" (p. 331). Rather, as Thompson (1992, p. 8) argued, housework and child care are at the heart of gender strategies in marriage.

Similarly, Thompson and Walker (1989) discuss the entanglements of women's unpaid labors in the home with a discourse of "love." The mundane, invisible, repetitive tasks that constitute women's work in the home have been constructed and naturalized not as labor but as demonstrations of maternal love. The practical reality of this love is demonstrated in child care practices where regardless of whether they have paid employment, women carry 90% of the burden of responsibility for child care. Interestingly, both men and women have tended to evaluate these skewed contributions as "fair" (Hochschild, 1989; Thompson, 1992). These evaluations speak volumes to the power of dominant discourses and practices to shape the structure of family feeling. Given the pervasive power of gender ideologies that constitute family work as a maternal act of love, men's minimal efforts will continue to count for more than women's monumental ones (Thompson, 1992).

Caring

The persistence of gender inequity in family work has caused a number of feminist scholars to deconstruct the certainties of caring and resituate caring as a nexus of the mutual construction of gender and family (Dressel & Clark, 1990; Ferree, 1990; Graham, 1983; Hochschild, 1989; Thompson, 1992; Wood, 1994). Dressel and Clark (1990) questioned why caring seemed self-evident and defied definition. What comprises family care and how is it expressed? They found some interesting gender differences in the way caring was defined. For example, women generally downplayed the importance of their practices of doing for and being with family members. Men, on the other hand, tended to valorize their comparatively paltry lists of contributions to family care. Interestingly, women showed much more dissonance between their caring activities and their thoughts and feelings about those activities than did men. Dressel and Clark (1990) concluded:

> These gender grounded observations suggest that family care may be a vehicle through which familial power relations are expressed at the very same time that it serves integrating functions both within and beyond the family. In short, who cares for whom, in what ways, under what circumstances, and to what end may be grounded in power relations that become mystified within the family and essentialized as "women's caring nature." It is a cruel irony if what endears women to their families also entraps them in an arrangement of subordination and provokes feelings and assessments by them that are at least partially and sometimes wholly negative. (p. 778)

Graham (1983) reconstructed caring as both labor and love. She critiqued the heavy symbolic load that the concept of "caring" embodies. Caring has been constructed as the key practice through which women achieve and demonstrate "femininity." Graham argued that once caring is stripped of its ideological cargo, it is reduced to "the obligatory transaction of goods and services which occurs within the patriarchal family" (1983, p. 17). Graham points to the transformative power in disengaging ideology from activity. Once we disentangle the knots of caring and feminine virtue, we expose the threads that connect practices of devalued labor to structures of economic power.

Kinwork

Di Leonardo (1984, 1987) opened another dimension in her discussions of "kinwork" in the way we think about gender, family, and labor. She argued that a reinterpretation of women's work and the family domain was needed to unearth relations among gender, kinship, and the larger economy. She focused on the conscious strategies of women's labors directed at the development and maintenance of kin networks (1987, pp. 441–442). Kinwork, she argues, has been a neglected dimension in understanding women as actors in these entangled arenas of family and economy. Women do the labor of maintaining kinship across households through diverse activities such as phone calls, letters, visits, and acknowledgments of birthdays and anniversaries, to the more symbolically loaded kinship celebrations at holidays. Kinwork is also an arena through which power among women is mediated. Through kinwork women may not only maintain family ties but also create obligations and claims to future reciprocity. Di Leonardo illustrates this with the account of a struggle between mother- and daughter-in-law over the venue of a holiday dinner. It is a struggle to claim the rights and obligations of kinwork, which reveals the intimate connections between self-interest and altruism (di Leonardo, 1987, pp. 451–452).

Kinwork gives us a new terrain for exploring women's agency, the capacity to reflect on, respond to, and perhaps change one's life circumstances. It suggests that the domestic domain is not only a place of women's subordination, but also one where women negotiate power, support, connections, and gratification (di Leonardo, 1987, pp. 449–450). The incorporation of kinwork into social work thinking and practice enables us to expand the discourse on gender and the family and think more critically about women's strengths as well as vulnerabilities (cf. Stack & Burton, 1993).

EXPANDING KNOWLEDGE OF FAMILY DIVERSITY

Thinking about gender and the family demands attention to lessons drawn from diverse cultural contexts and practices. In efforts to grasp the enmeshment of gender and family, we cannot afford to privilege gender to the neglect of race and ethnicity (Baca Zinn, 1990). And we cannot equate studies of gender with studies of women, making gender an issue only when women are under discussion (Arendell, 1992). To do so is to miss the relational dynamics of gender and power. The same holds for discussions of race, ethnicity, and sexual identity (Leslie, 1995). There is a tendency in the literature to take race, ethnicity, or sexual identity as an issue rather than as a given only when speaking of "people of color," those outside middle-class Anglo boundaries, or gays and lesbians. Such a view implicitly privileges a white, middle-class heterosexist orientation. It fails to address the processes through which racism, classism, and heterosexism are cultivated and reinforced, both within families and the larger society. Further, it limits our search for diverse lessons of strength and empowerment that might both inform "mainstream" practice and challenge the oppression inherent within it (Fine, 1993).

Baca Zinn (1990) encourages us to listen to and respect stories of survival and strength rather than pathology in understanding cultural diversity in the constructions of family and gender. The work of Zavella (1987) on Chicana families is a case in point. Zavella illustrates how women's family and wage labor responsibilities are entwined in larger systems of social, political, and economic inequality. She examines the many ways in which oppressive "borders" are created, and the constraints and contradictions women faced in their social locations as women, mothers, primary breadwinners, and Chicanas. She points to the need to examine the specific historic, economic, and cultural contingencies, and gendered strategies for responding to those circumstances rather than falling back on facile generalizations about gender, class, and ethnicity that may mask more than inform.

Segura and Pearce (1993) took this advice to heart. They critiqued Chodorow's theory of women's universal subordination through mothering by positing alternative constructions of multiple mothering within Chicana family systems (Chodorow, 1978). They point to the need to study the formation of gender identities in specific social, cultural, and historic contexts, and to recognize heterosexuality as an issue, not a given. Their study carefully examines distinct cultural features of familialism, *compadrazgo* (godparent relationships), and a collectivist orientation that shape the construction of gender and family in a working-class Chicano community. Their weaving of cultural patterns, political histories, and economic conditions challenges simplistic assessments of family differences under the gloss of "cultural traits." They show that culture is not a patchwork of traits, beliefs, habits, and tastes, but a dynamic, contested engagement of meaning and power, shaped by internal contradictions as well as external pressures. It is this notion of culture that we must struggle with in expanding practice knowledge.

Important work on gender and the family is also underway among scholars who have challenged the hegemony of heterosexism and have turned to the meanings and power of family among lesbians and gay men. Depoy and Noble (1992) have spoken to the exclusions inherent in formal institutions such as family that deny gay and lesbian couples a means to affirm commitments to their life partners (p. 51). They point to the everyday practices that reinforce these gender exclusions, from the messages on greeting cards to the ever-present threat of violence. They address the internal and external structural responses that lesbian couples may make in accommodating to and resisting those practices of oppression.

In her powerful ethnographic study, *Families We Choose: Gays, Lesbians, and Kinship* (1991), Weston disrupts deeply held certainties about family in the United States and exposes the contradictions behind the moral and political resistance to legitimizing gay families. She takes the concept "families we choose" as the focal point of her analysis and examines the complexities of delineating these choices, their connections to other experiences of family, and the inherent instability of the concept of "biological" family. "Coming out" stories told by gays and lesbians of their "moment of truth" exposed the uncertainty of supposedly enduring ties as gays and lesbians at times faced being disowned by their biological family on the basis of their gendered identities.

As gays and lesbians constitute family they are simultaneously rejecting the definition of family in terms of biological ties, and thus renegotiating the meaning and practice of kinship within the very societies that have nurtured the concept (Weston, 1991, p. 35). Weston plays with the ironies of family as she discusses the construction of family and co-parenting practices among gay men and lesbians. Such family constellations at once represent traditionally proscribed opposite-sex parenting as they disrupt the very gendered certainties of masculinity, femininity, and heterosexual identity upon which the traditional model is premised.

Weston's work has come under respectful criticism by Robson (1994), who questioned the meaning of this shift to the theory and practice of family among lesbians. She examines family as a legal construction and suggests that the position of lesbians vis-á-vis family should be one of resistance. Robson argues:

> Thus, rather than lesbians requesting inclusion into the privileged legal category of "family," what if lesbians advocated the abolition of benefits based on family status, the reconsideration of what constitutes "benefits," or even the abolition of the category "family" itself? And what would such advocacy mean for non lesbian feminists? (p. 991–992)

She concludes:

> Unnaming is an important, if under-utilized, form of resistance. Unnaming the family may be the most conceptually radical form of resistance to the family power to domesticate lesbianism; it has potentially important results for lesbian and feminist legal theorizing. At its most simple, such theorizing proceeds as if lesbians are not derivative of the family. (p. 992)

These groundbreaking analyses are both brave and provocative. They insert doubt into deeply held certainties. They challenge social workers to move beyond the comfortable terrain that traditional models have established and to engage with alternative discourse and debate where neither the map nor the territory is certain or familiar.

IMPLICATIONS FOR TEACHING PRACTICE WITH FAMILIES

Integrative knowledge development begins with family and gender as issues, not givens. It demands attention to both process and content and makes connections between personal struggles and political circumstances (Allen & Farnsworth, 1993; Fine, 1993; Walker, 1993). In so doing, we must make power a talkable theme in the classroom. Drawing from the insights of feminist methodology, we can begin by validating experiential knowledge of class members, recognizing the partiality of that knowledge, and questioning the certainties that inform our understandings of family (Hartman, 1990; Lather, 1988; Weiler, 1988).

We can start inductively, by asking rather than assuming "who is family." How do individual class members define family and their commitments therein? Weiler (1988) suggests that teachers can "seek dialogue with students and encourage them to unravel and understand the dynamics of their own life histories" (p. 149). As students and teachers articulate what they hold to be true about gender and family, we confront contradictions embedded in our multiple truths. The learning process demands that we grapple with those contradictions. Once we recognize the diverse experiences and practices of family among class members, we can challenge ourselves to build more inclusive understandings of this complicated arena of struggle and support. Reaching agreement on an inclusive definition of family could be a powerful consensus-building exercise for students of family practice.

A collective effort to craft an understanding of family that reflects the diversity of lived experience sets the stage for the study and critique of family theory. Theories, like families, are shaped by cultural, political, and historical conditions. Students need not only have an understanding of family theories; they also need critical questions to deconstruct the meaning and power of theoretical language. For example, in what historical context did the theory emerge? What is the source of data for theory building? To what theoretical positions or social circumstances is the theorist responding? What are the assumptions about the nature of gender, racial, or class differences? Do those assumptions support or challenge existing institutional arrangements and relations of power?

As students engage in the deconstruction of social theory, they may come to appreciate the political nature of social knowledge. For example, Coates (1992) offered a useful comparison of personal deficiency, ecological, and political economy approaches to social work practice. He outlined their contrasting assumptions about the person-society relationship, problem definition, responsibility for problem resolution, focus of intervention, and nature of the social worker-client relationship. He played out three distinct scenarios for intervention with a poor, single mother struggling to keep her job, care for her children, and recover from her marriage to a man who abused and abandoned her. A personal deficiency approach assumed that the woman was the problem and in need of treatment by a social work "expert." In contrast, a political economy approach looked to structural causation and promoted a collaborative change effort to redress the social injustices that resulted in personal pain.

Coates's approach provides a model for comparing the practice implications of differing theories of family. For example, an exchange theorist might focus on the resources available to the poor, single mother, and the rationality of her choices as strategies for survival. A theory of family informed by poststructuralist insights would consider the ways in which poor, single mothers have been constructed through the discourse and practices of a market economy, a patriarchal welfare system, and historically structured gender roles. A practice perspective would address the power of these social forces to shape the realities of women's lives and their beliefs about themselves. At the same time a practice perspective recognizes the transformative possibilities as women come to question, resist, and, at times, change the conditions of their lives.

Gender-relevant family intervention calls for articulating struggles through which family members try to fit their gender beliefs and emotional needs into the structural realities of their lives (Hochschild, 1989, as cited in Thompson, 1992, p. 8). Social workers need to help family members address gendered role expectations, economic resources, power differences, homophobia, and secrecy (Leslie, 1995). These are difficult issues that challenge our practice skills and personal biases. When these themes are the focus of open, critical dialogue in the classroom, students (and teachers) learn to reflect on their own assumptions, confront their biases, and guide others in the process of articulating their beliefs about gender, power, and family. The classroom process thus becomes a model for the family intervention process.

There are a number of theoretical and practical resources available for assessment and intervention that recognize the strength of family diversity and take gender seriously. When students are given hands-on opportunities to try out these resources, they will be better prepared to engage in gender-sensitive family practice and self-reflection. For example, Stack and Burton (1993) put forth the "kinscripts framework" as one approach to understanding the interdependence of the individual and family life course within a historical and political context. The authors present kinscripts as a framework for family research. It merits consideration by practitioners as a framework for family assessment as well. The kinscripts framework looks to the interplay of social structures, family norms and beliefs, and individual behaviors over the life course. It builds an understanding of family drawn from multigenerational ethnographic study of low-income African-American families in the United States. Thus, the understanding of family is not imposed on the basis of dominant norm; it emerges from the study of family "scripts," insiders' accounts of their individual life course constructed in a context of kinship and history.

The framework addresses three domains: kin-work, the labor necessary for intergenerational survival; kin-time, the timing and sequencing of transitions in the family; and kin-scription, the process of assigning kin-work to family members. Attention to the interplay among the domains helps to illuminate how intrafamily power is wielded, often along gendered lines. Attention to kinship in historical context allows insight into the impact of particular political and economic conditions on the individual and family life course. This framework holds promise for critical family practice that is grounded in the politics of everyday life. It recognizes the strengths of diverse family arrangements rather than imposing a limited and constricting "ideal."

Assessment tools such as the "gendergram" explicitly address gender dynamics in the family. In their carefully detailed article, White and Tyson-Rawson (1995) discuss the development and use of this tool to help couples and family members recognize and address assumptions about gender that often remain covert yet pervasive in family interaction. The gendergram "examines past and present significant relationships and influences on gender identity and the ways they have changed over time" (p. 254). It is an interactive tool through which clients can recall key events with significant same- and opposite-sex persons in their lives. Through a semi-structured interview, the worker helps the client explore the relationship among the timing of events in the life cycle, the nature of the relationship, and the messages received about gender identity that result. The process helps bring deeply ingrained gender themes to the level of the talkable.

Assessments that explore and evoke process, such as the telling of one's cultural story, also create possibilities for dialogue about gender. McGill (1992) suggests that families bring to therapy not only their particular family story, but also a larger story that reflects their relationship to their cultural community and larger society. The particular story has been constructed within and shaped by broader cultural accounts of family, gender, ethnicity, life cycle, and so on. Through their stories, family members can speak to the gendered expectations in their community and the larger society and the ways in which those expectations are reinforced and resisted within the family.

Walters et al. (1988) have argued the need to challenge the very concrete and specific ways in which patriarchal assumptions are perpetuated in family interventions. For example, there is a double bind in which cultural scripts frame emotionality, relatedness, and intimacy as "female" qualities, while women are labeled and blamed as "overinvolved" and "co-dependent" when they enact these scripts in the practice of family life (Walters et al., 1988, p. 23). Reframing and renaming become important practices for challenging these contradictions. Carter (1988) acknowledged the power of language in family practice and called for the need to challenge and re-create the slogans by which therapists are taught to work (p. 347). As we incorporate reframing, renaming, and, as Robson (1994) suggested, unnaming in the educational process, we can contribute to an alternative "common sense" regarding gender and family.

The field placement provides an important opportunity for putting critical knowledge of gender, power, and family diversity to practice. However, that practice needs to develop in the context of an open, ongoing conversation among faculty, students, and field supervisors. Many of the themes addressed here challenge deeply held assumptions about gender and family. All those involved in the teaching-learning process need opportunities to participate in critical and respectful dialogue that broadens the scope of mutual understanding. Students can be encouraged to develop learning objectives for the field placement that explicitly address gender. Participatory workshops on gender-sensitive family assessment and intervention would give students, faculty, and community practitioners the opportunity to critique accepted practices and consider the incorporation of alternative approaches that may both fit with and strengthen agency-based practice. Similarly, field supervisors, drawing on the ethnographic richness of practice knowledge, may help students build new frameworks for assessment and intervention that respect and respond to lived experience of the people they serve.

Field placements should offer a range of opportunities that reflect the social and cultural diversity of family experiences. Students working in diverse family contexts, from family support centers to women's shelters and refugee assistance programs, can be clustered together in the field seminar. They can reflect on the common ground and important differences among diverse structures and practices of family they encounter. Finally, family practice itself needs to be defined broadly in terms of field experience. Skills of advocacy and community action for affordable housing, child care, and health services are as important as knowledge of intrafamily intervention.

The abstract concepts of discourse and social construction discussed in this chapter can be translated into concrete learning activities in the classroom and the field. For example, in a course on women and the politics of welfare, class members maintained a "welfare scrapbook." We deconstructed the representations of gender and welfare that appeared in both popular media and professional literature, questioning the assumptions behind the words and images. Together, we were learning deconstruction as critical practice. Similar activities with constructions of gender and the family enable students to translate complex theoretical assumptions into concrete practices. Such activities also help students critically analyze the discourse of social policy that shapes the structure and practices of social service agencies.

We need to "seize the teachable moments" (Allen & Farnsworth, 1993; Walker, 1993) and encourage students to make connections between classroom and community issues. At both local and national levels, struggles are underway regarding the definitions of family and marriage. These struggles have direct implications for such issues as housing, insurance and benefits, and child custody. Through attendance at public meetings, development of position papers, and sponsorship of community forums students can engage with the family/gender system as a concrete political reality.

The learning process should disrupt we/they dichotomies and pathologizing of the "other," and focus instead on understanding the social construction of difference. The use of a broad and diverse literature mitigates against assumptions about single, monolithic truths. Historical accounts, ethnographies, biographies, and fiction are valuable resources for appreciating the diversity of gender/family systems (Walker, 1993). They provide resources for talking back to stereotypes and normative ideals. I have used family-based novels, such as *The Beans of Egypt, Maine* (Chute, 1985), to engage students in provocative discussions about violence, gender, and values in relation to family intervention. This novel offers a raw and poignant insider's account of rural poverty, marked by the stigma of welfare, violence against women, the resourcefulness of single mothers, and the hopeful and painful realities of family ties. Class members are asked to imagine themselves as social workers in Egypt, Maine, and to discuss how they would approach assessment and intervention with some of the characters they have come to know. As they try out social assessment tools on their clients, students come to question the values and assumptions embedded in those tools. The meaning and power of conflicting social realities is brought home.

The educational process should interrupt rather than facilitate the flow of dominant discourse. It is through a kaleidoscopic view of the gender/family system that old certainties are transformed to new questions. As students become entangled in other ways of knowing the world, they develop alternative frames of reference to better appreciate difference. Through reflexive teaching and learning, the classroom can become a site of struggle and a base for building new forms of knowledge, commitment, and action.

APPENDIX 6–1: FAMILIES IN SOCIAL WORK KNOWLEDGE AND PRACTICE

Course Description: This seminar provides a critical review of family theory, explores differing meanings and practices of family, and prepares students for practice in diverse social and cultural contexts. The course situates the study of family and family theory in historical and political context. Students will examine the social construction of family in relation to constructions of gender, ethnicity, race, class, and sexuality. A number of frameworks and tools for family assessment and intervention will be introduced. Class members will develop practice knowledge by utilizing these tools and critiquing their strengths and limitations in addressing themes of power, support, and diversity in families.

Course Objectives

1. Demonstrate theoretical understanding of family as a social construction and the implications for social work practice.
2. Describe at least three theoretical perspectives on family and critique them in terms of attention to gender, power, and racial, cultural, and class differences.
3. Employ a model of "discourse analysis" to understand the language and practices that shape family theory, policy, intervention, and lived experience.
4. Develop an inclusive definition of family that reflects and respects diverse arrangements of kinship and social ties.
5. Critique social work literature on family practice in terms of assumptions about appropriate family structure and function, and consider the implications for diverse family situations (e.g., single parent, multigenerational extended, and gay and lesbian families).
6. Develop skills in using assessment and intervention strategies that connect the experiences of family members to larger historical and political contexts.
7. Evaluate the effectiveness of these strategies as applied to a variety of family case studies.
8. Critically reflect on your personal experiences of and assumptions about family in light of these theoretical models, assessment tools, and intervention strategies.

Learning Units and Suggested Readings

Unit One: Defining Family: Contested Terrain. A review of diverse understandings of family, and an introduction to concept of social construction.

Selected Readings from: Thorne & Yalom (1982). *Rethinking the family;* Fine (1993). Current approaches to understanding family diversity; Gross (1992). Are families deteriorating or changing?; Flax (1982). The family in contemporary thought; Stacey (1990). *Brave new families.*

Unit Two: Theorizing Family. A review and critique of dominant family theories in historical context.

Selected Readings from: Burr et al. (1979). *Contemporary theories about the family;* Ingoldsby and Smith (1995). *Families in multicultural perspective;* Carter and McGoldrick (1989). *The changing family life cycle;* Cheal (1991). *Family and the state of theory;* Coates (1992). Ideology and education for social work practice; Ferree (1990). Beyond separate spheres.

Unit Three: The Social Construction of Family: Cultural, Historical, and Political Perspectives.

Selected Readings from: Gittens (1985). *The family in question;* Mintz and Kellogg (1988). *Domestic revolutions;* Jones (1984). *Labor of love, labor of sorrow;* Baber and Allen (1992). *Women and families;* Baca Zinn (1990). Family, feminism, and race in America; Collier and Yanagisako (1987). *Gender and kinship;* Jennings and Waller (1990). Constructions of social hierarchy; Weedon (1987). *Feminist practice and poststructuralist theory.*

Unit Four: Extending Family: Learning from Diverse Constructions of Family and Challenging "-isms."

Selected Readings from: Carter (1988). Remarried families; Depoy and Noble (1992). The structure of lesbian relationships in response to oppression; Weston (1991). *Families we choose;* Robson (1994). Resisting the family; Segura and Pearce (1993). Chicana/o family structure and gender personality; Dill (1988). Our mother's grief;

Herring (1989). The Native American family; Schmitz (1995). Reframing the dialogue on female-headed single parent families.

Unit Five: Family Living: Perspectives on the Politics of Everyday Life in the Context of Family.

Selected Readings from: Demo and Acock (1993.) Family diversity and the division of domestic labor; di Leonardo (1987). The female world of cards and holidays; Dressel and Clark (1990). A critical look at family care; Graham (1983). Caring: A labour of love; Hartmann (1981). The family as locus of gender, class and political struggle; Smith (1987). *The everyday world as problematic;* Googins and Burden (1987). Vulnerability of working parents; Thompson and Walker (1989). Gender in families; Komter (1989). Hidden power in marriage.

Unit Six: Family Assessment: Finding Strengths in Diversity.

Selected Readings from: Aldous (1990). Family development and the life course; Bray (1995). Family assessment; Mizan (1994). Family power studies; Stack and Burton (1993). Kinscripts; White and Tyson-Rawson (1995). Assessing the dynamics of gender in couples and families; McGill (1992). The culture story in multicultural family therapy; Congress (1994). The use of culturegrams to assess and empower culturally diverse families.

Unit Seven: Family Intervention: Building on Strengths in Arenas of Struggle.

Selected Readings from: Barrett et al. (1990). Feminist informed family therapy for the treatment of intra-family child sexual abuse; Leslie (1995). The evolving treatment of gender, ethnicity and sexual orientation in marital and family therapy; Carter (1993). Child sexual abuse: Impact on mothers; Goodrich (1991). *Women and power: Perspective for family therapy;* Walters et al. (1988). *The invisible web.*

Unit Eight: Application, Evaluation, and Critical Reflection. (Working with case studies and personal experiences of "family," class members will use and critique a variety of approaches to assessment and intervention).

Selected Readings from: Hartman (1992). In search of subjugated knowledge; Swigonski (1994). The logic of feminist standpoint theory for social work research; Thompson (1992). Feminist methodology for family studies.

Resources for Teachers

Allen and Farnsworth (1993). Reflexivity in teaching about families; Freire (1990). A critical understanding of social work; Schniedewind and Davidson (1983). *Open minds to equality;* Walker (1993). Teaching about race, gender and class diversity in United States families; Weiler (1988). *Women teaching for change.*

Ethnographic and Biographic Resources for Teaching About Family

Alpert (1988). *We are everywhere: Writings by and about lesbian parents.* Bell-Scott et al. (1992). *Double stitch: Black women write about mothers and daughters;* Campbell-Hale (1993). *Bloodlines;* di Leonardo (1984). *The varieties of ethnic experience;* Sheehan (1993). *Life for me ain't been no crystal stair;* Stacey (1990). *Brave new families;* Stack (1974). All our kin.

Novels for Teaching About Family

Campbell-Hale (1985). *The jailing of Cecilia Capture;* Chase (1983). *During the reign of the queen of Persia;* Chute (1985). *The Beans of Egypt, Maine;* Dorris (1988). *A yellow raft in blue water;* Erdrich (1984). *Love medicine.*

REFERENCES

Abramovitz, M. (1988). *Regulating the lives of women.* Boston: South End Press.

Aldous, J. (1990). Family development and the life course: Two perspectives on family change. *Journal of Marriage and the Family, 52*, 571–583.

Allen, K. & Farnsworth, E. (1993). Reflexivity in teaching about families. *Family Relations, 42*, 351–356.

Alpert, H. (Ed.). (1988). *We are everywhere: Writings by and about lesbian parents.* Freedom, CA: Crossing Press.

Aponte, H. (1991). Training in the person of the therapist for work with the poor and minorities. In K. Lewis (Ed.), *Family systems application to social work: Training and clinical practice* (pp. 23–40). Binghamton, NY: Haworth.

Arendell, T. (1992). The social self as gendered: A masculinist discourse of divorce. *Symbolic Interaction 15*, 151–181.

Armstrong, L. (1996). *Of 'sluts' and 'bastards': A feminist decodes the child welfare debate.* Monroe, ME: Common Courage Press.

Baber, K. & Allen, K. (1992). *Women and families: Feminist reconstructions*. New York: Guilford.

Baca Zinn, M. (1990). Family, feminism, and race in America. *Gender and Society*, (4), 68–82.

Barrett, M., Trepper, T. & Fish, L. (1990). Feminist informed family therapy for the treatment of intra-family child sexual abuse. *Journal of Family Psychology, 4*, 151–166.

Bell-Scott, P., Guy-Sheftall, B., Royster, J., Sims-Woods, J., Decosta-Willis, M. & Fultz, L. (Eds.). (1992). *Double stitch: Black women write about mothers and daughters.* Boston: Beacon.

Bose, C. (1987). Dual spheres. In B. Hess & M. Ferree (Eds.), *Analyzing gender*. Beverly Hills, CA: Sage.

Bourdieu, P. (1977). *Outline of a theory of practice*. (Trans. R. Nice). New York: Cambridge University Press.

Bray, J. (1995). Family assessment: Current issues in evaluating families. *Family Relations, 44*, 469–477.

Broderick, C. & Smith, J. (1979). The general systems approach to the family. In W. Burr, R. Hill, F. Nye & I. Russ (Eds.), *Contemporary theories about the family* (Vol 2). New York: Free Press.

Burr, W., Hill, R., Nye, F. & Russ, I. (Eds.). (1979). *Contemporary theories about the family* (Vol. 2). New York: Free Press.

Campbell-Hale, J. (1985). *The jailing of Cecilia Capture.* New York: Random House.

Campbell-Hale, J. (1993). *Bloodlines: Odyssey of a native daughter.* New York: Random House.

Carter, B. (1988). Remarried families: Creating a new paradigm. In M. Walters, B. Carter, P. Papp & O. Silverstein (Eds.), *The invisible web: Gender patterns in family relationships.* New York: Guilford.

Carter, B. (1993). Child sexual abuse: Impact on mothers. *Affilia, 8*, 72–90.

Carter, B. & McGoldrick, M. (1989). *The changing family life cycle.* Boston, MA: Allyn & Bacon.

Chafetz, J. (1988). The gender division of labor and the reproduction of female disadvantage. *Journal of Family Issues, 9*, 108–131

Chase, J. (1983). *During the reign of the queen of Persia*. New York: Harper & Row.

Cheal, D. (1991). *Family and the state of theory*. Toronto: University of Toronto Press.

Chodorow, N. (1978). *The reproduction of mothering: Psychoanalysis and the sociology of gender*. Berkeley, CA: University of California Press.

Chute, C. (1985). *The Beans of Egypt, Maine*. New York: Warner Books.

Clayton, R. (1979). *The family, marriage and social change* (2nd ed.) Lexington, MA: D.C. Heath.

Coates, J. (1992). Ideology and education for social work practice. *Journal of Progressive Human Services, 3*, 15–30.

Collier, J. & Yanagisako, S. (1987). *Gender and kinship: Essays toward a unified analysis*. Stanford, CA: Stanford University Press.

Congress, E. (1994). The use of culturagrams to assess and empower culturally diverse families. *Families in Society*, November, 531–539.

Cross, T. (1986). Drawing on cultural tradition in Indian child welfare practice. *Social Casework, 67*, 283–289.

Demo, D. & Acock, A. (1993). Family diversity and the division of domestic labor. *Family Relations,42,* 323–331.

Demos, V. (1990). Black family studies in *The Journal of Marriage and the Family* and the issue of distortion. *Journal of Marriage and the Family, 52*, 603- 612.

Depoy, E. & Noble, S. (1992). The structure of lesbian relationships in response to oppression. *Affilia, 7*, 49–64.

di Leonardo, M. (1984). *The varieties of ethnic experience: Kinship, class and gender among California Italian-Americans*. Ithaca, NY: Cornell University Press.

di Leonardo, M. (1987). The female world of cards and holidays: Women, families and the work of kinship. *Signs, 12*, 440–453.

Dill, B. (1988). Our mother's grief: Racial ethnic women and the maintenance of families. *Journal of Family History, 13*, 415–431.

Dorris, M. (1988). *A yellow raft in blue water*. New York: Warner Books.

Dressel, P. & Clark, M. (1990). A critical look at family care. *Journal of Marriage and the Family, 52*, 769–782.

Edwards, J. (1969). Familial behavior as social exchange. *Journal of Marriage and the Family, 31*, 518–526.

Ekeh, R. (1974). *Social exchange theory.* Cambridge, MA: Harvard University Press.

Elder, G. (1985). Families and lives: Some developments in life course studies. In G. Elder (Ed.), *Life course dynamics, trajectories and transitions*. Ithaca, NY: Cornell University Press.

Erdrich, L. (1984). *Love medicine*. New York: Holt, Rinehart and Winston.

Ferree, M. (1990). Beyond separate spheres: Feminism and family research. *Journal of Marriage and the Family, 52* , 866–884

Fine, M. (1993). Current approaches to understanding family diversity. *Family Relations, 42*, 235–237.

Finn, J. (1994). Contested caring: Women's roles in foster family care. *Affilia, 9*, 382–400.

Flax, J. (1982). The family in contemporary thought: A critical review. In J. Elshtain (Ed.), *The family in political thought*. Amherst: University of Massachusetts Press.

Foucault, M. (1978). *The history of sexuality, Vol. 1: An introduction.* New York: Vintage Books.

Fraser, N. (1990). Struggle over needs: Outline of a socialist-feminist critical theory of late-capitalist political culture. In L. Gordon (Ed.), *Women, the state and welfare* (pp. 199–225). Madison: University of Wisconsin Press.

Fraser, N. & Gordon, L. (1994). A genealogy of dependency: Tracing a keyword of the U.S. welfare state. *Signs, 19*, 309–336.

Freire, P. (1990). A critical understanding of social work. *Journal of Progressive Human Services, 1*, 3–9.

Giddens, A. (1979). *Central problems in social theory.* London: Macmillan.

Gilligan, C. (1982). *In a different voice*. Cambridge, MA: Harvard University Press.

Ginsberg, F. & Tsing, A. (Eds.). (1990). *Uncertain terms: Negotiating gender in American culture*. Boston: Beacon.

Gittens, D. (1985). *The family in question: Changing households and familiar ideologies.* London: Macmillan.

Glick, P. (1955). The life cycle of the family. *Marriage and Family Living, 17*, 3–9.

Goodrich, T. (Ed.). (1991). *Women and power: Perspective for family therapy.* New York: Norton.

Googins, B. & Burden, D. (1987). Vulnerability of working parents: Balancing work and home roles. *Social Work,32*(3), 295–299.

Gordon, L. (1990). Family violence, feminism and social control. In L. Gordon (Ed.), *Women, the state and welfare*. Madison: University of Wisconsin Press.

Graham, H. (1983). Caring: A labour of love. In J. Finch & P. Grove (Eds.), *A labour of love: Women, work and caring*. London: Routledge & Kegan Paul.

Gross, E. (1992). Are families deteriorating or changing? *Affilia, 7*, 7–22.

Haraway, D. (1987). Situated knowledge: The science question in feminism and the privilege of partial perspective. *Feminist Studies, 14*, 575–599.

Hare-Muston, R. (1991). Sex, lies and headaches: The problem is power. In T. Goodrich (Ed.), *Women and power: Perspective for family therapy*. New York: Norton.

Hartman, A. (1990). Many ways of knowing. *Social Work, 35*, 3.

Hartman, A. (1992). In search of subjugated knowledge. *Social Work, 37*, 483–484.

Hartmann, H. (1981). The family as locus of gender, class and political struggle: The example of housework. *Signs, 6*, 366–394.

Herring, R. (1989). The Native American family: Dissolution by coercion. *Journal of Multicultural Counseling and Development, 17*, 4–13.

Hochschild, A. (1989). *The second shift: Working parents and the revolution at home.* New York: Viking.

Holman, T. & Burr, W. (1980). Beyond the beyond: The growth of family theories in the 1970s. *Journal of Marriage and the Family*, November, 729–737.

Holter, H. (1970). *Sex roles and social structure.* Oslo: Universitetsforlaget.

Hutter, H. (1981). *The changing family: Comparative perspectives.* New York: Wiley.

Ingoldsby, B. & Smith, S. (Eds.). (1995). *Families in multicultural perspective.* New York: Guilford.

Jennings, A. & Waller, W. (1990). Constructions of social hierarchy: The family, gender and power. *Journal of Economic Issues*, 24, 623–631.

Jones, J. (1984). *Labor of love, labor of sorrow: Black women, work and family from slavery to the present.* New York: Basic Books.

Komter, A. (1989). Hidden power in marriage. *Gender and Society, 3*, 187–216.

Kuhn, A. (1974). *The logic of social systems.* San Francisco: Jossey-Bass.

Lather, P. (1988). Feminist perspectives on empowering research methodologies. *Women's Studies International Forum, 11*, 569–581.

Leslie, L. (1995). The evolving treatment of gender, ethnicity and sexual orientation in marital and family therapy. *Family Relations, 44*, 359–367.

Lewis, K. (Ed.). (1991). *Family systems application to social work: Training and clinical practice.* Binghamton, NY: Haworth.

Luckenbill, D. (1979). Power: A conceptual framework. *Symbolic Interaction, 2*, 97–114.

McGill, D. (1992). The culture story in multicultural family therapy. *Families in Society, 71*, 331–349.

Meyer, C. (1985). A feminist perspective on foster family care: A redefinition of categories. *Child Welfare, 64*, 249–258.

Mintz, S. & Kellogg, S. (1988). *Domestic revolutions: A social history of American family life*. New York: Free Press.

Mizan, A. (1994). Family power studies. *International Journal of Sociology of the Family, 24*, 85–91.

Nicholson, L. (1986). *Gender and history: The limits of social theory in the age of the family*. New York: Columbia University Press.

Oakley, A. (1974). *Women's work: The housewife, past and present.* New York: Vintage.

Ortner, S. (1984). Theory in anthropology since the sixties. *Comparative Studies in Society and History, 26*, 126–166.

Ortner, S. (1989). *High religion: A cultural and political history of Sherpa Buddhism.* Princeton, NJ: Princeton University Press.

Ortner, S. & Whitehead, H. (Eds.). (1981). *Sexual meanings: The cultural construction of gender and sexuality*. New York: Cambridge University Press.

Papp. P. (1988). The right to be a mother. In M. Walter, B. Carter, P. Papp & O. Silverstein (Eds.), *The invisible web: Gender patterns in family relationships* (pp. 321–324). New York: Guilford.

Parsons, T. (1954). The kinship system of the contemporary United States. In *Essays in sociological theory*. New York: Free Press.

Parsons, T. (1971). *The system of modern societies*. Englewood Cliffs, NJ: Prentice-Hall.

Rapp, R. (1982). Family and class in contemporary society. In B. Thorne & M. Yalom (Eds.), *Rethinking the family: Some feminist questions* (pp. 168–187). New York: Longman.

Reiter, R. (Ed.). (1975). *Toward an anthropology of women.* New York: Monthly Review Press.

Robson, R. (1994). Resisting the family: Repositioning lesbians in legal theory. *Signs, 19*, 975–996.

Rosaldo, M. & Lamphere, L. (Eds.). (1974). *Women, culture and society*. Stanford, CA: Stanford University Press.

Rosaldo, R. (1989). *Culture and truth: The remaking of social analysis*. Boston: Beacon.

Sabatelli, R. & Shehan, C. (1993). Exchange and resource theories. In P. Boss, W. Doherty, R. La Rossa, W. Schumm & S. Steinmetz (Eds.), *Sourcebook of family theories and method* (pp. 384–411). New York: Plenum.

Sacks, K. (1975). Engels revisited: Women, the organization of production, and private property. In R. Reiter (Ed.), *Toward an anthropology of women* (pp. 211–234). New York: Monthly Review Press.

Sarri, R. & Finn, J. (1992). Child welfare policy and practice: Rethinking the history of our certainties. *Children and Youth Services Review, 14*, 219–236.

Scanzoni, J. & Litton-Fox, G. (1980). Sex roles, family and society: The seventies and beyond. *Journal of Marriage and the Family, 42*, 743–756.

Schmitz, C. (1995). Reframing the dialogue on female-headed single parent families. *Affilia, 10*, 426–441.

Schniedewind, N. & Davidson, E. (1983). *Open minds to equality: Learning activities to promote race, sex, class and age equality*. Englewood Cliffs, NJ: Prentice-Hall.

Scott, J. (1988). *Gender and the politics of history*. New York: Columbia University Press.

Segura, D. & Pearce, J. (1993). Chicana/o family structure and gender personality: Chodorow, familism and psychoanalytic sociology revisited. *Signs, 19*, 62–91.

Sewell, W. (1992). A theory of structure: Duality, agency and transformation. *American Journal of Sociology, 98*(1), 1–29.

Sheehan, S. (1993). *Life for me ain't been no crystal stair.* New York: Vintage Books.

Smith, D. (1987). *The everyday world as problematic*. Boston: Northeastern University Press.

Smith, S. (1995). Family theory and multicultural family studies. In B. Ingoldsby & S. Smith (Eds.), *Families in multicultural perspective* (pp. 5–35). New York: Guilford.

Stacey, J. (1990). *Brave new families: Stories of domestic upheaval in late twentieth century America.* New York: Basic Books.

Stack, C. (1974). *All our kin: Strategies for survival in a Black community.* New York: Harper & Row.

Stack, C. & Burton, L. (1993). Kinscripts. *Journal of Comparative Family Studies, 24,* 157–170.

Stone, G. (1977). Personal acts. *Symbolic Interaction, 2*, 97–114.

Strasser, S. (1982). *Never done: A history of American housework.* New York: Pantheon.

Swigonski, M. (1994). The logic of feminist standpoint theory for social work research. *Social Work, 39*, 387–393.

Thompson, L. (1992). Feminist methodology for family studies. *Journal of Marriage and the Family, 54,* 3–18.

Thompson, L. & Walker, A. (1989). Gender in families: Women and men in marriage, work and parenthood. *Journal of Marriage and the Family, 51*, 845–871.

Thorne, B. & Yalom, M. (1982). *Rethinking the family: Some feminist questions*. New York: Longman.

Walker, A. (1993). Teaching about race, gender and class diversity in United States families. *Family Relations, 42*, 342–350.

Walters, M., Carter, B., Papp, P. & Silverstein, O. (1988). *The invisible web: Gender patterns in family relationships.* New York: Guilford.

Weedon, C. (1987). *Feminist practice and poststructuralist theory*. Oxford, England: Basil Blackwell.

Weiler, K. (1988). *Women teaching for change: Gender, class and power.* New York: Bergin & Garvey.

Weston, K. (1991). *Families we choose: Gays, lesbians and kinship*. New York: Columbia University Press.

White, M. & Tyson-Rawson, K. (1995). Assessing the dynamics of gender in couples and families. *Family Relations, 44*, 253–260.

Williams, R. (1976). *Keywords: A vocabulary of culture and society.* New York: Oxford University Press.

Wood, J. (1994). *Who cares? Women, care and culture*. Carbondale and Edwardsville: Southern Illinois University Press, 1994.

Zavella, P. (1987). *Women's work and Chicano families.* Ithaca, NY: Cornell University Press.

CHAPTER 7

Women, Communities, and Development

Marie Weil
Dorothy N. Gamble
Evelyn Smith Williams

INTRODUCTION

Women have skills, creativity, experience, and knowledge to contribute in all types of community practice. As the United Nations has noted, "Womens' Rights Are Human Rights," and full human participation means inclusion of women as equal partners in community, social, economic, and political life.

For social work education to respond to these challenges, gender-sensitive planning must integrate women's conditions, needs, and issues, and feminist theory throughout the curriculum. Community practice that reaches out to all society challenges educators to make certain that students can hear both women's and men's voices, understand their concerns, and facilitate their involvement in community leadership.

In this chapter, we focus on women, community, and development. We argue that social work practice and social work curricula need to recognize and incorporate both community practice as well as women's perspectives and contributions. Five areas of knowledge and skills are identified as needed in social work education: empowerment practice, community practice, participatory research, diversity/cultural competency, and social/sustainable development practice. We begin with a historical overview of women's contributions to community practice and the need to restructure education to focus on women as community leaders and as facilitators in organizing, planning, development, and change processes. We present feminist applications of community practice and emphasize community-based participatory research that can reflect women's perspectives as a major part of the empowerment focus of community practice. Given the growing awareness of the complexities of the global economy, attention is given to the importance of women's involvement and leadership in the accelerating worldwide movement toward sustainable development. We summarize the current community practice models and their feminist application. Finally, we conclude with assignments that can be used to apply some of the material presented in this chapter.

Community practice complements direct practice that is focused on empowerment, and greatly affects the programs, conditions, and policies under which direct services are provided. Currently, there are major political, economic, social, and technological challenges to social work and to many of the vulnerable and oppressed populations that social workers serve. The profession and its educational system need to respond proactively to these challenges. For practice to keep pace with the impacts of changing political, economic, social, and technological changes on people, particularly the poor, it is critical for social work education to reengage in community practice.

HISTORY OF COMMUNITY PRACTICE

The Role of Gender in the Development of Community Practice

Women comprise 51% of the U.S. population; historically, however, economic, political, and social forces have sentenced women, especially women of color and indigenous women, to second-class citizenship. Within the profession of social work these societal patterns have been echoed. Although social work as a profession is preponderantly female, leadership positions in administration, teaching, and research have been and remain mostly male (Brandwein, 1982; Hopps & Collins, 1995). Many of the pioneers who established methods of practice and the profession were women such as Jane Addams, Mary Parker Follett, and Mary Richmond, to name just the most obvious (see Edwards, 1995, for biographies).

Many other women emerged as powerful reformers. For example, Harriet Tubman, perhaps the best known of the women who led slaves from the South to freedom in the North, is recognized as a major advocate for abolition. Tubman was a highly skilled organizer, and a powerful proponent of social justice and policy change.

In its origins, community practice in the Settlement Movement focused on grass-roots neighborhood organizing, developing services for immigrant and low-income populations, social reform, and social policy, while the Charity Organization Society (COS) Movement focused on interagency planning and coordination. Community practice theories and methodologies greatly benefited from the pioneering work of Jane Addams and the women of Hull-House. They engaged in community organizing and neighborhood problem-solving, as well as in the development of new programs such as day care for low-income children, women's groups—organized around ethnicity, occupation, or skills training—and summer camps outside the city for women and their children. Equally important, Addams and her associates worked in the labor movement to establish fairer and safer working conditions for women and men and to protect children from economic exploitation. They developed methods to assess community strengths and needs. Additionally, they conducted environmental safety research in relation to parks, recreation, housing, and sanitation (Deegan, 1990; Weil, 1997).

The "taproots" of community organization in both the Settlement and COS movements reveal much about the perspectives that have shaped traditional practice (Betten & Austin, 1990). Addams's work and writings through the progression of her career increasingly emphasized citizen participation. As she developed stronger connections with the neighborhoods surrounding Hull-House, she separated from more paternalistic settlement leaders. She emphasized the involvement of people in solving their own and their neighborhoods' problems and focused on issues related to adult education, community-based planning and research, and social and political action. Democratic theory was a primary guide for many involved in the settlements, and Addams had a vision of radical democracy that was grounded in the conviction that all people are equal. Therefore she focused on action to build equality in social, political, and economic arenas. Addams was a staunch early feminist, a strong supporter of women's suffrage, and an activist in labor and child labor issues. Her philosophy can still serve to guide work with communities. She believed that people in industrial areas needed information and knowledge about their community situation and that they needed to learn how to use information to improve their social, economic, and political conditions (Lasch, 1965). Addams's analysis of the working conditions of her Hull House neighbors, many of whom were immigrants, eventually took her to Europe where she worked with other women through the Women's International League for Peace and Freedom to diminish the causes of war and replace conflict with mediation. She was awarded the Nobel Peace Prize in 1931 (Farrell, 1967).

Deegan documents the importance of the volume published by Addams and her colleagues, *Hull-House Maps and Papers* (1895), which illustrates programs, planning, and research activities. Research conducted by Addams, Florence Kelly, Grace and Edith Abbott, Julia Lathrop, and others formed the basis for sociological methods of studying urban neighborhoods and peoples (Deegan, 1990). Addams and her colleagues split with the male leadership of the sociology department of the University of Chicago over numerous issues, a rift that resulted in a departmental separation and establishment of the "applied" sociology section, which later became the School of Social Welfare. The most important reason for this division was the difference in perspectives regarding the relationship of the profession to the community. Male sociology leaders insisted on using the "community as a laboratory," however, Addams, her Hull-House colleagues, and other female faculty members insisted that researchers should work with the community in a mutual process of problem-solving, rather than as a laboratory experiment (Deegan, 1990). This early schism shows the application of feminist principles of mutuality and shared problem-solving in research in the early history of the profession.

Mary Richmond is recognized as a major contributor to the service coordination and interagency relations methods of the COS. Many women were involved in developing community organization strategies and in local service councils and planning, although their contributions are less widely known. The COS Movement developed approaches to interagency coordination and collaboration later embodied in health and welfare councils as well as federated planning and funding groups. Community social planning depended on joint work between professional staff carrying technical planning and coordination responsibilities and volunteers and board members engaged in resource development, planning, allocation, and monitoring of sponsored programs.

During the 1920s and 1930s Bessie McClenahan pioneered the "study, diagnosis, treatment" schema in community work designed to focus on both the generic problems of communities that reflect broad societal problems, and the uniqueness of each specific community

(Austin & Betten, 1990; McClenahan, 1922). She developed manuals of practice to assist organizers in the process of entering a community, establishing relationships with both community members and agency board members, and developing public relations campaigns for issues through the press (Austin & Betten, 1990; McClenahan, 1922). McClenahan was also interested in rural organizing and development and urged funding of agencies to extend "expert service to the local rural communities" (p. 134).

During the 1940s and 1950s, community organization practice and its literature grew rapidly. Several women made major contributions to this literature, and numerous women made contributions to practice. In 1959 the Council on Social Work Education's Curriculum Study on community organization (Lurie, 1959) included chapters by Violet Sieder, Genevieve Carter, Arlien Johnson, and Mildred Barry. Generally, however, in the 1940s and 1950s few women's voices were heard and contributions were disproportionately low in the literature and in the macro practice curriculum (Brandwein, 1982; and see Chapter 8 in this book).

During this period the community organization method of practice was further specified and it came to occupy a more salient place in the social work curriculum. A rich literature developed in this period that spanned grass-roots work and interagency coordination. Perspectives about women and women's issues, however, were underrepresented. Community workers at this time were called to respond to the aftermath of the Great Depression and to focus on major social problems (R. Perlman, 1971). Dunham (1940), McMillen (1945), and Newstetter (1947) contributed to the developing practice theory of community organization.

In the mid–1950s, Murray Ross (1955) specified three primary orientations to community organization: reform, planning, and process. He viewed the process orientation as the heart of practice and emphasized that these approaches could be merged or sequenced (Ross, 1955, 1958; Schwartz, 1965). Ross (1955) developed the first major theory-based literature for curriculum. He integrated a range of social science concepts and connected them to the achievement of goals through the community organization process. Ross connected relevant social science theories and social work values to construct his practice theory for community organization (Schwartz, 1965). Ross's emphasis on process and values relates more congruently to feminist community practice literature than do some of the later dominant emphases in the 1960s and 1970s.

Arthur Dunham was one of the chief architects of social planning and interagency methods. He drew from sociological theory, and group theory, and presented practice theory on community planning and service coordination (Dunham, 1959). To say that men's writings dominated the literature of this period is not to conclude that women were silent.

Genevieve Carter (1958b) codified generic elements of social work practice methods and elements specific to community practice. Her position paper in the Curriculum Study (Lurie, 1959) focuses on the responsibility of the profession for theory building and illustrates a spiral-like process of theory building that takes place through five levels: experience, systematic empirical inquiry, conceptualization, verification by scientific method, and practice testing (pp. 88–91). She emphasizes that "there is no professional practice without theory" because with every intervention a worker is operating with some "theory of the situation" and using principles and concepts with some consistency in similar situations (p. 86). Violet Sieder's CSWE position paper in the Curriculum Study outlines central tasks of the community organization worker (Sieder, 1959). Her earlier works provide a definition of the method and describe local-level social planning and action (Sieder 1947, 1950, 1956). The community organization method, she asserts in substantial agreement with Ross (1955, 1958), is grounded in "social work philosophy, principles and ethics, and depends upon knowledge of the social structure and dynamics of a community, social welfare program content, the science of human relations, and the art of professional practice" (Sieder, 1959, p. 250). The knowledge base for community organization guides its major tasks, which Sieder sees as an assessment of the reality factors in the community situation, diagnosis of the community situation, formulation of the community's social goals or objectives, implementation of the plan to achieve the goal; and reassessment of the community situation and setting of new goals (Sieder, 1959, pp. 250–256). Sieder and Carter were established leaders and scholars of community organization in the 1950s; their approach was to clarify the knowledge base and further specify the method (Carter, 1958a). As did other writers of their period, Carter and Sieder emphasized the community planning and interorganizational relations aspects of community social work. At this stage of theoretical development, the literature of the period gave little attention to women's issues and women as professional practitioners.

As community organization achieved increased emphasis in the 1960s and 1970s through major work on model specification, a rapidly increasing literature, and a growing number of schools offering a specialization in community organization or administration and community work, the predominance of men in academic, administrative, and research leadership escalated further (Brandwein, 1982). An explicit educational and practice strategy focused on the recruitment of men in the belief that social work would be taken much more seriously as a profession if it were to lose its designation as a "woman's profession" (Kadushin, 1976; for critique see, e.g., Kravitz, 1976). Preceding affirmative action policies, public and nonprofit agencies often openly expressed a preference for men as directors and as community workers.

Unfortunately, this effort to develop opportunities for men coincided with the advancement and expansion of macro practice, and a "fast track" emerged to leadership positions in teaching, research, and macro practice. "This pattern of male dominance has had a negative impact on the treatment of women's concerns and women's issues in macro-practice curricula" (Weil, 1995, p. 191). The emergence of the social action model with its emphasis on conflict theory and contest methods in the late 1960s and early 1970s is sometimes also linked to the predominance of men in macro-practice (Hyde, 1996; Rothman, 1995). The majority of writers in this era were men. While overt sexism was probably not intended, very little attention was given to women as community leaders and practitioners, and to approaches to community practice that emphasized feminist perspectives (Hyde, 1989, 1994; Weil, 1995). The climate in the 1960s and 1970s was decidedly "macho" in the preferred models, the preferences in hiring, and choice of leaders. However, influenced by societal changes, particularly the civil rights movement and the women's movement, a new generation of women enrolled in community and macro practice specializations. These women wrote and revised the literature and practice models to include women's realities.

Feminist Critique of Earlier Community Organization Theories

The combination of two major forces limited access to or easy availability of earlier knowledge, research, and literature on community practice that was developed by women, particularly those in the settlement movement. These forces, (a) the professionalization efforts within social work, and (b) the drive within sociology to emulate the scholarship and scientific methods of the natural sciences, operated with an overlay of the sexism that was prevalent in society at the time.

Within the developing schools of social work and applied social science, the emerging dominance of psychoanalytic and medical models of practice channeled much of the professional literature and curricula to individually oriented, psychoanalytic perspectives (Brieland, 1995; Hopps & Collins, 1995; Lubove, 1965; Popple, 1995). Despite social work's dual roots arising from the COS and the Settlement movements, the dominant presentations of social work theory still tend to ignore community practice and often give little attention to the women pioneers who developed theory, practice methods, and research methods. A notable exception is Simon's *The Empowerment Tradition in American Social Work* (1994), which presents a historical perspective on methods' development, and provides intellectual, historical, and theoretical underpinnings of these early efforts.

The dominance of casework perspectives in the early schools and departments of social work did not preclude course content in macro areas, but did limit both exposure and access for new generations of social workers. Although group work and community organization were recognized as bona fide methods of social work practice in 1939 in the Lane Report (Brieland, 1995; Lane, 1939; Lurie, 1959; Popple, 1995), fewer students were involved in macro courses. The appeals of Ross (1955, 1958), Carter (1959), Dunham (1959), Sieder (1956, 1959), Lurie (1959), and others who argued that all social workers need to have community practice skills went unheeded. Transmission of knowledge through generations of social work students focused much more on casework modalities than on community practice. Therefore the major research, practice methods, and theory birthed in community practice venues were passed on to smaller groups of students in community organization curricula. This twist in evolution to achieve professional status limited exposure to the social-reform and community-focused efforts of the settlement era and deprived generations of students of the pioneering knowledge, methods, and research developed by the settlement leaders and workers, particularly the women leaders.

The second major force that curtailed application of the pioneering work of Addams and others was the simultaneous effort in sociology to emulate the methods of the natural sciences along with the overlay of sexism in the development of the social sciences (Deegan, 1990). The lack of acknowledgment and exclusion in social work curricula of the research methods pioneered at Hull-House has also affected community and macro practice. While Addams and a number of women leaders in the settlement movement are often accorded "honorable mention" or "obligatory obeisances," the power of their research work in and with communities has received far too little notice—and has been largely missing from the "canon" of social work curriculum.

One consequence of this history is lack of recognition of the strong role that settlement movement pioneers (among them many women) played in development of practice models (in both group work and community work) and in research and practice theory building. The 1960s and 1970s witnessed a reemergence of community organization. For the generations of social work faculty trained from the late 1960s through the early 1980s, however, the available literature did not actively include women's perspectives as organizers, writers, researchers, and teachers of community organization. The major readings were Ross's work from the late 1950s and the newer, three-model approach codified by Rothman in successive editions of *Strategies of Community Organization*, published between 1979 and 1995 (Rothman, 1995), and the work of Gilbert and Specht (1968), Cox et al. (1970, 1984), Lauffer (1978), and Taylor and Roberts (1985), for example.

There were strong women community work scholars such as McClenahan, Carter, and Sieder. However, community and macro practice was largely a male preserve (Austin & Betten, 1990; Lubove, 1965; Lurie, 1959). While social work quickly became known as a "woman's profession" it is important to remember that for most of the profession's history it has been a profession with a preponderantly female membership but whose leaders in research, teaching, and publication have been predominantly male (Chernesky, 1980; Weil, 1996).

The effect of this "glass ceiling," especially in macro areas of curricula and practice, has limited the dissemination of knowledge about women's contributions and leadership in all aspects of community practice. As more women students gravitated toward community and macro practice during and following the social movements of the 1960s and 1970s, they began to raise questions about women's issues and feminist concerns.

FEMINIST KNOWLEDGE AND COMMUNITY PRACTICE

Development of Feminist Theory and Knowledge in Social Work

Social work has been greatly enriched by the development of feminist theory in sociology, psychology, anthropology, and political science. The development and adaptation of feminist theory, specifically theories related to empowerment, sexism, gender roles, structural analysis, and gender analysis, has been particularly useful for the analysis of social work interventions and guidance for social work practice. The development and adaptation of feminist theory by social work scholars now gives the profession a major opportunity to deal with gender as a central factor in micro, mezzo, and macro practice. New feminist principles guiding social work practice draw from both feminist theory and analysis and from social work theory.

As noted, women had always been involved in community practice as volunteers, workers, leaders, researchers, and scholars. Social workers were highly involved in the movement for women's suffrage and the first wave of feminism in America. Following that period, however, their writings were not widely published in the mainstream literature or used in teaching or theory development.

The second wave of feminist theory, with greater emphasis on working with women through empowerment models, began to burgeon in 1980. A literature emerged in social work that focused on women as clients/constituents, workers, organizers, planners, leaders, and administrators. Elaine Norman and Arlene Mancuso (1980) edited the first book to articulate feminist issues for a new generation of social work students, faculty, and practitioners. Also in 1980, Naomi Gottlieb edited *Alternative Social Services for Women*, containing articles that illustrated both individual and institutional mechanisms and effects of sexism in the helping professions. This book provided theoretical, programmatic, technical, and institutional ideas that innovatively addressed the special circumstances of women and provided a value and knowledge base to transform practice with women. At CSWE meetings during this time, Gottlieb spoke passionately about the need for a woman's perspective in practice and, with a number of colleagues, founded *Affilia*, the first social work journal devoted to women's issues.

In 1982, Anne Weick and Susan Vandiver edited a work, *Women, Power, and Change*, that explicitly articulated and integrated feminist theory and principles in social work practice in a variety of practice areas. In that book, a chapter by Brandwein specifically addressed the issues that confronted women in community and macro practice (1982, pp. 158–170).

Weil argued, in Van den Berg and Cooper's Feminist Visions for Social Work Practice (1986), that the lack of focus on women from the 1940s forward, coupled with efforts to recruit men for social work leadership positions, limited consideration of women's issues and women's organizations. Consequently, during that period in the literature and in social work education, it was "rare to find feminist case studies, a focus on organizing for and by women, or models employing feminist principles in organizing" (p. 192; reprinted in Rothman et al., 1995, p. 121). She argued for inclusion of women's content and perspectives in generalist practice courses, and for specialized practice courses focused on women's issues. In presenting the philosophical-theoretical foundation for feminist-oriented community practice, she delineated the following principles: actively using feminist values; valuing process; engaging in consciousness-raising and praxis; supporting wholeness and unity; reconceptualizing power as transactive and focusing on empowerment strategies; democratic structuring of groups, organizations, and services; remembering that the personal is political; and focusing on an orientation to structural change to eliminate sexism, racism, and other forms of oppression (Weil, 1995, pp. 201–203). Fortunately the feminist literature on social work and community practice has burgeoned since the late 1980s and once again emerged in the research literature.

Feminist Influence on Community Practice Research

Working with communities, organizations, and groups on their research agenda is a critical component of community practice. Community practice research that is done with, rather than on, communities can generate knowledge as well as empower and emancipate members, leading to a process of social change. Working collaboratively, community practice researchers help groups and organizations raise critical questions about their circumstances and voice self-defined concerns and goals. Serving as facilitators, teachers, and coaches, community practice researchers also help communities increase participants' skills and expand resources within the community that are available to document assets and needs, and to pursue goals. Production of knowledge is inextricably linked to actions that seek to change conditions that may be limiting, oppressive, and intolerable to the community.

Research with communities is inherently political. The community practice researcher must recognize the historical, cultural, political, economic, and social forces shaping current conditions and power relationships (Kincheloe, 1995). These forces provide a context that influences selection of the subject of inquiry, the research approaches, and relationships between the practitioners and community members.

When community practice research is influenced by feminist thought, it is conducted democratically; it accepts subjective experiences as valid sources of knowledge; it emphasizes both outcomes and process; and it strengthens the community or group so that individually and collectively, members are better able to act on their own behalf. Community practice research is grounded in values and processes that are empowerment-based. The process is participatory so that the researcher assumes a collaborative stance with members of the community. The researcher steps out of the expert professional role so that knowledge and skills are freely shared and taught to community members (Johnson, 1994). The relationship is consultative and egalitarian rather than expert-client. Through a process of praxis, the community practice researcher can facilitate a method of inquiry that rests upon action, reflection, and further action (Freire, 1990; Lee, 1994).

Action research methods are especially suitable for working with communities. Action research involves a simultaneous process of knowledge building, reflection, and action to promote change. Reinharz (1992) describes five approaches to "feminist change-oriented research" (p. 180): action research, participatory or collaborative research, prevalence and needs assessment, evaluation research, and demystification. Table 7–1 illustrates each approach in which the researcher engages with the research subject and generates knowledge that is intended to illuminate an inequity, raise consciousness, and mobilize advocates for change. Other research approaches, such as empowerment evaluation, share similar characteristics. According to Fetterman, empowerment evaluation is the "use of evaluation concepts, techniques, and findings to foster improvement and self-determination" (1996, p. 4).

Table 7–1: Feminist Influenced Approaches to Community Practice Research

Research approach	Characteristics	Examples
Participatory Action Research	• collaboratively involves members of the community in negotiating research topics, format, and data analysis • minimizes the distinction between the researcher and the "client"; the relationship is reciprocal both teaching and learning from the other • action results from increased critical consciousness	Gaventa, 1980; Hinsdale, Lewis & Waller, 1995; Johnson, 1994; Noponen, 1996; Sarri & Sarri, 1992
Needs/Assets Assessment	• provides data about the incidence of issues that are often "invisible" • provides data to be used by the community in advocacy work	Mauney, Williams & Weil, 1993; Thomas-Slayter, Polestico, Esser, Taylor & Matua, 1995; Noponen, 1996
Empowerment Evaluation	• uses "evaluation concepts, techniques, and findings to foster improvement and self-determination" (Fetterman, 1996, p. 4) • assesses the effectiveness of different types of actions in meeting needs or solving problems • increases capacity to self-evaluate	Andrews, 1996; Christiansen-Ruffman, 1995
Demystification	• illuminates the "invisible" • gives voice to the "voiceless"	Hyde, 1994; Slocum, Whichhart, Rocheleau & Thomas-Slaytor, 1995

CURRENT COMMUNITY PRACTICE

Community Practice and Generic Models

Community practice models are often grounded in sociological theory. For our purposes, a model is defined as "a simplification of reality that is intended to order and clarify our perception of that reality while still encapsulating its essential characteristics" (Jeffries, 1996, p. 101). The eight major practice models described in the *Encyclopedia of Social Work* (Weil & Gamble, 1995) include: (1) neighborhood and community organizing, (2) organizing functional communities, (3) community social and economic development, (4) social planning, (5) program development and community liaison, (6) political and social action, (7) coalitions, and, (8) social movements (p. 581).

Each of these eight models is grounded in the basic processes of organizing, planning, development, and change. The typology is based on a survey of the literature and the actual observation of current community practice interventions engaged in by social workers in recent years. The principles that guide the framework are: (1) *place*: the location of the intercommunication of those involved, (2) *purpose*: the goals or hoped for outcomes that would result from people coming together, and (3) *values*: the social, economic, and political values that undergird their goals. The models are also considered for their congruence with social work values. These three principles should guide the assessment of models and selection of strategies in any community practice situation.

There is considerable fluidity in the types of community practice models in existence. Real world community practice examples rarely follow such discrete patterns as are elaborated in the eight models of Weil and Gamble or in similar descriptions of community practice models (Hyde, 1996; Jeffries, 1996; Popple, 1996; Rothman, 1995). Community practice emerges from a variety of settings, molded primarily by two factors: (1) the physical, social, political, and cultural forces of the local place and/or the social issue and (2) the particular personal characteristics of the organizing leadership.

Brief descriptions of the eight discrete models are provided in Table 7–2 (for more detailed information on each model, see Weil and Gamble, 1995). Analysis of the characteristics of different community practice models from a feminist perspective requires an understanding of the needs of women and of organizational structures and strategies best suited to empower women. Learning about these issues is best done in a process, with the facilitator, organizer, and the members of the organization learning together. There are ample literature sources that provide excellent insight for analysis of community organization from the perspective of women (Brandwein, 1987; Ferree & Martin, 1995; Gutierrez & Lewis, 1995; Hooyman & Bricker-Jenkins, 1985; Hyde, 1986, 1989, 1996; Masi, 1981; Weil, 1995). In addition, Table 7–2 allows the practitioner to examine the models using specific questions that enable the organization to explore feminist perspectives. The table puts the issues in the form of questions rather than directives in order to engage participants in assessing the model's degree of sensitivity and responsiveness to the needs and strengths of women and girls.

Table 7–2 challenges community practice curriculum and practitioners in its application of a gender lens to practice. It should provoke reflection and analysis of women's conditions, roles, issues, concerns, and opportunities in all kinds of groups and organizations. It can provide a guide in assessing curriculum inclusion of women in a serious way—social work strategies when women *really* matter! The principles and ideas incorporated in the table provide some direction for dealing with the complexity of technological, social, political, and environmental change that is accelerating, and they provide a framework on which to test and analyze theory, research, and curriculum materials for their inclusiveness and relevance to women's realities.

Table 7–2: Community Practice Models with Feminist Application

Neighborhood and Community Organizing	**Theoretical Influence**	**Feminist Application Issues**
This kind of organizing would take place in a geographic location such as a neighborhood, parish, or rural county where face-to-face activity brings people together. The focus of the activities is to enhance the personal capacity of people to build and maintain organizations, and to build organizations that will have the capacity to change any community condition to improve the quality of life for all residents, especially for those most often excluded from official community planning and development processes.	Clearly, community and neighborhood must be delineated in each practice setting; however, the general concepts relating to how a community or neighborhood is defined and functions can be shaped by the conceptual frameworks of a wide range of community theorists and social work community practice theories (Bellah et al., 1985; Fellin, 1995; Fisher & Karger, 1997; Mondros & Wilson, 1994; Hyde, 1996; Martinez-Brawley, 1990; Rothman & Zald, 1995; Rubin & Rubin, 1992; Unger & Wandersman, 1985; Warren, 1978; Weil, 1995, 1996). In addition to concepts related to community, the practitioner working in community and neighborhood organizing will need grounding in group dynamics (Toseland & Rivas, 1995; Zander, 1985), change theory, especially as related to community groups (Bennis, Benne & Chin, 1985; Brager & Specht, 1973; Kretzmann & McKnight, 1993; Lipitt, Watson & Westley, 1958; Warren, 1971; Zander, 1990), and citizen participation (Gamble & Weil, 1995; Putnam, 1993; Rivera & Erlich, 1995; Wandersman, 1981).	• What are the best ways to maximize the participation of women at all levels of organization building? • What strategies are most successful to develop women's leadership capacities so that women are clearly seen in multiple roles, not just in organizational maintenance roles? • What are the most effective ways to empower women in local groups and representative groups? • How can organizations help women to practice roles in political and conflict arenas, and help men to practice roles in cooperative, supportive, and coalition arenas? • What strategies are most useful to help local organizations develop woman-centered programs to serve unique needs of women and girls?

Table 7–2 *(continued)*

Organizing Functional Communities	Theoretical Influences	Feminist Application Issues
This kind of organizing brings people together who have similar social/civic justice interests but who may not live in close proximity to each other. These are people who identify themselves as a "community of interest," and whose activities may focus on educational advocacy with a mission to develop new policies or change old policies, and who work generally to change attitudes and behaviors of public officials and the general public about issues or population groups. These groups may also provide services where a service vacuum exists for their constituent population. Communication among people in such groups who may be located some distance from each other could take place by fax, e-mail, websites, newsletter, meetings, and/or telephone conferences.	Practitioners working with functional communities draw from a range of research-based practice theory provided by those who have studied the formation and development of groups. Examples include women's groups (Burden & Gottlieb, 1987; Hooyman & Bricker-Jenkins, 1985; Hyde, 1986, 1996; Mauney, Williams & Weil, 1993; Van den Berg & Cooper, 1986; Weil, 1995; Weil & Gamble, 1995), groups organized by and for people of color (Rivera & Erlich, 1995), and groups organized for peace issues (Addams, 1922; E. Boulding, 1988). Theoretical concepts relating to social power (K. Boulding, 1989; Cartwright, 1959; Freire, 1973) and cultural competence (Fong & Gibbs, 1995; Gutierrez & Lewis, 1995; Rivera & Erlich, 1995) are also useful in understanding functional communities.	• How can alternative, woman-centered programs be developed to serve unique needs of women and girls? • What are the best ways to develop women's leadership capacities in organizing, planning, development, and change strategies? • How can women best be organized in functional communities around specific issues? • What are the best ways to build coalitions among women's groups and organizations—especially in the alternative service and domestic violence networks? • What strategies work best to develop coalitions among women across race, class, sexual preference, and other diversity issues—to build, articulate, and enact common women's agendas? • How can functional communities increase the accountability of political and service systems to women's concerns and concerns of other vulnerable populations?

Table 7–2 *(continued)*

Community Social and Economic Development	Theoretical Influences	Feminist Application Issues
This organizing activity brings together a group of people, especially a group that has been systematically excluded from the structures that provide economic and social capital in a region, to initiate social and economic development plans and programs. These groups will enable constituents to develop personal, social, organizational, and entrepreneurial skills. They will help people in the target area to gain access to increased resources such as community reinvestment funds, to identify their own capacities for development programs, and to make improved use of external social and economic investments in the region, especially investments in educational and training institutions. This model clearly connects both the social development activities (e.g., education and training, building organizations, establishing social support structures) and economic development activities (e.g., creating new sources of capital, housing developments, micro enterprise, community banking, and entrepreneurial support efforts). Sustainable development is a more recent development paradigm that focuses on the improved well-being of people in terms of health, production, cultural, and social needs without causing destruction to their environment in the near future and for coming generations.	Theories relating to this model are drawn primarily from development theories related to social development, economic development and sustainable development (Biddle & Biddle, 1965; Blakeley, 1979, 1989; Cernea, 1985; Christenson & Robinson, 1989; Clark, 1990; Dasgupta & Weale, 1992; Estes, 1993; Hanna & Robinson, 1994; Haq, 1995; Hoff & McNutt, 1994; Hinsdale & Lewis, 1995; Midgley, 1995; Raheim, 1995; Ross, 1955; Rubin, 1997; Rubin & Rubin, 1992; Sherrad-Sherrade & Ninacs, in press). Theories of social development, economic development, poverty, and sustainable development are summarized in the United Nations Development Report (1996).	• What are the best ways to include women's issues in social and economic development with an explicit acknowledgment of the value of women's social and "informal" economic contributions to the quality of life in any community? • What principles of development will make women's culture and women's values and concerns an equal part of the development process? • What are examples of strategies that have been employed to create sustainable development projects that protect populations and environments? • What are the best ways to develop and support women's full participation in decision making, and social and economic development planning, implementation, governance, and evaluation? • How can programs ensure the development of women's leadership capacities and opportunities for leadership at all levels of development.

Table 7–2 *(continued)*

Social Planning	Theoretical Influences	Feminist Application Issues
This model comprises organizing the activities of a group, organizations, boards, or groups of organizations to assess local or regional needs and assets in order to plan for and develop responses to social conditions. Groups may be formed through a single agency or government entity, or a set of organizations with similar missions. Planning involves the use of technical skills in assessment, data analysis, and evaluation. The process of planning increasingly emphasizes the involvement of grassroots consumer and constituency groups.	This model is informed primarily by change and planning theories (Bennis, Benne & Chin, 1985; Brager & Specht, 1973; Burke, 1979; Checkoway, 1995; Friedman, 1992; Kahn, 1969; Lauffer, 1978; Mandelbaum, Mazza & Burchell, 1996; Rothman & Zald, 1995), participatory planning, and particpatory research (Fetterman, 1996; Gaventa, 1980; Hinsdale & Lewis, 1995; Johnson, 1994; Noponen, 1996; Rothman & Thomas, 1994).	• What kinds of policies, programs, and activities will develop women's capacities (social planning professionals, organizational leaders in NGOs, and grass-roots women) in technical skills, management skills, monitoring skills, and evaluation skills? • How can women's groups and organizations be helped to apply technical planning and evaluation skills related to general organizing, planning, and development? • How can women's groups be involved in planning, organizing, and development related to the social, economic, and service needs of women, children, vulnerable populations, and oppressed populations? • How can we ensure that planning approaches will be grounded in the target population's experiences? What are the ways to validate and give credence to women's and other constituent groups' appraisals of needs and strengths? • What structures will ensure the democratization of planning processes? • How can planning processes be demystified and technical skills and analysis methods be made more appropriate to local culture and technology? • How can the inclusion of gender and diversity issues in planning processes be ensured? • What practices will ensure that cultural issues and women's perspectives and knowledge will be valued in planning processes? • In what ways can we intentionally use feminist theory, values, and principles in planning?

Table 7–2 *(continued)*

Program Development and Community Liaison	**Theoretical Influences**	**Feminist Application Issues**
This activity involves the initiation of new or expanded community services by an organization or collaboration of agencies to respond to unserved and underserved populations or new social issues. These new and expanded services are often established as the result of advocacy by, and in some cases consultation with, the constituent groups that are underserved in current delivery systems. The community liaison role is explicitly intended to seek ways for constituent groups and underserved populations to be actively engaged in the new or expanded programming.	This model draws heavily from theory relating to human service organizations and organization and program development (Gortner, Mahler & Nicholson, 1987; Gutierrez & Lewis, 1995; Hasenfeld, 1983, 1995; Hooyman & Bricker-Jenkins, 1985; Hyde, 1986; Kettner, Daley & Nichols, 1985; Kurzman, 1985; Perlmutter, 1989, 1994; Rivera & Erlich, 1995; Taylor, 1985). Practitioners using this model need to be grounded in theories relating to management of human services (Brody, 1993; Edwards & Yankey, 1991; Toch & Grant, 1982).	• How can we assure that women's issues are considered in the development of service networks and systems for service coordination? • What are the most successful strategies to broaden program development foci to include special needs of women—particularly in relation to issues such as health, mental health, or the disabling conditions of racism, or poverty? • How can connections and collaboration be strengthened between mainstream service systems and alternative programs developed by women of color or feminist groups? • How can programs ensure a focus on empowerment of and advocacy for oppressed groups? • How can programs develop closer, functional ties to constituent groups and populations invclved in services—sharing information, reconceptualizing, and sharing power? • What are the best strategies to involve constituent groups and service participants in governance?

Table 7–2 *(continued)*

Political and Social Action	Theoretical Influences	Feminist Application Issues
This kind of organizing engages people in a wide range of issue-oriented activities that could include advocacy, conflict model direct action, or partisan political activity (e.g., running for office, supporting specific candidates, organizing a political action group, etc.) The activities are often organized through a temporary coalition of organizations, and groups. The focus of this activity is for social and civic justice concerns.	This model draws from theories relating to political participation, power, conflict, and conscientization. The theoretical references that ground this model include Alinsky (1971), Bailey (1983), Bobo, Kendall and Max (1991), Brager and Specht (1973), Fanon (1966), Fisher (1984, 1995), Fisher and Karger (1997), Freire (1973), Gamson (1975), Kahn (1982), and Mondros and Wilson (1994). This model, like the model for organizing functional communities, is enriched by studies that look at gender roles and diversity in political and social action (Costain, 1992; Darcy, Welch & Clark, 1994; Verba, Scholzman, Brady & Nie, 1993; Woliver, 1996).	• How can women's power be increased to influence policy decisions? • What are the best ways to maximize the participation of women in political systems and institutions? • What activities will strengthen morale and build women's skills to participate in local political and advocacy groups? • How can we achieve the full representation of women in existing political structures, and develop strong women's political advocacy organizations? • What strategies successfully include women and women's issues in social and political decision-making processes with the goal of developing continued collective power? • How can we best increase political and service system accountability to women's and girls' concerns, and the concerns of other vulnerable populations?

Table 7–2 *(continued)*

Coalitions	Theoretical Influences	Feminist Application Issues
This organizing activity brings together, on a temporary or longer-term basis, organizations that have an interest in a common social, civic, or economic justice concerns for the purpose of building a power base large enough to influence policy decisions or secure needed resources. These coalitions are increasingly more involved in service delivery as well as influencing the shape of policy and the allocation of resources.	Useful theoretical perspectives that ground this model are those relating to conflict resolution, cooperation, coalition building, and interorganizational relationships. These concepts are drawn from Chong (1991), Coser (1956), Mizrahi and Rosenthal (1993), Pruitt (1972), Roberts-DeGennaro (1986, 1987), and Schopler (1994).	• How can organizations develop coalitions of women's groups for women's social and economic empowerment? • How can women's programs form coalitions that will strengthen service networks? • How can coalitions of alternative service networks be organized to advocate for particular needs of women such as Coalitions Against Domestic Violence? • How can women's groups and organizations be assisted to find common ground? • What are the best ways to facilitate groups in coalitions to deal with the inherent centripetal and centrifugal forces? • How can coalitions be formed, especially with men's groups, that work to eliminate sexism in society?

Table 7–2 *(continued)*

Social Movements	**Theoretical Influences**	**Feminist Application Issues**
From time-to-time the social and cultural conditions in a society allow for the expression and elaboration of new visions and new paradigms within which to reevaluate social justice issues. When these conditions are pervasive across the larger society, a wide range of leaders, organizations, and coalitions engage to become voices for community and societal change and to strengthen social justice.	Social movements are based on theories of social transformation and collective action. A summary of these theories is found in Morris and Muller (1992). More specific theoretical guidance is available on a variety of movements, for example, the women's movement (Costin, 1992), the civil rights movement (Chong, 1991), Appalachian and rural movements (Gaventa, 1980), and movements of poor people (Piven & Cloward, 1997).	• How can grass-roots women, NGO representatives, grantmakers, and academics best be engaged in the emerging movement for sustainable development? • What are the best strategies to engage women and men in the women's movement? • How can we assure that women's issues and concerns are dealt with in all social movements? Adapted from Weil & Gamble, 1995, and from Weil, 1995.

FEMINIST APPLICATIONS OF THE GENERAL MODELS

Each model of community practice can be strengthened by articulation of principles and strategies that bring attention to women and to issues of diversity. Despite the increasing numbers of women in community practice, organizing, planning, and development, there are still many challenges to women in these arenas. Weil (1995) noted that

> to function effectively as a woman organizer in community practice, one needs a heightened feminist consciousness, as well as the recognition that one will continually be tested as a woman and as an organizer. When feminists are involved in general community organization or social change, they must always work to include and expand feminist agendas. They must also maintain a dual focus with regard to both process and tasks, seeking to integrate feminist goals and approaches into the general problem-solving strategy. (p. 193)

Women in general community practice need to carry with them a feminist organizing model that acknowledges women's realities, strengths, and needs. They need to be able to deal with sexism as it affects women in communities and in organizations. With all of the models it is important to analyze the complexity of roles and issues from a feminist perspective. We have provided a framework to analyze feminist applications in the second assignment.

Critical Lenses for Community Practice: Gender, Diversity and Empowerment

Challenges of the twenty-first century will require a social work curricula with strengthened emphasis on community practice, paying particular attention to critical analysis of gender, diversity, and empowerment issues. If practice theory, methods, and strategies do not adequately consider gender factors, we can use gender analysis to examine roles, power, structure, and styles to ground practice approaches in the cultural, social, and community realities facing women and men. A gender lens can act as a "microscope," picking up factors in a particular situation that would be missed without magnification and specification. Conversely, a gender lens analysis can be used to magnify the broad effects of gender roles, expectations, and constraints at societal, cultural, and intercultural levels. Particularly since so many social workers are women, students need to be prepared to analyze gender issues in communities and organizations. More specifically in community practice, male and female students and practitioners need skills to assess the initial effect of their own "latent characteristics"—such as gender and age—on groups with which they work in different organizations, communities, and cultures.

Careful consideration and assessment of diversity and pluralism is increasingly important in a multicultural society such as the United States and in cross-cultural and international social work. A major challenge facing the nation is the value tension between concerns for common social values and the need to recognize, understand, and honor specific values of different cultural groups. Race and social class interact in the current political/social/economic system in ways that can further disadvantage the already economically disadvantaged. Women learn social/cultural expectations that emphasize their identification with their racial/ethnic group rather than with their gender, however, gender adds a specific dimension to issues of diversity. Some aspects of the backlash against feminism stem from this common expectation. Understanding the histories of racial/ethnic groups and their current opportunity structures provides a background for developing relevant practice approaches. If social work is to remain focused on social justice and equal opportunity during a period of increasing privatization and downsizing particularly in the public sector, community social work is a major means to act on those values with practice strategies that emphasize the strength in communal diversity and the importance of pluralism in democratic societies.

Both gender and diversity/pluralism are essential factors to consider in social work practices geared toward empowerment of individuals, groups, and communities. Empowerment concerns can be used as a lens to examine the operation of direct power blocks and the effects of inherent power blocks described by Solomon (1976) as the reasons that oppressed and disadvantaged communities and groups need practice strategies that focus on empowerment. Using empowerment as a concept provides a means to analyze these power blocks and see the complexity that can result in the combinations and interactions of gender, race, ethnicity, and socioeconomic class that affect individuals, groups, and communities.

An empowerment analysis provides a major analytic lens that is applicable in micro, mezzo, and macro practice. Although the term "empowerment" was coined relatively recently by Solomon (1976), the perspective connoted by the term has been a major stream of social work practice from its beginnings in the settlement movement (Simon, 1994). Simon illustrates, analyzes, and anchors this historic tradition illustrating themes and commonalities from the late nineteenth century to the present. Both Solomon's analysis and the documentation of the empowerment tradition can be used as groundwork for empowerment practice.

Empowerment-oriented practice occurs at individual, group, organizational, and community levels. Lee (1994) describes a "transactional view of political and personal change" illustrating "the unity of professional purpose in the empowerment approach" (p. 20). Through development and synthesis of principles and illustrations of practice strategies and skills, she defines and describes empowerment practice with individuals, groups, and communities (Lee, 1994). Empowerment practice at the community level operates simultaneously through individual leadership development and group capacity-building (Staples, 1990). In community practice, the focus is capacity-building activities guided by mutual analysis and learning, employing conscientization strategies and focusing on individuals, groups, community-based organizations, and communities (Freire, 1973, 1985; Rivera & Erlich, 1995). Rivera and Erlich stress the importance of analyzing power and racism, and developing critical consciousness in work with oppressed and disadvantaged groups. Critical consciousness is the development of knowledge and understanding of how "personal and political factors interact with each other and one's work, as well as how values, ideas, and practice skills are influenced by social forces and, in turn influence them" (p. 8).

It is critical for community practice to focus on the strengths, culture, needs, and diversity among different racial and ethnic groups. Rivera and Erlich provide an exciting "model-in-progress" approach to working with a community, and ten chapters in their book focus on community work with major population groups. They emphasize the importance of familiarity with customs, traditions, social networks, and values; knowledge of language, leadership styles, and development; analytical frameworks for political and economic analysis; knowledge of organizing strategies; and skills in conscientization and empowerment (pp. 13–15).

Lorraine Gutierrez and Edith Lewis (1995) provide a feminist perspective on organizing with women of color that offers a way to work on race and gender issues simultaneously. They state that the goal of feminist organizing is "the elimination of permanent power hierarchies between all people that can prevent them from realizing their human potential" (p. 98). Feminist organizing seeks to eliminate sexism, racism, and other forms of oppression through empowerment strategies that seek "individual liberation through collective activity, embracing both personal and social change" (Morell, 1987, p. 147). Gutierrez and Lewis identify the factors present in most feminist approaches to organizing and provide guidance for feminist organizing with women of color. Their analysis provides a useful framework for analyzing and implementing strategies and highlights the importance of adopting models and strategies that fit the vision and purposes of specific groups. They illustrate specific issues and concerns of women of color and suggest changes that may be needed in the organizer's behavior and interaction.

Women and Sustainable Development

Historically, as described earlier, social work has deep roots in community development beginning with the physical and social development of settlement house neighborhoods and continuing through to a major emphasis on community organization in the United States during the War on Poverty of the 1960s. In some countries, particularly developing countries such as India and Honduras, community-level interventions in social problems are much more prevalent than interventions directed at the individual level. In the United States, community development has often been more narrowly focused on a specific segment of community such as agriculture, housing, and economic development. These specific areas of community development more common in industrialized countries have traditionally been both directed by and toward men.

Social workers working with international organizations in community development have generally followed and been associated with the evolution of community development models as they have emerged in the past fifty years. In some cases, where models of community development have had untoward effects on the populations they seek to assist, social workers have literally "followed" these efforts as crisis assistance and rescue workers. Those development models originated from the West during the past five decades were based primarily on the theories of a free market economy. These approaches, often woefully shortsighted in their inappropriateness to cultures and environments, have been described as modernization, dependency, basic needs, and structural adjustment (McKay, 1990). Critique of these models has been very forceful in recognizing that the number of people who are poor in the world has increased during this period and the gap between rich countries and poor countries continues to grow larger (Carmen, 1994; Korten, 1995; UNDP, 1996).

In recent years social workers internationally have joined efforts, especially through the Inter-University Consortium on International Social Development (IUCISD), to focus more energy on community interventions under the model of social development. The journal *Social Development Issues* and many excellent books and articles have emerged to help direct the thinking and practice of social workers who are engaged in community practice (Billups, 1994; Chandler, 1986; Estes, 1984; Jones & Pandey, 1981; Midgeley, 1995). In explicating the model Midgeley notes that "social development offers a comprehensive macro-perspective that focuses on communities and societies, emphasizes planned interventions, promotes a dynamic change-oriented approach which is inclusive and universalistic, and above all seeks to harmonize social interventions with economic development efforts" (p. 8).

The most recent community development model, and one that has provided a framework welcoming women's voices, is sustainable development. The concept of sustainable development gained prominence in the development literature with the 1987 report of the World Commission on Environment and Development chaired by Gro Harland Bruntland, Our Common Future: From One Earth to One World. Generally, the meaning of sustainable development relates to a focus for development that is concerned, both now and in the future, about the healthy condition of the earth and the healthy condition of human populations. In his foreword for the 1996 *Human Development Report,* James Gustave Speth writes that "more and more policy makers in many countries are reaching the unavoidable conclusion that, to be valuable and legitimate, development progress—both nationally and internationally—must be people-centered, equitably distributed and environmentally and socially sustainable" (p. iii). While definitions of sustainable development that can provide guidance for concrete action are still being constructed, the meaning of sustainable development with its concern for healthy present and future human societies provides a hopeful and unifying development paradigm.

The work to develop helpful models and conceptual frameworks for sustainable development is directly relevant to social work's concern for the person-in-environment (Estes, 1993; Hoff & McNutt, 1994). Furthermore, because concern for the environment at the community level seems to be an active arena for grass-roots women leaders, sustainable development is also directly relevant to understanding women's ways of knowing and working as we develop a knowledge base for the critical tasks of preserving human societies and human ecology. If social work has a commitment to expand its person-in-environment perspective to include the biological and physical environment, then sustainable development offers the profession some guidance and many practice opportunities.

In recent years, ordinary citizen activists such as Lois Gibbs have surveyed the ill effects of the toxic waste dump at Love Canal in New York State on the children of her neighborhood in much the same way Jane Addams surveyed her neighborhood in Chicago to describe the bitter results of the industrial revolution (Addams, 1960). And currently across the globe we see, for example, women in the Greenbelt movement in Kenya work to reverse the effects of deforestation and women in the Andean Food Technology project promoting the growth of indigenous food as opposed to cash crops so that poor households can have more food on the table. Hundreds of actions taken by local, state, and regional groups across the globe have called attention to the need to stop business as usual, questioning routine life-styles, technological "progress," and industrial practices that have existed for a century (Berry, 1990; Korten, 1995; Marietta, 1995). Many of the leaders for environmental protection and alternative methods of development have been women (Abramovitz & Nichols, 1992; Dankelmann & Davidson, 1988; Harcourt, 1994; Leonard, 1995; Young, 1993).

Demand for development alternatives has spawned new organizations, many of them organized by women, such as Development Alternatives for Women in a New Era (DAWN), Women in Development (WID), Women's Environment and Development Organization (WEDO), ISIS International, National Congress of Neighborhood Women, Grassroots Organizations Operating Together in Sisterhood (GROOTS), International Alliance of Women, Sisterhood Is Global Institute, and others. International debates in which theories on population control are pitted against theories relating to the environment and development have been brought to the general population through the efforts of many nongovernmental women's organizations. These nongovernmental organizations (NGOs) energetically took the issues to United Nations conferences during the past several years including the UN Conference on Women in Nairobi in 1985; the International Conference on the Environment and Development in Rio de Janeiro in 1992; the UN Conference on Human Rights in Vienna in 1993; the International Conference on Population and Development in Cairo in 1994; the World Summit on Social Development in Copenhagen in 1995; and the Fourth World Conference on Women in Beijing in 1995; and especially the Habitat II Conference in Istanbul in 1996.

The international debates focused by the United Nations conferences and those relating to the critique of development models were particularly helpful in bringing forth feminist perspectives. Harcourt defines the feminist perspective as knowledge production and practice seeking "to bring out the different positions of the actors in order to allow for possible connections with others; feminist analysis aims to interpret, not claim, truth" (1994, p. 22). Women in particular have been active in organizing for and writing about alternative models of development that would include concern for women's needs and the needs of their children. The writings of ecofeminists, for example, focus on preserving life on earth (Merchant, 1992). Harcourt (1994, p. 3) describes a shift in some feminist circles from women in development (WID) to a more holistic, integrated view of women, environment, and alternatives to development (WED). The struggle to give practical meaning to the concept of sustainable development has played a large role in the search for alternatives to both traditional Western market-based development models and centralized government models. The conceptual framework for sustainable development has been influenced in large part by the organization and writing of women. (It is important to say both the organization and the writing because the key to feminist perspectives comes from understanding and analyzing relationships and previously unheard voices most often given life in face-to-face exchanges.)

The search for new development models has evolved with a parallel search for new ways to measure development progress. In 1984, Estes provided a significant contribution to rethinking the way we measure social progress beyond the simple and often distorted use of the gross national product (GNP). Since then, Henderson (1994) has provided a method for combining social and economic measures in a clear alternative to solely economic measures. She speaks of the need for competition and cooperation as equally useful economic strategies and poses the need for feedback loops of information for people affected by development decisions. Full-cost pricing (the cost of a product that takes into account the social and environmental costs incurred) would become a more accurate way to evaluate development and consumption costs. Henderson believes the GNP-growth models of economic development marginalize workers, especially those in the informal economy, the majority of whom are women. The informal sectors still provide "the basic safety nets in all societies, even those in the U.S., Canada and Western Europe" (p. 81).

The United Nations Human Development Index (HDI), developed largely through the leadership of Mahbub ul Haq (1995), takes a different approach to the gross domestic product (GDP) as the indicator of a nation's development. The Human Development Index is a composite score that calculates the GDP based on real purchasing power, not exchange rates; literacy rates and mean years of school; and life expectancy at birth. The move to measure human development in terms of economics as well as social, health, and educational attainment connects social work in a more integral way to development work.

The contributions of women to environmental and development issues make the work and words of women clearly linked to the sustainable development model. Social work is also clearly linked by its historical focus on the person-in-environment. Social work can easily and directly connect practice to sustainable development through its historically deep-rooted engagement with community practice described earlier in this chapter. Helping students of social work to make the connections with the contributions of women to community practice historically and the opportunities for practice within the sustainable development model will prepare students of social work for the next century.

CONCLUSIONS AND NEW EMPHASES FOR SOCIAL WORK EDUCATION

It is essential for social work education to further develop and expand community content and focus (Weil, 1996). In the face of rapid social change, a combination of knowledge and skills gained from content in community practice, social planning, citizen participation, community organizing, nonprofit management, and community development can keep practitioners grounded in the historical purposes of social work and enable them to meet new challenges. More specific content in participatory action research, needs/assets assessment, program evaluation, information management, resource development, and sustainable development is also requisite.

Education of social work students is effective only if it has incorporated social justice concerns. In our society, and in the face of sociopolitical tensions across the globe, all of the community content we describe can be useful to the social work practitioner only if it has been gained through the lenses of empowerment and diversity. Community practice that is associated with social work must display a sensitivity to the wide range of perspectives and interests in a community, especially those interests that have so often been ignored and undervalued. Furthermore, we must determine to change the kinds of structures and practices that keep some groups subjugated to others.

In this chapter we have provided a historical review of the development of community practice methods and theory. This review and critique outlined the influence of women's thoughts and experiences, first as pivotal forces in community practice development, then as voices in the background, and more recently as more prominent voices in developing theory and approaches to community practice. The chapter provides guidance for understanding the major influence women have had in shaping community practice research and sustainable development approaches. We presented eight general models for community practice along with feminist applications to women's organizations and women's issues. These feminist applications can help teachers and students analyze, plan, and implement practice focused on gender equity and special issues facing women. Finally, in the appendices at the end of the chapter, we have provided examples of assignments. The first recommended assignment has proven useful in helping students internalize some knowledge and skills needed for practice in sustainable development. The second assignment provides a tool for using a gender lens to analyze community practice.

APPENDIX 7–1: ASSIGNMENTS

Assignment A—Gender Issues in Sustainable Development

In order to understand gender issues in sustainable development, students will analyze aspects of sustainable development from a project of their choice. The project must have goals that help a community move toward sustainable development (e.g., ecotourism, sustainable agriculture, urban micro enterprise, education of women and girls, experiential environmental programs for young people, indigenous/natural wellness promotion, integrated health and development projects, etc.). The project can be selected from an example in the literature. It can be a project that has already started or that is planned for a specific community location anywhere in the world. The project must be analyzed from the perspective of a specific location so that local social, cultural, and political characteristics are incorporated in the analysis with particular attention to gender roles. The analysis must describe how these characteristics support or prevent a community's maintenance or initiation of a sustainable development project.

The analysis will include:

1. A description of the community location and general aspects of the social, cultural, and political characteristics, and gender role issues.

2. A description of the project identifying specifically the aspects of the project that would lead the community toward sustainable development. (This section should include your own final definition of sustainable development.)

3. A detailed description of a plan you would use to learn of the knowledge, structures, practices, and gender roles in the community that will affect the sustainable development project. (What do the people already know about their community and its sustainability? How will you learn about their knowledge of themselves, their community, and their world? What will you learn from women that you can't learn from men? What will you learn from men that you can't learn from women?)

4. An analysis of the community's social, cultural, and political characteristics as they relate to serving as barriers or helpers to the sustainable development project.

5. Your suggested proposals that incorporate knowledge, values, practices, and structures learned from the community that could enhance the life and strength of the project. What is the cultural wisdom you have learned from the community?

6. Your suggested proposals that incorporate knowledge you have of the world and sustainable development practice that could enhance the life and strength of the project. What knowledge

and skills do you bring as a facilitator to this community and proposed project?

7. To what extent does your own role, sex, race, culture, and value system influence the shape and subject of your project? Who are you from the perspective of community members?

8. To what extent are there conflicts between your expectations of your role and the gender role expectations of the community with whom you are working?

Assignment B—Gender Analysis of Community Practice Models; Assignment For Class or Field

Purpose: To enable students to become more sensitive to gender issues including the needs and strengths of women and girls. To plan leadership development strategies for women and girls, and to assure equal partnerships for women in community practice.

Use Table 7–2 from this chapter as a worksheet for this assignment. The exercise can be organized either for small groups in class or as a potential assignment with field placement community groups.

For a small group exercise in class: Divide the class into eight small groups. Each group will be assigned one of the eight models of community practice from Table 7–2. Ask groups to discuss the model, responding to each of the questions from the segment "Feminist Application Issues." Be sure that each group consists of both men and women. In responding to the questions, students should think about the needs and strengths of women and girls in order to facilitate their opportunities and involvement as well as development strategies to deal with priority issues. Each small group will report back to the class on their outcomes.

For an assignment that relates to field placement: Ask each student working in a field placement that involves community practice to complete the worksheet adapted from Table 7–2 by developing strategies that respond to specific issues. The student may do the assignment independently. A more useful approach would be to do the exercise with a small group of key people from the community with whom the students are working. The student would first have to analyze which sets of questions apply, since community practice in the real world often involves mixed or sequential models. Then, the student or group would respond to the most relevant questions and develop appropriate responses, again helping both the student and the organization to become more sensitive to the needs and strengths of women and girls and the complexity of gender relationships. The application could be even more sensitively applied by taking into consideration the ethnic, cultural, and class aspects of the community group. Thinking about feminist and gender issues with the additional lenses of diversity and empowerment would be the most useful application of this exercise.

Strategies to Insure Women's Equal Partnership to Community Practice: Sample Worksheet

Feminist Application Issues

Selected Model	Selected Strategies
A.	A.
B.	B.
C.	C.
D.	D.
E.	E.
F.	F.
G.	G.

REFERENCES

Abramovitz, J.J. & Nichols, R. (1992). Women and biodiversity: Ancient reality, modern imperative. *Development, Journal of SID, 2*, 85–90.

Addams, J. (1922). *Peace and bread in a time of war*. New York: Macmillan.

Addams, J. (1960). *A centennial reader*. New York: Macmillan.

Addams, J. & Residents of Hull-House. (1885). The settlement as a factor in the labor movement. In Residents of Hull-House (Eds.), *Hull-House maps and papers: A presentation of nationalities and wages in a congested district of Chicago, together with comments and essays on problems growing out of the social conditions*. New York: Crowell.

Alinsky. S. (1971). *Rules for radicals*. New York: Random House.

Andrews, A.B. (1996). Realizing participant empowerment in the evaluation of nonprofit women's services organizations: Notes from the front line. In

D.M. Fetterman, S.J. Kaftarian & A. Wandersman (Eds.), *Empowerment evaluation: Knowledge and tools for self-assessment and accountability* (pp. 141- 158). Thousand Oaks, CA: Sage.

Austin, M.J. & Betten, N. (1990). Rural organizing and the agricultural extension service. In N. Betten & M.J. Austin (Eds.), *The roots of community organizing, 1917–1939* (pp. 94–105). Philadelphia: Temple University Press.

Bailey, F. (1983). *The tactical uses of passion.* Ithaca, NY: Cornell University Press.

Bellah, R.N., Madsen, R., Sullivan, W.M., Swidler, A. & Tipton, S.M. (1985). *Habits of the heart*. Berkeley: University of California Press.

Bennis, W.G., Benne, K.D. & Chin, R.C. (Eds.). (1985). *The planning of change* (4th ed.). New York: Holt, Rinehart & Winston.

Berry, T. (1990). *The dream of the earth*. San Francisco: Sierra Club Books.

Betten, N. & Austin, M.J. (1990). *The roots of community organizing, 1917–1939*. Philadelphia: Temple University Press.

Biddle, W.W. & Biddle, L.J. (1965). *The community development process: The rediscovery of local initiative*. New York: Holt, Rinehart, and Winston.

Billups, J. (1994). The social develoment model as an organizing framework for social work practice. In R.G. Meinart, J.T. Pardeck & W.P. Sullivan (Eds.), *Issues in social work: A critical analysis* (pp. 21–38). Westport, CT: Auburn House.

Blakely, E.J. (1979). *Community development research: Concepts, issues and strategies*. New York: Human Sciences Press.

Blakely, E.J. (1989). *Planning local economic development: Theory and practice.* Newbury Park, CA: Sage.

Bobo, K., Kendall, J. & Max, S. (1991). *Organizing for social change: A manual for activits in the 1990s.* Washington, DC: Seven Locks Press.

Boulding, E. (1988). Image and action in peace building. *Journal of Social Issues, 44*, 17–38.

Boulding, K. (1989). *Three faces of power*. Beverly Hills, CA: Sage.

Brager, G. & Specht, H. (1973). *Community organizing*. New York: Columbia University Press.

Brandwein, R.A. (1982). Toward androgyny in community and organizational practice. In A. Weick & S.T. Vandiver (Eds.), *Women, power and change* (pp. 158–170). Washington, DC: NASW Press.

Brandwein, R.A. (1987). Community organizing. In D.S. Burden & N. Gottlieb (Eds.), *The woman client: Providing human services in a changing world* (pp. 111–125). New York: Tavistock Publications.

Brieland, D. (1995). Social work practice: History and evolution. In R.L. Edwards (Ed.), *Encyclopedia of social work* (19th ed., Vol. 3, pp. 2247–2257). Washington, DC: NASW Press.

Brody, R. (1993). *Effectively managing human service organizations*. Newbury Park, CA: Sage.

Burden, D.S. & Gottlieb, N. (Eds.). (1987). *The woman client: Providing human services in a changing world*. New York: Tavistock Publications.

Burke, E.M. (1979). *A participatory approach to urban planning*. New York: Human Sciences Press.

Carmen, R. (1994). The logic of economics vs. the dynamics of culture: Daring to (re)invent the common future. In W. Harcourt (Ed.), *Feminist perspectives on sustainable development* (pp. 60–74). London & New Jersey: ZED Books Ltd., in association with the Society for International Development (Rome).

Carter, G.W. (1958a). Practice theory in community organization. *Social Work, 3*, 54–69.

Carter, G.W. (1958b). Social work community organization methods and processes. In W.A. Friedlander (Ed.), *Concepts and methods of social work* (pp. 22–35). Englewood Cliffs, NJ: Prentice-Hall.

Carter, G.W. (1959). Practice theory in community organization. In H.L. Lurie (Ed.), *The community organization method in social work education, Vol. IV* (pp. 85–110). New York: Council on Social Work Education.

Cartwright, D. (Ed.). (1959). *Studies in social power*. Ann Arbor: Institute for Social Research, University of Michigan.

Cernea, M. (Ed.). (1985). *Putting people first: Sociological variables in rural development*. New York: Oxford University Press.

Chandler, S.M. (1986). The hidden feminist agenda in social development. In N. Van den Berg & L.L. Cooper (Eds.), *Feminist visions for social work* (pp. 49–162). Washington, DC: NASW Press.

Checkoway, B. (1995). Two types of planning in neighborhoods. In J. Rothman, J.L. Erlich & J.E. Tropman (Eds.), *Strategies of community intervention* (5th ed., pp. 314–327). Itasca, IL: Peacock.

Chernesky, R.H. (1980). Women administrators in social work. In E. Norman & A. Mancuso (Eds.), *Women's issues and social work practice* (pp. 241-261). Itasca, IL: Peacock.

Chong, D. (1991). *Collective action and the civil rights movement*. Chicago: University of Chicago Press.

Christenson, J.A. & Robinson, J.W., Jr. (1989). *Community development in perspective*. Ames, IA: Iowa State University Press.

Christiansen-Ruffman, L. (1995). Women's conceptions of the political: Three Canadian women's organizations. In M.M. Ferree & P.Y. Martin (Eds.), *Feminist organizations:Harvest of the new women's movement* (pp. 372–393). Philadelphia: Temple University Press.

Clark, J. (1990). *Democratizing development: The role of voluntary organizations*. West Hartford, CT: Kumarian.

Coser, L. (1956). *The functions of social conflict*. New York: Free Press.

Costain, A.N. (1992). *Inviting women's rebellion: A political process interpretation of the women's movement*. Baltimore: Johns-Hopkins University Press.

Cox, F.N., Erlich, J.L. Rothman, J. & Tropman, J.E. (Eds.). (1970). *Strategies of community organization*. Itasca, IL: Peacock.

Cox, F.N., Erlich, J.L. Rothman, J. & Tropman, J.E. (Eds.). (1984). *Tactics and techniques of community practice* (2nd ed.). Itasca, IL: Peacock.

Danklemann, I. & Davidson, J. (1988). *Women and environment in the third world: Alliance for the future*. London: Earthscan Publications.

Darcey, R., Welch, S. & Clark, J. (1994). *Women, elections, and representation* (2nd. ed.). Lincoln: University of Nebraska Press.

Dasgupta, P. & Weale, M. (1992). On measuring the quality of life. *World Development, 20*(1), 119–131.

Deegan, M.J. (1990). *Jane Addams and the men of the Chicago school: 1892–1918.* New Brunswick, NJ: Transaction Books.

Dunham, A. (1940). The literature of community organization. In *Proceedings of the National Conference of Social Work* (pp. 410–422). New York: Columbia University Press.

Dunham, A. (1959). *Community welfare organizations: Principles and practice.* New York: Crowell.

Edwards, R.L. (Ed.). (1995). *Encyclopedia of social work* (19th ed., pp. 2569–2619). Washington, DC: NASW Press.

Edwards, R.L. & Yankey, J.A. (Eds.). (1991). *Skills for effective human services management.* Silver Spring, MD: NASW Press.

Estes, R.J. (1984). *The social progress of nations*. New York: Praeger.

Estes, R.J. (1993). Toward sustainable development: From theory to praxis. *Social Development Issues, 15*(3), 1–29.

Fanon, F. (1966). *The wretched of the earth.* New York: Grove Press.

Farrell, J.C. (1967). *Beloved lady: A history of Jane Addams' ideas on reform and peace*. Baltimore: Johns Hopkins University Press.

Fellin, P. (1995). Understanding American communities. In J. Rothman, J.L. Erlich & J. Tropman (Eds.), *Strategies of community intervention* (pp. 114- 128). Itasca, IL: Peacock.

Ferree, M.M. & Martin, P.Y. (1995). *Feminist organizations: Harvest of the new women's movement.* Philadelphia: Temple University Press.

Fetterman, D.M. (1996). Empowerment evaluation: An introduction to theory and practice. In D.M. Fetterman, S.J. Kaftarian & A. Wandersman (Eds.), *Empowerment evaluation: Knowledge and tools for self-assessment and accountability* (pp. 3–46). Thousand Oaks, CA: Sage.

Fisher, R. (1984). *Let the people decide: Neighborhood organizing in America.* Boston: Twayne.

Fisher, R. (1995). Social action community organization: Proliferation, persistence, roots, and prospects. In J. Rothman, J.L. Erlich & J.E. Tropman (Eds.), *Strategies of community intervention* (5th ed., pp. 327–340). Itasca, IL: Peacock.

Fisher, R. & Karger, H.J. (1997). *Social work and community in a private world: Getting out in public*. White Plains, NY: Longman.

Fong, L.G.W. & Gibbs, J.T. (1995). Facilitating services to multicultural communities in a dominant culture setting: An organizational perspective. *Administration in Social Work, 19*(2), 1–24.

Freire, P. (1973). *Education for critical consciousness.* New York: Seabury.

Freire, P. (1985). *The politics of education: Culture, power and liberation.* Boston: Bergin & Garvey Publishers.

Freire, P. (1990). A critical understanding of social work. *Journal of Progressive Social Work, 1*(1), 3–9.

Friedman, J. (1992). *Empowerment: The politics of alternative development.* Cambridge, MA: Blackwell Publishers, Inc.

Gamble, D.N. & Weil, M.O. (1995). Citizen participation. In R.L. Edwards (Ed.), *Encyclopedia of social work* (19th ed., pp. 483–494). Washington, DC: NASW Press.

Gamson, W. (1975).*The strategy of social protest.* Homeward, IL: Dorsey Press.

Gaventa, J. (1980). *Power and powerlessness: Quiescence and rebellion in an Appalachian Valley.* Champaign-Urbana, IL: University of Illinois Press.

Gilbert, N. & Specht, H. (1968). *Community organizing.* New York: Columbia University Press.

Gortner, H.F., Mahler, J. & Nicholson, J.B. (1987). *Organization theory: A public perspective*, Chicago: Dorsey Press.

Gottlieb, N. (Ed.). (1980). *Alternative social services for women*. New York: Columbia University Press.

Gutiérrez, L.M. & Lewis, E.A. (1995). A feminist perspective on organizing with women of color. In F.G. Rivers & J.L. Erlich (Eds.), *Community organizing in a diverse society* (pp. 95–112). Boston, Allyn & Bacon.

Hanna, M. & Robinson, B. (1994). *Strategies for community empowerment*. Lewiston, NY: Edwin Melton Press.

Haq, M. ul. (1995). *Reflections on human development.* New York: Oxford University Press.

Harcourt, W. (1994). Negotiating positions in the sustainable development debate: Situating the feminist perspective. In W. Harcourt (Ed.), *Feminist perspectives on sustainable development* (pp. 1–25). London & New Jersey: ZED Books Ltd., in association with the Society for International Development (Rome).

Hasenfeld, Y. (1983). *Human service organizations*. Englewood Cliffs, NJ: Prentice-Hall.

Hasenfeld, Y. (1995). Program development. In J. Rothman, J.L. Erlich & J.E. Tropman (Eds.), *Strategies of community intervention* (5th ed., pp. 427–448). Itasca, IL: F.E. Peacock.

Henderson, H. (1994). Paths to sustainable development: The role of social indicators. *Futures, 26*(2), 125–137.

Hinsdale, M.A. & Lewis, H.M. (1995). Appendix A: Context and methodology. In M.A. Hinsdale, H.M. Lewis & S.M. Waller (Eds.), *It comes from the people* (pp. 340–347) Philadelphia: Temple University Press.

Hoff, M.D. & McNutt, J.G. (1994). *The global environmental crisis: Implications for social welfare and social work.* Brookfield, VT: Avebury.

Hooyman, N.R. & Bricker-Jenkins, M. (Eds.). (1985). *Not for women only: Models of feminist practice.* Washington, DC: NASW Press.

Hopps, J.G. & Collins, P.M. (1995). Social work profession overview. In R.L. Edwards (Ed.), *Encyclopedia of social work* (19th ed., 2266–2282). Washington, DC: NASW Press.

Hyde, C. (1986). Experience of women activists: Implications for community organizing theory. *Sociology and Social Welfare, 13*, 545–562.

Hyde, C. (1989). A feminist model for macro-practice: Promises and problems. *Administration in Social Work, 13*, 135–181.

Hyde, C. (1994). Commitment to social change: Voices from the feminist movement. *Journal of Community Practice, 1* (2), 45–64.

Hyde, C. (1996). A feminist response to Rothman's "Approaches to community intervention." In M. Weil (Ed.), *Community practice: Conceptual models*. New York: Haworth. (Also published as volume 3 (3/4) of the *Journal of Community Practice*, pp. 127–145.)

Jeffries, A. (1996). Modeling community work: An analytic framework for practice. In M. Weil (Ed.), *Community practice: Conceptual models*. New York: Haworth. (Also published as volume 3 (3/4) of the *Journal of Community Practice*, pp. 101–125.)

Johnson, A. (1959). Community method in casework agencies. In H.L. Lurie (Ed.), *The community organization method in social work education, Volume IV* (pp. 148–161). New York: Council on Social Work Education.

Johnson, A.K. (1994). Linking professionalism and community organization: A scholar/advocate approach. *Journal of Community Practice, 1* (2), 65–86.

Jones, J.F. & Pandey, R.S. (1981). *Social Development: Conceptual, methodological, and policy issues*. New York: St. Martin's Press.

Kadushin, A. (1976). Men in a woman's profession. *Social Work, 21*, 443- 454.

Kahn, A. (1969). *Theory and practice of social planning*. New York: Russell Sage.

Kahn, S. (1982). *Organizing: A guide for grassroots leaders.* New York: McGraw-Hill.

Kettner, P., Daley, J.M. & Nichols, A.W. (1985). *Initiating change in organizations and communities: A macro practice model.* Monterey, CA: Brooks/Cole.

Kincheloe, J. (1995). Meet me behind the curtain: The struggle for a critical postmodern action research. In P.L. McLaren & J.M. Giarelle (Eds.), *Critical theory and education research* (pp. 71–89). Albany: State University of New York Press.

Korten, D. (1995). *When corporations rule the world.* West Hartford, CT: Kumarian Press & San Francisco: Berrett-Koehler Publishers.

Kravitz, D. (1976). Sexism in a woman's profession. *Social Work, 21*, 421-426.

Kretzmann, J.P. & McKnight, J.L. (1993). *Building communities from inside out*. Evanston, IL: Northwestern University, Center for Urban Affairs and Policy Research.

Kurzman, P. (1985). Program development and service coordination as components of community practice. In S.H. Taylor & R.W. Roberts (Eds.), *Theory and practice of community social work* (pp. 95–124). New York: Columbia University Press.

Lane, R.P. (1939, June 18–24). *The field of community organization— report of discussions*. Paper presented at the National Conference of Social Work Sixty-sixth Annual Conference, Buffalo, NY.

Lasch, C. (Ed.). (1965). *Introduction to the social thought of Jane Addams.* Indianapolis: Bobbs-Merrill.

Lauffer, A. (1978). *Social planning at the community level.* Englewood Cliffs, NJ: Prentice Hall.

Lee, J.A.B. (1994). *The empowerment approach to social work practice*. New York: Columbia University Press.

Leonard, A. (Ed.). (1995). *Seeds 2: Supporting women's work around the world.* New York: Feminist Press.

Lippett, R., Watson, J. & Westley, B. (1958). *The dynamics of planned change: A comparative study of principles and techniques*. New York: Harcourt, Brace & World.

Lubove, R. (1965). *The professional altruist: The emergence of social work as a career, 1880–1930.* Cambridge, MA: Harvard University Press.

Lurie, H.L. (Ed.). (1959). *The community organization method in social work education, Volume IV.* New York: Council on Social Work Education.

Mandelbaum, S.J., Mazza, L. & Burchell, R.W. (Eds.). (1996). *Explorations in planning theory.* New Brunswick, NJ: Center for Urban Policy Research.

Marietta, D.E., Jr. (1995). *For people and the planet: Holism and humanism in environmental ethics.* Philadelphia: Temple University press.

Martinez-Brawley, E.E. (1990). *Perspectives on the small community.* Silver Spring, MD: NASW Press.

Masi, D.A. (1981). *Organizing for women: Issues, strategies and services.* Lexington, MA: Lexington Books.

Mauney, R., Williams, E. & Weil, M. (1993). *Beyond crisis: Developing comprehensive services for battered women in North Carolina*. Winston-Salem, NC: Z. Smith Reynolds Foundation.

McClenahan, B.A. (1922). *Organizing the community: A review of practical principles*. New York: Century Company.

McKay, J. (1990). The development model. *Development: The Journal of the Society for International Development*, 3/4, pp. 55–59.

McMillen, W. (1945). *Community organization for social welfare.* Chicago: University of Chicago Press.

Merchant, C. (1992). *Radical ecology: The search for a livable world*. New York & London: Routledge.

Midgeley, J. (1995). *Social development: The development perspective in social welfare*. Thousand Oaks, CA: Sage.

Mizrahi, T. & Rosenthal, B. (1993). Managing dynamic tensions in social change coalitions. In T. Mizrahi & J.D. Morrison (Eds.), *Community organization and social administration* (pp. 11–40). New York: Haworth.

Mondros, J.B. & Wilson, S.M. (1994). *Organizing for power and empowerment.* New York: Columbia University Press.

Morell, C. (1987). Cause is function: Toward a feminist model for integration for social work. *Social Service Review, 61*, 144–155.

Morris, A.D. & Mueller, C.M. (Eds.). (1992). *Frontiers in social movement theory*. New Haven: Yale University Press.

Newstetter, W.I. (1947). The social intergroup work process. In *Proceedings of the National Conference of Social Work* (pp. 205–217). New York: Columbia University Press.

Noponen, H. (1996, May 16–18). Presentation at the Women and Sustainable Development Conference, Chapel Hill, NC.

Norman, E. & Mancuso, A. (Eds.). (1980). *Women's issues and social work practice*. Itasca, IL: Peacock.

Perlman, R. (1971). Social planning and community organization approaches. In R. Morris (Ed.), *Encyclopedia of social work* (16th ed., pp. 1338-1345). Washington, DC: NASW Press.

Perlmutter, F.D. (Ed.). (1989). *Alternative social agencies: Administrative strategies*. New York: Haworth Press.

Perlmutter, F.D. (Ed.). (1994). *Women and social change: Nonprofit and social policy*. Washington, DC: NASW Press.

Piven, F. & Cloward, R. (1977). *Poor people's movements: Why they succeed and how they fail.* New York: Pantheon.

Popple, K. (1996). Community work: British models. In M. Weil (Ed.), *Community practice: Conceptual models* (pp. 147–180). New York: Haworth. (Also published as Volume 3 (3/4) of the *Journal of Community Practice*, pp. 147- 149.)

Popple, P. (1995). Social work profession: History. In R.L. Edwards (Ed.), *Encyclopedia of social work* (19th ed., Vol. 3, pp. 2282–2292).

Pruitt, D. (1972). Methods for resolving differences of interest: A theoretical analysis. *Journal of Social Issues, 28,* 133–154.

Putnan, R.D. (1993). *Making democracy work*. Princeton, NJ: Princeton University Press.

Raheim, S. (1995). Self-employment training and family development: An integrated strategy for family empowerment. In P. Adams & K. Nelson (Eds.), *Reinventing human services: Community and family-centered practice* (pp. 127- 143). New York: Aldine de Gruyter.

Reinharz, S. (1992). *Feminist methods in social research.* New York: Oxford University Press.

Rivera, F.G. & Erlich, J.L. (1995). *Community organizing in a diverse society.* Boston: Allyn & Bacon.

Roberts-DeGennaro, M. (1986). Factors contributing to coalition maintenance. *Journal of Sociology and Social Welfare, 13*, 248–264.

Roberts-DeGennaro, M. (1987). Patterns of exchange relationships in building a coalition. *Administration in Social Work, 11*, 59–67.

Ross, M.G. (1955). *Community organization: Theory and principles*. New York: Harper & Brothers.

Ross, M.G. (1958). *Case histories in community organization.* New York: Harper & Row.

Rothman, J. (1987). Three models of community organization. In F. Cox, J.L. Erlich & J.E. Tropman (Eds.), *Strategies of community organization* (4th ed., pp. 25–45). Itasca, IL: F.E. Peacock.

Rothman, J. (1995). Approaches to community intervention. In J. Rothman, J.L. Erlich, & J.E. Tropman with Fred Cox (Eds.), *Strategies of community intervention* (5th ed., pp. 26–63). Itasca, IL: Peacock.

Rothman, J., Erlich, J.L., Tropman, J.E. & Cox, F. (Eds.). (1995). *Strategies of community intervention* (5th ed.). Itasca, IL: Peacock.

Rothman, J. & Thomas, E.J. (Eds.). (1994). *Intervention research: Design and development for human services.* New York: Haworth.

Rothman, J. & Zald, M.N. (1995). Planning and policy practice. In J. Rothman, J.L. Erlich & J.E. Tropman (Eds.), *Strategies of community intervention* (5th ed., pp. 283–296). Itasca, IL: Peacock.

Rubin, H.J. (1997). Being a conscience and a carpenter: Interpretations of the community-based development model. *Journal of Community Practice, 4*(1), 57–90.

Rubin, H.J. & Rubin, I.S. (1992). *Community organizing and development* (2nd ed.) New York: Macmillan.

Sarri, R.C. & Sarri, C.M. (1992). Organizational and community change through participatory action research. *Administration in Social Work, 16*(3–4), 99- 122.

Schopler, J.H. (1994). Interorganizational groups in human services: Environmental and interpersonal relationships. *Journal of Community Practice, 1*(3), 7–27.

Schwartz, M. (1965). Community organization. In H.L. Lurie (Ed.), *Encyclopedia of social work* (15th ed., pp. 177–189). Washington, DC: NASW Press.

Sherrad-Sherraden, M. & Ninacs, W.A. (in press). Introduction to Community Economic Development. *Journal of Community Practice, 5*(1).

Sieder, V.M. (1947). The relation of agency and community welfare council structure to community organization. In D. Howard (Ed.), *Community organization: Its nature and setting* (pp. 44–59). New York: American Association of Social Workers.

Sieder, V.M. (1950). The community welfare council and social action. In *Proceedings of the National Council of Social Work* (pp. 84–97). New York: Columbia University Press.

Sieder, V.M. (1956). What is community organization practice in social work? In *Proceedings of the National Conference of Social Work* (pp. 76–87). New York: Columbia University Press.

Sieder, V.M. (1959). The tasks of the community organization worker. In H.L. Lurie (Ed.), *The community organization method in social work education, Vol. IV* (pp. 246–260). Alexandria, VA: Council on Social Work Education.

Simon, B.L. (1994). *The empowerment tradition in American social work: A history*. New York: Columbia University Press.

Slocum, R., Wickhart, L., Rocheleau, D. & Thomas-Slayter, B. (Eds.). (1995). *Power, process and participation: Tools for change*. London: Intermediate Technology Publications.

Solomon, B.B. (1976). *Black empowerment: Social work in oppressed communities.* New York: Columbia University Press.

Speth, J.G. (1996). Introduction. *Human development report 1996, United Nations Development Programme*. New York: Oxford University Press.

Staples, L. (1990). Powerful ideas about empowerment. *Administration in Social Work, 14*(2), 29–42.

Taylor, S.H. (1985). Community work and social work: The community liaison approach. In S.H. Taylor & R.W. Roberts (Eds.), *Theory and practice of community social work* (pp. 179–214). New York: Columbia University Press.

Taylor, S.H. & Roberts, R.W. (Eds.). (1985). *Theory and practice of community social work*. New York: Columbia University Press.

Thomas-Slayter, B., Polestdico, R., Esser, A.L., Taylor. O & Mutua, E. (1995) *A manual for socio-economic and gender analysis: Responding to the development challenge*. Worcester, MA: ECOGEN, Clark University.

Toch, H. & Grant, J.D. (1982). *Reforming human services: Change through participation*. Beverly Hills: Sage.

Toseland, R.W. & Rivas, R.F. (1995). *An introduction to group work practice* (2nd ed.). Boston: Allyn and Bacon.

Unger, D. & Wandersman, A. (1985). The importance of neighbors. *American Journal of Community Psychology, 13*, 139–169.

United Nations Development Program (UNDP). (1996). *Human Development Report, 1996*. New York: Oxford Press.

Van den Berg, N. & Cooper, L.B. (Eds.). (1986). *Feminist visions for social work practice*. Washington, DC: NASW Press.

Verba, S., Scholzman, K.L., Brady, H. & Nie, N. (1993). Citizen activity: Who participates? What do they say? *American Political Science Review, 87*, 303- 318.

Wandersman, A. (1981). A framework of participation in community organizations. *Journal of Applied Behavioral Science, 17*, 27–58.

Warren, R. (1971). *Social change and human purpose: Toward understanding and action.* Chicago: Rand McNally.

Warren, R.L. (1978). *The community in America* (3rd ed.). Chicago: Rand McNally.

Weick, A. & Vandiver, S.T. (Eds.). (1982). *Women, power and change.* Washington, DC: NASW Press.

Weil, M. (1995). Women, community and organizing. In J.E. Tropman, J.L. Erlich & J. Rothman (Eds.), *Tactics and techniques of community intervention* (3rd. ed., pp. 118–134). Itasca, IL: Peacock.

Weil, M. (1996). Community building: Building community practice. *Social Work, 41* (5), 433–576.

Weil, M. (1997). Community practice models: A historical perspective in M. Weil (Ed.), *Community practice: Conceptual models*. New York: Haworth. (Also published as volume 3 (3/4) of the *Journal of Community Practice*, pp.5–67.)

Weil, M.O. & Gamble, D.N. (1995). Community practice models. In R.L. Edwards (Ed.), *Encyclopedia of social work* (19th ed., pp. 577–594). Washington, DC: NASW Press.

Woliver, L.R. (1996). Mobilizing and sustaining grassroots dissent. *Journal of Social Issues, 52*(1), 139–151.

World Commission on Environmental Development. (1987). *Our common future: From one earth to one world*. New York: Oxford Press.

Young, K. (1993). *Planning development with women: Making a world of difference*. New York: St. Martin's Press.

Zander, A. (1985). *The purpose of groups and organizations.* San Francisco: Jossey-Bass.

Zander A. (1990). *Effective social action by community groups.* San Francisco: Jossey-Bass.

CHAPTER 8

Integrating Gender into Human Service Organization, Administration, and Planning Curricula

F. Ellen Netting
Mary K. Rodwell

INTRODUCTION

This chapter is written for educators committed to integrating gender into curriculum on human service administration, planning, and organization. This integration process requires a critical examination of one's assumptions about organizations and a willingness to struggle with how to create gender-sensitive environments. We view both "gender" and "organization" as socially constructed concepts. It is our hope that this chapter will assist the educator in guiding students: (1) to understand how organizations are anything but gender neutral and (2) to work to change human service organizations so that they become gender-sensitive.

First, we will examine the basic assumptions that underlie the theories and practice models that have been embraced by organizational theorists. Most organizational theories did not develop from the study of human service agencies, yet they have often been applied to these types of agencies as if there is a natural fit. With this application have come assumptions that may not support value-based social work practice, and that may actually dehumanize service delivery to vulnerable populations. In addition, principles of human service administration have been influenced by the same assumptions and have for the most part been viewed as gender-neutral (Gherardi, 1995, p. 17).

This background information can be introduced into the classroom, thus setting the stage for different ways of approaching and viewing human service organizations.

Second, we will focus on contemporary perspectives. Specifically, we highlight systems, power and politics, and organizational culture theories. We recognize that contemporary "management's romance with the technical" has not been inclusive of women's ways of knowing (Fenby, 1991, p. 20). Not only are the basic assumptions made by mainstream organizational theories not specific to human services, but they are typically formulated by men for profit-making corporate structures. Even contemporary approaches to understanding organizational culture and the movement toward quality, excellence, and empowerment have not always incorporated gender perspectives. The primary intent has been to increase productivity, more than to increase inclusiveness. Yet amid this neglect of gender-specific understanding, there is promising movement toward managing diversity within the workplace. Diversity includes not only gender but race and ethnicity (Thomas, 1991). In addition, there is a growing awareness of the effects that different structures have on power concentration, the generation of informal systems, and the pursuit of operative goals (Calas & Smirchich, 1996), as well as an emerging literature that challenges us to think differently about organizations (Clegg, Hardy & Nord, 1996). In this context, research has shown that the organizational behavior of women is significantly affected by the characteristics of the organizations in which they work, and that if given the choice, many women choose to work in certain types of "female" alternative organizations (Perlmutter, 1988).

Third, we will identify selected contemporary theories and practices vying for dominance and evaluate their relevance to empowerment and gender sensitivity using Weick's (1995) approach to "sensemaking." Weick's process for how a person within an organization understands the organization consists of seven sensemaking properties:

1. Identity. As individuals name, describe, and analyze organizations, they rethink their understandings based on their changing experiences and their effects on sense of self. Therefore, "making sense" of an organization is tied to a person's identity, and understandings about that organization change as the person grows and develops.

2. Retrospection. Understanding organizations is based on "lived" experience because people make sense of what happens after they have experienced reality. "Students of sensemaking find forecasting, contingency planning, strategic planning and other magical probes into the future wasteful and misleading if they are decoupled from reflective action and history" (p. 30).

3. Enactment. Organizations are understood in the context of the actions that are possible within them. Action in organizations such as enacting policies, writing rules, setting time lines, organizing space, establishing categories, and changing the environment in numerous ways give meaning to the organization and life within it.

4. Social. The actions that occur in organizations are interactive, people working with people. Shared experiences and processes do not always mean agreement or shared understanding, but there is shared history. How a person is socialized, and the groups to whom one looks for feedback, will influence what a person does and thinks about in organizational life.

5. Ongoing. Weick contends "that sensemaking never starts [because] people are always in the middle of things, which become things" (p. 43). Connecting events, seeing how things fit with the past, and even puzzling over interruptions to routines are ongoing. People's interests and experiences continue to change, and therefore understanding the organization itself is ongoing.

6. Extracted cues. Extracted cues are pieces of information from which people draw implications about organizations. What a person makes of an extracted cue depends first on themselves and their lived experience and then on context, both in terms of what cue is extracted and in how it is interpreted.

7. Plausibility. Sensemaking does not require that people in organizations know the "truth." In fact, they piece together extracted cues, so that they know enough to do current projects acceptably. This means that "sufficiency and plausibility take precedence over accuracy" (p. 62).

In this chapter, we will use these seven properties to create a lens through which to understand gender in organizations.

Finally, we will propose alternative theoretical and organizational practice approaches that consider the realities of both women and men in contemporary society. Obviously, there are a variety of approaches that derive from multiple theories that can lead to a gender-integrated approach. We will propose ways to design the planning and administration curriculum in social work so that gender can be integrated into course content. A proposed syllabus in the appendix to this chapter provides a sample approach to how a planning and administration course can be sensitive to gender issues. Suggested readings are also provided.

ASSUMPTIONS OF DOMINANT THEORIES AND PRACTICE MODELS

Numerous assumptions underlie any organizational theory, and practice models reflect these assumptions. We do not pretend to cover all such assumptions of dominant theories, but we will highlight some of the more basic ones. In this section we categorize theoretical development periods. We examine the language used to describe organizations because it is through the written and spoken word that assumptions about organizations are conveyed. More specifically, we will be particularly attentive to metaphors because of their ability to instruct about underlying assumptions. Lakoff and Johnson (1980) point out that metaphors are often so taken for granted that they are viewed as reality rather than related to thought or action. "Our ordinary conceptual system, in terms of which we both think and act, is fundamentally metaphorical in nature. . . . Since communication is based on the same conceptual system that we use in thinking and acting, language is an important source of evidence for what that system is like" (p. 3).

Several metaphors will be highlighted—"machine," "war," "sports," and others— that seem to have trapped us in familiar (male) categories (Langer, 1989). Though language has been metaphorically transformed during the highlighted theoretical periods, as have our images of organizations, today we remain with a basic erroneous assumption that organizational theories were and are gender-neutral. This is the case, even though Gherardi (1995) points out that all theories are cultural products and that gender neutrality would imply that there are "genderless organizations employing disembodied workers" (p. 17).

Early Theories

Shafritz and Ott (1987) categorize early schools of organizational thought as Classical Organization Theory, Neoclassical Organization Theory, and "Modern" Structural Organization Theory. The classical school was unquestioned until the 1930s, when the neoclassical theorists began to dispute many of its underlying assumptions. The modern structural theorists synthesized much of what had been produced by both the classical and neoclassical writers. They are termed "modern" simply because they wrote during the 1960s and 1970s, in contrast to the early classical theorists, who were also very structural in their thinking, but who wrote prior to World War II.

Of the writers who speak for these three schools, all are men and thus reflect one of the basic assumptions underlying early organizational theories — *that the important work of the world is done by men* (Waring, 1988, p. 17). Historically, these early theories were embraced at a time when women were relegated to the home and men to the factories and marketplace. The traditional metaphor that guided the classical theories was the organization as a machine or factory (Morgan, 1986). Bureaucratic theory was based on a mechanical metaphor in which human beings were literally viewed as interchangeable parts. Classical theorists also based their understandings on the military and the church, both bastions of hierarchical experiences. War, either secular or holy, was another organizational metaphor that was undergirded until the 1930s with other factorylike assumptions: Organizations existed to be economically productive; there was one best way to organize production; specialization and division of labor maximized production; and there were rational economic principles that people and organizations had to embrace (Shafritz & Ott, 1987, p. 21).

The neoclassical theorists questioned the classical assumptions and were viewed as the "anti-school." They sought to infuse the classical tradition with a more humane view of organizational members, with understandings of how administrative units interrelated and of how decisions were made, and that organizations had relationships with their environments. In questioning classical assumptions, these theorists (all male) led the way for new schools of thought that focused on human relations, modern structuralism, power and politics, and organizational culture. These perspectives emerged during changing times when more women were becoming involved in the labor force and as debates raged over whether women working outside the home would destroy the American family (Abramovitz, 1988).

The modern structural school somewhat expanded the assumptions of and departed from the classical theorists: Organizations were created to achieve objectives; objective achievement required defined rules, formal authority, control, and coordination; organizations had a "best" structure, appropriate to their objectives, environments, products/services, and technologies; in highly skilled organizations, specialization was best; and organizational problems could usually be resolved by restructuring (Shafritz & Ott, 1987, pp. 166–167). The organizational chart became the rallying cry of the structural school. But other voices warned that bureaucracy was on its way out. Bennis (1966) predicted that bureaucracies would disappear by the year 2000. Toffler discussed the coming of "ad-hocracy" in *Future Shock* (1970). These voices were male. The dialogue continued with men talking with men.

The place of women in modern organizations was the subject of debate well through the first half of the twentieth century. Whereas women were viewed by many as still belonging in the home, it is not surprising that they were not engaged in discussing organizational theory in the literature. Whether women should even be part of organizational life, not to mention their value as organizational members, was questioned. For example, from 1960 to 1980 women workers earned only 66 percent of men's wages in the United States. Jobs were devalued when they became "primarily female occupations," even though skills remained the same (Dinerman, 1992, p. 83). This was the political-economic environment surrounding gender into which contemporary organizational theories emerged.

Contemporary Perspectives

In this section, we focus on theories that currently dominate the organizational and management literature in social work. Although we will continue to draw from the works of multiple disciplines, we will emphasize what social work professionals are writing about human service organizations. As pointed out in the previous section, traditional mechanistic assumptions dominated the study of organizations for decades. Vestiges of these assumptions linger in social work practice today. Even though the intellectual debates have debunked many of the assumptions discussed earlier, they are often tenaciously and even unconsciously held. Two examples are illustrative. A leading social work text on management explains the relationship of the organization to its environment in this way, "Because a task environment that is hostile is not likely to reverse itself spontaneously to become more friendly, the only realistic way to negotiate successfully with it is to increase power over it" (Weinbach, 1994, p. 25). Power "over" implies a linear war metaphor or at least a zero sum game in which someone loses and someone wins. Similarly, a planned change model in a macro social work text discusses "strategies," "tactics," and "campaigns," which is the metaphorical language of business warfare (Netting, Kettner & McMurtry, 1993, pp. 248–264). Old assumptions die hard, even when females are writing for the future generation. But these assumptions must loosen if the curriculum in planning and administration is to be relevant and gender-sensitive.

As one approach for enacting this change to gender relevance, we suggest that following each section, the reader perform her/his own analysis of the material using Weick's model of sensemaking (1995), the seven properties of which were presented earlier in this chapter. In addition, we propose seven questions that educators can ask students who are studying various organizational theories. Our goal is to be gender-relevant so that both men and women are included in organizational thinking. We frame our questions to focus on women's experience only because women have typically been excluded. However, we recognize that there is no one way to look at women as a class because both men and women are highly diverse groups. Based on Weick's seven properties, our questions are:

1. Identity: What of this theoretical perspective makes sense for women's identity?
2. Retrospect: What of this perspective makes sense in the context of women's history?
3. Enactment: What here is enactive of sensible environments for women?
4. Social: What here is social/relational for women?
5. Ongoing: What here would allow ongoing sensemaking for women?
6. Extracted Cues: What here will allow for the extraction of meaningful cues for women?

7. Plausibility: What here allows the assessment of plausibility for women?

Keeping these questions in mind, we now highlight three influential theoretical perspectives: systems, power and politics, and organizational culture.

Systems Theory

With two works published by Katz and Kahn (1966) and Thompson (1967), the systems school came to the forefront. Perhaps timing is everything, and symbolically the late 1960s were ripe for opening eyes to the larger environment. Basic assumptions held by the systems school were: organizations and environments were a complex set of inputs, processes, outputs, and feedback loops; change in any element would cause change in others; and because interconnections are complex and dynamic, decisions made would always result in unanticipated impacts (Shafritz & Ott, 1987).

In early systems thinking, inputs were needed before one could have outputs, and process occurred before outcomes. Change was caused by other system components. Tired of the mechanical metaphors common in engineering and economics, systems metaphors derived from biology (Morgan, 1986). Organizations were likened to various species with diverse characteristics, and people were viewed as having diverse needs. Recognition of the importance of the environment, for example, Aldrich's (1993) population ecology perspective, led to the interest in inter- and intraorganizational relationships so essential in contemporary theory development. However, the language of systems theory did not include the power and politics issues within organizations nor did its assumptions challenge gender stratification so prevalent in the larger society (Walters, Carter, Papp & Silverstein, 1988).

Social work literature confirms the domination of systems theory. Texts in social work administration (Weinbach, 1994), human service organizations (Hasenfeld, 1992), social services in ethnic agencies (Iglehart & Becerra, 1995), macro practice (Netting, Kettner & McMurtry, 1993), and program planning (Kettner, Moroney & Martin, 1990) use systems language when discussing theoretical perspectives about human service organizations. In the "Management Overview" section of the *Encyclopedia of Social Work* open systems theory is acknowledged as particularly relevant to human service organizations, as is the political-economy framework that has emerged from systems analysis (Austin, 1995, p. 1652).

The increasing push toward "outcome measurement" in human service programs is tied to systems language. Not only are planned change models designed to produce outcomes that flow from the identification of inputs, throughputs, and outputs, but governmental and private human service organizations are being asked to identify outcomes. Managed care provides an illustration. In 1995 The Center for the Study of Social Work Practice held a conference on outcome measurement, and in September 1995, the lead article in *Social Service Review* addressed the difficulty in measuring social service outcomes (Lawlor & Raube, 1995). As long as funding sources demand outcome measurement, systems theory will continue to be a dominant influence in social work education.

Many of the sources that acknowledge the role of systems theory in understanding human service organizations also acknowledge a political economy framework that is rooted in systems thinking. Political economy highlights the role of the task environment in legitimizing and in providing resources for the organization. Hasenfeld (1992) indicates that this framework is very helpful in understanding politics inside and outside the organization, but recognizes that political-economy underemphasizes the role of various values and ideologies in influencing the organization.

Systems theory is problematic when it comes to gender. The language of inputs, throughputs, outputs, and outcomes when applied to human interactions in service organizations may sound dehumanizing. The denial of values is insensitive to social work as a profession. Outcome measurements are often determined by professional providers rather than by clients. Therefore, outcomes may not reflect quality-of-life changes as perceived by clients. Those measurements that do measure appropriate constructs are often not normed to special populations, much less women. Weick puts it this way:

> A crucial property of sensemaking is that human situations are progressively clarified, but this clarification often works in reverse. It is less often the case that an outcome fulfills some prior definition of the situation, and more often the case that an outcome develops that prior definition. (1995, p. 11)

Weick's statement flies in the face of linear thinking in which outcomes are assumed to be predetermined, and reflects the antithesis of what is often taught in systems approaches to program evaluation.

In support of systems theory, however, Flynn (1992) contends that original human systems thinking actually reflected several radical values that were somehow deemphasized when applied to organizations. Flynn suggests that if the basic principles of systems thinking are viewed from a sociocultural perspective, it is impossible to discount the values inherent in this theoretical orientation. He identifies four core systems concepts: indeterminateness, multifinality, non-summativity, and morphogenesis. Indeterminateness means that final states or outcomes are not fixed, linear, or simple. Multifinality means that "original conditions can result in multiple end-state conditions," and nonsummativity means "that the whole is different than or perhaps greater than or something other than the sum of its parts." Morphogenesis is the "recognition that human systems have the capacity to alter forms and processes" (pp. 87–89). Viewed by Flynn, systems theory offers options that have been underplayed by more traditional viewpoints, interpretations, and applications.

Power and Politics

Since the late 1960s when systems perspectives emerged, organizational perspectives have become more pluralistic. Reed and Huges (1992) explain:

> Some welcome this state of affairs with open arms, seeing it as an overdue vindication of a long intellectual march from sterile and stultifying orthodoxy which has finally culminated in an historical juncture characterized by considerable theoretical and methodological diversity and the innovative developments that the accelerated pace of intellectual change releases. (p. 1)

In the early 1970s the power and politics school of thought emerged. It was in this school that the first woman, Rosabeth Moss Kanter, is acknowledged for her work. In 1987 Kanter contended that "power is America's last dirty word" (p. 65) and with this statement came the possibility that power would become a central theme in organizational scholarship. Kanter's major contribution was in recognizing relationships between formal and informal structures.

Earlier assumptions that organizations were only concerned with formal power dynamics were rejected, and organizations were seen as collections of persons who used power and political activities in all their interactions. It was somewhat ironic that the earlier structuralists attempted to ignore power when it was Weber, the father of bureaucratic theory, who had originally proposed typologies of power and authority. Weber was concerned with why people comply and how to get people to do so. Whereas structuralists tended to focus on power as legitimized organizational authority (formal power), power theorists recognized that things get accomplished in organizations because members maneuver and bargain (wage war), forming coalitions around specific issues. The power and politics school acknowledged the conflict and tension that occurred within organizations. In the past twenty-five years, the literature on power and politics rapidly expanded.

Kanter (1987) examines how "women managers experience special power failures," and contends that formal and informal practices in organizations combine to "engender powerlessness" because women have been kept out of the mainstream of organizational life (p. 354). Without clout, women who do reach managerial positions are "rendered structurally powerless" (p. 354). Acknowledging the powerlessness of those persons who are "different," Kanter began to address the oppression of organizational structures and compliance mechanisms. She emphasized an old theme that women were "problems" in organizations because their differences did not fit in with male structures. In 1989, while editor of the *Harvard Business Review*, she broke metaphorical tradition with her book entitled *When Giants Learn to Dance*. She pronounced that giant corporations, chained by their unwieldy archaic structures, would have to learn how to develop relationships and to contend with rapid change or face their own extinction. More importantly, they would have to "dance" rather than "battle." A female voice was heard.

As we scanned the literature at this point, it was as if a box had been opened and all the invisible voices created a cacophony of sound. Women began writing about organizational culture and power, as did members of racial and ethnic minority groups. Unfortunately, however, most were still looking at ways for women to "fit in" rather than "be in" organizations, revealing a basic gender insensitivity in organizations built on the standard of being male. It may be in service organizations where we most have begun to hear female voices. Gherardi (1995) indicates that "business reverberates with the great male saga of conquest (of new markets) and of campaigns (to launch new products), while services echo to the language of care, of concern for need and of relationality" (p. 11).

Much creative thinking about power and politics has come from feminist writers, who have focused on empowerment. This concept has been seized by the popular press and has become somewhat of a buzzword in current political, organizational, and management discourse. Levy (1994) remarks that "the concept of empowerment has become one of the murkier terms in the American political and cultural lexicon. Empowerment has achieved the dubious distinction of being among the tiny handful of concepts, along with freedom, equality, and welfare reform, that signify opposite meanings to political antagonists" (p. xiii). Yet, for social work, empowerment is an established and respected concept that is centered in the social work value of self-determination for those persons who have been marginalized, impoverished, and oppressed. In addition, because the population groups with whom social workers work are those persons who have not traditionally been in positions of power, the concept of empowerment is central to understanding human service organizations and delivery systems. For women in the profession of social work, these issues are highly relevant in that these very women who serve disenfranchised populations have been marginalized in their own profession (see, e.g., Petchers, 1996). Empowerment is as much needed for women in human service systems as it is for their clients.

The concept of empowerment is that it transcends all the traditional boundaries within the social work curriculum. Historically, clinicians saw the concept as a way to individual, family, and group problem solving, just as community organizers have long recognized the importance of power and politics. The 1980s brought forward a new emphasis on power and politics across the curriculum. The emphasis on strengths perspectives was reinforced in direct client interactions, but also emerged as critical in assessing organizations and communities (Saleeby, 1996). Yet, Levy reminds us that the empowerment perspective is only one way in which social workers have approached their work. She cites the "benefactor" and the "liberator" perspectives as well, the former being "doing for" and the latter viewing social service consumers as victims. Both views are paternalistic or maternalistic. Rather than focusing on strengths, collaboration, and partnership, the benefactor seeks to lift the client up and the liberator leads the client to "a promised land mapped out previously or independently by the professional" (1994, p. 7). It is critical for our purposes to note that paternalistic/maternalistic approaches are deeply ingrained and that the alternative approaches that incorporate concepts of power, diversity, and gender-sensitive practice must be part of an organization's culture for empowerment to occur. Otherwise, workers within human service agencies will not be empowered, nor will they support empowerment approaches in their work.

Within the context of power and politics, there has been a surge of literature that examines feminist and alternative organizations. Perlmutter edited *Alternative Social Agencies: Administrative Strategies* (1988) followed by *Women and Social Change* (1994), in which she examines women's alternative organizations in a cross-national context. Alternative organizations are those that have identified a need or social problem that is not being addressed and that is not always valued by the larger society. Martin (1990) identifies alternative organizations as a strong product of the women's movement and sees these organizations functioning as nonbureaucratic, usually nonprofit ventures. These organizations are political forces and "have a range of organizational expressions" (p. 182). The literature on feminist organizations (Gottlieb, 1992; Hyde, 1992) and women and power (Odendahl & O'Neill, 1994) provides multiple perspectives on how power and politics are central in understanding human service organizations.

Organizational Culture

Acknowledging the critical role of power in organizations seemed to open a door for other schools of thought that departed from mainstream theorists. The organizational culture school that emerged in the 1980s questioned how organizations engaged in decision-making and how people behave in organizations by challenging the perspectives held by structuralists and systems thinkers. Whereas modern structuralists and systems theorists assumed that systems were self-correcting, that consensus existed, that coordination was accomplished by sharing information, and that organizational problems and solutions were predictable, the cultural school pointed out that deeply held (even subconscious assumptions) really drive behavior. Because people are different, the cultural school contended that every organization's culture is different. In spite of the diversity within this school of thought, there are still some assumptions upon which most cultural theorists would agree: Organizational cultures are somewhat unique and are socially constructed; organizational cultures provide members with a way of understanding and making sense of what happens; and organizational cultures become control mechanisms by accepting and rejecting certain behaviors (Shafritz & Ott, 1987, p. 378).

The term "corporate culture," like the term "empowerment," has become a buzzword in contemporary organizations whether they are for-profit, nonprofit, or public. There is general agreement that organizational culture theory has recently dominated the study of organizations and has been somewhat faddish. Even the excellence movement in the popular management literature (beginning with Peters & Waterman, 1982) has focused on identifying culture, changing culture, and becoming more consumer-driven. It is as if the concepts used in social work for the major portion of the life of the profession have been turned on their ear and shaken into the popular discourse of corporate America. For social workers this is somewhat confusing and paradoxical, since many of the time-honored patriarchal traditions have remained in place within various organizations and are being discussed in a new language that has a familiar ring. Levy's warning about empowerment, therefore, is relevant to the discussion of culture. These words are being used by different persons to mean very different things. Schein (1991) is helpful in our sensemaking. For him organizational culture is:

> A pattern of basic assumptions—invented, discovered, or developed by a given group as it learns to cope with its problems of external adaptation and internal integration—that has worked well enough to be considered valid and, therefore, to be taught to new members as the correct way to perceive, think, and feel in relation to those problems. (p. 9)

Schein's work identifies the problems of internal integration as developing a common language and conceptual categories; establishing group boundaries and criteria for inclusion or exclusion; developing power and status criteria; establishing ways to deal with friendship, intimacy, and love; knowing what is rewarded and what is punished; and establishing an ideology that will deal with unexplainable events. First the problem of language must be resolved before others can be addressed in that "if members cannot communicate with and understand each other a group is impossible by definition" (p. 66). Organizational culture as a theory base opens the doors that have been closed in looking at values, assumptions, multiple meanings, symbols, metaphors, and languages. Previously, instead of being central to understanding organizational life, these concepts were perplexing, but considered to be unimportant "soft" details.

Gender is defined and molded within these aspects of organizational culture. Gherardi (1995) has identified four processes in which gendered organizations are produced:

> (a) establishing divisions and patterns of jobs, wages and hierarchies that are based on gender; (b) developing symbols and images that justify or oppose established patterns; (c) reinforcing interactions among workers that enact domination; and (d) developing individual constructions of how organizations are understood that reinforce gender divisions. (p. 18).

Hasenfeld (1992) describes human services as gendered work because historically social work has been entrusted to women. Both front-line workers and their clients are typically women. Odendahl and O'Neill (1994) refer to a "gendered" and diverse nonprofit sector—"a large female work force . . . under the control of an elite male power structure" (p.14).

Organizational culture theory provides opportunities for examining the gendering of organizations and thus violates a basic assumption held by other theoretical orientations—that organizations are "de-gendered" because they uphold universal principles. "De-gendering is a social practice which exposes the power structure erected on the claim to universality and on suppression, not of gender but of only one of the (only) two genders. Silencing gender knowledge is a practice of power" (Gherardi, 1995, p. 18).

RECONSTRUCTION OF THEORIES AND PRACTICE MODELS

Assumptions

It is hoped that the sensemaking approach used up to this point has made clear the assumptions that construct both organizational and self-identity, and that the reader's and our analytical efforts have underscored the emerging thinking that is attempting to enact sensible environments for both genders. Continuing the sensemaking approach,

Weick's (1995) consideration of implications for women's identity, their history, their environments, and their relationships will be the framework for a gender-sensitive reconstruction of organizational theory. Also considered will be what in theories will allow ongoing sensemaking, meaningful cues, and assessment of the plausible for women. Gender-sensitive organizational sensemaking useful for curriculum building is the goal of our reconstruction. We have not "thrown out" or disregarded all theory to begin anew. Instead we offer a reconstruction of the assumptions that have been part of organizational theory so that gender sensitivity can occur. We also recognize that there are other resources available to educators that provide fertile ground for understanding organizations from multiple new and emerging perspectives (see, e.g., Hardy & Nord, 1996).

Assumption # 1: Organizations and environments are interdependent, are not always distinctive, and are mutually influential. From systems theory we see that organizations are interconnected, and from politics and power it is clear that their environments and boundaries are highly porous. Every environmental interaction is replete with dynamics of power and politics. Just as feminists have declared that the personal is political, so the organizational is political.

Whereas some systems theorists have perceived a distinct environment separate from an organization, others have viewed organizations as not always so well-defined. Organizations are reflective of and reflect on the environments in which they operate. Even when boundaries do not blur, a mutual shaping process occurs between organizations and environments, making them interdependent. In alternative agencies and social movement organizations, for example, clients may also be volunteers, and employees may be former clients. Whereas one person may be a client today, she may be a volunteer tomorrow. Today she is part of the environment, whereas tomorrow she is an intimate link in the organizational structure. Nice, neat job descriptions and organizational charts may not work well in these situations. The organization and the environment are highly interconnected.

Berlin (1990) reminds us of how convenient it is to think in terms of dichotomies and how much a part of Western thought it is to recognize contrasts by cutting our worlds up into distinctive, mutually exclusive, and static parts. The distinction between organizations and environments can be carefully drawn in times when alliances and coalitions frame the nature of social work practice and when the purpose is simplification of understanding. These distinctions, however, do not often work in the real world of planning and administration. There are multiple overlapping roles and relationships, and opportunities for infinite constellations, if we can tolerate the ambiguity of rethinking our polarities. The point is that context is everything. To overlook or attempt to dichotomize an organization and its environment is to overlook possibilities and underestimate challenges.

Women's ways of knowing, of seeing connections, and of considering relationships do not lend themselves to dichotomous thinking. Therefore, it is possible to draw from strengths that women bring in seeing the interrelationship between organizations and environments. Women have contributions to bring in seeing how family, home, profession, agency, and community interrelate.

Assumption # 2: Organizations are constantly changing within a changing global community. Decisions and actions to effect change occur in multiple ways. Systems and cultural theorists have referred to the uncertainty with which organizations face change as if it is a burden with which to cope. Early systems theorists indicated that organizations abhor this uncertainty, and managers in human service agencies have struggled to gain "control." We propose reframing uncertainty as an infinite range of possibilities and challenges. Weick (1995) suggests that it is not uncertainty that frustrates persons in organizations, but feelings of being overwhelmed when there is so much knowledge available from varied sources. This different view of uncertainty underscores a difficulty in deciding which information to use, but also avoids the power and control difficulties of aiming for the "right" decision. Managers in organizations who are not expected to know everything will be free to work collaboratively with colleagues because admitting uncertainty frees them to acknowledge that they, too, are seekers. With this comes a redistribution of expert power because many right decisions can be made in many ways.

Planned change models based on the dominant theories attempt to clarify and make sense of this uncertainty, but from entirely different premises. It is assumed that if we plan enough, study enough, read enough, and structure enough, programs can be developed that will deal with social problems. However, this assumes that we can plan in a linear fashion when the very problem we are targeting for change is altering as we plan. The outcomes that we define are becoming obsolete as programs are implemented. Nothing is static, so nothing is really controllable.

Managers are told that the functions of management are "planning, organizing, staffing, leading and controlling" (Weinbach, 1994, p. 17). These functions speak in a male voice steeped in the command terminology of machines and hierarchy (Morgan, 1986). Most revealing is the final function, "controlling." If it is important to feel in control in human service organizations, then managers will be sorely stressed and overwhelmed in an ever-changing environment. Our position is that there is a need to reframe the functions of management, administration, and planning to make sense in a rapidly altering world. For example, functions in contemporary human service management could include connecting, supporting, nurturing, and providing security against distress—functions akin to a female experience.

With an alternative perspective that recognizes the impossibility of stasis, educating the next generation of social work leaders will include leadership functions such as challenging, thinking, acting, empowering, and freeing. Relieved of the overwhelming burden of "control," social work managers would be trained to "challenge." The challenge would be to think critically, to act flexibly enough to change direction as needed, to empower ourselves to support and nurture employees, and to free ourselves and others to creatively change social conditions. With this, woman's voices of nurturance and relationship are heard. Lest this be perceived as too naive, let us now turn to assumptions with clear power dimensions.

Assumption # 3: Every decision made and every action taken is political, and represents a choice among values. Clearly, this assumption is informed by systems, power and politics, and culture theories. It is from the power and politics theorists that we understand the political nature of relationships, whether they are among individuals, groups, or organizations. Traditional decision-making theorists have used computer modeling to simulate the process. Everything from refined computer models to garbage can models have been proposed for understanding decision-making. Fuzzy logic and chaos theory begin to provide a vision of something different.

A theme that has persisted in many of our approaches to organizational decision-making is that the process is linear and technically clear. However, there are organizational theorists who have written for decades on nonlinear, tentative, and adaptive decision-making. Although these writings have not always been incorporated into our practice models and have not necessarily been written with a gender lens in mind, these approaches reflect how decisions are made in real organizations. For example, as early as 1959 Lindblom focused on decision-making in the public sector as a "halting 'incremental' [process] with periods of recycling, iteration and reformulation. The process was a non-linear one" (Miller, Hickson & Wilson, 1996, p. 299). Critical theorists point out that every action implies a value choice and that often those choices are made before a rationale has been constructed (Forester, 1980). For systems theorists who like to think in terms of inputs, throughputs, outputs, and outcomes, it may be somewhat disillusioning to realize that outcomes were determined before considering available inputs or that most people enter organizations in the middle rather than at the beginning of processes. The attraction of nonrational or values-based models of analysis (see, e.g., Stone, 1988; and Weick, 1995) is that it allows us to corral and articulate, if not control, what is occurring.

Recognition that choice is political and value-based also allows us to grapple with the real organizational challenges of gender stratification, occupational sex segregation, sex segregation within organizations, and the earnings gap between males and females. Employers discriminate because of beliefs about sex differences in abilities, because of different role expectations for men and women, because of a desire to control organizational friction, or because of some set of perceived preferences among and between employees and clients (Ainsley, 1993; England, 1992). These are political and value choices that can become open to critical analysis and potential change.

But with choice comes responsibility. If every choice is value-based, then it is important for social workers to consider the values represented by that choice. What possibility is being preferred over another and what might be the intended and unintended consequences of that choice? If values are implicit in every decision made and in every interaction, behaviors and actions to "make sense" must be value congruent. Espoused values of the organizational culture and the people within the organization should be reflected in behaviors and actions, both within organizations and in the larger society.

Assumption # 4: Language is political and symbolically communicates power. From organizational culture and power and politics theories come an overwhelming acknowledgment that language is important and that the words we use are powerful. Not only do they convey meaning, but they symbolize and shape entrenched attitudes, deeply held values, and cultural nuances. Social work managers, administrators, and planners can literally set the tone of the workplace. Remember, Schein (1991) indicates that without common concepts that are communicated, groups cannot be formed and organizational cultures will not bond.

Tannen's 1994 work on gender and communication has been pivotal in opening our eyes to the importance of words in our personal lives as well as in the workplace. As a sociolinguist studying conversational styles, Tannen uses the term "genderlects" to distinguish the focus of male and female voices. Female voices are defined as making connections, smoothing over situations, attempting to establish rapport, while male voices are often reporting, performing, and trying to establish a competitive position. Miscommunication occurs when communication styles do not mesh. It is not an issue of "right" or "wrong," but of "difference." Considering tone, inflection, style, intention, as well as the actual content of what is said, in addition to the languaging of diverse groups within an organization, makes it clear how complex communication is and how great the potential for miscommunication can be. It also points to the care that we must take with language to insure that power is distributed appropriately. If there is room for all the voices, then there must be room for the empowerment of multiple voices.

The power of language is evident, but we also want to emphasize the positive nature of power itself. In our experience, many women and many social work students and practitioners see power as a negative element with oppressive potential. This may be because to act powerfully, usually one must take on the words of the more powerful, usually male dominant group—an uncomfortable, paradoxical position. This rejection of the use of power is juxtaposed with empowerment as a cornerstone of social work practice. The empowerment concept allows the infusing of organizational thinking with the potential to use power (and words) in creative and constructive ways that can result in collective synergy for social change. This is not an "at-a-distance" concept. Empowerment in social work practice means that we must be comfortable with power in order to model our own empowerment for the disenfranchised. Organizations are microcosms of social work practice in which power of action, power of decision, power of understanding, and power of cross-gender and -cultural communication occurs.

Assumption # 5: Organization cultures are distinctive, and organizations are comprised of diverse persons with different realities. There are multiple rationalities and realities. Organizations will have their own group identities and their own cultures. This means that no two organizations will be exactly alike, although it does not negate the possibility that there are similarities between different organizations. Recognizing the culture within an organization requires an understanding of language, the meaning of concepts, artifacts, and symbols. Organizations do have distinctive features, but Weick (1995) and others (Boje, Gephart & Thatchenkery, 1996; Fox & Miller, 1995) have pointed out that groups of organizations that have to work together may also develop joint ways of making sense. Examples of this common sensemaking abound in the human service system and are called coalitions, alliances, and partnerships. The point is that differences among and between organizations do not mean only competition, but also mean collaboration for service survival. This collaboration cannot succeed by perpetuating the myth of uniformity. Instead, recognition of diversity and the infinite ways in which effective human behavior can be realized is a way to harness the collective potential and power of women, people of color, and others who are moving more and more into the work force. It is they who will define the real power in organizations and the future of the social work profession.

Recognizing multiple perspectives and realities, instead of presenting a threat to control, offers multiple opportunities and possibilities. If multiple perspectives are to provide advantage and richness, then the multiplicity must be recognized and honored for its strengths. This means that administrators and planners must hear the voices that have been ignored traditionally in systems that have affirmed only the voice of dominant groups. Decisions will still have to be made, but the action taken as a result of those decisions will be grounded in multiple insights.

Consequences of Assumptions

The five reconstructive assumptions are only a few of the many assumptions we could bring to our understanding of human service organizations if we carefully reflect about gender. Working within our reconstructed assumptions brings new challenges to the preparation of social work professionals. For the educator, this means preparing students with capabilities to examine organizations in multiple ways. They must approach organizations multitheoretically because there is no overriding theory with universal truths, but there are multiple realities that can be made plausible by the tentative application of theory in a precise time in the history of the organization.

For us, this also means that there is not one metaphor to fully explore the complexity of human service organizations. There are the old metaphors, as long as those do not ignore the ones that have developed with the recognition of a complex, diverse reality. And there are the new metaphors, as long as they, in making room for women and others, do not eliminate the voice of the other gender. There are patterned socially produced distinctions between female and male, feminine and masculine (Acker, 1992). These distinctions must enter into our analysis of organization. We resist the traditional genderless perspective in favor of a gendered organizational analysis (Milles & Tancred, 1992) that interprets the workplace reality of all workers.

What we espouse is not easy. Thomas (1991) defines managing diversity as "a comprehensive managerial process for developing an environment that works for all employees" (p. 10). Because it is a process, Thomas explains that managing diversity does not lend itself to "how to's." Instead, our students must learn that managing diversity, like managing chaos, is managing ambiguity and ambivalence. They must be prepared to change deep cultural values that are rooted in traditional assumptions and expectations. Clues to how this is accomplished can come from the proposed curricular revisions discussed in the next section.

PROPOSED REVISIONS: REDESIGN OF THE SOCIAL WORK CURRICULUM

In order to integrate gender content into the administration and planning curriculum, a sample syllabus based on our reconstructive assumptions is provided as an appendix to this chapter. As important as the substantive content is the process of education that must accompany the desired infusion. Our intent is to move beyond looking at women in comparison to men to the celebration of diversity. Here we are not even discussing whether diversity is a social work value (we think it is), but we are recognizing that it is the fact of today's and future organizations.

To do this, different ways of knowing and different cognitive and learning styles must be included in the classroom and beyond.

Halseth's 1993 article "Infusing a Feminist Analysis into Education for Policy, Planning, and Administration," though still placing women in comparison to men, is helpful in instituting a dialectic process. Her suggested assignments such as looking at the unique experiences of and demands on women in management, determining what could improve the climate for women, and the development of strategies for use at the individual, interpersonal, and organizational/structural levels (p. 235) can be helpful in recognizing differences. A move beyond her suggestions to the establishment of cross-gender exercises should serve as a consciousness-raising mechanism that would establish a classroom dialectic that normalizes the diversity theme without the "problem other" becoming the focus.

In addition, Hooyman (1994) raises the basic paradox of a female-dominated social work profession being the last of the helping professions to acknowledge how institutional sexism influences practice. Women comprise the majority of the members of the profession, but those who serve in administrative and planning positions are more likely to be men. Because of the power differential in administration and planning, it has been particularly difficult to hear female voices. For infusion, female voices must be heard in the classroom, even if the instructor is male. Successful female executives who have found authentic voices, not just those women who have progressed in hierarchies by fitting in, should be part of the classroom discourse. This poses the question of how one recognizes an authentic voice. What characterizes persons who "fit in" and persons who have their own voice? We believe that there really are not persons who conform to either prototype, but a range of styles. Perhaps there is the female leader of a local agency who is considered to be highly successful, but does not dress or act in terms of the standard norm for agency executives, one who is distinguished by drawing outside the lines. Such women could be invited to give presentations and to mentor both male and female field students.

Our intent is to incorporate sensitivity to persons regardless of gender in the recognition that traditional distinctions between male and female are no longer useful because there is no single male or female voice. We all speak with different voices, all of which can be heard. Our proposed focus on managing and celebrating diversity avoids the reductionistic dichotomies that have limited us. Students need to know why it is essential to have the complex harmony—new challenges, new answers, new visions for a very different multicultural reality. They also need to know that social work educators and professionals continue to struggle with this too (see, e.g., Longres, 1996). An alternative perspective can get beyond "either/or" to "both/and" based on the belief that organizational life is not a zero sum game in which if I give room for your voice I lose some of mine. We have a challenge to develop a complex harmony of voices. To underscore this complex harmony, exercises in nonrational analysis can be part of the critical thinking process both in classroom discussions and assignments. Students must be comfortable genuinely assuming various perspectives (perspectival thinking) and in managing paradoxes. Fox and Miller's *Postmodern Public Administration* (1995) and Stone's *Policy, Paradox and Political Reason* (1988) can provide solid frameworks for these activities.

Selected Alternative Practice Approaches

At this point, the reader may be asking, "So I hear all these voices, but what do I do? Organizations are created for purposes, not just to make people feel good because their voices are heard." In this section, we identify several practice approaches for incorporating gender into organizational culture. These alternative practice approaches focus on different organizational characteristics. We wish we had a plethora of models to present that would answer the question about what needs to be done. This is a struggle that we have had in writing this chapter. The approaches we have identified are only beginnings, and often we must begin with learning to recognize that different voices are speaking. It will be up to all of us, as educators, to develop the approaches and models that will go beyond the understanding of gender and the hearing of diverse voices, to actually transforming the actions taken in our organizations so that they are truly sensitive to employees and clients. Therefore, we present selected approaches we have identified, knowing that these writers may provide us a starting place in developing the models of tomorrow. Note the language used—whereas we are referring to "approaches" because the prescriptions are not well defined, some writers refer to their ideas as "models."

Thomas (1991) proposes that a cultural audit be incorporated into the ongoing life of the agency, serving as a reminder of gender and racial issues and concerns. Hyde (1989) offers a macro model focusing on women, whereas Fenby (1991) advocates for an action model. Acker (1992) provides a way to assess the processes involved in gendering organizations, while Fox and Miller (1995) focus on the importance of organizational discourse. We briefly touch upon each of these approaches. We encourage the reader to search for other approaches, as well as to engage students in developing their own alternative practice models for pursuing organizational change.

Thomas (1991), in recognizing the difficulties inherent in changing deep cultural values, describes an approach where diversity becomes an integrated cultural root in the organization. This is the organization that recognizes the values in all employees, regardless of gender, race, or any other characteristic. Starting with values and process, Thomas suggests that organizations do cultural audits to assess how well they are doing in getting beyond affirmative action, and even beyond valuing diversity, to actually manage a diverse work force. This cultural audit could become as important to managing organizations as program evaluations and financial audits. Students could be encouraged to work with field instructors in designing cultural audits for their local agencies. For example, one question that Thomas's instrument asks is: "Is it acceptable for you to discuss with your supervisor issues of racism, sexism, or other biases held by other employees?" (p. 69). We note that doing a cultural audit is only a beginning step, much like doing an assessment. It is what one does with the information learned in a cultural audit that moves an organization toward change. Since the literature does not provide a great deal of direction in this regard, this may be a starting point for students and field instructors to formulate approaches that take what has been learned and move the agency toward action.

Hyde (1989) and Fenby (1991) propose alternative approaches that focus on women in human service organizations. Hyde offers what she calls a composite model of feminist macro-practice with five practice principles: "The centrality of women's values, lives, and relationships; consciousness raising, linking the personal and political; the reconceptualization of power; democratizing processes and structures; and fundamental cultural and structural change" (p. 146). Fenby proposes an action model based on critical theory that shifts the focus from the technical aspects of management to self-reflection. This model encourages a look beyond the immediate actions and behaviors to the underlying values and perceptions guiding the desire for social change. Fenby provides an example of how one state bureaucracy separated treatment for substance abuse and mental illness, denying that some persons were dually diagnosed. A female manager advocated for the dual-diagnosis population and pressured the state hospital to designate a ward for this population group. This happened before it was fashionable to recognize dual diagnoses. Her belief in the importance of seeing connections, viewing people holistically and changing established patterns, illustrates the action model proposed by Fenby (1991, p. 34).

Acker (1992) lays out an inventory of gendered processes that recognize both the positive and negative potential of gendering organizations. She believes, as does Burrell and Hearn (1989), that gendering organizations is central to the production of better answers to questions about the organization of production and the reproduction of organization. Acker's first set of processes is the production of gender divisions because women and men are not alike, but the assumption that women are suited for certain work and men for other may mean that any reorganization will result only in the reorganization of male dominance. The second is the "creation of symbols, images, and forms of consciousness that explicate, justify, and more rarely, oppose gender divisions" (p. 253) to allow the voices of women to emerge and the construction of organizational cultures that contribute to success through diversity. The third set of processes involves the relational dimension of organizations, requires consciousness-raising about the power and politics that create divisions and dominance in order to establish the potential for change in the concrete work of the organization. The fourth dimension involves the cognitive activities of the individual members as they determine for themselves their understanding of the organization's work, opportunities, and demands. This work context should be gender-appropriate, not gender-neutral behaviors and attitudes (Cockburn, 1991; Pringle, 1989), in support of authentic individual development within the organization. The goal is to have this cognitive work become part of the organizational dialogue, women no longer need to "fit" in; they can "be in" organizations.

Perhaps the boldest alternative practice approach comes from Fox and Miller (1995), who seek to enhance organizational administration through improved discourse that operates within a publicly agreed upon set of rules and leadership selection. They see rules as socially constructed and, therefore, always open to reconstruction when they fail to serve the public good. For them, crucial to the quality of the practitioner's daily activities is discourse or "will formation" (p. xiv) that recognizes power transactions, social formations, and other dimensions of malleability and relativity. Discourse becomes the means to authentic communication within the organization and is based on the following norms. Authentic discourse requires trust between participants. It must be about contextually situated activities. It requires "vigorous, active, even passionate engagement" (p. 125). Finally, the discourse must make a substantive contribution to the dialogue. This is an intense, face-to-face method of honest dialogue where reality is a constructed consensus, based on recursive, sometimes conflictual discourse.

This last approach is the clearest in representing the level of discomfort that is involved in giving voice to the formerly unvoiced. Educators and students can grapple with what it means to have a plethora of voices and how they would incorporate various opinions and ideas into their organizational practice. Discomfort with this approach does not necessarily mean lack of effectiveness, so the next section offers ways for continual reevaluation that should guard against premature rejection of difficult ideas and processes.

Strategies for Reevaluation

Because the sensemaking concept was so useful in our own efforts to understand and make meaning in the creation of this chapter, we first suggest the use of Weick's dimensions for organizational sensemaking. Whether the reevaluation of assumptions, theories, or frameworks is aimed at the inclusion of women, other voiceless groups, or the power elite, Weick's framework provides an occasion of sensemaking and management of ambiguity and uncertainty. As a reminder, the following questions are suggested:

1. Is what is being evaluated grounded in identity construction?
2. Is it retrospective, in that it makes sense in the context of relevant history?
3. Does it allow the enactment of a sensible environment?
4. Is it social/relational?
5. Does it allow for ongoing sensemaking?
6. Does it allow for the extraction of meaningful cues?
7. Is it driven by plausibility rather than accuracy?

In order to capture the struggle for meaning in organization, we propose a series of additional questions in reevaluating alternative assumptions, theories, and models:

8. Is this approach sensitive to values, experience, and interpretation?
9. What are the implications of the language used?
10. Does this approach focus on processes and outcomes as interconnected?

Finally, in the assessment of authenticity of the discourse and behaviors in organizations guided by alternative assumptions, theories, and models, we borrow from the authenticity requirement for rigor in constructivist inquiry (Chambers, Wedel & Rodwell, 1992):

11. Does it promote fairness?
12. Is there evenhanded representation of all viewpoints?
13. Does it increase the awareness of the complexity of the social environment?
14. Does it increase appreciation of the complexities and a greater sophistication about the issues?
15. Is there an increased understanding of and respect for the value systems of others?
16. Do organizational stakeholders appreciate the constructions that are made by others and understand how those constructions are rooted in others' different value systems, each having merit and being worthy of consideration?
17. Is change a potential due to action being facilitated and stimulated?
18. Is empowerment or redistribution of power among organizational stakeholders made possible through stimulation to effective action?

The last two reevaluation questions clearly move from the assessment of knowledge for knowledge's sake to assessment of knowledge for action. It is our position that understanding the impact of being voiceless in organizations is not sufficient. Eventually, change must occur. This change may be possible through the redesign of the planning and administration curriculum. It is our hope that we have offered some suggestions that will assist the reader in moving toward curricular change.

CONCLUSION

If we move toward understanding organizations with gender lenses, social integration, respect for and the celebration of differences, and substantial equality we will change human service organizational life. In order to depart from the limits of traditional ways of knowing and doing that are barriers to successful application of the gender lens, a changed educational experience is necessary. For the social work administration and planning student to successfully manage the ambiguity, ambivalence, and uncertainty that are a part of openness, social work educators may begin with the content in this chapter. But this is only a beginning. We will all need to continue to seek new and different approaches to organizational work that are built on our new methods of communication and the insights of diverse voices, and that move us toward the implementation of client-centered, gender-sensitive models. Otherwise, sensitivity to diversity through the application of material provided herein will remain in the head, but not become a part of this profession's role in human service organizations.

APPENDIX 8–1: PLANNING AND ADMINISTRATION IN SOCIAL WORK PRACTICE

Course Description: 3 lecture hours. 3 credits. Emphasizes the importance of language and conceptual meaning in managing, administering, and planning in human service organizations. Presents rational and nonrational models of analysis. Focuses on decision-making as a value-based, political process. Offers knowledge for the understanding of changing human service agencies and their environments, and proposes approaches for addressing challenges and opportunities. Develops skills in leading and managing a diverse work force.

Course Objectives

1. In the context of rational and nonrational views, understand at least two organizational theories or frameworks, the metaphors

on which they are constructed, and their assumptions, strengths, and limitations.

2. Reconstruct the sociolinguistic assumptions within the verbal and written communication that occurs within at least one human service organization, paying particular attention to gender, race, and ethnicity.
3. Analyze at least two aspects of organizational culture and their underlying value assumptions in at least one human service organization.
4. Develop an understanding of contemporary complex human service environments and how the use and misuse of power affects individual and organizational behavior and decision-making.
5. Create a flexible human service program design, including service delivery intervention and evaluation that is considered sensitive to the needs of diverse consumers and stakeholders.
6. Identify and process ethical paradoxes and issues in human service program design and implementation, with particular attention to diversity.
7. Develop skills in leading and managing diverse employees. Diverse employees are persons of different gender, race, ethnicity, disabilities, age, sexual orientation, religion, and discipline.

Learning Units and Suggested Readings

Unit One: Assessing Organizational Culture, Values, and Assumptions: The language of which includes the nonrational, paradoxical, and cultural audit.

Berlin, S.B. (March 1990). Dichotomous and complex thinking. *Social Service Review*, 46–59.

Fenby, B.L. (1991). Feminist theory, critical theory, and management's romance with the technical. *Affilia*, *6*(1), 20–37.

Gherardi, S. (1995). *Gender, symbolism and organizational cultures*. London: Sage.

Morgan, G. (1986). *Images of organization*. Newbury Park, CA: Sage.

Unit Two: Understanding Organizational Behavior in the Context of Environment: The language of which includes politics, power, image, culture, communication, perspective.

Gottlieb, N. (1992). Empowerment, political analyses and services for women. In Y. Hasenfeld (Ed.), *Human services as complex organizations* (pp. 301–319). Newbury Park, CA: Sage.

Martin, P.Y. (June 1990). Rethinking feminist organizations. *Gender & Society*, *4*(2), 182–206.

Martin, P.Y., Harrison, D., & DiNitto, D. (1993). Advancement of women in hierarchical organizations: A multi-level analysis of problems and prospects. *Journal of Applied Behavioral Science*, *19*(1), 19–33.

Mason, M.A. (1992). Standing still in the workplace: Women in social work and other female-dominated occupations. *Affilia*, *7*(3), 23–43.

Weick, K.E. (1995). *Sensemaking in organizations*. Thousand Oaks, CA: Sage.

Unit Three: Creating Human Service Programs: The language of which includes voices, perspectives, multiple measures, multiple expectations.

Hyde, C. (1989). A feminist model for macro-practice: Promises and problems. *Administration in Social Work*, *13*(3/4), 145–181.

Hyde, C. (1992) The ideational system of social movement agencies: An examination of feminist health centers. In Y. Hasenfeld (Ed.), *Human services as complex organizations*. Newbury Park, CA: Sage.

Tannen, D. (1994). *Talking from 9 to 5 women and men in the workplace: Language, sex and power*. New York: Avon Books.

Unit Four: Managing Diversity: The language of which includes hermeneutics, dialectics, discourse, confrontation, conflict, empowerment, respect, risk, power.

Aguilar, M.A. & Williams, L.P. (1993). Factors contributing to the success and achievement of minority women. *Affilia*, *8*(4), 410–424.

Almeleh, N., Soifer, S., Gottlieb, N. & Gutierrez, L. (1993). Women's achievement of empowerment through activism in the workplace. *Affilia*, *8*(1), 26–39.

Gibelman, M. & Schervish, P.H. (1993). The glass ceiling in social work: Is it shatterproof? *Affilia*, *8*(4), 442–455.

Mallow, C. (1993). Coping with multiple roles: Family configuration and the need for workplace services. *Affilia*, *8*(1), 40–55.

Thomas, R. (1991). *Beyond race and gender: Unleashing the power of your total work force by managing diversity*. New York: AMACOM.

Zippay, A. (1994). The role of working-class women in a changing economy. *Affilia*, *9*(3), 30–44.

Zunz, S.J. (1991). Gender-related issues in the career development of social work managers. *Affilia*, *6*(4), 39–52.

REFERENCES

Abramovitz, M. (1988). *Regulating the lives of women*. Boston: South End Press.

Acker, J. (1992). Gender organizational theory. In A.J. Mills & P. Tancred (Eds.), *Gendering organizational analysis* (pp. 248–260). Newbury, CA: Sage.

Aguilar, M.A. & Williams, L.P. (1993). Factors contributing to the success and achievement of minority women. *Affilia*, *8*(4), 410–424.

Ainsley, S. (1993). *Sexual stratification in organizations*. Unpublished manuscript.

Aldrich, H.E. (1993). Incommensurable paradigms? Vital signs from three perspectives. In M. Reed & M. Huges (Eds.), *Rethinking organization: New directions in organization theory and analysis* (pp. 17–45). London: Sage.

Almeleh, N., Soifer, S., Gottlieb, N. & Gutierrez, L. (1993). Women's achievement of empowerment through activism in the workplace. *Affilia*, *8*(1), 26–39.

Austin, D.M. (1995). Management overview. In *Encyclopedia of social work* (19th ed., pp. 1642–1658). Washington, DC: NASW Press.

Bennis, W.G. (1966). *Changing organizations*. New York: McGraw-Hill.

Berlin, S.B. (1990). Dichotomous and complex thinking. *Social Service Review*,*64*, 46–59.

Boje, D.M., Gephart, R.P. & Thatchenkery, R.J. (1996). *Postmodern management and organization theory*. Thousand Oaks, CA: Sage.

Burrell, G. & Hearn, J. (1989). The sexuality of organization. In J. Hearn, D.L. Sheppard, P. Tancred-Shefiff & G. Burrell (Eds.), *The sexuality of the organization*. London: Sage.

Calas, M.B. & Smirchich, L. (1996). From "The woman's" point of view: Feminist approaches to organization studies. In S.R. Clegg, C.H. Hardy, W.R. Nord (Eds.), *Handbook of organizational studies* (pp. 218–257). London: Sage.

Chambers, D.E., Wedel, K.R. & Rodwell, M.K. (1992). *Evaluating social programs*. Boston: Allyn & Bacon.

Clegg, S.R., Hardy, C.H. & Nord, W.R. (1996). *Handbook of organizational studies*. London: Sage.

Cockburn, C. (1991). *In the way of women: Men's resistance to sex equality in organizations*. Ithaca, NY: ILR Press.

Dinerman, M. (1992). Is everything women's work? *Affilia, 7*(2), 77–93.

England, P. (1992). *Comparable worth: Theories and evidence*. Hawthorne, NY: Aldine de Gruyter.

Fenby, B.L. (1991). Feminist theory, critical theory, and management's romance with the technical. *Affilia, 6*(1), 20–37.

Flynn, J.P. (1992). *Social agency policy: Analysis and presentation for community practice*. Chicago: Nelson-Hall.

Forester, J. (1980). Critical theory and planning practice. *Journal of the American Planning Association, 46*(3), 275–286.

Fox, C.J. & Miller, H.T. (1995). *Postmodern public administration: Toward discourse*. Thousand Oaks, CA: Sage.

Gherardi, S. (1995). *Gender, symbolism and organizational cultures*. London: Sage.

Gibelman, M. & Schervish, P.H. (1993). The glass ceiling in social work: Is it shatterproof? *Affilia, 8*(4), 442–455.

Gottlieb, N. (1992). Empowerment, political analyses and services for women. In Y. Hasenfeld (Ed.), *Human services as complex organizations* (pp. 301–319). Newbury Park, CA: Sage.

Halseth, J.H. (1993). Infusing a feminist analysis into education for policy, planning, and administration. In T. Mizrahi & J.D. Morrison (Eds.), *Community organization and social administration* (pp. 225–241). Binghamton, NY: Haworth.

Hasenfeld, Y. (Ed.). (1992). *Human services as complex organizations*. Newbury Park, CA: Sage.

Hooyman, N.R. (1994). Diversity and populations at risk: Women. In F.G. Reamer (Ed.), *Foundations of social work knowledge* (pp. 309–345). New York: Columbia University Press.

Hyde, C. (1989). A feminist model for macro-practice: Promises and problems. *Administration in Social Work, 13*(3/4), 145–181.

Hyde, C. (1992). The ideational system of social movement agencies: An examination of feminist health centers. In Y. Hasenfeld (Ed.), *Human services as complex organizations* (pp. 121–144). Newbury Park, CA: Sage.

Iglehart, A.P. & Becerra, R.M. (1995). *Social services and the ethnic community*. Boston: Allyn & Bacon.

Kanter, R.M. (1987). Power failure in management circuits. In J.M. Shafritz & J.S. Ott (Eds.), *Classics of organizational theory* (pp. 349–363). Chicago: Dorsey Press.

Kanter, R.M. (1989). *When giants learn to dance*. New York: Simon & Shuster.

Katz, D. & Kahn, R. (1966). *The social psychology of organizations*. New York: Wiley.

Kettner, P.M., Moroney, R.M. & Martin, L.L. (1990). *Designing and managing programs: An effectiveness-based approach*. Newbury Park, CA: Sage.

Lakoff, G. & Johnson, M. (1980). *Metaphors we live by*. Chicago: University of Chicago Press.

Langer, E.J. (1989). *Mindfulness*. Reading, MA: Addison-Wesley.

Lawlor, E.F. & Raube, K. (September 1995). Social interventions and outcomes in medical effectiveness research. *Social Service Review, 69*(3), 383–404.

Levy, B.S. (1994). *The empowerment tradition in American social work*. New York: Columbia University Press.

Lindblom, C.E. (1959). The science of "muddling through." *Public Administrative Review, 19*(2), 79–88.

Longres, J.F. (1996). Can we have our cake and eat it too? *Journal of Social Work Education, 32*(2), 158–159.

Mallow, C. (1993). Coping with multiple roles: Family configuration and the need for workplace services. *Affilia, 8*(1), 40–55.

Martin, P.Y. (June 1990). Rethinking feminist organizations. *Gender & Society, 4*(2), 182–206.

Martin, P.Y., Harrison, D. & DiNitto, D. (1993). Advancement of women in hierarchical organizations: A multi-level analysis of problems and prospects. *Journal of Applied Behavioral Science, 19*(1), 19–33.

Mason, M.A. (1992). Standing still in the workplace: Women in social work and other female-dominated occupations. *Affilia, 7*(3), 23–43.

Miller, S.J., Hickson, D.J. & Wilson, D.C. (1996). Decision-making in organizations. In S.R. Clegg, C.H. Hardy & W.R. Nord (Eds.), *Handbook of organizational studies* (pp. 293–312). London: Sage

Milles, A.J. & Tancred, P. (1992). *Gendering organizational analysis*. Newbury Park, CA: Sage.

Morgan, G. (1986). *Images of organization*. Newbury Park, CA: Sage.

Netting, F.E., Kettner, P.D. & McMurtry, S L. (1993). *Social work macro practice*. White Plains, NY: Longman.

Odendahl, T. & O'Neill, M. (Eds.). (1994). *Women and power in the nonprofit sector*. San Francisco: Jossey-Bass.

Perlmutter, F.D. (Ed.). (1988). *Alternative social agencies: Administrative strategies*. New York: Haworth.

Perlmutter, F.D. (Ed.) (1994). *Women and social change*. Washington, DC: NASW Press.

Petchers, M.K. (1996). Debunking the myth of progress for women social work educators. *Affilia, 11*(1), 11–38.

Peters, T.J. & Waterman, R.H. (1982). *In search of excellence*. New York: Warner Books.

Pringle, P. (1989). *Secretaries talk: Sexuality, power, and work*. New York: VERSO.

Reed, M. & Huges, M. (Eds.). (1992). *Rethinking organization: New directions in organizational theory and analysis*. London: Sage.

Saleeby, D. (1996). The strengths perspective in social work practice: Extensions and cautions. *Social Work, 41*(3), 296–305.

Schein, E.H. (1991). *Organizational culture and leadership*. San Francisco: Jossey-Bass.

Shafritz, J.M. & Ott, J.S. (1987). *Classics of organizational theory* (2nd ed.). Chicago: Dorsey Press.

Stone, S. (1988). *Policy, paradox and political reason*. New York, NY: Harper Collins.

Tannen, D. (1994). *Talking from 9 to 5 women and men in the workplace: Language, sex and power*. New York: Avon Books.

Thomas, R. (1991). *Beyond race and gender: Unleashing the power of your total work force by managing diversity*. New York: AMACOM.

Thompson, J.D. (1967). *Organizations in action*. New York. McGraw Hill.

Toffler, A. (1970). *Future shock*. New York: Random House.

Walters, M., Carter, B., Papp, P. & Silverstein, O. (1988). *The invisible web: Gender patterns in family relationships*. New York: Guilford.

Waring, M. (1988). *If women counted*. San Francisco: Harper & Row.

Weick, K.E. (1995). *Sensemaking in organizations*. Thousand Oaks, CA: Sage.

Weinbach, R.W. (1994). *The social worker as manager: Theory and practice*. Boston: Allyn & Bacon.

Zippay, A. (1994). The role of working-class women in a changing economy. *Affilia, 9*(3), 30–44.

Zunz, S.J. (1991). Gender-related issues in the career development of social work managers. *Affilia, 6*(4), 39–52.

CHAPTER 9

Gender and Social Welfare Policy

Ann Nichols-Casebolt

INTRODUCTION

Women are much more likely to be poor than men; women make up the largest share of recipients of some of the most controversial social welfare programs (e.g., AFDC); and women are most typically the providers of social welfare services through their overrepresentation in such professions as social work, nursing, and teaching, and as the mainstay of the voluntary sector. The gendered nature of the social welfare system, however, is seldom addressed in mainstream interpretations of social welfare policies. Although societal expectations based on gender have influenced the development of the social welfare system and the delivery of social welfare services, traditional analyses have often ignored issues of gender in their assessment of welfare policies (as they have ignored issues of race and class). This both limits and distorts our understanding of the provision of social welfare. A great deal of social policy does relate to "women's concerns" (i.e., home and family); however, many of these policies are based on ideologies and outdated assumptions about women's proper role in society. Policies that assume women's primary functions are in the home and that women should assume primary responsibility for caretaking, or policies that view the two-parent family as the only appropriate family structure, result in a social welfare system that is inequitable for both women and men and do not accurately reflect the life circumstances of many who are affected by such policies.

The social welfare policy content taught in schools of social work is generally no exception to this portrayal. Although most courses discuss issues such as poverty and domestic violence and thus necessarily focus on topics related to women, covering content on women does not mean that policies and issues are examined from the perspectives of women, or that gender assumptions that drive our social welfare system are challenged. For example, the discussion of women's poverty is often done without an acknowledgment of the gender segregation of the labor market, and discussions of domestic violence often exclude examination of the sexist, racist, and classist attitudes that continue to influence the implementation of laws and policies in this area (see, e.g., Sheffield, 1995). In addition, the language that is used often obscures the importance of gender in understanding social policies and programs. Gender-neutral terms such as "welfare recipients" and "welfare dependents" mask the fact that we are primarily referring to women and their children.

The integration of women's content into the policy area of the curriculum is particularly crucial because it is here that students are expected to develop "perspectives, values, and sensitivities that enrich and shape" their practice of social work, and to learn "knowledge and skills to participate in the policy changing process" (Jansson, 1994a, p. 51). Without an understanding of how gender—as well as race/ethnicity and class—continues to shape social welfare policies, the perspectives students receive will conform to what is, and policy changes will continue to reflect dominant biases.

In this chapter the topics or themes typically covered within social welfare policy courses are presented. I do not, however, provide in-depth knowledge of social welfare programs and policies; it is my assumption that the reader already has an understanding of the American social welfare system. Instead, I briefly outline the topics and critically examine the theories and assumptions of their major components; the ways in which gender categories remain invisible; and how this has limited our understanding of the issues. The chapter concludes with recommendations for curricular revisions to integrate gender issues into social policy courses.

TRADITIONAL KNOWLEDGE IN SOCIAL WELFARE POLICY

Social policy has been variously defined as "a collective strategy to address social problems" (Jansson, 1994b, p. 4); "those social security, social service, and health programs, activities and organizations, public and private, intended primarily to promote the well-being of individuals who society felt needed and deserved help (Trattner, 1994, p. xxxii) and "anything government chooses to do, or not to do, that affects the quality of life of its people" (DiNitto, 1991, p. 2). It is clear from these definitions that the scope of social welfare policy is very broad, covering content on public and private social service delivery systems, particular programs, political processes, and an understanding of social problems and issues. Because of this breadth there is no agreement as to the particular topics that social welfare curriculum must cover. According to the Council on Social Work Education's "Curriculum Policy Statement" there is, however, an expectation that all students must obtain knowledge about

> the history and current patterns of provisions of social welfare services, the role of social policy in helping or deterring people in the maintenance or attainment of optimal health and well-being, and effect of policy on social work practice. Students must be taught to analyze current social policy within the context of historical and contemporary factors that shape policy. (Council on Social Work Education, 1994, p. 141)

The following section presents an overview of the typical mainstream view of the historical factors that have influenced the development of our social welfare system. It then moves to a discussion of the place of gender in understanding that development. In the next section various models for analyzing social policies are described, and their attention to identifying underlying assumptions and biases that may be influencing policy alternatives are examined.

The Historical Context for Understanding Social Policy

While it has been argued that many schools do not place much emphasis on historical analyses (Jansson, 1988, p. 2), most courses on social welfare policy include aspects of the historical development of major welfare programs and the welfare state (Ginsberg, 1994). This historical information is used to provide a context for understanding our current system of social welfare. It helps us to understand the social forces—ideological, political, and material—that shaped, at specific historical periods, the welfare enterprise.

Historical explanations of social policy generally focus on an examination of the economic, social and political factors that have influenced policy choices and the development of social welfare programs. The typical approach relies upon an exploration of the effects of the private market economy on government intervention (or lack thereof), social conditions that give rise to societal problems and social structures that are available to meet the needs of society, and ideological and political forces that have determined which problems and solutions resulted in social welfare interventions at various points in time (see, e.g., Axinn & Levin, 1982; Day, 1989; Jansson, 1988; Trattner, 1994).

Mainstream social policy scholars generally agree that the theory of the liberal state and its concepts of individualism and laissez-faire, or free market, economics are key to understanding the historical development of American social welfare policies. This theoretical perspective argued that pursuing individual self-interest would maximize both personal and societal benefits and that any interference with the interests of the individual would undermine what was in the best interests of society. "The welfare of the whole was seen as the function of the activities of the members rather than the welfare of members being determined by the desires of the whole" (Mencher, 1967, p. 63). Under the philosophy of laissez-faire, individuals acting out of their own competitive self-interest would be naturally regulated by the "invisible hand of the market" to channel their activities into those that would promote the welfare of all. Under this model, the market rather than government regulates society and provides rewards to its members.

Implicit in this theory is that individual initiative will lead to economic prosperity for both the individual as well as society (Bell, 1983; Sapiro, 1990,) and that any interference by government to assist individuals outside the market—such as providing financial assistance to the poor—will undermine the economic system by eroding individual initiative and work effort (Smith & Stone, 1988). This predominance of individualism and the "work ethic" perspective during the nineteenth and early twentieth centuries is used to explain our country's relatively laggard development of a social welfare system to meet the needs of its citizens.

The belief in the attributes of the free market and its accompanying assumptions were strengthened in the 1800s by Spencer's and Sumner's views of the "survival of the fittest" and the application of Darwin's theory of evolution and natural selection. This view reinforced the notion that poverty was the fault of the individual, attributable to sinful acts or personal failings such as idleness, spendthriftiness, intemperance, and gambling (Day, 1989). It also equated economic success with morality. Not surprisingly then, during this period employment was seen as both an economic as well as a moral enterprise—those who worked were viewed as "moral," and those who did not were viewed as "immoral." This sent a clear message: Providing aid to the poor would not only support the "unfit" but would also be rewarding individuals for their immoral behavior.

The Charity Organization Movement, considered the beginning of social casework, was founded upon the notion of the importance of the work ethic, moral virtue, individual achievement, and the concern for dependency. Families were investigated as to their need for relief, and if aid was given, "for assuring its connection to work" (Axinn & Levin, 1982, p. 100). Pauperism was seen as a threat to an economic system that was working properly, and relief as an aid to immorality.

In addition to the ideology of the work ethic, a major factor in mainstream explanations of the historical development of welfare state policies was the value our society placed on the family for meeting the economic and social needs of its members. Families, like the marketplace, were considered best served by minimal "interference" unless they did not adequately perform their role. The interplay between the work ethic and the role of the family was evident in the view that a "good" family was one that was self-reliant and in which the values of work were instilled in the children (Axinn & Levin, 1982).

While the values of individualism and the work ethic argued against the provision of public assistance, by the end of the nineteenth century the social problems that had come with industrialization and urbanization prompted reformers to advocate for government intervention to assist families (Bell, 1983). The social welfare policies and programs that developed recognized that the market and the family might at times not be able to deal with the vagaries of the economic and social system. The majority of the programs, however, continued to reinforce the traditional view that work and family should be the primary social supports, and that both could be destroyed if public aid was not given wisely. Nowhere is this view more evident than in the Social Security Act of 1935.

It was not until the 1930s when the country was gripped by a massive depression that the view that adherence to work would result in economic self-sufficiency was called into question (Bell, 1983), and government took an active role in the design and provision of social welfare services. But, even then, the social welfare system that developed was tied closely to the work ethic, and resulted in a two-tiered system of provision: The social insurance programs were the most generous and provided cash benefits to those who had a past history of work in designated jobs; the public assistance programs were means-tested and directed to those who were poor and unable to work because of age, disability, or family obligations. The two social insurance programs included Unemployment Compensation and Social Security for the aged, and were based on an *institutional* perspective that viewed social welfare as necessary for protecting individuals—initially only workers and later their dependents—from the risks inherent in a modern industrial society (Wilensky & Lebeaux, 1965). The programs were fashioned after a private insurance model. They were designed to provide benefits to individuals who had worked and made prior financial contributions to the system, much like a private insurance plan. On the other hand, public assistance programs such as Aid to Dependent Children (now AFDC), Old Age Assistance, and Aid to the Blind largely reflected the residual perspective which "holds that welfare institutions should come into play only when the normal structures of supply, the family and the market, break down" (Wilensky & Lebeaux, 1965, p. 138). Social insurance programs were seen as an entitlement, whereas public assistance programs were seen as helping those who were deemed to be justifiably out of the labor force, but somewhat less deserving because they "had not made the most of opportunities to work or save" (Day, 1989, p. 291).

This two-tiered welfare system and the notions of deserving and undeserving persist today. The largest program in terms of numbers and beneficiaries is Social Security, but AFDC continues to be the most controversial and the one that receives the most criticism. Current debates and discussions about welfare reform are most often centered around the historic issues of reinforcing the notion of work, self-sufficiency, and family responsibility.

The Place of Gender in the Historical Context

The understanding of our social welfare system from this mainstream historical approach is generally perceived to be "gender-neutral." Yet if we examine the development of social welfare policies and programs within the context of gender roles and expectations we find that the value of the work ethic and our concern about dependency do not adequately reflect the experience of women and that individualism and economic self-reliance are not universally applied. Historically, social policies have instead "supported individualism, independence, and self reliance for some people (primarily men) and dependence and reliance on paternalism for others (primarily women)" (Sapiro, 1990, p. 42). Interestingly, there does not appear to be a recognition in mainstream analyses that at the same time we were establishing expectations for "people" to be in the labor force, women were expected to be wives and mothers, not workers. While industrialization and urbanization were creating significant social problems they were also creating a division between work and family—the public and the private spheres—and the roles of workers and dependents. Increasingly during the 1800s the proper role for married women was seen to be in the home, and in support of their husbands who needed to work outside the home in the new industries and commercial enterprises to provide for the family (Gerstel & Gross, 1995).

The support of women and men within prescribed gender roles has been termed the "domestic code" or "family ethic" (Abramovitz, 1988). The family ethic is based on the expectation that the appropriate female role is that of wife and mother providing support within the home, while that of the male is as the breadwinner. This sexual division of labor not only made women's dependence on men acceptable, but also made it desirable, for it was when women were carrying out the domestic responsibilities that men were able to pursue their obligation to economically support the family.

> Fundamentally patriarchal, nineteenth-century industrial society constructed the home as sanctuary. Men, increasingly subject to the rigors of industrialized laissez-faire, needed wives as home managers, child rearers, and sources of emotional support. The wife and mother in the home was to be the source of higher moral and ethical values than were found in the business world. Women were valued for piety, purity, and submissiveness. Children now became the center of women's activity. The home and children constituted women's "separate sphere," which was seen as part of the "natural" social order. (Handler & Hasenfeld, 1991, p. 52)

The portrayal of women as the upholder of moral values became the Victorian cult of true womanhood that "cast women as moral guardians—pious, nurturant, and naturally domestic. Wives' proper place became the home; their proper duties, housework and mothering" (Gerstel & Gross, 1995, p. 95). The outcome of this ideology was to make economic dependency as much a moral "obligation" for women as work for pay was a moral obligation for men, and, not coincidentally, effectively kept women from competing with men for jobs in the market. Unfortunately, not all women could afford to be, or desired to be, economically dependent upon men. However, society's adherence to the domestic code has historically curtailed the ability of women to be economically self-sufficient and to pursue their own individual interests.

During the early 1800s when the theory of the liberal state argued that individualism was a virtue, there were laws that prohibited women from voting and serving on juries, prohibited married women from owning property and signing contracts without their husband's consent, and made women "technically the property of their husbands" (Jansson, 1988, p. 34). Denying women fundamental rights of citizenship effectively kept them as dependents in an era when dependency was viewed as a moral failing. In addition, although educational opportunities for women expanded by the end of the 1800s, institutions of higher education were often sex segregated, and women were at times prohibited from areas of employment outside of the domestic sphere or denied employment within some professions (such as teaching) if they married or became pregnant (Sapiro, 1990). Educated middle-class women who aspired to opportunities outside of the home were channeled into activities that were fitting for "true womanhood"—attacking immorality by addressing such issues as prohibition, child labor, and peace (Day, 1989).

Mainstream historical analyses have not typically discussed the contradictory expectations and experiences of women. For example, under the domestic code women were expected to be dependent upon their husbands, but the model of the liberal state argued that dependent individuals were morally inferior. And, under the liberal state the work ethic was a valued principal, but women who attempted to carry out the goals of the work ethic by seeking employment were stigmatized as breaking the domestic code. Yet, those that adhered to the domestic code by "working at home" were not rewarded by the market, making them vulnerable to poverty and potential dependency on the state if their husbands were unwilling/unable to support them.

The domestic code of the 1800s also clearly had a class and race bias. Poor women and women of color have historically had to work for wages to support their families. However, because of the emphasis on the appropriate role of women as within the domestic sphere, when women were employed during the 1800s they were not only seen as "selfish and neglectful of their families" (Handler & Hasenfeld, 1991, p. 52), but they were typically paid low wages and channeled into sex-segregated jobs that mirrored their work in the home. "Wherever they worked, however, women's low earnings barely supplemented a husband's income or supported a husbandless family. . . . Urban newspapers reported women toiling at 'starvation rates' and 'in a constant fight with starvation and pauperism'" (Abramovitz, 1988, p. 142). The employment opportunities for black women were even more restricted, it was estimated that in the 1890s almost all black women in the labor force worked in either personal service or agriculture (Gerstel & Gross, 1995).

The gender roles embodied in the family ethic also determined socially acceptable roles for men. Men were expected to be employed, and through work it was assumed they could adequately support their families. Thus when a married woman worked she was not only "violating" the domestic code for women, but her employment was an indication that her husband was not able to fulfill his responsibilities. The recognition that the prevailing wages earned by some men might not be enough to support a family did not change the view that men should be the sole breadwinner for the family. Instead, some early legislative proposals supported by the male-dominated labor movement argued for the provision of a "family wage" that would enable husbands to support their family without the assistance of a wage-earning wife (Michel, 1993).

It needs to be remembered, however, that this view of the proper role of men and women was largely reflective of the white middle-class family and its experiences, and often placed women of color in an untenable position.

> Society's treatment of women of color clearly indicated that their value as laborers took precedence over their domestic and reproductive roles. On all fronts, the families of poor and immigrant women and women of color experienced a series of assaults not faced by middle-class White women. (Abramovitz, 1988, p. 39)

Social legislation that was instituted to "protect" women and provide for their economic needs can also be viewed from the perspective of reinforcing gender roles and undermining the ability of women to become self-sufficient. For example, protective labor legislation was promulgated on the notion that women needed protection because of their role as mothers, but many of the laws also effectively kept women out of competition with men for jobs that often paid higher salaries. Labor unions were, in fact, a major force behind this legislation because men were increasingly seeing women as competitors for their jobs (Freeman, 1995; Handler & Hasenfeld, 1991). As one labor leader was quoted as saying in 1879: "We cannot drive the females out of the trade, but we can restrict their daily quota of labor through factory laws" (Freeman, 1995, p. 368). It has also been pointed out that such protective labor legislation "has generally been applied less strenuously to 'female' than to 'male' jobs. Hours and weightlifting limits, for example, were never applied to domestic labor, paid or unpaid" (Sapiro, 1990, p. 44). The exclusion of domestic and agricultural work from labor legislation was also a clear indication of inherent race bias since most African-American women worked as domestics (Boris, 1993, p. 216).

The barriers to women's labor force participation had serious implications for women who lacked the support of a male breadwinner. Single women, including significant numbers of single mothers, were left economically vulnerable in a system that demeaned female labor and provided very little in the way of social welfare supports. Then (as now), poor women and women of color were caught in a system that expected them to work, often in the lowest-paid and most menial jobs, yet condemned them for working and abandoning their family responsibilities. Violation of the domestic code by women who entered the world of work did not go unpunished!

Social welfare intervention in the area of child protection during the late 1800s put single working mothers in a particularly difficult position.

> The very life-style of these single women was morally suspect. They had to work outside of the home to survive, but lack of supervision became one of the defining elements of child neglect. Almost by definition, they failed at mothering and at playing the proper feminine role. And because they were very poor they were also suspect as paupers. Because caseworkers generally saw these mothers as incapable of maintaining a home and earning a living, they frequently found neglect, and, rather than help the mothers maintain the home,

> they often recommended that the children be removed. (Handler & Hasenfeld, 1991, p. 24)

The mothers' pension movement in the early part of the twentieth century was, in part, prompted by the changing view that children in single mother families would be better off if their mothers could be home caring for them. While mothers' pensions provided financial assistance to women (primarily white widows) who were deprived of the income of a breadwinner, it was also expected that such benefits would serve to keep women in the home and out of the labor market (Abramovitz, 1988). The reality, however, was that pension benefits were not enough to adequately support a mother and her children, requiring many recipients to continue to work for wages, which again put them at odds with the family ethic. The additional financial support from pensions also had the negative effect of undercutting political strategies which argued that working women's wages should be increased because many working women, like men, had dependents to support (Michel, 1993).

These gendered messages of the ideal liberal market society and its domestic code—that men should be dependent on the market and women dependent on men—were institutionalized in the Social Security Act of 1935. The social insurance programs served primarily white men who were most likely to be employed in jobs covered under the Act. The initial exclusion of certain groups of workers, mainly those in agricultural and domestic employment, meant that many working women (particularly women of color) were not eligible for these benefits in their own right as workers. The programs within the Social Security Act that served predominantly women were designed to benefit women as wives and mothers, not workers, and within those programs, women who most closely conformed to the domestic code and the prescribed role of wife and mother were treated more generously. Widows of covered workers could receive benefits through their husband's contributions to the system, whereas single mothers who were not eligible for these social insurance benefits were reliant upon ADC, a stigmatizing, poorly funded program that left most in poverty (Miller, 1990).

This discussion of the role of gender in the development of the social welfare system is not, however, "simply a matter of male policy makers keeping women subordinate" (Gordon, 1990, p. 14). A critical analysis of the historical development of the social welfare system would be incomplete without an understanding of the reform efforts of women themselves in the enactment of programs and policies—and the views those women brought to the issues that influenced the design of social welfare programs. Most historical accounts highlight the achievements of such women as Dorothea Dix, Jane Addams, Florence Kelly, and other notable women, but mainstream discussions often do not explore the role of women as an interest group in the development of social policies. Yet it has been argued that "to an extent unequaled elsewhere, middle-class American women were crucial and central to the responses state, and federal governments made to social pressures created by massive immigration and rapid industrialization and urbanization" (Sklar, 1993, p. 44). Through women's clubs and other types of organizations, women exercised considerable influence at the local, state, and national levels at the turn of the century. Unlike men, women did not have access to the public authority and institutional power, but they were extremely successful in grass-roots organizing. Through the efforts of women, American social policy developed with a distinctive focus on bettering the lives of women and children.

As noted previously, women's volunteer work in the social welfare arena was sanctioned as an extension of their domestic role. Women made significant contributions through voluntary organizations that both provided social services and served as vehicles for political action. The philosophy of minimal government intervention coupled with a domestic code that kept many women from entering the paid labor force created opportunities for women to become involved in social welfare issues. Women, particularly middle-class women who had been college educated, engaged in charitable work that eventually evolved into more direct political action.

At times, however, the efforts of these white middle-class reformers were oblivious to the reality of the lives of poor women and women of color. There were times when "disagreements over control of the workplace and household divided women along the lines of class, race, ethnicity, and religion" (Koven & Michel, 1993). On the other hand, while it is evident that most reformist women accepted the traditional middle-class view of women's roles and the place of family, "within the political culture of middle-class women, gender consciousness combined with an awareness of class-based injustice, and talented leaders combined with grass-roots activism to produce an impressive force for social, political, and economic change" (Sklar, 1993, p. 75). These changes created a system that protected and supported women in their role as mothers; however, at the same time these changes were detrimental to their independence and ability to be economically self-sufficient.

Demographic, social, and political changes during the past several decades have had a dramatic effect on the welfare system and the view of women's roles that it embodies. Whereas white widows were the primary recipients of AFDC until after World War II (Abramovitz, 1988), by the mid–1960s most recipients were divorced or never-married mothers and a large percentage were people of color. In addition, caseloads and costs were increasing at what was seen as an alarming pace—from 2 million in 1950 to 9 million by 1970 (Handler & Hasenfeld, 1991). Women, including married women (in part due to a drop in men's wages), were also entering the labor market in unprecedented numbers, calling into question the view that government should be supporting women to stay home and care for their children. All of these factors contributed to AFDC policy changes that began to officially link welfare receipt with a work obligation. As Abramovitz stated:

> The strengthened work orientation marked a shift in the notion of mutual obligation between the ADC mother and the state. Until this time, in theory at least, the government supported mothers at home as an entitlement, so that they could raise their children to be productive citizens. The new stress on work conveyed the doctrine that recipients should be obligated to become self-sufficient in exchange for government assistance. The punitive character of the amendments derived from a perception of welfare mothers as unmotivated and unwilling to work. (pp. 339–340)

The assumption continued to be, of course, that if these women were willing to work they would be able to find a job that paid them enough to support their children, but that was never the case. Women continued to be overrepresented in the low-skill, low-wage sector of the labor market, and in all occupational categories and at all educational levels they earned less than their male counterparts; the labor market continued to be gender-segregated, with occupations that mirror the traditional "caring" roles of women (e.g., nurses, teachers, child care workers, etc.) almost exclusively filled by women (Thornborrow & Sheldon, 1995); and supports such as health care and day care were often not available. In addition, as discussed in Chapter 6 on gender and families, women continued to carry the majority of home and child care even when they were employed.

While AFDC policies are reinforcing the notion of work for welfare, our two-tiered system of benefits remains intact. Widows with young children whose primary role has been as wife and mother are eligible to receive social security payments as an entitlement based on their husband's employment record without a work expectation. It is clear that our current social welfare system continues to reward dependency on men in some programs, while punishing dependency on the state in others; it continues to treat some groups as deserving of assistance and others not, basing that distinction on historic views of gender roles and acceptable behavior that has ironically often led to women's dependency and potential need for welfare programs. It has been argued that

> in fact, the social welfare system has been designed to perpetuate a system in which women's place is in the nuclear family. The divorce rate, women's emergence in great numbers into the labor force, and the growth in out-of-wedlock births has challenged the status quo, in spite of incentives to the contrary. Yet policy makers hesitate to make changes that would have implications for fundamental notions of gender roles that remain strong in American culture. (Miller, 1990, p. 3)

These traditional values and gender roles are particularly evident in the Personal Responsibility Act signed into law on August 22, 1996 (P.L. 104–193). This legislation has been touted as reinforcing what are considered to be the "fundamental" values of work, responsibility, and family. Its most far-reaching provision is the imposition of time limits on the receipt of AFDC. Welfare mothers can receive benefits for a maximum of only two years at one time, and cannot receive benefits more than five years over their entire lifetime. This legislation has made a clear statement that "merely" raising children is not sufficient to fulfill one's obligation to work, responsibility, or family. Women are no longer guaranteed a claim on social benefits exclusively through their role as mothers. . . . They must also be wives/widows or workers. On the surface, the emphasis of the legislation appears to be on reinforcing work among women on welfare. However, because it gives little or no consideration to the structural barriers to women's economic independence, these mothers' ability to support their families or to claim benefits in their own right as workers, will continue to be severely limited.

Examining gender roles and the gendered assumptions of social welfare policy not only provides a more complete understanding of the historic development of our social welfare system, but provides an important context for a critical analysis of current policies and change proposals. Unless we approach policy analysis with an understanding of the "traditional" assumptions about gender (and class and race), policies will continue to be evaluated against such values as the work ethic and individual responsibility, without recognizing their inherent gender bias.

POLICY ANALYSIS MODELS FOR EVALUATING SOCIAL POLICY ALTERNATIVES

It is increasingly recognized that an important component of the social policy curriculum is presenting knowledge and skills in policy analysis (Jansson, 1994a). "The purpose of policy analysis is to provide reliable information to policy-makers about a problem they must consider, in order to guide policy-making activities to appropriate conclusions" (Dobelstein, 1990, p. 61). The importance of policy analysis skills for practitioners is to support their professional commitment to the promotion of social justice and social change, as well as their responsibilities as deliverers of social services that are directly influenced by the policies implemented (Gilbert, Specht & Terrell, 1993).

There are numerous policy analysis models provided in a range of social welfare texts (e.g., Chambers, 1993; Day, 1989; Dobelstein, 1990; Flynn, 1992; Gilbert, Specht & Terrell, 1993; Iatridis, 1994; Jansson, 1994b; Moroney, 1991; Stone, 1988). These models are presented as tools for guiding analysts in making recommendations for policy interventions. While the details of the models may vary, they typically include criteria for clarifying the problem to be addressed, and generating and evaluating alternatives for solving the problem.

Traditional policy analysts generally approach the process from a "rational" perspective, using scientific principles and what are perceived to be objective data. The assumptions under the rational approach are that (a) the policy analyst is a technical expert providing needed information to the policymaker, (b) analysis is primarily a research function that examines the dimensions of a particular problem and explores the costs and benefits of various policy alternatives, (c) the costs and benefits associated with the policy can be used to assess the most cost-effective policy for achieving the desired outcome, and (d) policymakers take the information provided by the analyst and design appropriate policies.

The sources of data and information used in the rational approach to policy analysis are typically quantitative in nature, including such sources as census data, surveys, agency records, or interviews (Einbinder, 1995). Courses that use this approach to policy analysis to assist students in understanding social policies "have the merit of exposing students to social science and research literature, structured investigation, and methods of framing positions" (Jansson, 1994a, p. 67). But, as Jansson and others (see, e.g., Moroney, 1991; Stone, 1988) accurately point out, rationality and research do not adequately explain many resulting policy decisions.

The view that policy-making is a purely rational and scientific process has been challenged on many fronts—from the criticism that there are neither the resources nor capabilities to identify all the costs and benefits associated with a particular policy alternative, to the political interests that affect the final outcome of most policy choices, to the values that influence every step of the process from problem identification to the criteria used for evaluating alternatives. To address these shortcomings, many current policy analysis texts include aspects of the rational approach as well as an explicit examination of the value and (to a somewhat lesser extent) political bases of policy choice within their analysis models (DiNitto, 1991; Dobelstein, 1990; Jansson, 1994b; Moroney, 1991; Stone, 1988).

Inclusion of value criteria into policy analysis models is seen as "especially appropriate for a practice-oriented profession bound by its code of ethics" (Flynn, 1992, p. 35). This value-analytic approach as described by Moroney (1991) is "systematic inquiry into the nature of values . . . and policy analysis, at least in part, is an attempt to improve the quality of decision-making by tracing through the fact-value implications of alternative courses of action" (p. 30). That does not mean, however, that the analysis models presented either share a common set of values or incorporate values in the same way within the model. Analysis models have variously focused on the values the analyst brings to the activity (e.g., values central to social work that might guide an evaluation of a particular policy intervention); the societal values that need to be considered in formulating and evaluating policy alternatives (e.g., values such as individual freedom that need to be preserved); and recognizing the values of the decision-maker in preparing recommendations (e.g., values of those currently in political power that will influence the feasibility of particular policy outcomes). Whatever the primary emphasis, the value-analytic approach uses values—rather than just dollar costs and benefits—to establish the criteria for selecting among policy alternatives.

A third approach to social policy analysis is really less a model than it is a method. "The social policy context of social work practice is being transformed from strictly descriptive, historical and conceptual orientations that exclude practice realities to a prescriptive, problem-solving, action- and practice-oriented interventive method for social policy reform" (Iatridis, 1995, p. 1855). Policy practice, as this method has been labeled, provides knowledge and skills in developing and/or changing social policies. Some of these skills are the policy analysis skills used in the rational and value-analytic approaches, but in addition, the policy practice approach focuses on providing skills in advocacy and political action. The goal in policy practice is to prepare social work professionals to intervene in the policy arena in an effort to address social issues. Social workers, it is argued, have an obligation to engage in policy practice as part of their commitment to social and economic justice, making policy intervention as important to their practice as individual intervention (Figueira-McDonough, 1993).

The Place of Gender in Applying Policy Analysis Models

Recent poverty statistics indicate that 14.3 percent of all U.S. adult women are poor, compared to 9.3 percent of adult men, making them 54 percent more likely to be poor than men; black and Hispanic women have the highest poverty rates, with over 32 percent of black women and 27 percent of Hispanic women counted as poor in 1992; overall, women represent 57.4 percent of the poverty population (Kemp, 1995, p. 461). In addition to poverty, women, compared to men, are more likely to experience many other social problems. For example, women who head families are more likely than men to be unemployed, and females have a higher rate of school dropout than males (Committee on Ways and Means, 1994, pp. 1096,1142).

In spite of these data, many models of analysis do not explicitly include an examination of the gender (or class or race) assumptions that might constrain definitions of policy problems and establish the criteria for prioritizing solutions. For example, most analysts recognize that even the rational model is not value neutral, but there does not appear to be the same universal recognition that the model is also not gender-, race- or class-neutral. As is discussed in Chapter 10 on research, the way data are gathered and interpreted is influenced by the worldview of the researcher. The voices of women and other marginalized groups are often not heard in analyzing policy issues, and traditional models of analysis do not explicitly require the analyst to attend to diverse voices. Even if their voices are heard, for example, in surveys of the population, the questions asked and the interpretation of the answers are often based on the analyst's point of view, which is typically male, but certainly is not the view of those who are most often the targets of social welfare policy.

There is a growing recognition that an individual's reality is shaped by the context in which she/he experiences events and that context varies significantly by gender, socioeconomic status, and race. (For a discussion of this issue see Hartman, 1992; Riger, 1992; Tyson, 1992). In addition, statistics are not always gathered on concerns relevant to women, and the way they are gathered frequently keeps women invisible (e.g., excluding women from studies such as those on unemployment; not including the "home" work women do in labor force statistics). This is particularly troublesome because many studies that have examined an issue as it affects women have found that it is not valid to generalize findings from studies on men to conclusions about women (see, e.g., Donovan, Jaffe & Pirie, 1987). The way we use language also often obscures the gendered nature of many social issues. Phrases such as "spousal" abuse disguise the fact that women are the ones most often abused, and a critical area of study

> hides under the term one-parent families. The term suggests that single motherhood and single fatherhood can be lumped together. The studies cannot help showing that gender counts more than single parenthood. But the attempt to "legitimize" single mothers under the umbrella "families" also disguises the fact that most such "families" are female-headed, and that an overwhelming factor in their situation is lack of a male wage. (Pascall, 1986, pp. 3–4)

Analysis also needs to be attentive to differences among women and the diversity of their experiences. While gender provides one lens through which we can view social problems and policies, race and class are also important to our understanding.

Too often our understanding of a policy issue takes the identification and definition of social problems as a given (Scheurich, 1994), thereby constraining the policy solutions we generate. Yet identifying which social conditions we identify as social problems is influenced by gender, race, and class biases and assumptions. For example, we accept the identification of the dependency of women on public welfare as a social problem rather than seeing it "as a vital source of income for single mothers whose economic choices are constrained by the myriad of ways that racism and sexism structure economic life" (Amott, 1990, p. 280). Because most analysis models do not question the naming of the problem itself (Scheurich, 1994), our policy alternatives are most often focused on changing the behavior of women on welfare rather than changing the societal structures that are barriers to economic independence.

Feminists make a similar point when they argue that the personal is the political, and criticize policy interventions for focusing on the individual rather than the sociopolitical environment in which the social problem occurs. An example of this is provided by Davis and Hagen (1992) in their discussion of the problem of wife abuse. Wife abuse, they argue, is increasingly being defined as one problem among many that results from dysfunctional families, rather than as a social problem whose primary roots are in women's powerlessness and dependency. An emphasis on the former results in policies that are designed to change individual behavior, whereas an emphasis on the latter would result in strategies for changing the social context that supports men's violence toward women.

One of the criticisms of policy analysis has been that models are presented and evaluation of alternatives are conducted without needing to take a stand on which alternative is better or worse, and without questioning the value framework that is guiding the selection of alternatives (Chambers, 1993). Feminist models of analysis, on the other hand, explicitly take a value stance that starts from the premise that women are oppressed in our society. Whether from a liberal, socialist, or radical framework, feminist analysis seeks to expose the gendered nature of social welfare policies. For example, Naples's feminist evaluation of the Family Support Act of 1988 (Naples, 1991) revealed how such features of the Act as gender-neutral language (e.g., using the word "parent" rather than "mother"), stigmatization of particular family forms, and the maintenance of women in their caretaking roles do not adequately reflect the reality of women's lives and serve to reinforce women's subordination in society. Unlike much of more mainstream analysis, feminist analysis not only challenges the traditional norms and values of society, but the outcome of the analysis is a proposal that often includes strategies for implementing change. Feminists acknowledge that they are not neutral analysts, but rather advocates for policies that promote empowerment for women, and for the development of more just policies.

There is a growing recognition that social workers must be involved in analyzing and formulating social policy. "Because social policies are at the heart of the practice of human service professions, understanding what those policies are and developing the capacity to think about and suggest alternatives to them is a requirement for human services professionals" (Ginsberg, 1994, p.175). Social work's commitment to social justice makes it imperative that social workers not only develop skills to analyze policy, but that they learn skills to formulate and change policies. By virtue of their professional code all social workers should be involved in analysis activities that are "directly related to the implementation of the social justice goal" (Figueira-McDonough, 1993, p. 180). This begins with analyzing and formulating policy that adheres to principles of social justice. With this perspective, the policy-practice approach holds potential for challenging gender-neutral models of policy analysis by explicitly incorporating gender equity as a component of social justice. A social justice perspective requires that we are able to critically apply policy analysis models in ways that will expose and challenge the gender, race, and class assumptions and biases that are implicit in most American social welfare policies and programs.

A feminist perspective on policy practice also encompasses "not only the context and outcome of social policy, but also brings to bear a different perspective on the process of policy formulation and change" (Hooyman, 1994, p. 336). As part of the feminist critique of the traditional approaches to policy formulation and change has been the concern that most policymakers are men. Although over half the U.S. population is female, across all levels women hold less than 25 percent of the elected offices or executive positions in this country (Mandel, 1995, p. 415). Among women in elective office, the representation is greatest at the lower levels of government, with a greater percentage of women in state and local governments than at the national level. In

1996, 11 percent of the U.S. Congress was women, whereas, approximatley 21 percent of state legislators, mayors, and municipal council members were women (Center for the American Woman and Politics, 1996). While still very underrepresented, having greater numbers of women in state and local offices may bode well in an era of devolution of authority to lower levels of government.

It is argued that unless more women are involved in the process their views and perspectives will not be adequately represented in the decisions that are made.

> The fact that women do not seem to leave the "private" behind when they enter the "public" world suggests that they might show a greater sensitivity and concern than men traditionally have for issues such as child care, consumer protection, care of the elderly, and teen pregnancy. They also might be more likely than men to consider the possible implications for families and family life of policy proposals dealing with work. (Carroll, 1989, p. 64)

Studies have, in fact, indicated that women and men bring different considerations to the policy arena. In surveys of both national- and state-level officeholders, women were more likely than their male colleagues to address issues such as child care, health care, and welfare that are traditionally seen as women's concerns (Carroll, 1989; Mandel, 1995; Saint Germain, 1989). This suggests that integral to a policy-practice model that promotes social justice for women is the need to identify strategies for including more women in positions of policy-making authority.

There are, however, many other arenas for promoting social justice for women. Figueira-McDonough (1993) presents four methods of policy-practice that have the potential for affecting change: legislative advocacy, litigation, social action, and policy analysis. It is important that we understand how we can influence the process of policy formulation and change across legislative, judicial, and organizational decision-making bodies, as well as how we can mobilize for change through community organizing and grass-roots advocacy. We can be watchdogs for legislative issues that might potentially have an adverse effect on women; we can be instrumental in supporting litigation that will increase women's rights (such as in the case of *Roe* v. *Wade*, 1973); and we can participate in community and organizational advisory boards and councils to assure that supports and services to women are in place. We must also be knowledgeable about how to influence policy formulation and implementation at all policy-making levels—from agency boards through federal laws.

"Attempts to achieve change are blocked because of inherent cultural and situational biases that often go unnoticed by many of the individuals who shape policies. Given this analysis, the best hope of achieving real change lies in changing the biases that block progress" (Miller, 1990, p. 152). It is my belief that knowledge can begin to accomplish that change.

CURRICULAR REVISION

The previous discussion highlighted the implications of neglecting gender as a framework for analysis in understanding the historical foundations of social welfare policy, in examining policy alternatives, and in advocating for policy change. The challenge to social work educators, however, is in transforming the policy curriculum in ways that will be inclusive of content on women and other marginalized groups. Paralleling the previous sections, this section begins by addressing strategies for revision in course content that provide the historical context of policy development.

Integrating Gender into Historical Content

Paludi (1991) discusses three goals for teaching women's history:

1. Compensatory history, in which "lost" or "overlooked" women are found and placed back into historical accounts.
2. Contributory history, in which women's contributions to the field of study are noted and discussed.
3. Reconstructive history, in which the gendered past is recognized and history is reconstructed through the perspective of women.

To bring lost women back into social welfare history and to examine their contributions to social policy changes over time, the curriculum needs to include content about and by women in the development of the welfare state. This means not only highlighting the contributions of such famous women as Dorothea Dix and Jane Addams, but also women we rarely read about such as Mary McLeod

Bethune and Mary Church Terrell (Giddings, 1984; Peebles-Wilkins & Francis, 1990).

It also means that we need to attend to the role of women in general in influencing social policies. For example, historical accounts of women's activism in the development of Worker's Compensation and Mother's Aid legislation is an important story that often goes unnoticed. Readings that present information about women's contributions over time can be found in Freeman (1995), Giddings (1984), Gordon (1990), Koven and Michel (1993), and Peebles-Wilkins and Francis (1990). The primary sources listed in the readings in these books are also valuable resources for faculty and students to explore.

However, for students to gain a more complete understanding of the role of women in the development of the welfare state, the curriculum must go beyond just describing contributions by women and move to reconstructive history. Students need to be challenged to examine how the gender roles ascribed to women (and men) were constructed historically; how those may have varied by class and race; and how gender expectations and assumptions have influenced social welfare programs and policies over time. An understanding of the welfare state is not only limited by our exclusion of lost women, but more importantly, by the loss of any discussion of the place of gender and gender role expectations in its development. Integration of this concept into the curriculum requires that gender influences on social policy become a central theme—along with such concepts as the work ethic—in courses teaching this content. Readings that discuss the gendered nature of the development of the welfare state include Abramovitz (1988), Miller (1990), Mink (1990), Sapiro (1990), and Sklar (1993).

Traditional descriptive historical accounts can easily lead students to believe that history is an objective presentation of facts, rather than one explanation among many concerning events that occurred. Although the goal of this discussion is to present strategies for integrating women's perspectives into the policy curriculum, history that is reconstructed only through the perspective of women is merely a partial picture. Taking a critical approach to understanding social welfare history requires that we examine various historical accounts and then explore other ways in which the same event can be explained. Students need to be exposed to a range of views including feminist (e.g., Abramovitz, 1988) and radical (e.g., Ehrenreich, 1985; Piven & Cloward, 1982). Of particular importance in the social work curriculum is to examine social policy from the perspective of those affected by the policy or experiencing the social problem. There are many writings that have examined social welfare history from the perspective of women, but far fewer that have expressed the experiences of poor women, people of color, and other marginalized groups from their own perspectives. Requiring students to search out and read original source material that captures the voices of diverse women would help them to gain this perspective. Resources that present welfare participants' views of a current social welfare program include Hagen and Davis (1994) and Edin (in press).

Identifying strategies for integrating women's content into the policy curriculum is not to suggest that most instructors are not currently incorporating some of this material into their courses. However, a typical approach is a presentation of the more "mainstream" explanation of the historical development of the welfare state, and then discussing the status of women as a special issue, or presenting a feminist analysis as an alternative explanation. This tends to marginalize the issue of gender and give less authority to alternative views— particularly when the mainstream view is the one with which most students are familiar. One strategy for moving gender to the center of the policy curriculum and challenging mainstream views is to develop course content around what is typically seen as an alternative perspective. For example, a course on the history of social welfare policy might use a text such as Mimi Abramovitz's *Regulating the Lives of Women* (1988) or Phyllis Day's *A New History of Social Welfare* (1989) as the primary text and supplementing those chapters with readings from the more traditional analyses.

Integrating Gender into Analysis Models

Curriculum content that focuses on analyzing contemporary social policy issues and interventions also needs to incorporate analysis models that examine underlying gender biases and assumptions. A model using a gender lens would require the analyst to ask continually the following questions:

1. How is this policy issue being defined and by whom?
2. What are the stated and unstated assumptions about women and men in this policy?
3. What effects would this policy have on women and on men?

4. Does this policy take into account the diversity among women (Women who work outside the home and those that do not? Poor women and nonpoor women? White women and women of color? etc.).

5. What evidence/information is used to support the conclusions about these effects?

6. How credible are the sources of this information and what gender, race, and class biases might exist in those sources?

As in the discussion about the historical understanding of policies, it is also important for students to examine current policies from various perspectives. Being able to compare and contrast the underlying values and assumptions of several analysis models will give them a broader picture of why conflicts arise in the policy arena. In addition to the rational and value-analytic models of analysis most typically discussed, students should have an understanding of feminist models and feminist critiques of the more traditional models. Texts such as Miller (1990) and Stone (1988) provide a contrast to the mainstream view of policy analysis.

The application of a gender-sensitive policy analysis model can assist students in their understanding and evaluation of national and state social welfare policies, but it can also assist them as they examine agency policies and programs. As Flynn (1992) has pointed out, social workers are more often called upon to do small-scale agency policy analysis. As students learn skills in policy analysis, they need to be given opportunities to apply those skills across a variety of policies and policy settings. As one learning activity they could be required to do a gender-sensitive analysis of agency policies as part of their field practicum experience. This might include an analysis of policies that guide social service programs which the agency implements as well as policies under which the agency itself operates. Students most typically have to demonstrate an understanding of agency policies and procedures as part of their field learning, but that could be extended to require that they do a critical analysis of some of those policies, particularly as they relate to assumptions about women and other marginalized groups. An examination of policy issues also needs to be included in all practice courses, not just confined to the policy curriculum. Students should be continually challenged to step back from the individual-level interventions to examine the social and political context in which clients' problems arise. Another potential activity is presented by Finn in Chapter 6 on gender and families. She discusses a "welfare scrapbook" activity that helps students examine assumptions about gender and welfare in the popular media.

Integrating Skills in Policy Practice

Students need to go beyond understanding how gender influences social policy, to formulating and evaluating policy options that provide "the means whereby a significant portion of the society could become more economically secure and less dependent and vulnerable" (Sapiro, 1990, p. 51). Social work values of social and economic justice require that students learn skills for policy practice, not just policy analysis. Figueira-McDonough (1993) has outlined several methods for policy practice that should become part of the knowledge building in social work if we are committed to social justice. These include legislative advocacy, reform through litigation, and social action, along with policy analysis. The relationship of policy-practice skills to the integration of women's content in the curriculum is obvious. Unless we educate social work students to the policy change process they will not have the skills to advocate for policies that are fair and socially just for women and other disadvantaged groups. Figueira-McDonough provides numerous suggestions in her article for building knowledge and skill in policy-practice that can be incorporated into the social work curriculum.

Policy practice courses also need to educate students to the biases that policymakers bring to the policy-making process. Hooyman (1994) suggests that students interview women and men decision-makers to observe differences in perspectives that they may bring to the process. Students also need to examine their own perspective and how they may differ from the individuals for whom they are advocating. Advocating on behalf of others is not the same as understanding issues from their point of view.

CONCLUSION

In light of the latest attacks on AFDC and other social programs, understanding the gendered nature of social welfare policy is particularly critical as we educate our students about such concepts as social justice and empowerment. Students need to know that family caps and two-year time limits are not merely gender-neutral strategies for reducing welfare costs and caseloads. Integrating women's content into the policy curriculum will hopefully not only claim half the human experience, but provide knowledge for shaping policies which value that experience.

APPENDIX 9–1: POTENTIAL LEARNING ACTIVITIES FOR SOCIAL POLICY COURSES

Course Title: Introduction to Social Welfare Policy

Course Description: Presents a critical historical perspective on the development of U.S. social welfare policies within a social, political, and economic context. Introduces students to theoretical frameworks for understanding and critically analyzing social welfare policies. Emphasis on examining ideologies and assumptions on which policies are based, with particular attention to those related to gender, race, ethnicity, and class.

Texts

Abramovitz, M. (1988). Regulating the lives of women: Social welfare policy from colonial times to the present. Boston: South End Press.

Gordon, L. (1990). Women, the state and welfare. Madison: University of Wisconsin Press.

Piven, F. and Cloward, R. (1971). Regulating the poor. New York: Vintage.

Handler, J.F. & Hasenfeld, Y. (1991). The moral construction of poverty: Welfare reform in America. Newbury Park, CA: Sage.

Quadagno, J. (1994). The color of welfare: How racism undermined the war on poverty. New York: Oxford University Press.

Learning Activity: The Anywoman family[1]

Case Name: Anita Anywoman, age 20
Arlene Anywoman, age 53 (Anita's mother)
Minor children of Anita:
Billie, age 3

1. I want to thank Dr. Fred Seidl for originally "introducing" me to members of the Anyperson family and a variation of this assignment when I was an MSW student in his policy class.

April, age 6 months
Father of minor children:
Bill, Sr., age 30

Presenting Problem: Anita is a single mother with two young children and no means of support. She is not sure of the whereabouts of the children's father. He left several weeks ago to look for work, and she has not heard from him since.

Anita is very distraught. She and the baby seem to cry continuously.

Billie, age three, appears to be out of control. Anita says that he won't mind her. He hits and bites her, and she is concerned that he may harm April.

Arlene, Anita's mother, is partially paralyzed from a stroke, but otherwise is in apparent good health.

Family Background: Bill and Anita have lived together for over three years, but they have never been married. They moved with their children to Urbania when the marginal farming operation that supported the family in Bucolia, a rural community, failed to provide even subsistence. In the three months since coming to Urbania, they have been living "hand to mouth," mostly from handouts from relatives. When their welcome wore out and Bill was unable to find work, he left Urbania and his family. Anita doesn't know where he is, but stated that she is somewhat relieved that he is gone because he would often hit her and the children. She also stated that she has no money and no food.

The family came to the attention of authorities through a minister when Billie was found crying and hungry on the church steps.

Assignment: Choose three of the following years and discuss how the community might have responded to the plight of the Anywoman family. Compare/contrast the perspective of at least two different theoretical frameworks to explain the community's response during that period.

1800 1840 1920 1940 1960 1996

Within each theorectical perspective, address the following points in your response:

1. The social, political, and economic context of the time period and the assumptions about the poor that are likely to influence the community's potential response to the needs of the Anywoman family.
2. The assumptions about gender that are likely to influence the potential community response for this family, including the view of family responsibility during that period and the role of women and men within the family.
3. The assumptions about race/ethnicity that are likely to influence the potential community response for this family.

As a final component to your paper, using your two theoretical perspectives, discuss why the community response to this family changed over time. Include a discussion of the reform efforts of women and other groups.

Course Title: Policy Analysis and Practice

Course Description: This course builds on the historical foundation of the Introduction to Social Welfare Policy course. It presents various policy analysis models for evaluating current and proposed social policies. It examines contemporary policy issues and presents strategies for policy change through methods of policy-practice.

Readings

Chambers, D.E. (1993). Social policy and social programs: A method for the practical public policy analyst (2nd ed.). New York: Macmillan.

Figueira-McDonough, J. (1993). Policy practice: The neglected side of social work intervention. Social Work, 38(2), 179–188.

Flynn, J.P. (1992). Social agency policy: Analysis and presentation for community practice (2nd ed.). Chicago: Nelson-Hall.

Haskins, R. & Gallagher, J.J. (Eds.). (1985). Models for analysis of social policy: An introduction. Norwood, NJ: Ablex.

Jansson, B.S. (1994). Social policy: From theory to policy practice (2nd ed.). Pacific Grove, CA: Brooks/Cole.

Naples, N. (1991). A socialist feminist analysis of the Family Support Act of 1988. Affilia, 6(4), 23–38.

Prigmore, C.S. & Atherton, C.R. (1979). Social welfare policy: Analysis and formulation. Lexington, MA: D.C. Heath.

Stone, D. (1988). Policy paradox and political reason. Glenview, IL: Scott Forseman.

Learning Activity: The development of a gender- and ethnic/race-sensitive policy analysis model[2]

The purpose of this assignment is to facilitate a gender- and ethnic/race-sensitive understanding of a current policy issue of interest. The outcome will be a set of questions that will comprise a model that anyone could use in analyzing a policy for its sensitivity toward gender and race/ethnicity, and its promotion of social justice.

Assignment: Using some of the traditional policy analysis models as a starting point, develop a new model that will examine your selected social policy in relation to the promotion of gender, racial/ethnic, and economic justice. Once the set of questions that comprise the model has been developed, provide a rationale for why you would ask these questions and why answering them will promote social justice. You will want to draw from scholarly literature on gender/racial/ethnic and economic justice to ground your rationale.

REFERENCES

Abramovitz, M. (1988). *Regulating the lives of women: Social welfare policy from colonial times to the present.* Boston: South End Press.

Amott, T.L. (1990). Black women and AFDC: Making entitlement out of necessity. In L. Gordon (Ed.), *Women, the state and welfare* (pp. 280–298). Madison: University of Wisconsin Press.

Anderson, E.A. & Hula, R.C. (Eds.). (1991). *The reconstruction of family policy*. Westport, CT: Greenwood Press.

Axinn, J. & Levin, H. (1982). *Social welfare: A history of the American response to need* (2nd ed.). New York: Longman.

Bell, W. (1983). *Contemporary social welfare.* New York: Macmillan.

Boris, E. (1993). The power of motherhood: Black and White activist women redefine the "political." In S. Koven & S. Michel (Eds.), *Mothers of a new world* (pp. 213–245). London: Routledge.

Carroll, S.J. (1989). The personal is political: The intersection of private lives and public roles among women and men in elective and appointive office. *Women and Politics, 9*(2), 51–67.

---

2. This assignment was developed in collaboration with Ellen Netting.

Center for the American Woman and Politics. (1996). Women in elective office 1996: Fact Sheet. New Brunswick, NJ: National Information Bank on Women in Public Office, Eagleton Institute of Politics, Rutgers University.

Chambers, D.E. (1993). *Social policy and social programs: A method for the practical public policy analyst* (2nd ed.). New York: Macmillan.

Committee on Ways and Means. (1994). *1994 green book*. Washington, DC: U.S. Government Printing Office.

Council on Social Work Education. (1994). Curriculum policy statement for master's degree programs in social work education. In *Handbook of accreditation standards and procedures* (4th ed., pp. 134–144). Alexandria, VA: Council on Social Work Education.

Davis, L.V. & Hagen, J.L. (1992). The problem of wife abuse: The interrelationship of social policy and social work practice. *Social Work, 37*(1), 15- 20.

Day, P.J. (1989). *A new history of social welfare*. Englewood Cliffs, NJ: Prentice-Hall.

DiNitto, D.M. (1991). *Social welfare: Politics and public policy* (3rd ed.). Englewood Cliffs, NJ: Prentice-Hall.

Dobelstein, A.W. (1990). *Social welfare: Policy and analysis*. Chicago: Nelson-Hall.

Donovan, R., Jaffe, N. & Pirie, V.M. (1987). Unemployment among low-income women: An exploratory study. *Social Work, 32*, 301–305.

Edin, K.J. (in press). *Making ends meet: How single mothers survive welfare and low-wage work*. New York: Russell Sage Foundation.

Ehrenreich, J.H. (1985). *The altruistic imagination: A history of social work and social policy in the United States*. Ithaca, NY: Cornell University Press.

Einbinder, S.D. (1995). Policy analysis. In *Social work encyclopedia* (19th ed., Vol. 2, pp. 1849–1854). Washington, DC: NASW Press.

Figueira-McDonough, J. (1993). Policy practice: The neglected side of social work intervention. *Social Work, 38*(2), 179–188.

Flynn, J.P. (1992). *Social agency policy: Analysis and presentation for community practice* (2nd ed.). Chicago: Nelson-Hall.

Freeman, J. (Ed.). (1995). *Women: A feminist perspective* (5th ed.). Mountain View, CA: Mayfield.

Gerstel, N. & Gross, H.E. (1995). Gender and families in the United States: The reality of economic dependence. In J. Freeman (Ed.), *Women: A feminist perspective* (5th ed., pp. 92–127). Mountain View, CA: Mayfield.

Giddings, P. (1984). Black braintruster: Mary McLeod Bethune and the Roosevelt administration. In P. Giddings, *When and where I enter: The impact of Black women on race and sex in America* (pp. 217–231). Toronto: Bantam Books.

Gilbert, N., Specht, H. & Terrell, P. (1993). *Dimensions of social welfare policy* (3rd ed.). Englewood Cliffs, NJ: Prentice-Hall.

Ginsberg, L. (1994). *Understanding social problems, policies, and programs.* Columbia: University of South Carolina Press.

Gordon, L. (Ed.). (1990). *Women, the state, and welfare.* Madison: University of Wisconsin Press.

Hagen, J.L. & Davis, LV. (October 1994). *Implementing jobs: The participants' perspective.* Albany, NY: Nelson A. Rockefeller Institute of Government.

Handler, J.F. & Hasenfeld, Y. (1991). *The moral construction of poverty: Welfare reform in America.* Newbury Park, CA: Sage.

Hartman, A. (1992). In search of subjugated knowledge. *Social Work, 37*, 483–484.

Hobson, B. (1993). Feminist strategies and gendered discourses in welfare states: Married women's right to work in the United States and Sweden. In S. Koven & S. Michel (Eds.), *Mothers of a new world* (pp. 396–429). London: Routledge.

Hooyman, N.R. (1994). Diversity and populations at risk: Women. In F.G. Reamer (Ed.), *The foundations of social work knowledge* (pp. 309–345). New York: Columbia University Press.

Iatridis, D. (1994). *Social policy: Institutional context of social development and human services.* Pacific Grove, CA: Brooks/Cole.

Iatridis, D. (1995). Policy practice. In *Social work encyclopedia* (19th ed., Vol. 2, pp. 1855–1856). Washington, DC: NASW Press.

Jansson, B.S. (1988). *The reluctant welfare state: A history of American social welfare policies.* Belmont, CA: Wadsworth.

Jansson, B.S. (1994a). Social welfare policy. In F.G. Reamer (Ed.), *The foundations of social work knowledge* (pp. 51–87). New York: Columbia University Press.

Jansson, B.S. (1994b). *Social policy: From theory to policy practice* (2nd ed.) Pacific Grove, CA: Brooks/Cole.

Kemp, A.A. (1995). Poverty and welfare for women. In J. Freeman (Ed.), *Women: A feminist perspective* (5th ed., pp. 1–21). Mountain View, CA: Mayfield.

Koven, S. & Michel S. (1993). *Mothers of a new world*. New York: Routledge.

Mandel, R. (1995). A generation of change for women in politics. In J. Freeman (Ed.), *Women: A feminist perspective* (5th ed., pp. 405–429). Mountain View, CA: Mayfield.

McInnis-Dittrich, K. (1994). *Integrating social welfare policy and social work practice*. Belmont, CA: Wadsworth.

Meenaghan, T.M. & Kilty, K.M. (1994). *Policy analysis and research technology: Political and ethical considerations*. Chicago: Lyceum.

Mencher, S. (1967). *Poor law to poverty program*. Pittsburgh: University of Pittsburgh Press.

Michel, S. (1993). The limits of maternalism: Policies toward American wage-earning mothers during the Progressive Era. In S. Koven & S. Michel (Eds.), *Mothers of a new world* (pp. 277–320). London: Routledge.

Miller, D.C. (1990). *Women and social welfare: A feminist analysis*. New York: Praeger.

Mink, G. (1990). The lady and the tramp: Gender, race, and the origins of the American welfare state. In L. Gordon (Ed.), *Women, the state and welfare* (pp. 92–122). Madison: University of Wisconsin Press.

Moroney, R. (1991). *Social policy and social work: Critical essays on the welfare state*. New York: Aldine de Gruyter.

Naples, N. (1991). A socialist feminist analysis of the Family Support Act of 1988. *Affilia, 6*(4), 23–38.

Paludi, M.A. (1991). Placing women psychologists in the psychology of women course. *Teaching Psychology, 18*(3), 172–174.

Pascall, G. (1986). *Social policy: A feminist analysis*. London: Tavistock.

Peebles-Wilkins, W. & Francis, E.A. (1990). Two outstanding Black women in social welfare history. *Affilia, 4*(1), 33–44.

Piven, F.F. & Cloward, R. (1982). *The new class war: Reagan's attack on the welfare state and its consequences*. New York: Pantheon.

Riger, S. (1992). Epistemological debates, feminist voices: Science, social values, and the study of women. *American Psychologist, 47*, 730–740.

Saint-Germain, M.A. (1989). Does their difference make a difference? The impact of women on public policy in the Arizona legislature. *Social Science Quarterly, 70*, 956–968.

Sapiro, V. (1990). The gender basis of American social policy. In L. Gordon (Ed.), *Women, the state and welfare* (pp. 36–54). Madison: University of Wisconsin Press.

Scheurich, J.J. (1994). Policy archaeology: A new policy studies methodology. *Journal of Education Policy, 9*(4), 297–316.

Sheffield, C.J. (1995). Sexual terrorism. In J. Freeman (Ed.), *Women: A feminist perspective* (5th ed., pp. 1–21). Mountain View, CA: Mayfield.

Sklar, K.K. (1993). The historical foundations of women's power in the creation of the American welfare state, 1830–1930. In S. Koven & S. Michel (Eds.), *Mothers of a new world* (pp. 43–93). London: Routledge.

Smith, S.R. & Stone, D. (1988). The unexpected consequences of privatization. In M. Brown (Ed.), *Retrenchment and social policy in America and Europe* (pp. 232–251). Philadelphia: Temple University Press.

Stone, D. (1988). *Policy paradox and political reason*. Glenview, IL: Scott Forseman.

Thornborrow, N.M. & Sheldon, M.B. (1995). Women in the labor force. In J. Freeman (Ed.), *Women: A feminist perspective* (5th ed., pp. 1–21). Mountain View, CA: Mayfield.

Trattner, W. (1994). *From poor law to welfare state: A history of social welfare in America* (5th ed.). New York: Free Press.

Tyson, K. (1992). A new approach to relevant scientific research for practitioners: The heuristic paradigm. *Social Work, 37*, 541–553.

Wilensky, H.L. & Lebeaux, C.N. (1965). *Industrial society and social welfare*. New York: Free Press.

CHAPTER 10

The Role of Gender in Practice Knowledge: Research

Paula S. Nurius
Cynthia Franklin

INTRODUCTION

When we prepared to write this chapter on issues of gender in research, we found ourselves bumping up against a whole strata of issues related to research in general that complicate our efforts. As each chapter in this book attempts to illustrate, concern for the role of gender in the expansion of practice knowledge involves more than an "add-women-and-stir" concept. With respect to research, we will identify areas of content that reflect an underrepresentation of women as researchers as well as a neglect of topics of concern to women. Equally important, however, is the difference that a gender-sensitive and gender-inclusive perspective brings to bear in how we think, what we pursue, toward what, guided by what, and why. In the next section, we will identify some critiques of traditional research methods from a gender analysis perspective. The thrust of our chapter, however, will be in considering alternatives currently under discussion, as well as issues related to evaluating alternatives and their applicability and utility for social work education.

Many who have taught research have encountered some of these impediments associated with the "R word": feelings of unease and resentment; attitudes about research as irrelevant, rigid, boring, and detached. One of our goals in writing this chapter is to change that image. We aim to reframe what "research" means, its relationship to practice, the contributions that students and practitioners can and do make on an ongoing basis, the issues that need critical analysis and creative problem-solving, and ways through which research in varied forms will increasingly become a part of one's professional reality as current and future trends continue to unfold.

If students do not see research as having much to do with their sense of mission, their consciousness and development of expertise, or what they need in order to be ethical and effective practitioners, then it is unlikely that they will see the hard work of undertaking an analysis of the role of gender in research as a worthwhile endeavor. And this would be a real loss. Many people find it far easier to see how gender analysis with respect to human behavior theory, psychopathology formulations, policy, and practice with individuals, families, groups, organizations, and communities yields important insights. Part of our goal is to illustrate ways of assisting our students and colleagues to understand how science, scholarship, and the politics of knowledge development are permeated by gender bias, neglect, and oppression.

WHAT'S WRONG WITH THE WAY THINGS ARE?

The role of gender in the expansion of knowledge for social work practice is complex. First, to examine if gender has been included in the development of practice knowledge, we must identify a knowledge base that undergirds social work practice, as well as the research methods used to generate this knowledge base. Second, we must develop a critical stance for evaluating gender input into practice theories. For example, how will we know if gender considerations were included in our practice knowledge and the methods of knowledge building through research? We first discuss some general critical stances that have been developed by feminist researchers for thinking about whether gender is included in practice knowledge, and criticisms of the research methods used to construct social science theory.

Limitations in Traditional Research

Criticisms concerning traditional research have been constructed over a number of years. Many of the challenges to traditional epistemology and research methods within the social sciences and helping professions emerged from each field's biases and distortions in the study of women (Fonow & Cook, 1991). These criticisms are germane to this book's focus on knowledge expansion in practice theory research because many of the concerns involve lack of gender representation and many apply to the practice theories and methods used in social work.

Jayarante and Stewart (1991) summarize specific feminist criticisms of social science research. It is important to keep in mind that there is variation in what is included in feminist and gender-sensitive analysis of traditional research. The following issues are not meant to be wholly inclusive, but rather to provide illustrations of some central issues. Within the work cited below, readers can pursue related writing to more fully capture this variation (Gottlieb & Bombyk [1987] offer an earlier perspective in social work; Worell & Etaugh [1994] offer a model for feminist research that reflects an interdisciplinary approach).

The first of these criticisms addresses sexism and elitism in the selection of research topics (Frieze, Parsons, Johnson, Ruble & Zellman, 1978; Grady, 1981; Jayarante & Kaczala, 1983; Scheuneman, 1986) and the absence of research on questions of central importance to women (see Parlee, 1975; Roberts, 1981). A common complaint about university researchers, for example, is that the research has little to do with the real-world problems of women but rather focuses on issues of importance to a select group of individuals who are supported by the societal norms. Saulnier (in press), for example, points out that social work researchers have neglected to address women who are employed in the sex industry in their research, social policies, or advocacy work. Relative neglect of concerns specific to women in mainstream fields of practice have also been noted, such as issues related to new reproductive technologies (Moss, 1988), self-concept among elderly women (Heidrich, 1994), and effects of gender-related variables in education, particularly science education (Hanson, 1996). Emergence of the women's movement has promoted some increase in attention to women's issues among researchers, but, even among social work journals, this increase has not yet been sufficient, particularly related to minority women, older women, and lesbians (Quam & Austin, 1985).

A second concern centers on the use of research designs and sampling methods that are markedly biased to include male subjects (Grady, 1981; Lykes & Stewart, 1986). Major theoretical models such as Kohlberg's theory of moral development was based on male subjects (Gilligan, 1982) and presumed to generalize to all people. This approach to theory development and testing treats one group's (males, and generally young, white, middle-class given other design and sampling biases) perspectives and experiences to be a universal standard. Rather than operating on the basis of presumption, this generalization should be systematically tested, as evidenced by findings of gender differences across the life span (see Riger, 1992, for examples, and Frieze, Sales & Smith, 1991 for findings regarding differences in the central life events experienced by men and women at different life stages and how these affect achievement-related choices and behaviors). This kind of sampling bias can often be unintended and at least partially a function of convenience samples such as the military, higher education, and some workplace settings that have a greater proportion of male participants. It can stem also from indirect sources such as research on topics that are likely to be of greater interest or relevance to males and lack of attention to factors that can inhibit women's participation—such as the need for transportation and child care to make participation in the research realistic. We would add to this criticism the relative lack of males in certain lines of research, such as investigations of children, nurturing, and family functioning and the need for inclusion of both mothers and fathers to obtain more complete understandings (see Phares, 1996).

A third criticism focuses on the exploitative nature of relationships between the researcher and subject (Jayarante, 1983; Mies, 1983; Oakley, 1981; Reinharz, 1979; Stanley & Wise, 1983) and within research teams (Birke & Silvertown, 1984; Harding, 1987) that often characterizes traditional research. This is by no means always the case, but too often is implicit or minimized. In addition, feminist research teams may not be exempt from these types of human political problems. For example, A. Walker (1994) describes behind-the-scenes political struggles within an egalitarian research team in which she participated. Feminist researchers wish to do research *for* women instead of just *on* women, striving to have a positive effect on women's lives and issues that is consistent with the sociopolitical nature of feminism. There are, however, complicated ethical nuances, such as whether there is any way to really know if a research study will be harmful or helpful to the people involved (Saulnier, in press). Can we really guarantee that our research will empower women? What constitutes our own accountability (e.g., in subjecting to public scrutiny the specific methods of data collection, analysis, and interpretation that we used to enable evaluation and replication)? Feminist researchers themselves do not agree on these points. For example, some feminist researchers would claim that their research represents the viewpoints of women whom they are studying. Other researchers would object to this position, saying that they represent the women's viewpoints as channeled through the elitist views of the researchers (Saulnier, in press).

The illusion of objectivity, especially associated with the positivist approach, is a fourth area of critique (Bleier, 1984; Jayarante, 1983; Jayarante & Stewart, 1991; Lykes & Stewart, 1986; Stanley & Wise, 1983; Wallston, 1981). This is a multifaceted issue, which includes, for example, underlying beliefs that there is an objective truth, a view of the researcher as being an uninvested observer, assumptions that use of certain methods or tools will prevent the research experience from influencing the phenomenon or participants, and so forth. Consider the potentially distorting or misleading effects that inattention to social context in research can produce. The laboratory experimental paradigm, for example, implicitly assumes that subjects leave their social status, history, beliefs, and values at the door or that random assignment cancels out effects of such factors (Riger, 1992). Tools such as controlled designs or statistical control techniques are indeed extremely valuable in dealing with enormous complexities and increasing confidence in the validity of findings. Consider their value when comparing the relative effectiveness of three forms of family therapy, for example, or in distilling focus on a specific aspect of a phenomenon to better understand its functioning. The worrisome question, though, is what it means to divorce people's actions from their social roles and institutions, and to tacitly assume that research outcomes reflect choices made by free and self-determining individuals with little to no consideration of sociocultural realities related to power, control, values, and perceived consequences (Riger, 1992). Consequently, context and the analysis of history and power relations plays a significant role in feminist research (see Deaux & Major, 1987; Eagly, 1987; Sherif, 1987, for examples).

The objectivity of science and other issues concerning a value-free science have been discussed for many years within the philosophy of science. Social work researchers have also been involved in debating these issues for more than fifteen years (see Atherton, 1993, for a review of these debates). Traditionally, science was assumed to be capable of obtaining a value-free stance, to rise above or control subjectivities such as feelings, values, and biases. The goals of researchers were to be as objective as possible, making valid quantitative measurements of variables and maintaining a dispassionate distance from what was being researched, so as not to contaminate what was being discovered. Assumptions and assertions of neutrality and objectivity have nearly come to be equated with logical positivism. We will discuss later ways in which critique has at times overly simplified and caricaturized differences and ways in which efforts to pursue alternative methodologies introduce weaknesses of their own.

The potential for negative influence of objectivity is certainly not limited to men. Allen (1994) discusses, for example, ways in which women researchers can become lulled into allowing their belief in objectivity to keep them from gaining relevant information about women. She illustrates her points through her own experience as a researcher who failed to ask pertinent questions about the sexualities of single women in her study.

Fifth, the limitations of relying on any one method of obtaining information have been indicated (Jayarante, 1983). This criticism maintains, for example, that discussing the dilemma of women's (or anyone's) lives solely within a framework of statistics or statistical models is sometimes hollow and narrow if not complemented with other methods, such as qualitative processes, that have different types of strengths and foster more open-ended thinking and reflection. The main interpretation of statistics usually comes from the researchers themselves and thus can all too easily exclude the voices of women and other research participants (see Allan's, 1994, example of disagreement by subjects with concepts of "success" and "failure" used to classify outcomes in a weight-management study). Postmodernist feminist researchers, for instance, insist that in order to capture the position of women in research, research participants should be provided opportunities to engage in self-reflection and that this self-reflection should be given the same weight as mainstream methods of statistics-based knowledge (Lather, 1991, cited in Saulnier, in press). This is not to say that any one method is inherently more or less "correct" in study of women—although there are differences of perspective on this point. Rather, reliance on highly restrictive methods for obtaining information can inadvertently lead to circularity; such as gathering information only through currently available standardized measures that may be inherently gender-biased and limited in both the theoretical and sampling base from which they were derived. By the same token, rigid adherence to only one set of qualitative tools will inherently limit the scope and generalizability of what one finds. We will explore options and issues related to a multimethods approach later in the chapter.

Sixth, concerns about improper interpretation and overgeneralization of findings have been raised (Jayarante & Kaczala, 1983; Lykes & Stewart, 1986; Westkott, 1979). An example of this is the application to females of theory tested exclusively on male subjects (comparable concerns related to race have been raised given the high reliance on European-American research subjects) as well as use of person-blame explanations. One area that illustrates risks of distorted understanding of women involves using standards of males and patriarchy in studying family socioeconomic status. The socioeconomic status of women and children has been based on the income of the male head of the household. Of course, there are many female-headed households and joint-income households where women contribute equally or perhaps even more to the family income. Family researchers, however, have continued to use this outdated method of gathering information about the socioeconomic status of women and then to interpret findings and implications based on the flawed picture that this method presents (Smith & Graham, 1995).

A seventh criticism has to do with inadequate data dissemination and utilization (Jayarante, 1983; Tangri & Strausburg, 1979). In general, research does not reach the masses, remaining instead in academic and, to a lesser extent, professional circles. Many feminist researchers advocate for using more public vehicles for dissemination so that research may influence grass-roots constituencies and social policies toward women as well as simply be accessible to individuals who could directly benefit from the information if it were more easily available and consumable (Saulnier, in press). Information technologies offer new possibilities for supporting broader dissemination (although these technologies also introduce new challenges to locating information that fits one's needs given the tidal wave of unfiltered content through which one must navigate). The future will require more than ever thoughtful efforts to pursue, report, and disseminate research findings in ways that subject them to public as well as professional scrutiny and thereby widen the net of utilization.

Amidst the current conversations and debates, we do not see that feminism or concern about gender representation is associated with a single point of view or single methodology. Moreover, rather than a single definition of feminism today, there are "feminisms" that incorporate some distinct yet overlapping theoretical, philosophical, methodological, political, and pragmatic tenets (Henderson, 1994). Freeman (1990) outlines differences between feminists and nonfeminists and differences among feminist perspectives as well as implications she sees for social work education and research. Difficulties in reconciling differences among social work researchers who value and see themselves applying a feminist perspective reflect underlying complexities and concerns (e.g., Davis, 1990, 1994; Ivanoff, Robinson & Blythe, 1987; Marsh, 1994).

The plurality of thought regarding what values are feminist makes it difficult to formulate an alternative research method based on feminist values. However, a number of factors have become fairly widely embraced (see Ferree, 1990; Reinhartz, 1992; Riger, 1992; Worell, 1996). These include the need for more interactive, contextualized methods of research that are consciously applied in service of emancipatory goals. It includes the need for new knowledge about aspects of women's lives that have remained relatively unaddressed or deemed as lower-level importance in the world of science. Illustrations of this point are projects that study life experiences unique to women (e.g., pregnancy, breastfeeding, menopause) and experiences tied to women's position in the sex/gender system (e.g., violence against women by partners, sexual harassment, sexual discrimination; see Grossman et al. (1997) for a related discussion of core purposes). This is a view of research as a mechanism of change; for example, moving beyond study *of* women but also *for* women, whereby the choices at each stage of research and the manner of its conduct is geared toward changing the world as well as describing it. Emphasizing that there are no consensual standards of feminist research, the following tenets are advocated by Gergen (1988; as cited in Riger, 1992; see also Reinhartz, 1992; Wilkinson, 1986; Worell & Etaugh, 1994):

1. Recognizing the interdependence of experimenter and subject.
2. Avoiding the decontextualizing of the subject or experimenter from their social and historical surroundings.
3. Recognizing and revealing the nature of one's values within the research context.
4. Accepting that facts do not exist independently of their producers' linguistic codes.
5. Demystifying the role of the scientists and establishing an egalitarian relationship between science makers and science consumers.

These tenets concerning research are consistent with social constructionism and postmodern belief systems that are discussed in more detail in the following sections.

Feminism and Postmodernism in Research

Many feminist researchers are postpositivists (Small, 1995) and advocate for a "socially constructed" or postmodernist view of science that acknowledges the sociopolitical nature of science and seeks to dethrone science as a kingpin in providing knowledge about everyday life. These views are believed to be consistent with the sociopolitical mission of feminism as a social change philosophy (Osmond & Thorne, 1993). Postmodernists, in particular, see science as socially constructing knowledge within and for an elitist (powerful) class of people who ignore or oppress all other people (often called voices). The term "subjugated knowledges" is used to express the idea that many common people are not involved in constructing knowledge or setting up cognitive schemes for how to understand the world. In addition, the ideas of people (the lost voices) are often not taken seriously because they are not "scientific" (Gorman, 1993; Marshall, 1992).

Even though feminists often embrace or are sympathetic to social constructionist and postmodernist views, authors have pointed out that there are inherent tensions among philosophical views (Allen & Baber, 1992; Burman, 1990). Coverage of the philosophical tensions are beyond the scope of this chapter and thus will not be reviewed here (however, Chapter 1 of this book offers a useful overview). Due to the considerable blurring of feminist and postmodernist writing, it is important to keep in mind that no particular epistemology or approach to research is necessarily feminist (DeVault, 1996; Small, 1995) and there can be wide variations in which any method is applied. Moreover, criticism that feminist researchers have brought toward science does not mean that feminists as a group believe that science should be abandoned, that all "traditional methods" are bankrupt of utility, or that women should stop conducting or consuming research. Critical stances are meant instead to bring attention to the limitations in the way that current research is being conducted, especially in areas involving, or should we say, dis-involving women. Advocates for gender analysis and inclusion strive primarily to open up a way for new and improved methods for conducting research that is more gender-sensitive and possibly also more effective for research on women's issues. Pugliesi (1992) provides an interesting example of ways in which differing streams of feminist thought that have remained relatively independent have been seen by some as contradictory—one stream examines features of women's lives that enhance or undermine well-being and another involves a more critical analysis of methodology and conceptions of mental health and illness (both offer important ingredients of a general feminist perspective that would profit from greater interarticulation and synthesis).

Increasingly, many feminist researchers have come to the conclusion that research methods are not categorically bad or good in themselves, but that any type of research method could be misused in studying women (Reinhartz, 1992). Many feminist researchers who advocated for the exclusive use of qualitative methods now see the limitations of believing that a research method can protect us from the perils of unethical and unrepresentative research (Small, 1995). Allen and Baber (1992), for example, raise a number of ethical questions. Is feminist postmodernism "postfeminist"? Are qualitative methods more feminist than quantitative ones? Whose aims are served, feminists or their collaborators? To think that any method can do so is to commit the same type of thinking errors of the logical positivists. For example, Freud relied on qualitative methods such as case studies with women participants to formulate his theory. Yet, it is widely accepted that he came to many harmful and erroneous conclusions concerning women, including denying their experiences of sexual abuse. Freud's qualitative method did not protect him from taking an authoritarian and patriarchal stance in his work. Qualitative research is not exempt from all the abuses often associated with quantitative research (Peplau & Conrad, 1989; see Ashford, 1994, for a discussion of similar points with respect to research about and with people of color).

In the same light, quantitative research can be used to empower and help women and to stop oppression just as well as qualitative research. For example, Hyde (1994) demonstrated how meta-analysis, a quantitative technique for synthesizing outcome studies in literature reviews, may be used to confront commonly held myths about women that have been passed down from the interpretations of individual studies and their narrative (qualitative) reviews. She believes that the methodology of meta-analysis is transformative in that a researcher is able to use this methodology to reconstruct knowledge about women. Meta-analysis is used to show that the common beliefs, such as gender differences between mathematics performance and spatial ability, do not hold much validity, for example. In addition, it is used to discover new differences in sexual attitudes that have implications for the sexual functioning of women.

In the same manner, quantitative and qualitative research may be used together to study women's issues and to empower women. For example, Rank (1992) combined these methods to help him better understand the childbearing patterns of women who were welfare recipients. On the one hand he was able to draw from a large data base on households of welfare recipients, and on the other hand he undertook in-depth interviews with women and fieldwork of welfare systems. In the quantitative portion of his study, Rank found that the fertility rate of women on welfare was lower than women in the general population. These findings debunked common stereotypes of women on welfare. Based on the results of the quantitative analysis, Rank used the in-depth interviews to explore why women on welfare were not having very many children. What he found in the qualitative portion of his study complemented his quantitative findings. Most women on welfare indeed did not want to have more children for a variety of personal and economic reasons.

The Challenge of Maintaining Balance and Accountability

In saying that social work researchers are moving to a position of not seeing one research epistemology or set of research methods as being inherently superior over others (e.g., see the recent debate by Grinnell, et al., 1994, and Tyson, 1994), we are not suggesting that social work researchers as a whole are coming to agree that all research methods should be accepted as equal. A common belief in the social sciences has been that there is a hierarchy of research methods and within this scheme qualitative research is on the bottom and quantitative research is on the top (Hoshmand & Martin, 1995a, 1995b; Sells, Smith & Sprenkle, 1995). Others, however, see qualitative research as being intrinsically most relevant to social work practice and would like to see social workers do less quantitative research and more qualitative research (Davis, 1994; Reissman, 1994). For an interesting overview, see the recent special issue of the journal *Social Work Research* (1995, volume 19) on qualitative research methods for discussions of these issues and the place of qualitative research in social work (e.g., Allen-Meares, 1995; Fraser, 1995; Gambrill, 1995; Mullen, 1995; Wakefield, 1995; as well as Tyson's 1995 advocacy for a heuristic paradigm).

Feminist theorists and researchers have worked to assure that gender is included in the theories and methods produced by social science researchers (e.g., Belensky, Clinchy & Goldberger, 1986;

Bernard, 1973, Gilligan, 1982; Miller, 1976; Peplau & Conrad, 1989; Sherif, 1987; Unger, 1979). These efforts have made important gains regarding the goals of gender equality, recognition of the historical oppression of women and their exclusion from a prominent place in public life, and advocacy for women to be included in research as important topics of study. Many of the critiques of traditional research methods have prompted constructive questions and consideration of alternatives. As with many arenas of challenge and change, there have also been excesses and limitations in the critique itself.

Sometimes in the midst of advocating for women and proposing neglected gender differences, some research took on the tone of suggesting that women were not only uniquely different than men but possibly better. Recent critiques refer to this as being "essentialist" and point out that one of the limitations is that essentialist research stereotypes women and implies that women cannot have characteristics different than those proposed by the research. Essentialist theories about gender differences deny the diversity that exists within groups of women, and the situational contexts that produce individual circumstances (Bohan, 1993). As limitations and gaps are receiving increased attention (e.g., such as insufficient replication or attention to race and class issues), so too are ways in which to update and retain currency of feminist research given new substantive and technological arenas (Levy & Fivush, 1993; Reid & Comas-Diaz, 1990; Riger, 1992; Tittle, 1986; Williams & Heikes, 1993).

Extremes of traditional logical positivist stances for research are not the wholesale model of correctness that they once were held to be, nor are they rigidly pursued by most philosophers of science, and have not been for some years. Researchers working from experimental and positivist views of science have increasingly adopted new stances such as critical realism, hypothetical realism, fallibilistic realism, and transcendental realism (Anastas & MacDonald, 1994; Franklin, 1995; Guba, 1990; Mahoney, 1991). In part these efforts reflect a postpositivist effort to move away from prior claims of objectivism to a science that recognizes perspectival approaches, the influence of values, and the inherent biases attendant in interpretation of any set of observations. While many recognize that one can never really obtain full knowledge of "the truth" and that all scientific inquiries are theory-driven and influenced by concepts and the views of the researcher, this does not argue for sweeping abandonment of traditional methods nor embracement of absolute relativism (see Gambrill, in press, for a discussion related to practice relevance). Many simply acknowledge that there are limitations with any one epistemology and set of methods and bring a less dogmatic and more open and flexible approach to scientific inquiry. These approaches take into account the inherent nature of bias in cognitive processes and the value-laden nature of theory generation in the research process. In addition, nontraditional perspectives such as the heuristic paradigm forcefully advocate the research process as being consistent with the naturalistic role of practitioners, who are mostly women.

In short, the world of research has not remained frozen. Rather than strictly divided groups, many contemporary researchers recognize the inescapable nature and relevance of bias, the necessity for critical thinking in all research endeavors, and the utility of various research tools to match the nature of the research question. This includes increasingly prevalent blended approaches that strive to combine the strengths of multiple research methods (e.g., Dennis, Fetterman & Sechrest, 1994), although there are also a number of concerns about blurring of epistemology and methodology (see Smith & Heshusius, 1986).

Thus, some of the criticisms aimed toward positivist researchers by feminists have an outdated view of research epistemologies and may no longer apply in the same manner as they have in the past (Franklin, 1995; Greenwood, 1991; Taylor, 1991). Although considerable progress is still needed, a critical thinking and pragmatic stance is now emphasized and is the essence of research that we see as essential to the future of social work and allied arenas (Hoshmand & Martin, 1995a). Critical thinking is also the hallmark of intellectual inquiry and, we believe, important in assuring that gender is included in practice knowledge. For example, a critical thinker will see the flaws in not considering context in research and will not accept faulty assumptions such as making assertions about women without including them in samples of their data. Marsh (1994) illustrates a pragmatic stance in noting that "restricting feminist research to one set of tools or another necessarily limits the type of questions that can be asked and answered" (p. 71). "Despite evidence of progress, there is no question that there is significant work to be done to transform the 'patriarchial construction of reality.' And I say let us get to work—with all the energy and tools at our disposal" (p. 69).

Internal examination of potential weaknesses or caveats of research methods that have been advocated as alternative to traditional methods is growing. For example, many issues arise in the research process, such as how to resolve disagreements about interpretations of findings between researchers and participants, or how to manage feelings of betrayal or abandonment that participants may experience when the researcher terminates the relationship (Allen & Baber, 1992; Riger, 1992). In addition, there is the ongoing issue of who benefits from the research, the participants or the researcher? Concerns have been voiced, for instance, about whether ideological adherence to certain methods may be deepening rather than diminishing a researcher-centered approach to knowledge building (Hoshmand & Martin, 1995b). Perhaps, despite the intent to the contrary, some interpretive researchers may be appropriating women's voices and experiences; filtering these through themselves as the instrument for interpretation and thereby implicitly claiming their unique subjectivity as the most appropriate vehicle for inquiry and knowledge building.

TEACHING METHODOLOGICAL DIVERSITY IN RESEARCH

Given the emphasis on methodological diversity of research methods it seems to us to be important for social work educators to focus attention on teaching practice students a variety of research methods and teaching them how to critically analyze and examine these methods in relationship to their historical perspectives within the social sciences and their usefulness for social work research. Methodological diversity and a multimethods approach equips the researcher (whether in the agency or the academy) to address a range of different types of questions, under different types of conditions—a flexible set of competencies that are important to broadening rather than telescoping gender sensitivity and inclusiveness in research. Below, we offer several suggestions for the types of information that should be covered in a classroom setting.

One of the premises of this book is that critical thinking and analysis are important prerequisites to growth and change. However, critiquing the current state of affairs, whether it be in the realm of policy, practice, or research, is a first step, not an end point. Thus, if we find deficiencies, what are the remedies to pursue? Our approach with respect to teaching research is one of methodological diversity—examining the potential appropriateness and utility of a range of research methods and tools and making reasoned selections. That is, to understand the events and experiences in both women's and men's lives and to use our knowledge to provide the best possible services, it is necessary to rely on all existing methods of inquiry. This approach to research highlights the purpose of the enterprise and reflects concern that narrowing what to study and how to study it commensurably narrows the questions we are able to ask and the tools we are able to apply (Marsh, 1994; see Stanley & Wise, 1983, and Collins, 1986, for contrasting views).

This may sound sensible and straightforward, but it is neither an easy nor a particularly straightforward approach to maintain in teaching or in conducting research. It is about as complex as being able to develop a responsible approach to eclecticism in practice, and students may benefit from a discussion of how different approaches to eclecticism in practice (e.g., theoretical eclecticism, technical eclecticism, meta-theoretical eclecticism) may be used to think about how to solve the dilemmas encountered in a methodologically diverse approach to research. For example, if students are to take a meta-theoretical approach to eclecticism in research in the same manner as in practice, this would involve them choosing methods of research that are philosophically compatible in their underlying assumptions and beliefs (e.g., radical feminism and action research). If they are to take a theoretical approach, this would involve them selecting out common elements across different approaches to research (i.e., the interview); and if they are to take a technical (pragmatic) approach, this involves them using criteria to select out the best approach for a given research situation. Below, we will illustrate the more pragmatic approach further.

Choosing methodological diversity in research entails a professional obligation to be sufficiently informed about the options to be able to make sound judgments whether as a teacher, consumer, or producer of research, and a stance on how and why differing methods from different schools of thought concerning research may be used together. The "rule book" becomes not only considerably larger in terms of the available research repertoire, but choices must now take a number of contextual variables into account. For example, what is the purpose of the research? What is the state of the current relevant knowledge base and how does this inform subsequent query? What individuals or systems will be involved and how do their needs or attributes need to be taken into consideration? What are the available resources, expertise, risks, and safeguards? In what ways have women and other marginalized groups been or not been included in the prior research and knowledge-building foundation?

If this sounds familiar, it is because there are parallels between judgments one makes in practice and those one makes in research. Drawing these parallels as mentioned above in relationship to eclecticism is likely to prove a useful teaching method for social work practice students. Assessment (such as the questions posed above) is vital to both in order to select methods and plans that are appropriate and likely to yield fruitful outcomes. All the while meaning that the making and awareness of one's own meta-cognitions or how one makes sense of the research problems becomes a self-reflective exercise that no clinician or researcher may disregard if we are to defend a justifiable use of various methods.

Underlying an approach of methodological diversity is a recognition that all methods have both strengths and limitations and that these differences form a complementarity—for example, between quantitative methods and qualitative methods, generally (although not necessarily) associated with hypothetic-deductive and interpretive paradigms, perspectives—that collectively offer more than any one set of tools is capable of when it stands alone. In cross-cultural research, one often sees distinctions framed in terms of etic (objective, behavioral) and emic (subjective, phenomenological) approaches (e.g., Landrine, Klonoff & Brown, 1992). Leading students through case studies of research situations may enhance the understanding of this process. Sells et al. (1995), for example, provide a detailed example of how a research team combined quantitative and qualitative research methods in their studies on the process of reflecting teams as used in family therapy. These researchers provide a bidirectional and multimethod research model that shows the linear nature of time but at the same time recognizes the reciprocal and bidirectional impact of quantitative and qualitative methods on one another. Sells et al. chronicle how they made decisions back and forth between quantitative and qualitative approaches to research in a series of studies that built on one another and took place across time. This type of example is excellent for illustrating to students the rationale for using various methods and how both quantitative and qualitative methods may be logically combined to study practice.

TEACHING MULTIPLE RESEARCH STRATEGIES

Student learning may be enhanced by the use of diverse research examples that parallel social work practice, problems, and settings. It is important, for example for students to realize that quantification helps provide a broad-based picture of patterns and trends. Having representative evidence that 20 to 25 percent of college women experience sexual aggression and that the vast majority of all women experience sexual aggression at some point in their lives (Kilpatrick et al., 1985; Koss, Gidycz & Wisniewski, 1987) is powerful information that helps influence policy and mobilize response. If we have questions about prediction and control, such as whether one policy or service intervention is more effective than another or whether significant differences in outcome are evident for males and females or other subgroup comparisons, quantitative methods are likely to be most informative and accessible.

From a pragmatic point of view, think about the information that is needed to answer a host of agency questions and the utility of quantitative methods in addressing them. Are we serving the populations and needs that we seek to reach? Are we using our resources as optimally as possible? How fully are desired goals and outcomes being attained? To what extent do our services appear to be effective—to be the causes of positive outcomes? In a similar vein, consider the utility of measurement tools in the context of managed care. Accepting that all measurement strategies are limited and fallible, an extremely important skill for future practitioners involves the ability to locate, employ, and interpret valid, reliable, and sensitive measurement tools whether they be about attitudes, feelings, perceptions, beliefs, relationships, environment, or behavior.

In general, qualitative tools are particularly useful for providing detailed, rich descriptions of phenomena, for exploring questions or populations for which there is little prior inquiry, and for determining new insights and understandings with minimal influence of preconceptions or preexisting prevailing frameworks. Tools labeled "qualitative" vary greatly in their origins and their character and have been grouped in different ways; for example, Marsh (1994) illustrates different roots of ethnography (from anthropological traditions), phenomenology (from philosophy), ethnomethodology (from sociology), and hermeneutics (from theology, philosophy, and literary study), whereas contributors in Sherman and Reid (1994) differentiate among ethnographic methods, heuristic methods, grounded theory methods, narrative methods, discourse analysis, and qualitative approaches to evaluation.

It quickly becomes apparent that "qualitative research" is not a single method but rather a complex and variegated set, much like the range from randomized experimentation, quasi-experimentation, single case analysis, survey interview and questionnaire methods, and cost-benefit analyses within quantitative methods. Students will benefit from this broad-based appreciation for the complexity of the qualitative approaches to research. Building upon the work of Patton (1990), and Murphy and O'Leary (1994), we provide the following general list of characteristics of qualitative methods, with contrasting characteristics of quantitative approaches in parentheses:

1. Naturalism. Fieldwork on real-life situations without manipulating variables (vs. experimentation and artificial laboratory conditions).

2. Inductive reasoning. Deriving categories, dimensions, or associations from detailed descriptive information (vs. deductive hypothesis testing).

3. Holism. A focus on systematic interdependencies and emergent system properties (vs. elementalism, the reduction of complexity to a small number of specific variables).

4. Qualitative data. In-depth description of people's experience and perspective (vs. quantification of specific variables).

5. Personal contact. Attempts to form close human bonds with research participants to increase understanding (vs. objective detachment).

6. Unique case orientation. The thorough analysis of each unique case before aggregating data (vs. nomothetic orientation toward group norms).

7. Context sensitivity. An emphasis on specific local effects of history, culture, and society (vs. a search for general or universal truths).

8. Design flexibility. The use of research strategies that emerge and change during the course of a study (vs. a priori study design specifications).

9. Data collection and data analysis. Each often reciprocally affects the other (vs. separation of the activities to promote standardization within each).

10. Strategic selection of participants to pursue specific questions (vs. efforts to representatively sample a population).

Such a set of characteristics may be used to help students draw beginning distinctions between qualitative and quantitative approaches to research. Once students have a sense of the distinctions between qualitative and quantitative research and can understand the importance of including differing methods, they are ready to learn how to combine these methods in research and how to pursue more gender-sensitive inquiry.

Learning to Combine Quantitative and Qualitative Methods

As previously noted, there are increasing trends toward various forms of bridging qualitative and quantitative approaches. We have seen in our own research programs and those of colleagues that a common integration is to undertake a sequence of methods that build one upon the other. Practice students may benefit from learning how this process has been used before within social science research (Sells, Smith & Sprenkle, 1995). This often starts with employing exploratory, interactive methods (such as unstructured or semistructured interviewing, naturalistic observation) at early stages, followed by development of measures and hypotheses reflective of this input, followed by interactive pilot testing and small-scale studies to ascertain the validity and utility of the methods, measures, and theories, followed by larger-scale and more controlled survey or experimental designs to test hypothesized relationships across diverse individuals or to assess the impact of an event or intervention (see Follingstad, Rutledge, Berg, Hause & Polek, 1990; Murphy & O'Leary, 1994; Norris, Nurius & Dimeff, 1996; Yllo & Bograd, 1988, for examples in research related to violence against women).

Of course some researchers use qualitative research in the opposite manner, moving from the deductive to the more inductive to provide understanding of patterns they are observing in larger quantitative data sets. The example cited above about Rank's (1992) research on childbearing patterns of welfare recipients illustrates this point in that he used the in-depth interviews as a means to more fully understand the patterns he was observing in his quantitative analysis. In a like manner in the Sells et al. (1995) program of research (also mentioned above), researchers confirmed observations from a qualitative study using content analysis and returned to further qualitative interviewing to better understand the meaning of their confirmed observations. Rather than being handled as strictly separate, elements of both qualitative and quantitative approaches can provide a balancing of the strengths and limitations of each. Students may benefit from several illustrations of this point.

Another means of applying methodological diversity involves matching method to question. Sometimes methodological choices are fairly straightforward, but there are times when assistance in sorting out the relative pros and cons of various possibilities is useful. In examining the relative fit of methods to questions in the arena of sexual violence, White and Farmer (1992) suggest use of pragmatic, organizing frameworks such as the circumplex typology of research strategies (Runkel & McGrath, 1972). Using this type of framework in teaching may assist students as a heuristic for thinking about choosing methods in research studies. White and Farmer's framework clarifies the circumstances under which more controlled or more naturalistic approaches would likely yield the kind of information needed, given the primary concerns of the researcher. This model essentially charts the controlability of research operations, how context-dependent or -independent the nature of the phenomena is, and how important it is to observe analog or spontaneous real world behavior and then locates research strategies within this grid.

If the question, for example, is to examine the effects of sexually violent stimuli on aggression toward women and attributions of responsibility, some form of experimental simulation or analog may be the best means (e.g., Donnerstein, 1980; Linz, 1989). If the question is centered more around understanding how men and women convey nonverbal signals regarding interpersonal interest, a field study such as that by McCormick (1988), coding male-female interactions in bars, may be most useful. In some cases, questions motivating the research have to do with establishing the prevalence and/or incidence of an experience and the factors that appear associated with that phenomenon. Here, survey approaches are often useful, such as Koss et al.'s (1987) nationwide survey of college students' experience with unwanted sexual contact and Muehlenhard and Linton's (1987) convenience sample survey that helped to establish an understanding of situational and attitudinal factors that appeared most highly associated with risk. This circumplex typology is but one of a variety of tools to sort out methodological options. (See Sells, Smith & Sprenkle, 1995 for another example that is useful in teaching.) The point is that students will likely benefit most from concrete steps and examples of how to carry out research using multiple perspectives and methods. Guiding students through the steps of the research process with an eye to gender integration may further aid their learning.

HELPING STUDENTS LEARN THE RESEARCH PROCESS

Students must first do their homework in clarifying the research question(s), the state of the relevant knowledge base, and the context within which inquiry will be undertaken; then research methods selections can be made with these factors in mind. Thus, they will be employing research methods in the service of the need rather than the other way around. The following sections provide directions to guide students in the learning process of preparing themselves to do research on their topic as well as becoming more astute evaluators and consumers of research. We suggest that the metaphor of the dialogue or conversation be used as a way to communicate to students the socially based, interactive, conceptual, and problem-solving features of research. We see this applying to research in general as well as to the goals of this book to foster a more gender-integrative perspective as part of one's professional development.

Dialogue

Establish a conversation with researchers and the grass-roots constituencies or local context (consumers, participants, funders, etc.) involved in the research for the purpose of defining the questions to be answered. After this research is complete, what do they want to know? This process is very much like practice in defining a goal-oriented or solution-focused set of questions that will guide the outcomes of the research. Consistent with an egalitarian view, students may wish to take the role of learner during dialogues with the local context, thus playing down their role as an expert. We also believe that this is consistent with the role of women in conversations and provides a isomorphism for learning from the female voice. A good question to ask is: Has anyone else asked the questions or similar questions that these folks are asking? If so, how did they approach the research? If not, what is the closest question that someone has asked and what research methods did they use? This requires a dialogue with other researchers in the field of study. One way students form a conversation with other researchers is to read their studies and perhaps to communicate with them directly by phone or e-mail for clarification purposes.

Questions are usually defined in relationship to constituent groups in which the research benefits. What do they want to know that will benefit them? How do the grass-roots constituencies (i.e., battered women, agencies serving battered women, funding agencies, etc.) define the important questions to be answered in relationship to how researchers define the questions? How does this questioning process relate to the current researcher's agenda to provide services or research information?

Method Options

Following assessment of underlying research questions and needs that motivate the research comes examination of research methods. What are the available method options? What factors have been or could be used to make selections among methodological alternatives? Careful and thorough reading of the studies published on a given topic is an essential step in this assessment. Systematic approaches to charting methodological patterns can be helpful toward getting an overarching picture, such as outlining research methods used and rationales developed for why these methods were used. Similarly, listing strengths and weaknesses of existing studies and clarity of rationales for their methodological choices can be useful in illuminating the trade-offs with any given method as well as gaining an aggregate view of the knowledge base on the topic at hand.

Field Context

The location of students in the field (e.g., in practica, employment) offers an opportunity for students to engage in active dialogue as well. An example of this would be students spending time with local practitioners or grass-roots constituencies to discuss the methods and findings that have emerged from research (and in this manner establishing a three-way dialogue among the researchers, the local context, and student). What do local practitioners (micro, meso, or macro) think of the approaches and advice of the researchers? Including the advice of the researchers as options, students may brainstorm alternatives for what might work to answer the current research questions. New ideas for methods may also emerge that are better suited for the local context.

Selecting Preferences for Methods

The outcome of such interactions would profitably be a set of research methods that students could consider for use in future study. This might entail generating more than one option for a set of methods and rank-ordering them in preference (providing rationales for the rank order). The rank-ordering and preferences should include the input from people in the field. Thus, to make the research go well it is important always to work on the relationship aspects of the research. We also believe that this provides a further isomorphism for the way that most women prefer to interact. Part of the point here is to move beyond critique to application or a working relationship that moves the research project forward. It is easy for researchers' to become overly critical of the local context and their ideas for carrying out the research, and of other researchers' projects as far as that goes. Yllo (1994) points out that researchers often discount the voices of people in the field in their research. In family violence research, for example, activists and shelter workers are often discounted because they are not "experts." As pointed out by Yllo it is wrong to discount these individuals as experts because they spend "everyday working with abused women and helping them negotiate the bureaucracies of welfare, and criminal justice and this is hardly a non expert role" (p. 224).

It is easy, however, for a type of elitism to creep into the researchers' approach. We believe that such an elitist and overcritical method should be avoided because it shuts down the dialogue, especially with the local context. Consistent with the notions of gender representativeness it is important that as many voices as possible be heard. After all, it is one thing to point out the flaws and limitations in others' work and another to tackle the complexities oneself, grappling with inherent compromises and constraints.

Using a "Dialogic" Approach

Assuming that students are undertaking the conduct of research as part of their learning process, an additional challenge is to "continue the conversations" across the life of the study. What are ways of building in feedback loops (e.g., continue looking for new literature that is relevant and keep talking to the local context to assess the pros and cons of the methods as they are being implemented)? Being open to change and modifying or expanding one's research approach as new information emerges is often more difficult than it sounds. What are the challenges and opportunities students see in their own work?

Franklin et al. (1993) illustrate this type of dialogic approach to research. These authors used an egalitarian, combined bottom-up and top-down approach to design an outcome-based assessment system in a youth agency. Franklin et al. outline twelve process steps that were used to help researchers follow this type of approach and to select the research methods in the study reported. This case study and the steps outlined may be used as a teaching example to help students understand the dialogic approach to carrying out the research process in an agency setting. Students may also be given assignments to carry out a small study that includes these components.

What should become clear to students through this process is that there is no "one size fits all" or single correct methodological choice and that the process of research varies depending on context and need. Sources such as Katzer et al.'s (1991) review of ways in which various methods for acquiring knowledge are subject to different forms of error can also be helpful in getting this point across. When time and resources allow, a third means of applying methodological diversity is to use several methods to study the same problem or question. This allows one to cross-check observations and to obtain a more complete picture than would be otherwise attainable from any single method. In developing a grant proposal, for example, Nurius and Norris (1994) specified a combination of focus group methods, survey interviews of retrospective experiences, and prospective methods in the form of experimental simulations to achieve collectively a well-rounded picture of the intrapersonal, interpersonal, and environmental variables associated with women's perception of risk of sexual aggression and coping responses. As a class exercise, students may be divided into research teams that will use their expertise to carry out a miniature study triangulating different methods as a cross check. Or this approach may be built into the small research study as suggested above. Once students gain competencies in understanding different research methods and gain some experience on how the research process works, they will more readily be able to evaluate and critique different knowledge-generation methods.

TEACHING STUDENTS TO EVALUATE

Knowledge-Generation Methods

What are the limitations of methods for knowledge generation in social work practice? And are all approaches to knowledge generation truly a research process? After all, many new epistemologies and research methods are being proposed today, and the common understandings concerning science are being deconstructed (Franklin, 1995). How do we teach students to decide which methods are appropriate modes of inquiry for science? Are all knowledge-generation methods science? When is an approach of gathering information really a research method verses another type of method such as clinical process, a philosophical inquiry, a spiritual journey, or journalism, for example? Should we accept all methods as research if they help us find out pertinent information about the lives of women and other research participants? Where do we draw the line in our acceptance of various methods?

As the spectrum of available research tools and methods expands, how do we evaluate the scientific credibility of differing methods when they stem from diverse ontological and methodological understandings of the research process? Some social welfare scholars might argue in favor of the inclusion of all epistemologies and research methods because inclusiveness and acceptance are consistent with feminist, postmodernist, and social work values. But, if we endorse a blanket affirmative answer to the question of inclusion, we quickly see that we create as many problems as we attempt to resolve. For example, does every type of inquiry that comes along qualify as research just because it is so labeled? What do we use to distinguish high-quality work and products from those of substantially lower quality? What do we use to determine which tools and methods are most appropriate or most likely to yield optimally useful findings in differing types of circumstances or with differing types of information needs? How can we best link the information needs of the field and profession (e.g., regarding effective policies, direct services, administrative practices, and so forth) with the discourse about research methods and approaches?

In order to move beyond these types of questions and to facilitate critical thinking and effective teaching, we offer six criteria to be considered in evaluating the scientific basis of knowledge-generation methods. These criteria are not intended to be exhaustive, but rather are intended to provide a tangible starting point (e.g., for developing an assignment or a course outline that helps address some of the above-noted questions). We believe that these criteria follow the spirit of research methodologists such as Guba (1990), who proposes criteria for categorizing different types of research and tracing the development of the different approaches within social science disciplines.

1. The method should be consistent with the history and purposes of science, which generates new knowledge and human technologies.
2. The method should show a clear connection with previous modes of inquiry that have been used in the social sciences (e.g., phenomenology, hermeneutics, experimental methods, etc.). In this regard it should also demonstrate that it follows standards proposed for credible research within those research paradigms.
3. The method should demonstrate the presence of critical thinking in its process, including the recognition of its own meta-theoretical assumptions, values, and limitations. Researchers should communicate a sense of self-reflexivity.
4. Research methods should be inclusive and representative of context including gender and other characteristics of the participants in which we are seeking to develop knowledge. Multiple viewpoints (within group differences) and individual explanations should also be evident within gender and other classifications.
5. Researchers should demonstrate that their methods are the best available alternatives for their study.
6. Research methods and knowledge generated from research should be conducted and communicated in such a way as to submit to a critical review and analysis. Subsequently, researchers should learn from this critique and incorporate their learnings into their research and practice knowledge.

While we see these six criteria as a method for critically analyzing different methods, we realize that some teachers may not agree with the criteria or may feel more comfortable having students in their classes develop their own scheme for decision-making. Outlining an assignment where students develop their own criteria for decision-making may prove to be a useful teaching exercise. Whatever scheme for analyzing appropriate research methods is used, however, we believe that the profession should strive toward and be prepared to distinguish between higher and lower quality work that reflects sufficient rigor, meticulousness, and specificity to permit others to evaluate the merits of the research process and product and to attempt replication. This goal would require, for example, that social workers work toward developing clear criteria and exemplars for what comprises good quality qualitative and quantitative research. Such criteria should include attention to gender as well as other historically marginalized groups. These criteria may assure greater inclusion of different types of studies in social work journals, as well as serving as a mechanism for maintaining the standards of science in our practice knowledge generation.

Teaching students to critically analyze research from multiple perspectives may serve as a method for enhancing their competencies for including multiple perspectives in research programs. We also believe that the social work preference for both inclusion and effectiveness in practice may be modeled through this process. Once students master content in this area they are ready to think critically about the broader mission of social work and how that research may be used in our work to enhance the social functioning of people, including but not limited to gender sensitivity.

TEACHING RESEARCH THROUGH A SOCIAL WORK LENS

Students may benefit from analyzing the mission of research through the lens of social justice. In addition to understanding research methods, their history, meta-theoretical assumptions, and current context in social science, teachers may challenge students to analyze specific themes that may be used in the analysis of gender inclusion in research. Worrell and Etaugh (1994), for example, identify six guiding themes that have appeared in the feminist research literature in psychology:

1. Challenging the tenets of traditional science, such as a value-free science and producing a more inclusive science.

2. Focus on the experience and lives of women, such as focusing on women separately and studying within group differences in women.

3. Viewing power relations as the basis of the patriarchal political arrangements, such as questioning power relations and stereotypes toward women and shifting attributions of blame from victims to perpetrator.
4. Recognize gender as an essential category of analysis, including the multiple interpretations of gender and the socially constructed nature of gender.
5. Attention to the use of language and power to name social issues such as sexual harassment, woman battering, date rape, etc.
6. Promoting social activism toward the goal of societal change, such as reductions in power asymmetries and gender justice, and creating a science that will benefit rather than oppress women. (pp. 447–448)

We believe that these themes are based on the values of equity, diversity, and self-determination that are consistent with social work practice knowledge. Teaching themes from feminist research literature may serve as heuristics for evaluating social work research, and students may be challenged to see the connections between these points and the mission of the social work profession. For example, an assignment might be to take the above gender themes and decide how they connect with the mission of the social work profession. See the teaching exercises at the end of the chapter for further suggestions for how to engage students in analyzing gender relations and research. Beyond the critical analysis of feminist psychology, however, we believe that students can gain a broader perspective and learn to be even more inclusive of both genders if we teach them to critique the assumptions in the above points and expand them further. An assignment could be to think about the underlying assumptions of the themes found in feminist psychology literature and how these assumptions can be used to guide research. Teachers may proceed to guide students in a broader analysis concerning the underlying themes of social justice in the feminist psychology literature and further explore what impact this type of analysis has on the roles of social work researchers.

Points to Be Made in Discussing Feminist Research and Social Justice Issues

First, feminist research points out the need to critique science, which assumes that science has a tendency to become myopic, one-sided, and resistant to multiple viewpoints. Bias is a well-researched human attribute (see Brower & Nurius, 1993; Gambrill, 1990; Nurius & Gibson, 1990). In this way science becomes biased and elitist, and is not inclusive of a range of diverse perspectives (e.g., neglecting the viewpoints of women, people of color, different classes, subcultures, and other marginalized groups). The question of how to be completely inclusive and representative is quite a challenge in that social work researchers are not omnipotent. They may not have the power to represent life flawlessly in all its complexities. One research study, for example, cannot represent a full spectrum of analysis. We need to teach students to think in terms of programs of research where multiple researchers conduct research that builds on the work of one another. Perhaps one of the best policies a social work researcher can follow is honest humility. Be honest about the many limitations of the knowledge one is developing, and do not represent it for more than it can actually represent. For example, if your measurement instrument was tested only on predominantly male freshman college students do not try to generalize your findings. It is better for the knowledge to stand as it is with all its limitations. From this perspective, we are going to suggest a paradox in that one of the ways that we may apply better critical thinking in research is to become more accepting of the limited capacities of researchers and the knowledge produced.

Second, feminist research focuses on the lives of women, which assumes that women should be full participants in the research process. It also assumes that because of the unequal power distribution, women have been kept out of the research enterprise. Scarborough and Furumoto (1987) and Slack et al. (1996) provide examples of ways in which women researchers have historically been constrained in their contributions and how their contributions have been obscured. Women must be included in all facets of research from participants to investigators. But we must also recognize that any person or group of people may be kept out and that their voices may be silenced. Women are not alone in social oppression. As researchers and practitioners, we must continue to ask ourselves, who are the people that need to be participating in this research? Is my practice knowledge inclusive of the groups with whom I am practicing? Local knowledges become imperative in that there are many subtle regional, communal, and cultural differences that keep knowledge from being transferable from one practice setting to another. Thus, in the research on the development of standardized measurement instruments it is often recommended that we develop local norms (Jordan & Franklin, 1995). Of course, practically, we cannot develop a new knowledge base every time we encounter a new group of clients. But we can maintain a critical stance that is constantly questioning our practice knowledge for different groups. In addition, we can continually inquire from our clients concerning the utility of our approaches, and be open to developing new approaches that are more suitable to our clients.

Third, feminist research emphasizes keeping power relations in mind as the basis of patriarchal political social arrangements assumes that a power structure is in place that is unfavorable to women and favorable to men. Social workers focus on a mission to empower disadvantaged groups. The so-called "haves" and "have nots," however, are an old human story and go beyond gender constructions. Power is a relative and dynamic process, and students should be taught that the relative power of individuals and groups should be considered in one's global assumptions. For example, a professional woman with a medical degree may have more relative power than a man who is a high school dropout. So, broader critical social analysis is needed in our research programs if we are to keep power relations fully in mind.

Fourth, gender as an essential category of analysis assumes that gender is an important social construction that has an impact on other areas of inquiry. Gender differences as social construction have an impact on practice knowledge and must be considered in analysis. For this reason social workers must consider both the gender of women and men, as well as the limits of this categorization and its political uses on practice knowledge.

Fifth, feminist research uses the power of research programs to name hidden phenomena such as social oppression against women and assumes that these inequities will remain hidden unless uncovered and forcefully brought to the attention of the public. This is a humanistic goal for researchers to serve as ambassadors and mediators in human oppression. It also takes advantage of the researcher's relative status as an "expert" whose knowledge is afforded credibility in society. The existence of social oppression and issues become "real issues" as the researcher confirms their presence. As social work researchers, we must broaden our understanding of human oppression, and as we do, we will be evaluating our research based not only on gender justice but also on social justice in all its many forms. We believe also that this idea is consistent with social work practice as well as feminist research.

Finally the feminist goal toward social activism and societal change assumes that it is the responsibility of the researcher to use her/his research to improve social conditions and the lives of women, and other groups. In evaluating social work research, it is important to ask, does our research have potential truly to make a difference in the lives of those involved—both women and men. A cautionary point is needed here. Students often do not have the training or experience to fully understand the range and progression of research. Students may need to be assisted to see how basic research, for example, can form the backbone of subsequent preventive or remedial interventions that will be field tested or to see ways in which systems research or policy analysis can be importantly related to advancing effective and appropriate services. Social work students' commitment to advocacy can incline them to believe that any research that is not explicitly political or rabble-rousing in nature is irrelevant. Indeed, some research is pretty irrelevant. Moreover, as Gelles (1994) illustrates, differences between the purposes and needs of research and advocacy should not be trivialized nor should difficulties in their simultaneous pursuit be underestimated. But the answers to today's complex social welfare questions regarding women and all people require a wide range of interdisciplinary research endeavors.

CONCLUSION

This chapter focuses on gender and the many ways in which it is related to the knowledge base and knowledge-building processes of social work. Clearly, women and gender-related issues are by no means the only areas of neglect. In this regard, much of what we have discussed goes beyond focus on women as a group or gender as a socialized status per se, and is part of an approach that reinforces

1. a constructively critical perspective;
2. the capacity to problem-solve and engage in alternatives (e.g., regarding gender inclusiveness and correcting prior neglect and disenfranchisement);

3. the necessity of developing competencies in the inclusion of, and critical analysis of, multiple perspectives and diverse research methods;
4. a willingness to engage in dialogue with others as a means of designing and evaluating studies;
5. a commitment not just to gender justice but to the broader issues of social justice in our research endeavors; and
6. a pragmatic ability to do whatever is necessary to complete the job in today's service and knowledge-building contexts.

There are many reasons for pursuing research. In this chapter, however, we focus on the use of research-generated knowledge in practice. As professional helpers working with vulnerable populations, we have an obligation to draw upon the best knowledge available as part of our practice and professional conduct. We each have a continual obligation to update, diversify, and push the boundaries of knowledge and its use in practice. Research must serve to strengthen practice (we use this term to span the different levels and forms, including policy practice): to strengthen, for example, our understanding of needs and problems, our formulation of interventive responses, our capacity to determine the utility and appropriateness of our efforts, our openness to change in the face of evidence and relevant new questions, and our commitment to lifelong learning as our knowledge base continually undergoes expansion and change. Exactly how we go about this expansion of alternatives and what we use as referents is, of course, powerfully influenced by gender analysis.

Today's practice context emphasizes more than ever practitioners' ability not only to understand issues and be consumers of research, but to apply and oversee the conduct and application of research-related activities in practice. Consider, for example, the presence of factors such as managed care, outcome measurement requirements, and varied forms of public scrutiny, accountability, and cost containment. Further, consider the increasing presence and roles of computer/information technology in the human services (Nurius, 1995; Nurius & Hudson, 1993). For example, the impact (both positive and negative) on what information is seen as important, how it is collected, and how it gets interpreted and applied as these affect service providers and the clients with whom they work. Consider our growing appreciation of the need to understand more fully and include diversity (e.g., gender, race, culture, class, age, sexual orientation, ableness) in our knowledge development and in our practice. This is certainly not an exhaustive list of contextual factors that are shaping today's practice. Our point is to illustrate that the rapidly changing and complex nature of practice settings increasingly closes the gap between research and practice, between the roles of researcher and practitioner.

As we look to practice and research in the years to come, we find that there is no one-size-fits-all answer, no neat package for how to best grapple with our information needs and challenges. More than black and white, right and wrong, with-us or against-us divisions, there is instead a lot of gray area and complexity. To be constructive contributors over the long haul, we must have the capacity not only to tolerate this uncertainty and ambiguity, but to persevere with a creative and tolerant spirit toward better and better solutions. We could present you with a self-contained model of "correct" gender-sensitive research tenets, topics, methodologies, forms of data and analysis, and so forth, but we see this as not only unrealistic but inconsistent with a gender-sensitive perspective. We are encouraging contextualized inquiry—an approach to bridging research and practice that takes the context of the prevailing human needs, goals, strengths, and limitations into account. Rather than "an" alternative method or a "this is it" set of answers, we have highlighted issues and questions to bolster students' critical reasoning as well as a range of research methods and tools for consideration in moving beyond critique to creative application.

A commitment to changing our societal assumptions, our educational institutions, and our service systems to be more reflective of diversity (our focus here is on gender, but, obviously, the issues generalize to other marginalized groups) requires a commitment to both challenge and cooperation. We believe that an analysis of gender as well as many other contextual variables will continue to guide research in social work and allied disciplines pointing to the need for us to change the way we teach research to include the critical, pragmatic perspective that we have suggested in this chapter.

APPENDIX 10–1: TEACHING EXERCISES FOR EXPANDING THE KNOWLEDGE OF GENDER IN PRACTICE RESEARCH

Exercise #1: General Discussion Questions: Gendered Alternatives for Research

1. Are there certain methods of conducting research that are seen as higher quality or more correct? On what beliefs and assumptions are such judgments based?
2. Can social science be objective and is there an objective reality? What do we draw upon as evidence or argument in defending our answers to these questions?
3. Why is there such a marked underrepresentation of women in theory development and subjects in research? Why do women play such limited roles as researchers?
4. Why are topics predominantly of concern to women so often underrepresented in the literature and in research funding priorities? What do we need to understand about the agenda-setting context of research to find answers to questions such as these?
5. Do the research methods that we employ affect what we ask? How do we ask it? What is experienced or provided by the research participant? How do we interpret and present results? What do we assume about the validity or generalization of findings?

Further Reading

Allen, K.R. (1994). Feminist reflections on lifelong single women. In D.L. Sollie & L.A. Leslie (Eds.), *Gender, families and close relationships: Feminist journeys* (pp. 97–119). Newbury Park, CA: Sage.

Bleier, R. (1984). *Science and gender: A critique of biology and its theories on women.* Elmsford, NY: Pergamon.

Fonow, M.M. & Cook, J.A. (1991). Back to the future: A look at the second wave of feminist epistemology and methodology. In M.M. Fonow & J.A. Cook (Eds.), *Beyond methodology: Feminist scholarship as lived research* (pp. 1–15). Bloomington: University of Indiana Press.

Frieze, I.H., Sales, E. & Smith, C. (1991). Considering the social context in gender research: The impact of college students' life stage. *Psychology of Women Quarterly, 15*, 371–392.

Jayarante, T.E. (1983). The value of quantitative methodology for feminist research. In G. Bowles & R.P. Klein (Eds.), *Theories of women's studies* (pp. 140–161). Boston: Routledge & Kegan Paul.

Jayarante, T.E., & Kaczala, C.M. (1983). Social responsibility in sex difference research. *Journal of Educational Equity and Leadership, 3*, 305–316.

Jayarante, T.E. & Stewart, A.J. (1991). Quantitative and qualitative methods in the social sciences: Current feminist issues and practical strategies. In M. M. Fonow & J.A. Cook (Eds.), *Beyond methodology: Feminist scholarship as lived research* (pp. 85–106). Bloomington: University of Indiana Press.

Lykes, M.B. & Stewart, A.J. (1986). Evaluating the feminist challenge to research in personality and social psychology: 1963–1983. *Psychology of Women Quarterly, 10*, 393–412.

Roberts, H. (Ed.). (1981). *Doing feminist research*. Boston: Routledge & Kegan Paul.

Saulnier, C.F. (in press). *Feminist theories and social work: Approaches and applications*. New York: Haworth.

Scheuneman, J.P. (1986). The female perspective on methodology and statistics. *Educational Researcher, 15*, 22–23.

Stanley, L. & Wise, S. (1983). *Breaking out: Feminist consciousness and feminist research.* Boston: Routledge & Kegan Paul.

Wallsten, B.S. (1981). What are the questions in the psychology of women? A feminist approach to research. *Psychology of Women Quarterly, 5*, 597–617.

Westkott, M. (1979). Feminist criticism in the social sciences. *Harvard Educational Review, 49*(4), 422–430.

Exercise 2: What Is the Difference Between Gender and Sex?

Gender is both a concept and a set of socially constructed relationships that are produced and reproduced through people's actions. The term "sex" tends to be used more to distinguish biologically based differences, whereas the term "gender" refers to cultural distinctions associated with sex—such as socially mediated distinctions, perceived differences, and relationships of power. Ideas and relationships such as those associated with gender emerge from social and historical settings and form a social structural context that deeply infuses and shapes people's understandings of "reality," what is "normal," and how things are "supposed to be." This is not unique to gender. Clearly, concepts about culture, race, class, age, sexual orientation, ableness, religion, and other social categories similarly shape perceptions. Knowledge and skills that support a constructively critical gender analysis can similarly support analyses related to other statuses. Gender affects us all!

1. What relation might these differences have to research?
2. Given the differences between sex and gender, which do you think might have a greater impact on a person?
3. How might these differences be a challenge for researchers?

Further Reading

Hare-Mustin, R.T. (1986). The problem of gender in family therapy theory. *Family Process, 26*, 15–27.

Henderson, K.A. (1994). Perspectives on analyzing gender, women, and leisure. *Journal of Leisure Research, 26*, 119–137.

Henderson, K.A., Bialeschki, M.D., Shaw, S.M. & Freysinger, V.J. (1989). *A leisure of one's own: A feminist perspective on women's leisure*. State College, PA: Venture.

Scott, J.W. (1986). Gender: A useful category for historical analysis. *American Historical Review, 91*, 1053–1075.

Exercise #3: Thinking About Research from the Viewpoint of Social Construction of Gender

For many, thinking about research is somewhat akin to thinking about technical or mechanical activities such as working with computers, electronics, physical structures, or machines. For example, images of males engaged in these tasks come to mind more quickly than do images of females. Assuming that we can move beyond these stereotypes, consider the following:

1. What does gender really have to do with research?
2. Aren't the steps and principles pretty much laid out so that you can learn them and carry through the steps—whether it's conducting a survey study, writing a computer program, or overhauling an engine?

3. From the viewpoint of the social construction of reality, what is wrong with this type of thinking?
4. How does gender play a role in how we interpret research and what steps we follow in conducting research?

Further Reading

Allen, K.R. (1994). Feminist reflections on lifelong single women. In D.L. Sollie & L.A. Leslie (Eds.), *Gender, families and close relationships: Feminist journeys* (pp. 97–119). Newbury Park, CA: Sage.

Bleier, R. (1984). *Science and gender: A critique of biology and its theories on women.* Elmsford, NY: Pergamon.

Fonow, M.M. & Cook, J.A. (1991). Back to the future: A look at the second wave of feminist epistemology and methodology. In M.M. Fonow & J.A. Cook (Eds.), *Beyond methodology: Feminist scholarship as lived research* (pp. 1–15). Bloomington: University of Indiana Press.

Frieze, I.H., Sales, E. & Smith, C. (1991). Considering the social context in gender research: The impact of college students' life stage. *Psychology of Women Quarterly, 15*, 371–392.

Jayarante, T.E. (1983). The value of quantitative methodology for feminist research. In G. Bowles & R P. Klein (Eds.), *Theories of women's studies* (pp. 140–161). Boston: Routledge & Kegan Paul.

Jayarante, T.E. & Kaczala, C.M. (1983). Social responsibility in sex difference research. *Journal of Educational Equity and Leadership, 3*, 305–316.

Jayarante, T.E. & Stewart, A.J. (1991) Quantitative and qualitative methods in the social sciences: Current feminist issues and practical strategies. In M.M. Fonow & J.A. Cook (Eds.), *Beyond methodology: Feminist scholarship as lived research* (pp. 85–106). Bloomington: University of Indiana Press.

Lykes, M.B. & Stewart, A.J. (1986). Evaluating the feminist challenge to research in personality and social psychology: 1963–1983. *Psychology of Women Quarterly, 10*, 393–412.

Roberts, H. (Ed.). (1981). *Doing feminist research*. Boston: Routledge & Kegan Paul.

Saulnier, C.F. (in press). *Feminist theories and social work: Approaches and applications.* New York: Haworth.

Scheuneman, J.P. (1986). The female perspective on methodology and statistics. *Educational Researcher, 15*, 22–23.

Stanley, L. & Wise, S. (1983). *Breaking out: Feminist consciousness and feminist research.* Boston: Routledge & Kegan Paul.

Wallsten, B.S. (1981). What are the questions in the psychology of women? A feminist approach to research. *Psychology of Women Quarterly, 5*, 597–617.

Westkott, M. (1979). Feminist criticism in the social sciences. *Harvard Educational Review, 49*(4), 422–430.

Exercise #4: Social Work Research, Gender, and the Ecosystems Perspective

Systems theory including the ecosystems model has been criticized for being too abstract, mechanistic, and deterministic to benefit social work practice. Research that undergirds these models came from fields such as biology, mathematics, and cybernetics. These fields are all dominated by men, and subject to the same limitations and research caveats that have been discussed in the feminist research literature summarized in this chapter. The life model and other ecological-systems models developed within social work relied on a more humanistic and organismic interpretation of systems theory and partly corrected some of these limitations by being more responsive to the interactional nature of human systems and social environments.

It is not clear how the limitations in the basic research and reifications that went into the formulation of systems models have been corrected. How are they sensitive to the special conditions of women, for example? In fact indications are that systems models such as those developed within family practice may not be very sensitive to women. Feminist practitioners and researchers have continually critiqued family therapy models, suggesting that they were patriarchal models developed by men, inadvertently reifying the inequitable power relations that exist between men and women in society. Recently Wakefield (1995, 1996a, 1996b) challenged our basic notions about the ecosystems model.

Analyze the above critiques and decide how the systems or ecosystems model may be used to design a gender-sensitive study.

1. How would one graph the nature of relationships among factors in an ecological framework that would guide data analysis?
2. How clear or unclear is an ecological model regarding how to interpret findings (e.g., how things are related to one another and what is the most important chain of relationships in relation to gender)?

Further Reading

Franklin, C., DiNitto, D.M. & McNeece, C.A. (1997). In search of social work theory. In D.M. DiNitto & C.A. McNeece (Eds.), *Social work: Issues and opportunities in a challenging profession* (2nd ed). Needham Heights, MA: Allyn & Bacon.

Hare-Mustin, R.T. (1986). The problem of gender in family therapy theory. *Family Process, 26*, 15–27.

Wakefield, J.C. (1996a). Does social work need the eco-systems perspective? Part 1. Is the perspective clinically useful? *Social Service Review, 70*, 1–32.

Wakefield, J.C. (1996b). Does social work need the eco-systems perspective? Part 2. Does the perspective save social work from incoherence? *Social Service Review, 70*, 183–213.

Wakefield, J.C. (1995). When an irresistible epistemology meets an immovable ontology. *Social Work Research, 19*, 9–17.

Exercise #5: The Status of Women and the Social Work Profession: Implications for Research

David Austin (1988) suggested that the emphasis of private practice and other forms of more lucrative practice positions in social work parallel the changing role of women in society, and that other professions such as nursing are following those trends. To put it plainly, women professionals are no longer willing to work for nothing, and they seek more money, power, and prestige in their jobs. In the 1980s private practice and specialized forms of clinical practice changed the status of practice positions, making them more lucrative and entrepreneurial. The managed care environment with its emphasis on competition and limited resources is likely to continue this trend even though the overall earning potential of some private practitioners may decrease in the short term. Social work educators are concerned about the numbers of women who want jobs as private psychotherapists because they believe that social work's historic mission may be lost in the shuffle for better paying jobs. Women, however, may aspire to these jobs not because they wish to abandon the poor or disadvantaged who social work is committed to helping but because they wish to improve the social status of themselves and their children.

Changes in the relative status in the role of women in social work and in their potential future contributions to practice may be partly dependent on the changing socioeconomics and the fact that women are no longer willing to go along with the previous inequitable social arrangements. What implications do these changes have for social workers serving the poor and oppressed, including women who are impoverished, and the research that social workers may conduct on those populations? (Although their research focuses on women researchers rather than practitioners in social work, it would be instructive for students to read Bentley, Hutchison & Green's [1994] findings about the way that men and women who are "successful" social work scholars differ and overlap in their experiences.)

Exercise #6: Grappling with the Practice/Research Split

Social work has long struggled with the relationship between research and practice. What do we mean by and include in the term "research"? Are these activities that take place as special projects separate from the conduct of everyday agency or practice life (e.g., surveys undertaken by NASW, treatment outcome studies done by university researchers, special questionnaires sent out to service providers by a central agency administrative office)?

As you reflect on this, consider the following questions. Are the measurement and related information-collection activities that are part of practice assessment included in the concept of research? What about the design factors that are part of client or service monitoring? The analysis and interpretation activities that go with case evaluation and, on a more aggregate level, program or system evaluation? What about the processes that practitioners go through in triangulating information, generating working hypotheses about the nature of the client's problems and the most helpful ways to meet their changing needs, considering alternative explanations, and then iteratively experimenting with intervention components to determine what will work most effectively with this particular individual or group—are these related to research?

If you were to graph the relationship between research and practice, what principles, knowledge, skills, or activities would be wholly unique to each? What would overlap? Are there aspects of each that may be relatively independent but that would inform or guide understandings or undertakings in the other realm? What are these aspects and how would you draw the arrows of influence?

Now, add to this picture a gender analysis. Are there ways in which research or practice is undertaken (by whom, or under what conditions) that limit the overlap and the utility of one realm to the other? If so, what are some of these factors? Do you have ideas about what would help reduce the impediments?

Further Reading

Fonow, M.M. & Cook, J.A. (1991). Back to the future: A look at the second wave of feminist epistemology and methodology. In M.M. Fonow & J.A. Cook (Eds.), *Beyond methodology: Feminist scholarship as lived research* (pp. 1–15). Bloomington: University of Indiana Press.

Grossman, F.K., Gilbert, L.A., Genero, N.P., Hawes, S.E., Hyde, J.S., Marecek, J. & Johnson, L. (in press). Feminist research: Practice, problems, prophecies. In J. Worell & N. Johnson (Eds.), *Feminist visions: New directions for education and training in feminist practice*. Washington, DC: APA.

Harding, S. (1987). *Feminism and methodology*. Bloomington: Indiana University Press.

Grossman, F.K., Gilbert, L.A., Genero, N.P., Hawes, S.E., Hyde, J.S., Marecek, J. & Johnson, L. (1997). Feminist research: Practice, problems, prophecies. In J. Worell & N. Johnson (Eds.), *Feminist visions: New directions for education and training in feminist practice*. Washington, DC: APA.

Reinharz, S. (1979). *On becoming a social scientist.* San Francisco: Jossey-Bass.

REFERENCES

Allan, J.D. (1994). A biomedical and feminist perspective of women's experiences with weight management. *Western Journal of Nursing Research, 16*, 524–543.

Allen, K.R. (1994). Feminist reflections on lifelong single women. In D.L. Sollie & L.A. Leslie (Eds.), *Gender, families and close relationships: Feminist journeys* (pp. 97–119). Newbury Park, CA: Sage.

Allen, K.R. & Baber, K.M. (1992). Ethical and epistemological tensions in applying a postmodern perspective to feminist research. *Psychology of Women Quarterly, 16*, 1–15.

Allen-Meares, P.A. (1995). Applications of qualitative research: Let the work begin. *Social Work Research, 19*, 5–8.

Anastas, J.W, & MacDonald, M.L. (1994). *Research design for social work and the human services*. New York: Lexington Books.

Ashford, J.B. (1994). Are traditional empirical research methods inherently biased against people of color? No. In W.W. Hudson & P.S. Nurius (Eds.), *Controversial issues in social work research* (pp. 29–34). Boston: Allyn & Bacon.

Atherton, C.R. (1993). Empiricists verses social constructionists: Time for a cease fire. *Families in Society, 74*(10), 617–624.

Austin, D. (1988). Women's career choices and human service organizations. *Social Work, 33* (6), 551–555.

Belensky, M.F., Clinchy, B.M. & Goldberger, N.R. (1986). *Women's ways of knowing: The development of self, voice, and mind*. New York: Basic Books.

Bentley, K.J., Hutchison, E.D. & Green, R.G. (1994). Women as social work scholars: An empirical analysis. *Affilia, 9*, 171–189.

Bernard, J. (1973). My four revolutions: An autobiographical history of ASA. In J. Huber (Ed.), *Changing women in a changing society* (pp. 11–29). Chicago: University of Chicago Press.

Birke, L. & Silvertown, J. (1984). *More than the parts: Biology and politics.* London: Pluto Press.

Bleier, R. (1984). *Science and gender: A critique of biology and its theories on women.* Elmsford, NY: Pergamon.

Bohan, J.S. (1993). Regarding gender: Essentialism, constructionism, and feminist psychology. *Psychology of Women Quarterly, 17*, 5–21.

Brower, A.M. & Nurius, P.S. (1993). *Social cognition and individual change: Current theory and counseling guidelines*. Newbury Park, CA: Sage.

Burman, E. (1990). Differing with deconstruction: A feminist critique. In I. Parker & J. Shotter (Eds.), *Deconstructing social psychology* (pp. 208–220). London: Routledge.

Carter, C., Coudrouglou, A., Figueira-McDonough, J., Lie, G.Y., MacEachron, A.E., Netting, F.E., Nichols-Casebolt, A., Nichols, A.W. & Risley-Curtiss, C. (1994). Integrating women's issues in the social work curriculum. *Journal of Social Work Education, 30,* 200–216.

Collins, P.H. (1986). Learning from the outsider within: The sociological significance of Black feminist thought. *Social Problems, 33*, 14–32.

Davis, L.V. (1990). Empirical clinical practice from a feminist perspective: A response to Ivanoff, Robinson, and Blythe. *Social Work, 34*, 557–558.

Davis, L.V. (1994). Is feminist research inherently qualitative and is it a fundamentally different approach to research? Yes. In W.W. Hudson & P.S. Nurius (Eds.), *Controversial issues in social work research.* Boston: Allyn & Bacon.

Deaux, K. & Major, B. (1987). Putting gender into context: An interactive model of gender-related behavior. *Psychological Review, 94*, 369–389.

Dennis, M.L, Fetterman, D.M. & Sechrest, L. (1994). Integrating qualitative and quantitative evaluation methods in substance abuse research. *Evaluation and Program Planning, 17*, 419–427.

DeVault, M.L. (1996). Talking back to sociology: Distinctive contributions of feminist methodology. *Annual Review of Sociology, 22*, 29–50.

Donnerstein, E. (1980). Aggressive erotica and violence against women. *Journal of Personality and Social Psychology, 39*, 269–277.

Eagly, A.H. (1987). *Sex differences in social behavior: A social-role interpretation*. Hillsdale, NJ: Erlbaum.

Ferree, M.M. (1990). Beyond separate spheres: Feminism and family research. *Journal of Marriage and the Family, 52*, 866–884.

Follingstad, D.R., Rutledge, L.L., Berg, B.J., Hause, E.S. & Polek, D.S. (1990). The role of emotional abuse in physically abusive relationships. *Journal of Family Violence, 5*, 107–120.

Fonow, M.M. & Cook, J.A. (1991). Back to the future: A look at the second wave of feminist epistemology and methodology. In M.M. Fonow & J.A. Cook (Eds.), *Beyond methodology: Feminist scholarship as lived research* (pp. 1–15). Bloomington: University of Indiana Press.

Franklin, C. (1995). Expanding the vision of the social constructionist debates: Creating relevance for practitioners. *Families in Society, 76*(7), 395–407.

Franklin, C., Nowicki, J., Schwab, J.A., Trapp, J. & Peterson, J. (1993). A computerized assessment system for brief, crisis oriented youth services. *Families in Society, 74*, 602–616.

Fraser, M.W. (1995). Rich, relevant, and rigorous: Do qualitative methods measure up? *Social Work Research, 19*, 25–28.

Freeman, M.L. (1990). Beyond women's issues. Feminism and social work. *Affilia, 5*, 72–89.

Frieze, I.H., Parsons, J.E., Johnson, P.B., Ruble, D.N. & Zellman, G.L. (1978). *Women and sex roles: A social psychological perspective*. New York: Norton.

Frieze, I.H., Sales, E. & Smith, C. (1991). Considering the social context in gender research: The impact of college students' life stage. *Psychology of Women Quarterly, 15*, 371–392.

Gambrill, E. (1990). *Critical thinking in clinical practice*. San Francisco: Jossey-Bass.

Gambrill, E. (1995). Less marketing and more scholarship. *Social Work Research, 19*, 38–48.

Gambrill, E. (in press). *Helping clients*. New York: Oxford University Press.

Gelles, R.J. (1994). Research and advocacy: Can one wear two hats? *Family Processes, 33*, 93–95.

Gergen, M.M. (1988). Building a feminist methodology. *Contemporary Social Psychology, 13*, 47–53.

Gilligan, C. (1982). *In a different voice: Psychological theory and woman's development.* Cambridge, MA: Harvard University Press.

Gorman, J. (1993). Postmodernism and the conduct of inquiry in social work. *Affilia, 8*(3), 247–64.

Gottlieb, N. & Bombyk, M. (1987). Strategies for strengthening feminist research. *Affilia, 2*, 23–35.

Grady, K.E. (1981). Sex bias in research design. *Psychology of Women Quarterly, 5*, 628–636.

Greenwood, J.D. (1991). *Relations and representations: An introduction to the philosophy of social psychological science.* New York: Routledge.

Grinnell, R.M. et al. (1994). Social work researchers' quest for respectability. *Social Work, 39*, 469–470.

Grossman, F.K., Gilbert, L.A., Genero, N.P., Hawes, S.E., Hyde, J.S., Marecek, J. & Johnson, L. (1997). Feminist research: Practice, problems, prophecies. In J. Worell & N. Johnson (Eds.), *Feminist visions: New directions for education and training in feminist practice*. Washington, DC: APA.

Guba , E.G. (1990). *The paradigm dialog*. Newbury Park, CA: Sage.

Hanson, S.L. (1996). Gender, family resources, and success in science. *Journal of Family Issues, 17*, 83–113.

Harding, S. (1987). *Feminism and methodology*. Bloomington: Indiana University Press.

Hare-Mustin, R.T. & Marecek, J. (1988). The meaning of difference: Gender theory, postmodernism, and psychology. *American Psychologist, 43*, 455–464.

Heidrich, S. (1994). The self, health, and depression in elderly women. *Western Journal of Nursing Research, 16*, 544–555.

Henderson, K.A. (1994). Perspectives on analyzing gender, women, and leisure. *Journal of Leisure Research, 26*, 119–137.

Henderson, K.A., Bialeschki, M.D., Shaw, S.M. & Freysinger, V.J. (1989). *A leisure of one's own: A feminist perspective on women's leisure.* State College, PA: Venture.

Hoshmand, L.T. & Martin, J. (1995a). Method choice. In L.T. Hoshmand & J. Martin (Eds.), *Research as praxis: Lessons from programmatic research in psychology* (pp. 3–28). New York: Teachers College Press.

Hoshmand, L.T. & Martin, J. (1995b). The inquiry process. In L.T. Hoshmand & J. Martin (Eds.), *Research as praxis: Lessons from programmatic research in psychology* (pp. 29–47). New York: Teachers College Press.

Hyde, J.S. (1994). Can meta-analysis make feminist transformations in psychology? *Psychology of Women Quarterly, 18*, 451–462.

Ivanoff, A., Robinson, E.A.R. & Blythe, B.J. (1987). Empirical clinical practice from a feminist perspective. *Social Work, 32*, 417–423.

Jayarante, T.E. (1983). The value of quantitative methodology for feminist research. In G. Bowles & R.P. Klein (Eds.), *Theories of women's studies* (pp. 140–161). Boston: Routledge & Kegan Paul.

Jayarante, T.E. & Kaczala, C.M. (1983). Social responsibility in sex difference research. *Journal of Educational Equity and Leadership, 3*, 305–316.

Jayarante, T.E. & Stewart, A.J. (1991). Quantitative and qualitative methods in the social sciences: Current feminist issues and practical strategies. In M.M. Fonow & J.A. Cook (Eds.), *Beyond methodology: Feminist scholarship as lived research* (pp. 85–106). Bloomington: University of Indiana Press.

Jordan, C. & Franklin, C. (1995). *Clinical assessment for social workers: Quantitative and qualitative methods*. Chicago: Lyceum.

Katzer, J., Cook, K.H. & Crouch, W.W. (1991). *Evaluating information: A guide for users of social science research.* New York: Hill.

Kilpatrick, D.G., Best, C.L., Veronen, L.J., Amick, A.E., Vileponteaux, L. A. & Ruff, G.A. (1985). Mental health correlates of criminal victimization: A random community survey. *Journal of Consulting and Clinical Psychology, 53*, 866–873.

Koss, M.P., Gidycz, C.A. & Wisniewski, N. (1987). The scope of rape: Incidence and prevalence of sexual aggression and victimization in a national sample of higher education students. *Journal of Consulting and Clinical Psychology, 55*, 162–170.

Landrine, H., Klonoff, E. & Brown, C.A. (1992). Cultural diversity and methodology in feminist psychology: Critique, proposal, empirical example. *Psychology of Women Quarterly, 16*, 145–163.

Levy, G.D. & Fivush, R. (1993). Scripts and gender: A new approach for examining gender-role development. *Developmental Review, 13*, 126–146.

Linz, D. (1989). Exposure to sexually explicit materials and attitudes toward rape: A comparison of study results. *Journal of Sex Research, 26*(1), 50–84.

Lykes, M.B. & Stewart, A.J. (1986). Evaluating the feminist challenge to research in personality and social psychology: 1963–1983. *Psychology of Women Quarterly, 10*, 393–412.

Mahoney, M.J. (1991). *Human change processes*. New York: Basic Books.

Marsh, J.C. (1994). Is feminist research inherently qualitative and is it a fundamentally different approach to research? No. In W.W. Hudson & P.S. Nurius (Eds.), *Controversial issues in social work research* (pp. 69–72). Boston: Allyn & Bacon.

Marshall, B.K. (1992). *Teaching the postmodern: Fiction and theory*. New York: Routledge.

McCormick, N. (May 1988). *Flirtation and seduction*. Paper presented at Nags Head Interdisciplinary Conference on Sex and Gender. Nags Head, NC.

Mies, M. (1983). Towards a methodology for feminist research. In G. Bowles & R.P. Klein (Eds.), *Theories of women's studies* (pp. 43–61). Boston: Routledge & Kegan Paul.

Miller, J.B. (1976). *Toward a new psychology of women*. Boston: Beacon.

Moss, K.E. (1988). New reproductive technologies: Concerns of feminists and researchers. *Affilia, 3*, 38–50.

Muehlenhard, C.L. & Linton, M.A. (1987). Date rape and sexual aggression in dating situations: Incidence and risk factors. *Journal of Counseling Psychology, 34*, 186–196.

Mullen, E.J. (1995). Pursuing knowledge through qualitative research. *Social Work Research, 19*, 29–32.

Murphy, C.M. & O'Leary, K.D. (1994). Research paradigm and spouse abuse. *Journal of Interpersonal Violence, 9*, 207–223.

Norris, J., Nurius, P.S. & Dimeff, L. (1996). Through her eyes: Factors affecting women's perception of and resistance to acquaintance sexual aggression threat. *Psychology of Women Quarterly, 20*, 123–145.

Nurius, P.S. (1995). Critical thinking: A meta-skill for integrating practice and information technology training. *Computers in Human Services, 12*, 109–126.

Nurius, P.S. & Gibson, J.W. (1990). Clinical observation, inference, reasoning, and judgment in social work: An update. *Social Work Research & Abstracts, 26*, 18–25.

Nurius, P.S. & Hudson, W.W. (1993). *Human services practice, evaluation, and computers: A practical guide for today and beyond*. Pacific Grove, CA: Brooks/Cole.

Nurius, P.S. & Norris, J. (1994). *Response to sexual aggression in dating and courtship*. Bethesda, MD: National Institute for Mental Health.

Oakley, A. (1981). Interviewing women: A contradiction in terms? In H. Roberts (Ed.), *Doing feminist research* (pp. 30–61). Boston: Routledge & Kegan Paul.

Osmond, M.W. & Thorne, B. (1993). Feminist theories: The social construction of gender in families and society. In P.G. Boss, W.J. Doherty, R. LaRossa, W.R. Schumm & S.K. Steinmetz (Eds.), *Sourcebook of family theories and methods: A contextual approach* (pp. 591–622). New York: Plenum.

Parlee, M.B. (1975). Psychology. *Signs, 1*, 119–138.

Patton, M.Q. (1990). *Qualitative evaluation and research methods* (2nd ed.). Beverly Hills, CA: Sage.

Peplau, L.A. & Conrad, E. (1989). Beyond nonsexist research: The perils of feminist methods in psychology. *Psychology of Women Quarterly, 13*, 379–400.

Phares, V. (1996). Conducting nonsexist research, prevention, and treatment with fathers and mothers: A call for a change. *Psychology of Women Quarterly, 20*, 55–77.

Pugliesi, K. (1992). Women and mental health: Two traditions of feminist research. *Women & Health, 19*, 43–68.

Quam, J.K. & Austin, C.D. (1985). Coverage of women's issues in eight social work journals. *Social Work, 29*, 360–365.

Rank, M.R. (1992). The blending of quantitative and qualitative methods in understanding childbearing among welfare recipients. In J.F. Gilgun, K. Daly & G. Handel (Eds.), *Qualitative methods in family research* (pp. 281–300). Newbury Park, CA: Sage.

Reid, P.T. & Comas-Diaz, L. (1990). Gender and ethnicity: Perspectives on dual status. *Sex Roles, 22*, 397–408.

Reinhartz, S. (1992). *Feminist methods in social research*. New York: Oxford University Press.

Reinharz, S. (1979). *On becoming a social scientist.* San Francisco: Jossey-Bass.

Riessman, C.K. (1994). *Qualitative studies in social work research*. Thousand Oaks, CA: Sage.

Riger, S. (1992). Epistemological debates, feminist voices: Science, social values, and the study of women. *American Psychologist, 47*, 730–740.

Roberts, H. (Ed.). (1981). *Doing feminist research*. Boston: Routledge & Kegan Paul.

Runkel, P. & McGrath, J. (1972). *Research on human behavior: A systematic guide to methods.* New York: Holt.

Sands, R.G. & Nuccio, K. (1992). Postmodern feminist theory and social work. *Social Work, 37*, 489–494.

Saulnier, C.F. (in press). *Feminist theories and social work: Approaches and applications.* New York: Haworth.

Scarborough, E. & Furumoto, L. (1987). *Untold lives: The first generation of American women psychologists.* New York: Columbia University Press.

Scheuneman, J.P. (1986). The female perspective on methodology and statistics. *Educational Researcher, 15*, 22–23.

Scott, J.W. (1986). Gender: A useful category for historical analysis. *American Historical Review, 91*, 1053–1075.

Sells, S.P., Smith, T.E. & Sprenkle, D.H. (1995). Integrating qualitative and quantitative research methods: A research model. *Family Process, 34*, 199–218.

Sherif, C.W. (1987). Bias in psychology. In S. Harding (Ed.), *Feminism and methodology* (pp. 37–73). Bloomington: University of Indiana Press.

Sherman, J.A. & Reid, W. (1994). *Qualitative research in social work.* New York: Columbia University Press.

Slack, J.D., Myers, N., Nelson, L. & Sirk, K. (1996). Women, research, and mentorship in public administration. *Public Administration Review, 56*, 453–458.

Small, S.A. (1995). Action-oriented research: Models and methods. *Journal of Marriage and the Family, 57*, 941–955.

Smith, J.K. & Heshusius, L. (1986). Closing down the conversation: The end of the quantitative-qualitative debate among educational inquirers. *Educational Researcher, 15,* 4–12.

Smith, T.E. & Graham, P.B. (1995). Socioeconomic research in family research. *Journal of Marriage and the Family, 57*, 930–940.

Stanley, L. & Wise, S. (1983). *Breaking out: Feminist consciousness and feminist research.* Boston: Routledge & Kegan Paul.

Tangri, S.S. & Strausberg, G.L. (1979). Can research on women be more effective in shaping policy? *Psychology of Women Quarterly, 3*, 321–343.

Taylor, C. (1991). The dialogic self. In D.R. Hiley, J.F. Bohman & R. Schusterman (Eds.), *The interpretive turn: Philosophy, science and culture* (pp. 304–314). Ithaca: Cornell University Press.

Tittle, C.K. (1986). Gender research and education. *American Psychologist, 4,* 1161–1168.

Tyson, K. (1994). Author's reply: Response to "Social work researcher's quest for respectability." *Social Work, 39*(6), 737–741.

Tyson, K. (1995). *New foundations for scientific social work and behavioral research: The heuristic paradigm.* Boston: Allyn & Bacon.

Unger, R.K. (1979). *Female and male: Psychological perspectives.* New York: Harper & Row.

Wakefield, J.C. (1995). When an irresistible epistemology meets an immovable ontology. *Social Work Research, 19*, 9–17.

Wakefield, J.C. (1996a). Does social work need the eco-systems perspective? Part 1. Is the perspective clinically useful? *Social Service Review, 70*, 1–32.

Wakefield, J.C. (1996b). Does social work need the eco-systems perspective? Part 2. Does the perspective save social work from incoherence? *Social Service Review, 70*, 183–213.

Walker, A.J. (1994). You can't be a woman in your mother's house: Adult daughters and their mothers. In D.L. Sollie & L.A. Leslie (Eds.), *Gender, families and close relationships: Feminist journey*? (pp. 74–96). Newbury Park, CA: Sage.

Walker, B.G. (1994). Science: The feminists' scapegoat? *Research on Social Work Practice, 4*, 510–514.

Wallston, B.S. (1981). What are the questions in the psychology of women? A feminist approach to research. *Psychology of Women Quarterly, 5*, 597–617.

Westkott, M. (1979). Feminist criticism in the social sciences. *Harvard Educational Review, 49*(4), 422–430.

White, J.W. & Farmer, R. (1992). Research methods: How they shape views of sexual violence. *Journal of Social Issues, 48*, 45–59.

Wilkinson, S. (1986). Sighting possibilities: Diversity and commonality in feminist research. In S. Wilkinson (Ed.), *Feminist social psychology: Developing theory and practice* (pp. 7–24). Milton Keynes, England: Open University Press.

Williams, C.I. & Heikes, E.J. (1993). The importance of researcher's gender in the in-depth interview. *Gender & Society, 7*, 280–291.

Worell, J. (1996). Opening doors to feminist research. *Psychology of Women Quarterly, 20*, 469–485.

Worrell J. & Etaugh, C. (1994). Transforming theory and research with women: Themes and variations. *Psychology of Women Quarterly, 18*, 443–450.

Yllo, K. (1994). Reflections of a feminist family violence researcher. In D.L. Sollie & L.A. Leslie (Eds.), *Gender, families and close relationships: Feminist journeys* (pp. 213–236). Newbury Park, CA: Sage.

Yllo, K. & Bograd, M. (Eds.). (1988). *Feminist perspectives on wife abuse*. Newbury Park, CA: Sage.

CHAPTER 11

Designing and Implementing Curricular Change

Josefina Figueira-McDonough
F. Ellen Netting
Ann Nichols-Casebolt

INTRODUCTION

The overriding task that we embrace in this book is how to promote curricular change in social work education so that it incorporates both female and male experiences. This is not a simple task. Given the ways that knowledge is constructed in academia, this undertaking calls for a major transformation, since women's realities and experiences have traditionally been marginal or absent in such constructions. In fact, acceptance of new curricula implies a major cultural shift whereby fundamental tenets are challenged. It is likely to be resisted by those who have built their careers on these tenets. In other words, the curricula suggested in the preceding chapters have the characteristics of a second-order change, a change that occurs at the very core, the very essence of the academic enterprise, requiring a paradigmatic shift (Shaw & Walton, 1995).

Although the changes proposed in this book appear, from our point of view, to be both necessary and common-sensical, they involve a renegotiation of the dominant beliefs, assumptions, values, and attitudes that guide the behavior of groups and individuals in higher education and that provide a frame of reference within which the meaning of events and actions on and off campus is interpreted (Smith, 1994). The purpose of this renegotiation is to introduce new beliefs and establish a new order that transforms the system. Naturally, this new order will be viewed as threatening to the controllers of the old culture.

Awareness of the type of change (and its ramifications) in which we are getting involved has to be the first step in considering strategies of implementation, but equally important is an understanding of the settings in which the changes are to take place.

It is important to recognize that although this book is written with the basic premise that current curricula in schools of social work across the country have not reached the point where gender is fully integrated, there are other educators who do not see this as a problem. One sociologist who was attempting to integrate gender content into her courses remarked: "To me, the striking thing about the traditional curriculum is that no one notices that there is a problem. Women's experiences are invisible" (Yllo, 1989, p. 658). She goes on to elaborate that true curriculum transformation will not occur with an "add women and stir" approach. Methodology and pedagogy must be changed as well.

Going from defining the situation of not having the voices of both genders heard to defining this as a problem will encounter resistance. It is one thing to say that more gender content needs to be incorporated into all course work. It is another thing to frame this as a problem in dire need of rectification, for that means that everyone must change what they teach. These changes may not only require modifications and adjustments in course content, but may also require a complete rethinking of how one approaches the educational experience itself. Regardless, varying degrees of resistance to change will occur.

We begin this chapter by identifying the target of change—schools of social work. Since schools of social work are part of larger university and college settings, they are viewed as subsystems within larger structures. Universities and colleges, in turn, are nested within larger environments that are uncertain at best and often somewhat turbulent. Each of these systems will be examined prior to our focus on strategies that faculty might use to infuse gender into the curriculum.

SCHOOLS OF SOCIAL WORK AS TARGETS OF CHANGE

Although schools of social work are well-positioned to not only promote gender integration in their curriculum, but to also be the trigger for such curricular transformation in other academic subsystems, our focus at this time will be exclusively on schools of social work. We focus on schools as organizational sub-units within larger systems. Second-order change can be achieved within a subsystem; it is not contingent on the transformation of the whole system (Levy & Merry, 1986). At the same time, the culture of the school cannot be dissociated from the culture of the university to the extent that they may share a common view of scholarship, the nature and purpose of higher education, and the role of faculty.

UNIVERSITIES AS THE CONTEXT

Recent analyses of colleges and universities underscore the functional and structural complexity of these organizations. They can be examined simultaneously as institutions, enterprises, and agencies (see, e.g., Balderston, 1995). Because our goal is not to revolutionize or remake the institution, but to transform curricula, it is important to locate the target of change precisely. Academic institutions have a mixed organizational character. They have administrative elements, often hierarchically organized, with explicit rules of performance and criteria of efficiency. They also have academic or faculty elements, characterized by collegial decision-making, internalized norms, and work autonomy. Although such mixed organizations are interconnected through an elaborate system of committees and boards that permit both a certain level of autonomy as well as coordination (Litwak, 1961), it is the academic focus that is of greater interest to our project, because the dominant culture that we are interested in challenging is maintained by it. To be more precise, it is the academic subsystem of schools of social work that should be the target of change in order to implement the proposals in this book.

The goals of the university, teaching, scholarship, and service are differently weighted and measured by different constituencies in different environments (Balderston, 1995). Beyond the types of support (public or private funding) on which the existence of universities directly depends, there are a variety of publics that applaud or question their functioning, indirectly increasing or decreasing their legitimization and funding claims. These publics vary by type of institution and so does what they expect from it. As an example of this diversity, Balderston (1995) uses a simple typology of universities and other institutions of higher education examining the different publics and their expectations. For example, private colleges and universities depend on endowments, alumni gifts, and the willingness of parents to pay high tuition. Alumni and parents are paying for association with an institution that is often viewed as prestigious, may be tied to certain values that they hold dear, or has a reputation that they value. To maintain that reputation, the institution has to enforce consistent standards in admission of students and in hiring of faculty. Public universities exist in an equally complex environment, requiring both reputation and accessibility to in-state students. Extramural funding, crucial to graduate training and to the maintenance of good faculty, may depend on its reputation as a research institution. National recognition, in turn, legitimizes the claims of funding from the state. On the other hand, its legitimization as a public institution is very much tied to the number of in-state students that it educates, making high standards of admission unpopular.

Whatever the environmental pressures felt by universities, and whether they vary greatly by auspice, the point is that they exist in highly politicized environments. All are preoccupied by funding constraints, maintaining relationships with multiple constituencies, and trying to survive in a changing environment. These are the systems in which schools of social work are nested.

Culture Within Schools of Social Work

While departments and schools might share in the culture of the institution and of the national system of higher education, they vary among themselves in their organizational cultures and the commitments that they command from their faculty and students (Smith, 1994). Lahiry (1994) identifies types of cultures that might emerge in academic units, the structural organization that accompanies them, and the types of commitments they generate. *Constructive cultures* encourage achievement and self-actualizing among the faculty and students, and they encourage experimentation and nurture support and teamwork. The administration in these units shares the academic norms of the faculty and facilitates individual efforts, integrating them in as part of the overall unit's achievements. *Defensive cultures* usually associated with authoritarian administration are of two types: (1) passive-defensive cultures—organizational cultures determined by the need of approval from the administration (e.g., dean, director)—that tend to be conventional and promote avoidance of any innovation; or (2) aggressive-defensive cultures—characterized by forceful approaches by the individual faculty to protect their status and security, along with oppositional competition for power and perfectionism. In both types of defensive cultures, faculty are quite dependent on the authority of the dean or director, but in the passive-defensive case the person in authority has not internalized academic norms of achievement, whereas in the aggressive-defensive she/he has. In the passive-defensive culture, participation of students in school affairs may be ritualized, while in aggressive-defensive cultures participation might follow a two-tier structure where students have little power.

Assessing what type of culture a school of social work has is very important to identifying who will serve as agents of change. Note that these cultural types are based on who provides leadership *within* the school. In constructive cultures, leadership is a shared responsibility and is less tied to formalized power or authority. According to Levy and Merry (1986), it would be easier to enter and challenge constructive cultures than defensive cultures, since the former support innovation. For schools sharing this culture, the point of entry for second-order change would be the faculty. Smith's (1994) study suggests that working with senior faculty would be especially important. He argues that it is senior faculty who embody more strongly the department's culture and are more committed to the progress of the unit. He found that if full professors do not move immediately after their promotion, but instead decide to remain at the school, they will probably stay there until retirement, and therefore, their commitment to the unit will increase (Smith, 1994). In constructive cultures, faculty change agents will generally emerge.

In defensive cultures, leadership is held by persons in positions of authority. In these situations, without a dean or director's support, major change is unlikely to occur. Approaches to second-order change in the aggressive-defensive culture would have to be initiated from the top down, through the conversion/cooperation of the dean or director. The passive-defensive culture would probably represent the most difficult situation for the curricular change we propose. A culture based on insecurity and fear will resist innovation. Even if change were to be imposed from above (an improbable circumstance), the response would more likely be ritualistic on the part of an insecure faculty.

Obviously, there are variations on these types. For example, some schools of social work may have what might be called *partnered cultures* in which an authoritarian dean steps back and defers to faculty on curricular matters. Therefore, to initiate an effort to integrate gender content into the curriculum it is important to know who assumes leadership for curriculum development and innovation, since this is the focus of change. It is conceivable that even in a passive-defensive culture some change could occur if the person in authority is not particularly concerned about controlling curriculum content. Also, it is important to consider that even in constructive cultures, change may be problematic if senior faculty members oppose gender infusion. Without an aggressive-defensive leader to declare that gender will be infused into the curriculum in this situation, change could be averted by one or two strong faculty leaders who advocate for the status quo.

Leadership Within Schools of Social Work

Schein (1991) identifies ways in which leaders embed culture into their organizations. The most powerful embedding mechanisms are

1. what leaders pay attention to, measure, and control;
2. leader reactions to critical incidents and organizational crises;
3. deliberate role modeling, teaching, and coaching by leaders;
4. criteria for allocation of status and rewards; and
5. criteria for recruitment, selection, promotion, retirement and excommunication. (pp. 224–225)

Each embedding mechanism provides clues to how the leaders within schools of social work might approach integration of gender content into the curriculum. If leaders pay attention to gender content issues that are raised, and are committed to change, then a foundation is laid. Reaction to critical incidents may also become an opportunity for change. For example, if during a site visit from CSWE (a critical incident in social work education), leaders respond with concern when site visitors ask why gender content is missing, this is a sign that gender content is worth a response. The level of commitment of accreditation team members to enforce the requirement of gender content within the curriculum can make a considerable difference in the outcome. Organizational crisis, such as the threat of a school's loss of autonomy (e.g., going from an independent school to becoming a department in another college) can also be used as an opportunity for curriculum innovation. It could be an argument to preserve autonomy or a way of establishing the unit's distinctiveness in the new organizational context.

Probably most important in achieving gender sensitivity is the third mechanism identified by Schein, in which leaders model, teach, and coach. For example, the efforts begun at one school of social work was championed by a full professor who took the opportunity to demonstrate in her own collaborative manner how feminist principles could actually guide the process of curricular renewal. A fourth area identified by Schein is that of the allocation of rewards. If performance, tenure, and promotion reviews have built-in mechanisms to reward those persons who fully integrate certain content within their courses, then faculty will have incentives to follow through. When these reward processes fail to recognize the significance of these types of contributions, then a faculty person's only reward is in the richness this content brings to the classroom. It would be nice to say that this is enough in itself, but most faculty (especially when untenured) appreciate and need recognition for their efforts at the school level.

Last, the very selection of who teaches in a school of social work will effect the way in which curriculum develops. When search committees recruit faculty, if there is a clear message that the integration of gender content is a respected and honored part of the curriculum, then new faculty will be socialized to its importance from the beginning. If, however, no attention is paid to recruiting faculty who have already made contributions to this area, or who are interested and willing to work toward integration of gender content, then the likelihood of this message becoming a part of the school's culture is greatly reduced. On an optimistic note, the hiring of female assistant professors, regardless of the orientation of the school, might contribute to the support for curricular gender integration. Younger or more recently trained faculty cohorts tend to have had greater exposure to epistemological critiques, to be less tolerant of gender biases, and to be less constrained by prior history in constructing course syllabi.

In summary, we propose that there are different types of cultures within schools of social work. These cultures are highly related to the formal and informal types of leadership patterns that develop. Carefully assessing a particular school's culture will provide clues for how much resistance to change there may be. In addition, looking for ways that leaders embed and reinforce cultural characteristics is essential for assessing how change can proceed.

Structural Units Within Schools of Social Work

No two schools are structured exactly the same, even if their formal organizational charts look similar. There will always be variations on a theme, given the ways in which informal communication and faculty relationships develop within (or even in protest to) the formally agreed upon structure. With this caveat, however, comes the suggestion that one must understand the structure, both formally and informally, in order to effect change. It is critically important to know what units within the school deal with curriculum development and approval. For this book chapter authors were asked to write about particular curricular areas, knowing full well that courses actually taught may cut across chapter topics. For example, a policy course (the content of Chapter 9) may be combined with content from both administration (Chapter 8) and community (Chapter 7). Psychopathology content (Chapter 4) may be combined with content on human behavior, the subject of Chapter 2. Having been schooled and having taught in multiple schools of social work, we are aware of the ways in which course content will vary and how it is structured. Knowing how the content is conceptualized is a necessary first step.

Beyond the conceptual organization of the curriculum, however, are the actual vehicles for changing what appears on an approved course syllabus or outline. Are there curricular content groups (sequences, teaching groups, etc.) in which course content is first explored and developed? Are there lead faculty persons who are responsible for coordination and oversight of specific courses? Are there program committees through which courses must proceed on their way to approval? Is there a curriculum committee that serves as a gatekeeper for course approval? Who serves on these structural units and who has the power to make change? Are there "sacred" courses that no one ever touches because they are viewed as "belonging" to a master teacher? Are there courses that are ripe for change if someone would just decide to take them on? Understanding the structure, as well as the power and politics in which these units operate, will be a next step in identifying where change can occur.

An example may be helpful. In one school of social work a change in curriculum had left several faculty disgruntled and unhappy about certain courses. As a result, persons who had taught these courses for years were searching for other courses to teach, anxious to let someone else teach what appeared to be an oversubscribed set of courses. A window was therefore open for new faculty to step in and teach these courses. In the process of teaching them for the first time, they identified a number of areas that needed updating. They also found that gender content was virtually missing. They began to put together syllabi revisions that would eventually go through the school's curriculum committee. Since faculty who had taught these courses for years had little remaining investment, they were willing to let the new faculty make changes. This provided an opportunity to integrate gender as well as to rethink the courses in their entirety. When these windows open, syllabi can be changed in a fairly rapid manner as long as there are persons willing to make those changes and to carry them through.

Another example speaks to the use of team teaching in courses that are undergoing revision and rethinking. Paludi (1991) writes that "exposure to many women can contribute to students' growth [and] self-concept development" (p. 172). Certainly, this approach is warranted, yet we would go even further. This book seeks to incorporate gender into the curriculum, not to eliminate content on men and replace it with content on women. A way to challenge ourselves is to team female and male faculty members in courses that seek to integrate gender and have them talk frankly about the challenges they face in dealing with this content. This approach models what we are seeking to do—to integrate gender into the curriculum. There will be uncomfortable moments, but change is uncomfortable if that change truly challenges underlying assumptions.

Beyond units established for curricular purposes, there are other units and constituencies within schools of social work that can be mobilized to support change. Student associations, advisory councils, committees that are part of the governance structure, and a host of ad hoc committees that function within schools of social work may provide support for efforts that focus predominantly on curricular change. For example, if a student association sponsors a series of speakers on gender concerns, then this becomes a logical stepping-off point to ask how courses within the school can better integrate this content. In the parlance of planned change, this process is the identification of various stakeholders who may support or oppose new initiatives. It is particularly important to know who opposes these changes so that these persons can be co-opted into the process.

RESOURCES FOR PROMOTING CHANGE

Promoting change in schools of social work also requires consideration of what additional school, university, and external environmental forces can be used to support the change. There are some general resources available to any unit pursuing the same program of change, whereas others use environmental resources specific to professional schools.

Student Resources

Students can be one of the major forces for curricular change in a university. This is particularly true in schools of social work where accreditation standards require that students have a voice in curriculum matters. Student feedback through course evaluations as well as their participation in the governance of the school can be used to advantage when attempting to make curricular changes.

Because CSWE standards mandate the incorporation of content on women and minorities in the curriculum, most course evaluation forms ask specific questions related to coverage of this content in the course. A starting point for fostering change might be to take seriously the feedback students provide on these questions and identify curriculum areas that seem particularly weak in this content. Beyond this, however, is engaging students in a discussion of what is meant by "gender integration" and how this is or is not occurring in the curriculum. Once students are brought into the process of identifying gaps in the curriculum, they can also be enlisted to help in the restructuring. Special course activities, independent study projects, and the myriad of sample assignments provided in each of the chapters in this book not only increase the students' knowledge about gender in the content area, but they can also be used as a resource for additional curricular changes. For example, a course assignment that requires students to examine critically the gender, race, and class assumptions underlying a particular practice theory may identify assumptions and issues the faculty member had not considered.

Students may, of course, be resistant to curricular change that brings gender to the center of the curriculum. A common "complaint" from some students when there is an attempt to address gender more directly in courses is that "women's content was being rammed down their throats" (Ray, Murtry, Matison & Tucker, 1990, p. 23); or that women's content took up too much space in the class (Peterson, 1991). As Higginbotham (1990) has noted, however, these reactions may be a function of attempting merely to add this content, not integrate it. "Students can tolerate a certain amount of cultural enrichment, but if this material exceeds more than one or two lectures, they lose their patience because they think the instructor is deviating from the core" (Higginbotham, 1990, p. 14). If the material is integrated—and therefore seen as part of the core material—this problem can be avoided.

The development of critical thinking skills among students may be the best means for both overcoming resistance to the introduction of this content, as well as fostering a process that continually challenges the assumptions held by students and faculty alike. Encouraging students to examine critically how gender, race, class, culture, and other attributes influence knowledge development and their own ways of knowing helps to "reduce the marginalization of women and minorities in the classroom" (Tice, 1990, p. 139). Such an approach also challenges the traditional teaching style that assumes faculty are knowledge givers and that students are knowledge receivers. Continual examination of assumptions requires that students and faculty engage in dialogue that increases self-reflection. Feminist scholars have long advocated that a gender-sensitive learning environment must include informal discussion that allows for recognition of differences, expression of opinions, and continual questioning of the "truth" (Tice, 1990).

Another student resource that is often overlooked when addressing issues of curriculum revision are doctoral students. In some ways these students may be our best hope for major curricular change, for they are the faculty of the future. Raising their awareness and understanding of gender issues makes it more likely that the next generation of faculty will view gender integration as a necessary component of curricular development.

The University as a Resource

Several important political dimensions and pressures affect both the internal and the external dimensions of universities. In an environment of reduced resources and greater demand for productivity, coalition-building and bargaining have emerged as important features of the role of presidents and academic leaders. Political pressures have become more powerful at all levels of the external environment, requiring that university representatives make persuasive arguments for institutional support to political leaders, regents, and boards. One contemporary force for both private and public institutions is that parents and the public at large are increasingly concerned that students are taught by full-time faculty and that teaching is viewed as the primary focus of an educational system. For example, at the undergraduate level, change agents in schools of social work must be aware that parents are concerned about size of classes, who teaches their children, and the relation of training to employability. While awareness of external expectations is important, these constituencies may be neutral rather than supportive forces for curricular transformation. However, university responses to parental concerns might facilitate the transformations proposed here. For example, small classes are favorable to interactive learning. Also, the pressure for senior professors to teach introductory courses can, under certain circumstances, have a positive effect. If senior faculty are committed to gender-integrated curriculum, raising such issues at the beginning of the student's academic career will be important. In addition, senior status might carry with it greater academic discretion in designing critical courses and impart greater credibility to students.

Another force that is driving change in colleges and universities is the recognition that the world of practice is highly interdisciplinary. Although universities may espouse interdisciplinary values in their strategic plans and vision statements, it is important to realize that educational institutions are the most professionally and disciplinarily segregated organizations in modern society. Educational institutions have built their reputations on educating students to perform certain roles that are highly specialized. In graduate-level education, students frequently move through lock-step curricular programs with little chance for interaction with students from other fields of study. In schools of social work this is especially true, given the number of required courses. It is in field practicum experiences that opportunities are occasionally offered for students to interact with persons from other helping professions. Recognizing the predisposition of universities and colleges to organize themselves according to professional and disciplinary boundaries, one strategy that can be used to break with tradition is to engage colleagues from other units in assisting with internal curricular change. This not only works to promote interdisciplinary collaboration such as team teaching and scholarship, but it may also change some of the power dynamics among social work faculty. While this is a reasonable and often discussed strategy, the enormous costs of team teaching and the reluctance of departments to support interdepartmental teaching must not be underestimated.

Parallel movements or interest in other departments concerning gender integration of the curriculum could be used for internal leverage, as could any support from the university administration. For example, Peterson (1991) writes about gender integration in speech communication courses, Yllo (1989) elaborates on the process of integrating gender into sociology classes, Stevens-Smith (1995) focuses on gender issues in counselor education, and Paludi (1991) focuses on incorporating the work of women psychologists into psychology courses. Furthermore, any groups in the university environment that would be especially interested in women's education could have the type of political influence that weakens internal resistance to change. For example, if a distinguished and respected scholar from another department assists in the development of curriculum, faculty within the school who have resisted change may defer to an outside person.

Resources Within the Larger Environment

More specific to professional school environments are stronger links with community organizations and the role of accrediting bodies. Professional schools develop, for their own purposes, specifications of educational content, staffing, and resource standards that must be met by a school that is seeking certification. Accrediting organizations provide a means of enforcing some conventions of legitimacy and quality control. Accreditation reviews affect the position of the school within the university and simultaneously affect the university by reinstating or questioning the credibility of one of its units. The potential influence of the accrediting body in the matter of gender integration in the curriculum could be far reaching.

CSWE accredits schools of social work and has established standards for integrating content on women into the curriculum. Three groups are targeted for required inclusion: women, people of color, and gays and lesbians. Other groups are noted for inclusion as well. However, it has been our experience that the inclusion of women's content has been played down in the reaccreditation process. The CSWE Women's Commission has developed guidelines for curricular inclusion, but the power of their voices seems to have been somewhat reduced in light of multiple groups that have voiced concerns about curriculum content. This may be a function of the fact that the majority of faculty are women, but women are not the majority of CSWE members. Therefore the CSWE has to forge a link to women nonmembers to increase their influence within the organization. Certainly, this book targets schools of social work for change, but we strongly encourage the leadership within CSWE to use its contents for reinforcing their own standards. If we manage to target both CSWE and schools of social work simultaneously, we could not hope for more. As things stand now, the verbiage is in the standards, but the power of enforcement must come from those persons who conduct site visits and who scan syllabi and dialogue with faculty to identify clear indications that gender has been infused within the curriculum.

Professional schools, by the nature of their applied training, have to establish ongoing links with professional organizations in the community. In the case of the social work schools, instruction requirements (field internships) make this imperative. Depending on how these links are developed and nurtured by the schools, these professional organizations can become a strong constituency for or against change in the schools. The NASW and its National Commission of Women's Issues might also contribute to the creation of reinforcing links by shaping a professional culture aware of the imperatives of gender integrated social work.

EXAMINING AND OVERCOMING RESISTANCE TO CHANGE

Whatever strategies are adopted in trying to implement gender-integrated curricula, factors of inertia, cultural resistance, and fear will be present. That is what Eccles (1994) calls "organizational viscosity." This type of resistance is likely to be stronger in schools of social work than in the disciplines because it is based both on traditional academic and professional cultures. As mentioned in the introduction to this chapter, the curricular changes proposed would modify not only conceptualizations and meaning of social problems but also practices of intervention.

The dominant culture provides a frame of reference within which meaning of events and actions is interpreted. It is shared with a community of people, it has its own "lingua franca" and distinctive modes of interpretation. In fact, it forms a self-contained cognitive whole within which patterns of thinking and logic repeat themselves, producing more of the same with respect to action and behavior. Traditional cultures lead at best to a dynamic conservatism reproducing an infinity of permutations of the old. This is why reorganizations from generalist approaches to specialist approaches, special sections in the curriculum dealing with women's issues or even special courses on women, cannot bring about the second-order change intended in our proposal. This type of change cannot be derived from the dominant culture (Huber & Glick, 1993).

To implement a gender-integrated curriculum, we are faced with the necessity of changing the old intellectual and professional culture and creating a new one that brings to the center the reality of women. Understanding the functions of the old culture tells us that we will face strong resistance. This resistance is not necessarily based on personal hostility but on the threat that any cultural transformation represents to the order that many faculty have embraced, been socialized in, and practiced. For example, following a CSWE site visit in one school of social work, a senior faculty member circulated a protest via the Internet about the politically correct tyranny of infusion for an assortment of population groups. Protesting that there was already a "minorities" course within the curriculum that was supposed to cover various population groups, he argued that the quality of education was seriously at risk if courses were required to include this content. Under these types of circumstances, it is to be expected that proposals of new models, approaches, and concepts derived from a new paradigm might at first appear illogical, blurred, and unfamiliar because they are based on a framework that cannot be understood within the structure of the dominant culture. Consciousness-expansion will be a long and exhaustive process.

Given the resistance to second-order change, Cunningham (1991) proposes that it is unwise to espouse a single approach. Schuster and VanDyne (1983, pp. 27–34) report on experiments carried out in institutions of higher education using three types of approaches: top-down, bottom-up, and piggyback. For example, at the University of Montana, the project "Women in the Curriculum" was supported by the administration and was implemented in introductory courses. However, the integration of women's experiences in those courses was not very successful, and therefore had no impact in the department's structure. On the other hand, Smith College experimented with a bottom-up approach whereby courses already taught were linked with public lectures emphasizing a new gender-integration paradigm. The lack of an ongoing structure made such an approach discontinuous and its effects hard to measure. Finally, the piggyback approach was used by Lewis and Clark College in Oregon. The principle was to implement gender integration in interdisciplinary courses, on the assumption that such courses are by definition more open to different disciplinary cultures and, therefore, less resistant to transformation. The result of this approach was partial success; it seems to have generated dichotomous approaches based on the gender of the teaching faculty.

Cunningham (1991) concludes that to achieve cultural transformation, the approach has to be multidimensional, including top-down and bottom-up initiatives, as well as central, lateral, and environmental strategies.

We agree with Cunningham in that multiple approaches must occur simultaneously. Certainly, courses can be changed and innovative classes may result, but if there are no mechanisms to institutionalize the integration imperative, these courses will be attached to creative faculty members rather than become cultural roots of the school. As faculty come and go, such innovations will come and go as well. Finding ways to institutionalize gender-integrated curricula will take time, but it is a necessary condition for the success of our proposal.

PARAMETERS, IDEAL TYPES, AND FLEXIBILITY IN PROMOTING SECOND-ORDER CHANGES

Understanding the school of social work's culture, leadership, and structure, the institutional setting, the environment, and various constituencies will condition the assessment of resources available as well as the anticipated resistance to the curricular innovation proposed in this book. Bates (1994) argues that to achieve second-order change certain design parameters have to be met regardless of whether strategies start at the top or the bottom of the academic unit, and/or in its environment (pp. 202–211). We will briefly examine each of those parameters: expressiveness, commonality, infiltration,[1] adaptation, and institutionalization.

Expressiveness

Expressiveness has to do with how the consciousness of the issue is raised, how it is presented, how attention is attracted to it, and how it becomes visible. Evidence of bias, and inequity, and their consequences, and use of symbols in relating these symptoms contribute powerfully to the process of conscientialization as does the ability of connecting with experiences felt but not expressed. The objective is to provoke and challenge the audience to question the status quo. Communication should be direct and uncomplicated,

---

1. The original word used by Bates was "penetration." In the context of the discussion we feel uncomfortable by the Freudian male connotation of the term. Therefore we have substituted the word "infiltration."

demonstrating with examples how the new curriculum would bring conflicting and marginalized issues into an integrated whole. It should also make clear how tinkering within the old framework will not achieve the proposed goals. In sum, the role of this parameter is to convey a new vision (Mendez-Morse, 1992).

It is critical to consider who will communicate this message or convey this new vision. Selecting a faculty member who has charisma and credibility with peers is extremely important. If a person or task force is seen as "forcing" others to buy into this vision, then faculty will nod accordingly, but they will continue doing what they have always done. If the person(s) is not seen as credible within the system, faculty will disregard the messenger even if the message is an important one to hear. Who raises the issue will set the stage for whether there is any possibility of change.

Commonality

Commonality refers to solidifying adherence to the new ideas and proposals by potential supporters of the gender-integrated curriculum. This requires much more interaction to achieve an understanding of the purpose and implications of the proposed change. Often the translation of feminist language unfamiliar to many of these potential supporters is necessary to make the connection with other common interests (Schram, 1995). The use of respected scholarly authority and of commitment to the school's progress as well as practice improvement helps, especially to establish common ground with interested senior faculty. Thus, commonality addresses the mechanisms of expanding the nucleus of supporters of change around common commitments.

Commonality requires building alliances and coalitions within and across the school's informal and formal structural units. For example, informally, some faculty concerned with research courses that are exclusively quantitative may join the effort for gender integration because they see a chance to build a more diverse research program. Commonality also requires a recognition of formalized structures within the school. If, for example, direct practice or a clinical group decides that gender integration is important, they may want to take examples of how this would change the courses for which they are responsible to the curriculum committee. Once the curriculum committee approves these changes, then getting on the agenda for a full meeting of the faculty may be a next step. In this way, there is gathering ownership of various groups within the school before commonality from the larger whole is sought.

Infiltration

Infiltration is the process of spreading the new vision across all school members, but primarily to the faculty not included in the innovation nucleus. This is an effort of "conversion" involving established internalized academic and professional norms. Promoters of gender integration in the curriculum have to be prepared to address a variety of objections derived from the latent assumptions of the dominant culture. Aiken and associates (1985) describe a similar experience with gender integration at the University of Arizona and list an array of manifestations of resistance they encountered: accusations of ideological rather than scholarly foundations of their project; denial of evidence of knowledge bias in the treatment of women's experiences, debates based on the certainty of biological determinism, complaints that responding to all claims of minority groups would make it impossible to address the substance of the courses, and defensiveness regarding the identification of dominant and oppressive knowledge as being male.

Three avenues might help to deal with such resistance. First, appeals to higher values are often effective in managing internalized norms (see, e.g., Rossi, 1972; Hefferman, 1992). For example, among academics, Kuhnian principles of discontinuous transformation of knowledge are commonly accepted, and it can be argued that the curricular change fits this interpretation. Professionally, social work educators are committed to effective help, responding to clients' distinctive experiences. This constitutes another example of appeal to higher values consistent with our proposal. However, conversion cannot rest only on intellectual and cultural persuasion. It requires involvement and participation. New approaches need "mid-wifing"; we hope that in part such is the role of this book. As faculty with a diversity of backgrounds, both intellectual and experiential, examine the new proposal, it might be necessary to make accessible to them literature they have not been acquainted with and the rationale of how that literature might contribute to shaping the courses they teach. For example, one school's efforts at integration were enhanced through the establishment of a Women's Resource Center that made reference materials available to faculty (Ray, Murtry, Matison & Tucker, 1990).

Third, it is important to create open spaces, where together and individually faculty create their own responses to the new ideas, and are encouraged to design their own development to gender-integrated curriculum, deliberate alternatives, and become problem-solvers and researchers of their own plans (Gamston & Eblan, 1988).

Adaptation

Adaptation is especially important in cases when the university administration is not supportive or is simply indifferent to curricular change. In this situation, all possible available resources, supporting coalitions, in the university and in its environment, need to be marshaled to maintain a visible political presence vis-á-vis the administration. Equally important is to be open to all opportunities that might enhance the development of the change. Therefore, flexibility in designing the implementation (avoiding being typecast as a dogmatic program and instead projecting an image of "work in progress") is strategically advantageous to maximize opportunities without deviating from the goal of curricular gender integration. Aiken and associates (1985), analyzing their experience at the University of Arizona, underscore the need for external funding as a means of public legitimization to the unit's effort and facilitating information and training seminars at all levels of the institution.

Institutionalization

The most critical design parameter for lasting change is institutionalization. We will not pretend to cover this parameter here because it will take years to achieve, no matter the success of any gender integration project. Schools of social work are continually revising curriculum, and this is as it should be. Course descriptions, objectives, units of study, readings, and so on will change as students provide feedback and as faculty revisit and revise what they have taught. New faculty will come in, and incrementally, courses will change. However, the test of this change strategy is whether the integration of gender becomes a part of the school's culture.

It took many years for those concepts and visions that define current cultures to be established. Baca Zinn, Cannon, Higginbotham, and Dill write:

> Institutions are organized to facilitate White middle-class men's smooth entry into and mobility in positions of power. These men establish criteria for the entry of others into similar positions, defining success, the reward system, the distribution of resources, and institutionalized goals and priorities in a way that perpetuates their power. In higher education, as in other areas, women—even White middle-class women—have been excluded from many of these activities. . . . Over the past decade, women have made gains in approaching those centers of power, but the institutional barriers have been formidable, and the fight to break them down has left many women scarred. (1986, pp. 291–292)

Placed in this context, one could feel overwhelmed in even attempting the changes proposed in this book. On the other hand, not to attempt them is unthinkable in a profession that espouses social justice as a rallying concept. We have no choice, but we reassert how very difficult these changes are to make and we see this as an ongoing process.

CULTURAL TRANSFORMATION STRATEGIES

Bates (1994, pp. 212–234) formulates approaches to cultural transformation characterized by different strengths of the parameters just discussed. The *aggressive approach* is led by groups that not only espouse the imperative of the transformation but also believe that change is overdue. Their message is delivered assertively and with passion, carrying with it a high level of expressiveness. However, the attitude of "demand for change," or if one is in a position of authority, "imposition of change," runs against the formation of coalitions. The discovery of commonalities and its solidification requires extensive joint exploration through give-and-take. The flexibility necessary to engage in this dialogue is not present in the aggressive approach. Without a limited coalition, the likelihood of effective infiltration will also be low. The ability to deal with resistance from faculty embracing the dominant culture, and create open spaces to let them engage in trial involvement with the new curriculum, runs counter to the urgency of the commitment to change that is characteristic of the aggressive approach. Finally, a messianic zeal might cloud the perception of opportunities for less direct and lengthier routes to change.

The *indoctrinative approach* specializes in communicating core messages delivered by respected academic authorities, using a variety of channels to enhance its message: special events, lectures, courses. This approach tends to be successful in awakening community feelings and in promoting commonality in academic settings. It can achieve reasonable levels of infiltration to an institution's members, especially students. However, attachment to an intellectual ideal, logically integrated in a vision of a new order, constrains its adaptability.

The *conciliatory approach* attempts to pursue pluralism and balance. It tends to dilute its message of change, lowering its expressiveness. Because it calls for high participation and operates in the consensus mode, it fosters trust and is able to promote high commonality. Its framework is appropriate for dealing with long-term change and therefore is consistent with strategies involving training, seminars, solicitation of proposals, demonstration projects, and so on. Such strategies enhance infiltration. Also, to the extent that the approach is open-ended, it can accommodate new views and new situations, making it adaptable.

The *corrosive model* is characterized by pragmatism and manipulation of the dominant culture. It does not declare openly its goals and is careful to propose changes, downplaying potential conflicts. This approach is likely to generate mistrust even among those sympathetic to the goals. Conversely, its pragmatism can be effective in impacting the everyday life of the institution. Infiltration might occur without much conversion. And because it follows an opportunistic strategy, it has the capacity to adapt quickly to a variety of situations.

Table 11–1 summarizes the strengths and weaknesses of each approach along the design parameters that Bates (1994) proposes are requirements for second-order change.[2] These are ideal types, helpful only to the extent that they identify clusters of characteristics ordered by an assumption of internal consistency. In practice, the variety of approaches is much larger. The use of ideal types merely facilitates the analytic projection of interactions among different dimensions. We suggest that multiple or mixed approaches will most likely maximize the strength of each design parameter, and maximize the achievement of second-order change. For example, combining the aggressive with

2. To the extent that the proposals in this chapter focus on initiating and promoting change, institutionalization is not included in the following discussion.

the conciliatory and corrosive approaches, at different stages, could maximize the strength of each.

Table 11–1: Different Approaches to Second-Order Change

Parameter	Aggressive	Indoctrinaire	Conciliatory	Corrosive
Expressiveness	H	H	L	L
Commonality	L	H	H	L
Infiltration	M	M	H	M
Adaptation	L	L	M	H

CONCLUSION

We have argued that the curricular change proposed in the book has the characteristics of secondary change and that therefore it will be resisted at various levels. The corollary of this proposition is that those committed to gender integration in schools of social work will have to proceed with a clear understanding of their schools, of the resources available, and of the strategies that match both. This procedure replicates classical social work intervention. Since the change toward a gender-integrated curriculum is to take place within schools of social work, the change agents need to have a good understanding of the type of culture characterizing the school, the variety of leaders available, and the opportunities that might activate effective leadership, as well as the contingencies set by the structural frame of curricular decisions.

The assessment of available resources, within the school and in its relevant environment (e.g., students, recruitment of faculty, coalition with other academic units moving in the same direction, university changes, etc.), constitutes another step in mapping the elements necessary for planned change.

Having suggested guidelines to identify dimensions of resistance as well as facilitators to change, we searched for methods designed to implement second-order change, especially in academic settings. The conclusion from a variety of experiments that we reviewed was that, given the expected resistance to this paradigmatic change, all known methods should be used. However, in a more theoretical and analytic fashion, some authors called for exact identification of the characteristics of different methods of intervention. The choice of methods can then be based on their potential to bring about a specific outcome. This permits a more reasoned approach that takes into consideration the unit's profile in terms of resistance and facilitating resources. The use of multiple approaches should be framed by a hierarchy and sequencing of intended outcomes.

The arguments in favor of this discriminating approach to secondary changes has the merit of logical coherence, sensitiveness to diversity of circumstances, and openness to imaginative possibilities. Its effectiveness in affecting secondary changes in academic settings has, however, not been tested. Therefore, more specific and concrete suggestions will have to come from the experience of faculty in different schools of social work committed to the gender-integrated curriculum. Reports from those experiences will be crucial to advance our knowledge of how to attempt such revolutionary change in different settings with varied resources. It is the gathering of this information that will be essential to the clearer specification of how to implement gender-integrated curricula in schools of social work.

REFERENCES

Aiken, S.H., Anderson, K., Dinnerstein, M., Lensink, J.N. & MacCorquodale, P. (1985). Changing our minds: The problematics of curriculum integration. In S.H. Aiken, K. Anderson, M. Dinnerstein, J.N. Lensink & P. MacCorquodale (Eds.), *Changing our minds: Feminist transformations of knowledge* (pp. 135–162). Albany: State University of New York Press.

Baca Zinn, M., Cannon, L.W., Higginbotham, E. & Dill, B.T. (1986). The costs of exclusionary practice in women's studies. *Signs: Journal of Women in Culture and Society, 11*(2), 290–303.

Balderston, F.E. (1995). *Managing today's university: Strategies for viability, change and excellence.* San Francisco: Jossey-Bass.

Bates, P. (1994). *Strategies for cultural changes.* Oxford, England: Butterworth-Heinman.

Cunningham, J.B. (1991). Leadership in planning and problem solving. *Leadership and Organization Development Journal, 12* (4), 22–27.

Eccles, T. (1994). *Succeeding with change: Implementing action-driven strategies*. New York: McGraw-Hill.

Gamston, R.J. & Eblan, D.D. (1988). Visions, decisions, and results: Changing school culture through staff development. *Journal of Staff Development, 9* (2), 22–27.

Hefferman, W.J. (1992). *Social welfare policy: A research and action strategy*. New York: Longman.

Higginbotham, E. (1990). Designing an inclusive curriculum: Bringing all women into the core. *Women's Studies Quarterly, 1*, 7–23.

Huber, G.P. & Glick, W.H. (1993). What was learned about organization change and redesign. In G.P. Huber & W.H. Glick (Eds.), *Organizational change and redesign: Ideas and insights for improvising performance* (pp. 383–392). New York: Oxford University Press.

Lahiry, S. (1994). Building commitment through organizational culture. *Training and Development* (April), 50–52.

Levy, A. & Merry, V. (1986). *Organizational transformation: Approaches, strategies, theories*. New York: Praeger.

Litwak, E. (1961). Models of bureaucracy which permit conflict. *The American Journal of Sociology, 67*(September), 177–184.

Mendez-Morse, S. (1992). *Leadership characteristics that facilitate school change*. Austin, TX: Southwest Educational Development Laboratory.

Paludi, M.A. (1991). Placing women psychologists in the psychology of women course. *Teaching of Psychology, 18*(3), 172–174.

Peterson, E.E. (1991). Moving toward a gender balanced curriculum in basic speech communication courses. *Communication Education, 40*, 60–72.

Ray, J., Murtry, S.A., Matison, S.C. & Tucker, J. (1990). Women's content: Involving faculty and students in organizational change. *Journal of Teaching in Social Work, 4*(2), 19–36.

Rossi, P. (1972). Testing for success and failure in social action. In P. Rossi & W. Williams (Eds.), *Evaluating social programs* (pp. 11–57). New York: Seminar Press.

Schein, E.H. (1991). *Organizational culture and leadership*. San Francisco: Jossey-Bass.

Schram, S.F. (1995). *Words of welfare: The poverty of social science and the social science of poverty*. Minneapolis: The University of Minnesota Press.

Schuster, M.R. & VanDyne, S.R. (1983). *Feminist transformation of the curriculum: The changing classroom, changing the institution (Working Paper #125)*. Wellesley, MA: Wellesley College, Center for Research on Women.

Shaw, R.B. & Walton, A.E. (1995). *Discontinuous change: Leading organizational transformation*. San Francisco: Jossey-Bass.

Smith, T. (1994). Changing university culture through promotion policies. *Proceedings of the Frontiers in Education Conference*, Session 5D3. New York.

Stevens-Smith, P. (1995). Gender issues in counselor education: Current status and challenges. *Counselor Education and Supervision, 34*, 283–293.

Tice, K. (1990). Gender and social work education: Directions for the 1990s. *Journal of Social Work Education, 26*(2), 134–144.

Yllo, K. (1989). How the new scholarship on women and gender transforms the college curriculum. *American Behavioral Scientist, 32*(6), 658–667.

Contributors

Janice Andrews received her BA from Augsburg College, her MSW from Washington University, and her Ph.D. from the University of Maryland. She taught at Winona State University for nine years and directed the BSW Program. She currently is in her seventh year at the College of St. Catherine/University of St. Thomas School of Social Work where she teaches in the MSW Program and directs the Distance Education Program. She has edited a book, *From Vision to Action: Social Workers of the Second Generation*, published by the University of St. Thomas, and authored numerous articles on social welfare, history, feminism, radicalism, and McCarthyism. She is under contract with Garland Publishing to write a book co-authored with Michael Reisch on *Radicalism and Repression in Social Work: A Historical Perspectus*. She has over 20 years experience as a clinical social worker and currently facilitates women's groups in the Twin Cities.

José B. Ashford is Professor of Social Work and Interdisciplinary Ph.D. Program in Justice Studies and Law and the Social Sciences at Arizona State University. His doctorate is in Sociology with a specialization in criminology/social deviance from Bowling Green State University (1984), and he has an MSW with a concentration in clinical practice from Ohio State University (1976). Dr. Ashford teaches courses in psychopathology, human behavior and the social environment, law and social work, and law and the social sciences. He is co-author of *Human Behavior in the Social Environment: A Multidimensional Perspective* by Brooks/Cole Publishing, and *Introduction to Social Work and Social Welfare* by Merrill (an Imprint of the Macmillian Publishing Company). He is also co-author of the forthcoming book *Treating Adult and Juvenile Offenders with Special*

Needs by the American Psychological Association, and has written numerous journal articles on justice and other forensic social work issues. Dr. Ashford often serves as an expert witness in capital murder cases where he testifies on the role of human development, psychopathology and other human behavior issues in assessments of mitigating factors.

Iris Carlton-LaNey is Associate Professor of Social Work at the University of North Carolina at Chapel Hill School of Social Work. She received her BA in Social Work from North Carolina Agricultural & Technical State University (1972), her MA from the University of Chicago (1974), and her Ph.D. from the University of Maryland at Baltimore (1981). Dr. Carlton-LaNey has taught social work on the BSW and MSW levels for nearly eighteen years. Currently she is director of the Aging Concentration at UNC-Chapel Hill. She has served as guest editor for special issues of the *Journal of Sociology and Social Welfare* and the *Journal of Community Practice*. She co-edited, with Dr. N. Yolanda Burwell, *African American Community Practice Models: Historical and Contemporary Responses* (1996), and has written a monograph entitled "Elderly Black Farm Women as Keepers of the Community and the Culture" (1989). Her most recent article entitled, "Elizabeth Ross Haynes: An African American Reformer of Womanish Consciousness 1908–1940" has been accepted for publication by *Social Work*.

Josefina Figueira-McDonough is Professor of Justice Studies at Arizona State University. She was trained in social work and sociology at the University of Michigan, held faculty positions at the University of Michigan, Michigan State University, and Vanderbilt University and has lectured in Puerto Rico, Portugal, Italy, Ireland, Taiwan and Korea. Her research has focused on issues of social justice, more specifically on gender, deviance and control and on the environmental context of poverty. Her studies have been supported by federal agencies (e.g., NIH, NIMH, NSF, NIE, NIC, NIJ, OJJDP) as well as by private foundations, and the results of her research have been published in social work, sociology and criminology journals. She is presently working on a book to be titled *Community Analysis and Intervention: In Search of the Civil Society*.

Janet L. Finn is Assistant Professor of Social Work and Adjunct Professor of Anthropology at the University of Montana. She received her BA in Psychology from the University of Montana (1978), her MSW from Eastern Washington University (1982), and her PhD in Social Work and Anthropology from the University of Michigan (1995). Prior to doctoral studies she was a social work supervisor in Child and Family Services with the State of Montana and a social worker for the Casey Family Program. She currently teaches courses in social work intervention with individuals, families, groups and communities, women and the politics of welfare, and women and social action in the Americas. Her current research includes assessment of welfare reform in Montana and a cross-national comparative study of women's grassroots initiatives entitled "Women Building Community: Lessons from the Andes to the Rockies." Dr. Finn is the author of the forthcoming book, *Tracing the Veins: Mining Copper, Culture and Community in Butte, Montana, USA and Chuquicamata, Chile* (Berkeley and Los Angeles: University of California Press.)

Cynthia Franklin is Associate Professor at the University of Texas at Austin, School of Social Work where she teaches courses on clinical practice and research. Dr. Franklin has numerous publications on clinical assessment, practice theories, research methods, and child and family practice. She is co-author (with Dr. Catheleen Jordan) of *Clinical Assessment for Social Workers: Quantitative and Qualitative Methods*, and a forthcoming text, *Practicing Constructivism*, co-edited with Dr. Paula Nurius. Dr. Franklin maintains a part-time clinical practice, specializing in marriage and family therapy.

Dorothy "Dee" N. Gamble is Assistant Dean for Student Services and Clinical Assistant Professor at the University of North Carolina at Chapel Hill School of Social Work. She received her BA from the University of Colorado, Boulder (1962) and her MSW from Columbia University (1966). She was a Peace Corps Volunteer in Bucaramanga, Colombia (1962–64) and has done community organizing in Colombia, New York City, and rural North Carolina. She serves on the NASW-NC Legislative Action and Peace and Justice Committees. She teaches courses in citizen participation and sustainable development and was a co-project director for an international forum at UNC-Chapel Hill on Women, Community, and Sustainable Development. She is co-author of two articles in the Encyclopedia of Social Work (19th ed.): Citizen

Participation, and Community Practice Models. She continues to consult with and supervise students in community practice settings.

Lorraine Gutierrez is Associate Professor in the School of Social Work and Department of Psychology at the University of Michigan. She received her BA in History from Stanford University, her MA in Social Service Administration from the University of Chicago, her MA in Psychology from the University of Michigan, and her PhD in Social Work and Psychology from the University of Michigan. Her research focuses on multicultural social work practice with large and small systems. Current projects include evaluating gender and ethnically relevant AIDS prevention interventions, identifying multicultural issues in organizational and community practice, and defining culturally competent and ethnoconscious social work practice.

Elizabeth D. Hutchison is Associate Professor of Social Work at Virginia Commonwealth University. She received her BA in Sociology from Maryland College (1967), her MSW from the George Warren Brown School of Social Work at Washington University (1969), and her PhD from the State University of New York at Albany (1988). Prior to joining the faculty at VCU in 1987, Dr. Hutchison directed a BSW Program at Elms College, Chicopee, Massachusetts. She has taught social work practice and human behavior courses in the MSW and PhD programs at VCU. Her research interests are in the areas of child welfare, social work practice with involuntary clients, substance abuse, and faculty productivity. She is currently writing a human behavior textbook.

Edith Lewis is Associate Professor of Social Work and Women's Studies at the University of Michigan. She has an MSW from University of Minnesota and PhD in Social Welfare from the University of Wisconsin-Madison. Dr. Lewis has taught in the areas of culturally competent social work practice, family relationships, group process, and behavioral theory and interventions. Her research has focused upon African-American mothers' use of traditional helping networks to offset their role responsibilities, and interventions for use with pregnant substance-dependent women. She has recently given presentations on network utilization as a social work intervention strategy; race, ethnicity, and gender conflict in organizations;

multicultural teaching at the university level; and the empowerment of people of color in higher education.

Jill Littrell is Assistant Professor at Georgia State University in the Social Work Department. She graduated from the University of Nebraska in 1971 with a degree in Social Welfare. In 1972, she received her MSSW from the University of Wisconsin. In 1981, she received her PhD in Clinical Psychology from Arizona State University. Prior to becoming an academic, she worked in a variety of human service areas including employment in a state hospital system, at Cigna Health Plan's Substance Abuse Department, in the Arizona child welfare system, and in a residential treatment facility for juvenile offenders.

F. Ellen Netting is Professor of Social Work at Virginia Commonwealth University. She received her BA in Sociology from Duke University (1971), her MSSW from the University of Tennessee-Knoxville (1975), and her PhD from the University of Chicago (1982). After teaching both social work and gerontology courses at Arizona State University for ten years, the last four years she has taught courses in policy practice, and administration and planning in the BSW and MSW programs at VCU. She is co-author of *Social Work Macro Practice* published by Longman, and has written numerous journal articles. Currently she is co-investigator for the John A. Hartford Foundation Generalist Physician Initiative with a team of health administration, physician, and public health colleagues. This multi-site demonstration examines how multiple disciplines can team within community-based physician practices to serve frail elders. Other research interests include the Long Term Care Ombudsman Program, continuing care retirement communities, and religiously affiliated nonprofit organizations.

Ann Nichols-Casebolt is Professor and Associate Dean in the School of Social Work at Virginia Commonwealth University. Dr. Nichols-Casebolt received her PhD and MSSW at the University of Wisconsin-Madison where she also was employed as a Research Associate at the Institute for Research on Poverty. Prior to assuming her administrative position at VCU, Dr. Nichols-Casebolt was a faculty member at Arizona State University where she taught social policy courses in the BSW, MSW, and PhD programs. Her research interests are in the area of single-parent families and poverty, with a particular focus on issues of child support and paternity establishment for children born outside of marriage. She has most recently co-authored an article on this topic entitled "The Economic Well-Being of Never- and Ever-Married Single Mother Families: A Cross-National Comparison" that will be published in the *Journal of Social Service Research*. Dr. Nichols-Casebolt is currently co-investigator of an evaluation of a Housing and Urban Development (HUD) funded human services integration demonstration project in the city of Richmond.

Paula S. Nurius is Professor and Doctoral Program Director at the University of Washington School of Social Work. She received her BA from the University of Texas, MSW from the University of Hawaii, and MA in Psychology and PhD in Social Work and Psychology from the University of Michigan. In addition to teaching and administration of the doctoral program, Dr. Nurius is Principal Investigator of the National Institute for Mental Health (NIMH) funded prevention-oriented research related to women's risk appraisal of, and response to acquaintance sexual aggression and serves on the governing board of the UW Social Work Center for Prevention Research. Her research interests include social cognitive analysis of risk appraisal and response to threat, self-concept development and functioning, and social cognitive factors involved in practice reasoning and judgment. She is particularly interested in women's issues such as coping with intimate sources of threat (e.g., acquaintance violence, breast cancer) and self-concept functioning related to sex role socialization and marginalization. She publishes extensively on these and related topics and is actively involved in strengthening doctoral education and funding for doctoral research training.

Robert Ortega is Assistant Professor of Social Work at the University of Michigan. He has an MSW, MS in Social Psychology, and PhD in Social Work and Social Psychology from the University of Michigan. His teaching and research interests are in the areas of relationship development, treatment interventions, and service utilization, particularly in the realm of mental health and child welfare. Dr. Ortega has presented and written on these topics with a special focus on issues of race/ethnicity and gender.

Beth Glover Reed is Associate Professor of Social Work and Women's Studies at the University of Michigan. Dr. Reed received her PhD in Psychology at the University of Cincinnati. Her work focuses on the ways in which social and organizational structures and processes maintain and recreate patterns of inequities related to gender, race, ethnicity, sexual orientation, and other markers of status. She also studies strategies to change these processes. Professor Reed has conducted research and published on policy issues and treatment services for alcohol and other drug problems in women, feminist group work and organizations, multicultural teaching and social change, and various other topics related to race and gender dynamics in small groups, communities, and organizations.

Mary K. Rodwell is Associate Professor in the School of Social Work at Virginia Commonwealth University where she teaches in the MSW and PhD programs. She received a BS in Art from Immaculate Heart College, Hollywood, CA., and her MSW and PhD from the University of Kansas. Prior to entering academics, Dr. Rodwell was a member of the Peace Corps in Brazil and had extensive direct and administrative practice experience in child welfare both in state government and the nonprofit sector. She is the co-author of *Evaluating Social Programs*, is currently finishing *Constructivist Research for Social Work Practice*, and has written numerous journal articles with a particular focus on child welfare issues or constructivist research methods. She was a Fulbright scholar in Brazil where she taught constructivist research in Portuguese and conducted constructivist research with street children. Her current research involves focus groups with children to assess the impact of a sexual abuse prevention intervention.

Marie Overby Weil is Professor and Director of the Community Social Work Program at the School of Social Work at the University of North Carolina at Chapel Hill. She received her BA in philosophy from UNC-Chapel Hill in 1963, her MSW from the University of Pennsylvania in 1967, and her DSW from the Graduate Center of the City University of New York in 1977. She previously taught courses in program evaluation, macro practice and family policy at the University of Southern California for 11 years and has been at UNC-Chapel Hill since 1988. She is Associate Director of the Jordan Institute for Families and teaches community practice and family policy and the foundation course for the PhD program. She recently edited *Community*

Practice: Conceptual Models and *Community Practice Models in Action*, both published by Haworth Press. Recent articles include "Community Building: Building Community Practice," "Model Development in Community Practice: An Historical Perspective," "Community Practice Models," co-authored with Dee Gamble in the 19th edition of the *Encyclopedia of Social Work*, and a book chapter entitled "Women, Community and Organizing." With Evelyn Williams, she has just completed an Aspen Institute funded study of nonprofits in North Carolina, and is Principal Investigator of the ACYF funded North Carolina Family Preservation and Family Support Project evaluating sixty programs throughout the state.

Evelyn Smith Williams is a Clinical Assistant Professor and Associate of Field Education in the School of Social Work at the University of North Carolina at Chapel Hill. She earned her BA in psychology at Duke University in 1973, and her MSW at UNC-Chapel Hill in 1976. Ms. Williams is currently a doctoral candidate in adult education at North Carolina State University pursuing research on cultural competence and mental health services for children and families. In addition to her field education responsibilities, Ms. Williams teaches macro practice and diversity at UNC-Chapel Hill. She co-authored curriculum material on diversity and on cross-systems management for a children's case management curriculum used nationally to train service providers and supervisors. With Marie Weil, and in collaboration with the North Carolina Center for Nonprofits, she recently completed an Aspen Institute funded study of nonprofits in North Carolina. Her research interests include planning in grassroots programs, knowledge utilization by human service professionals, and program development in domestic violence organizations.

Leanne Wood Charlesworth is a doctoral candidate in the School of Social Work at Virginia Commonwealth University. She received her MSW from the State University of New York at Albany (1993) and a BA in government from Cornell University (1991). Ms. Wood teaches Human Behavior in the Social Environment and the Foundations of Research in Social Work Practice in the MSW Program at VCU. Her doctoral dissertation focuses on the impact of welfare reform on women and children.

Index